ID0646858

DIRTY LITTLE SECRETS OF WORLD WAR II

ALSO BY JAMES F. DUNNIGAN AND ALBERT A. NOFI

Dirty Little Secrets

ALSO BY JAMES F. DUNNIGAN

How to Stop a War (with William Martel)
A Quick and Dirty Guide to War (with Austin Bay)
How to Make War
The Complete Wargames Handbook
Getting It Right (with Raymond M. Macedonia)

ALSO BY ALBERT A. NOFI

The Alamo and the Texas War for Independence
The Civil War Treasury
Eyewitness History of the Civil War
The Gettysburg Campaign
Napoleon at War
The War Against Hitler: Military Strategy in the West

DIRTY LITTLE SECRETS OF WORLD WAR II

Military Information No One Told You About the Greatest, Most Terrible War in History

James F. Dunnigan and Albert A. Nofi

WILLIAM MORROW AND COMPANY, INC.
New York

For
Marilyn J. Spencer
and
Lori Fawcett,
In Loving Memory

ACKNOWLEDGMENTS

SPECIAL THANKS TO:

Barney Dombrowski, Dennis Casey, Richard L. DiNardo, George Blagowidow, the editors and the staff of *Strategy and Tactics* magazine, the members of the New York Military Affairs Symposium, Fun H. Fong, Jr., Brian Sullivan, Patrick Abbazia, Wayne McKinney, Kathleen Williams, Steve Laroe, Susan Leon, Bob Shuman, Richard Garczynski, John Boardman, David E. Schwartz, Roger Covington, Linda Grant DePauw, Steven J. Zaloga, Norman Friedman, Tom Holsinger, Mike Peterson, Tom Trinko, and Mary Spencer Nofi, who has to put up with one of us.

CONTENTS

INTRODUCTION

This is not a history of World War II, but revelations about many of the lesser-known details. Because it is a book of facts, you don't read it from beginning to end, but rather you jump in wherever it strikes your fancy. There are over three hundred separate items, each a complete story in itself.

As a rule, much of the information found in one section of the book will usually also be applicable to the others as well. After all, although aircraft carriers are inseparably associated with the Pacific war, they also performed yeoman service in the Atlantic and Mediterranean, while the problems of troop transport transcended theater.

After reading this book, you'll never look at World War II the same way again. We have not changed the story of that conflict; we are providing information about it that is not generally known. We often look at the same subject from several different angles, giving you a better appreciation of, for example, how a blitzkrieg was conducted, what it took to supply partisans, and why the U.S. Army had more ships than the U.S. Navy.

World War II was the most enormous human drama in history. No one volume could ever really come close to examining all of the unusual, and often important, aspects of this, history's greatest war. So much has had to be left out, from the drama of Dunkirk to the U.S. Navy's coal-burning, paddle-wheel aircraft carriers on the Great Lakes; from the Marine Corps's Navaho communications specialists to the

Japanese Navy's "American" pilots; not to mention the improbable adventures of FDR's son, the extraordinary antiarmor tactics of the Finns, and the secret missions of Harry Hopkins. Also left out are many interesting items from the "secondary" theaters such as China, Burma, Finland, and the Middle East. Moreover, the end of the Cold War has thrown open the Soviet World War II archives. Much fascinating material is coming out. We were shown a volume (in Russian) of some of the newly revealed material already being published in Russia and realized that we could have added several dozen pages of previously unknown goodies for this book from that one Russian volume alone. Well, if we sell enough copies of this book, there may be more. We certainly have enough to fill several more volumes.

This book undoubtedly displays an "American" bias. This is natural, given the audience. Without much difficulty the authors could produce a book of similar length with a "British" or "German" or "Chinese" bias which, while being somewhat repetitive, would still manage to include a lot of unusual and interesting material. World War II was the most enormous human drama in history, and there is far more to be told about it than can possibly be included between the covers of a single book.

1

THE ROAD TO WAR

World War II didn't begin in a vacuum. The clouds were forming throughout the 1930s and the scene was set in a complex movement of political, social, and economic forces.

BE AFRAID, BE VERY AFRAID

From 1935 onward, the world had to endure one nerve-racking crisis after another as Italy, Germany, and Japan flexed their muscles in East Africa, central Europe, and East Asia. Then, during the first week of September 1939, when Germany invaded Poland, World War II was under way, as most of the major powers set their armies and navies in motion. America, however, the greatest industrial power on the planet, proclaimed neutrality and showed no enthusiasm for getting involved. This would eventually change, and not solely because of the Japanese attack on Pearl Harbor.

Here is a list of the chief heart-stopping events you would have read about in the newspapers, seen in the newsreels (anyone remember newsreels?), or heard on the radio from 1935 onward. Read it and you will understand how the whole mess called World War II began. In 1935, for Americans World War I was still a recent memory and the Great Depression gave most of them more immediate problems to deal with than war in Europe and Asia. Yet, throughout the world, you could see that something else was happening. And that something else was not good. Most of these prewar events have faded into the murky background of history. But the war did not begin for no reason. There were plenty of reasons, and plenty of signs that it was coming. (And these signs still reappear, indicating to those in the know that another world war is possible.)

March 1935. Germany renounces the terms of the Treaty of Versailles, which ended World War I, and, in effect, begins openly rearming.

There had been several serious disarmament conferences during the 1920s and a series of naval disarmament treaties had been signed and carried out. Germany had been effectively disarmed after World War I by the Versailles Treaty. During the early 1930s only the Soviet Union, Japan, and Italy were rearming (Germany was secretly getting ready to). But then Germany announced its intention to rearm and many Europeans and Americans feared the worst. Germany felt it had gotten a raw deal after World War I. The Germans had not been innocent participants in that war; all of the great powers were responsible for the conflict and the disaster it brought upon Europe. But the Germans lost the war, and the French had a big say in the peace terms. Germany was stripped of much territory and humiliated in general. A competent historian could have predicted, and several did, that on the basis of past experience this almost guaranteed another major war. On a more immediate note, the end of World War I was also the end of several empires. Many ethnic groups that had long been kept quiet by imperial armies and police were now free to settle ancient scores. Thus Germany wasn't the only nation looking for "revenge" in the 1930s, a lot of others had gripes too: the Soviet Union, Hungary, and Bulgaria had lost big time in 1918; and, not least, Italy and Japan, who had been among the winners back then, felt cheated of the loot. They all got their revenge, as well as a new crop of grudges. And now Germany, the most feared military power for the last seventy years, was arming itself again.

August 1935. The U.S. Congress passes a neutrality act, which forbids loans or arms sales to participants in foreign wars.

This act was brought about partially by the 1934–1936 Nye Committee investigation, which left many Americans with the erroneous impression that U.S. entry into World War I was largely an effort to make bankers and arms manufacturers ("the Merchants of Death") rich. This led to a resurgence of isolationism, particularly in light of the subsequent Italian invasion of Ethiopia, what the Japanese euphemistically called "incidents" with China, the Spanish Civil War, and the rearming of Germany. Too, many of the emigrants who had fled to America in the 1840s and 1930s had done so to escape military service, wars, and ethnic strife in the Old Country. So there was in the American mind a strong aversion to participation in foreign wars. Most American politicians played to this attitude and the result was an American electorate that strongly resisted sending U.S. troops "over there."

October 1935. Italy invades Ethiopia without warning (after a year of low-level hostilities). The League of Nations (the precursor of the UN) condemns the aggression and imposes sanctions (including an embargo), but has no effect beyond allegedly cutting off the supply of tennis balls to Italy.

By May 1936 Ethiopia was conquered and annexed by Italy. Mussolini had created the first Fascist state in Italy. While fascism contained elements of nationalism and socialism, the "might makes right" angle caused the most problems. Although most nations condemned the Italian invasion of Ethiopia, and the use of chemical weapons, no one was willing to do anything about it. But then Ethiopia in 1935, unlike Kuwait in 1990, didn't have anything (like oil) the rest of the world needed.

March 1936. Germany sends troops into the Rhineland region, which under the treaty of Versailles is to remain free of German troops.

Adolf Hitler decided to go for broke and march some troops in. France did not resist. This was the first of Germany's diplomatic gains through the use, or threatened use, of military force that would lead to World War II.

July 1936. Civil war breaks out in Spain between conservative Nationalists and Leftist Loyalists. Within weeks, Fascist nations, Italy and Germany, begin sending aid to the Nationalists, while the Soviet Union supports the Loyalists, as do sixty thousand Soviet-recruited individuals from many other countries. This is the first war to see wide use of modern aircraft and armored vehicles. Fighting continues until March 1939.

Nearly half a million people died in this conflict, a foretaste of World War II. The world was impressed by, and justifiably fearful of, the performance of German troops and weapons in this war.

November 1936. Japan signs the "Anti-Comintern" Treaty with Germany and Italy, allegedly designed to counter Communist influence.

This was the beginning of what the Italian dictator Benito Mussolini called the Axis (because the world would revolve around them), against which the Allies later fought. The treaty was mostly for show but starkly divided the world into "good guys" and "bad guys." The Soviet Comintern was the Communist International, an organization of Marxist parties preparing for the "Red Crusade" to spread world revolution. This had caused a lot of nervousness in the 1920s but was now only something for Fascists to rail against. The Communist threat would not become a big issue again until the late 1940s. In any event, the Soviets formally dissolved the Comintern as a favor to their allies before World War II was over, and hardly anyone noticed.

May 1937. The War Policy Act is passed by the U.S. Congress, which modifies the Neutrality Act of 1935 to give the president (Franklin D. Roosevelt) some discretion in allowing loans and arms sales to foreigners.

Many U.S. politicians saw that America might not be able to stay out of any future world war, and the War Policy Act was one of several efforts to deal with the problem by helping potential allies before trouble started.

July 1937. Japan openly wars on China after years of incursions, raids, skirmishes, and occasional battles.

The Japanese occupied much of the Chinese countryside in the late 1930s and committed enough atrocities for American journalists to get a steady supply of gruesome stories, what with their troops' penchant for conducting bayonet practice on Chinese prisoners and similar horrors. The situation in China was thus always quite an issue in America, although less so in Europe (where they had Hitler and his Nazis to make them nervous).

March 1938. The *Anschluss,* Germany invades and annexes Austria, adding six million more German-speaking people to its population.

This was part of Hitler's (domestically quite popular) policy of uniting all members of the "German race" in one nation. Unfortunately, most Europeans soon realized that there were substantial German minorities in Czechoslovakia, Poland, the Soviet Union, and other nations.

July 1938. Fighting erupts between Japanese and Soviet troops on the Russian-Korean-Manchurian border.

The Soviets won. Little was known of this in the West until after the war. But reports of "friction between Japanese and Soviet troops in Manchuria" added to the general sense of unease in America.

September 1938. After threats to march into western Czechoslovakia and seize the German-populated territories, Germany is approached by Great Britain and France with offers of compromise. At a conference in Munich, Hitler explains that this means giving him what he wants in return for a promise to behave in the future.

As a result of this Munich Pact, Germany annexed the western portions of Czechoslovakia (containing three million German-speaking Czechs) without bringing on a general European war. Czechoslovakia had been allied with France and several other countries, but these agreements were ignored as part of the Munich Pact.

October 1938. As part of the Munich agreement, Polish troops occupy the Teschen area of Czechoslovakia (which they have long claimed is Polish-inhabited), taking advantage of Czechoslovakian helplessness in the face of German aggression, while Hungary takes a slice of the southern part of the country as well (for similar "reasons").

January 1939. President Roosevelt proposes a defense budget that, in effect, begins to rearm the United States.

The votes in Congress were still close, and it would take quite a traumatic event to push America into a major war.

March 1939. Germany annexes the Lithuanian port of Memel (more Germans "reunited" with Germany, this time via a vote of the largely German inhabitants). Pressed about Germans living on its soil, Poland successfully resists demands for more annexations of German-populated areas. Germany secretly decides to invade Poland.

March 1939. German troops occupy what is left of Czechoslovakia and take pieces for themselves, in direct violation of the 1938 Munich Pact, while Hungary and Romania snip off little pieces for themselves, and Slovakia (eastern Czechoslovakia) proclaims its independence.

April 1939. Hitler renounces Germany's 1935 naval agreement with Great Britain, under the terms of which Germany voluntarily agreed to limit its fleet to about a third the size of Great Britain's.

This signaled Germany's intention to rebuild its fleet and challenge Great Britain's control of the oceans. Germany had been rebuilding its fleet since 1935, and had been bending the terms of the treaty anyway by building ships larger than the official treaty limitations.

April 1939. Mussolini invades Albania, which has for centuries (back to the Roman Empire) frequently been ruled by Italian states.

The Duce saw this as yet another building block in his new Roman empire. The rest of the world saw it as another exercise in naked aggression.

April 1939. A German diplomatic note to Poland denounces the ten-year non-aggression treaty the two countries had signed in 1934, and requests Polish acquiescence to the annexation of the formerly German "Free City of Danzig" to Hitler's Reich as well as to Germany's control over railway and highway connections across Poland to east Prussia, which is separated from the rest of Germany by Polish territory, another vexing result of World War I.

July 1939. The United States gives notice of its intention to terminate its commercial treaty of 1911 with Japan, which granted the latter "most-favored nation" status.

This was intended to hurt Japan economically and force the Japanese to cease their attempts to conquer China.

August 23, 1939. Germany signs a nonaggression treaty with the Soviet Union. A secret clause allows both nations to partition Poland.

This treaty (even without their knowing of the secret clauses) came as a shock to everyone (especially the Communists), as Germany had been rabidly anti-Communist (and thus anti–Soviet Union) up to this point, while the Soviets had been enthusiastically anti-Nazi. It had been expected that the heavily armed Soviet Union would keep Germany from being too aggressive. Now Germany didn't have to worry about Russia, which had effectively become its ally.

August 24, 1939. Great Britain and Poland sign a formal treaty of mutual assistance.

This meant that if Germany invaded Poland, Great Britain would declare war on Germany and a general war would begin.

August 1939. Japan has a rough month. It denounces its anti-Communist treaty with Germany, because Germany and the Soviet Union have just signed their non-aggression pact. Japan has also just been defeated in a major border battle with the Soviets in Mongolia.

September 1, 1939. Germany invades Poland. Great Britain and France issue an ultimatum demanding that Germany cease its aggression within forty-eight hours or they will declare war. Italy declares its neutrality and proposes a new conference like the Munich conference.

September 3, 1939. Germany not having replied to their note of September 1, Great Britain and France declare war.

September 17, 1939. The Soviet Union invades Poland from the east, under the terms of the Nazi-Soviet pact.

September 29, 1939. A new German-Soviet treaty is signed, resulting in the partitioning of Poland and various trade agreements.

November 1939. The Soviet Union invades Finland. The Finns fight back successfully, by a combination of heroic resistance and Soviet ineptitude, and obtain an end to the war, on terms favorable to the Soviets, albeit less than what Stalin wanted, in March 1940.

November 1939. The U.S. Congress allows arms sales to certain foreign nations (particularly Finland, Great Britain, and France).

January 1940. American defense spending is increased to more than six times 1939 levels. The "Two Ocean Navy" bill increases shipbuilding so dramatically that the United States will be the world's largest naval power within three years.

Still, there was strong isolationist sentiment in America. It was one thing to be prepared, quite another to get involved.

April 1940. Germany invades Denmark and Norway.

May 10, 1940. Germany invades the Netherlands, Belgium, and France. Quickly demonstrating its military superiority, the German Army defeats all of its enemies and forces the British to retreat from the continent via the beaches near Dunkirk.

June 1940. The Germans enter Paris; France surrenders soon afterward. American military leaders (and Americans in general) are shocked at the speed with which Germany has defeated the British, French, and several smaller armies. Lurid (and highly inaccurate) newspaper accounts tell of the Germans using 50-ton tanks with 90mm guns (something the Germans would have in four years) and flamethrowers that cut through metal (this has not appeared on any battlefield yet).

August 1940. The Battle of Britain begins, as German and British air forces struggle for air supremacy. The battle ends in September with a British victory.

September 1940. Italy invades Egypt, which is occupied by British troops.

September 1940. The Japanese begin the occupation of French Indochina. America protests and puts an embargo on shipments of scrap metal to Japan.

America was a primary source of scrap metal for the Japanese, who were greatly dependent on this resource for their metals industries.

September 1940. A German-Italian-Japanese ten-year military-economic-alliance treaty is signed.

September 1940. The United States introduces "selective service," the draft.

October 1940. The Italians invade Greece, and the Greeks successfully resist.

December 1940. The British in Egypt chase the Italians back into Libya.

January 1941. The British launch another offensive against the Italians in North Africa while also invading Italian-held Ethiopia and Somalia.

March 1941. The U.S. Congress introduces the Lend Lease Act, which allows for the "loan" of massive amounts of weapons and equipment to nations fighting the Axis.

March 1941. British troops land in Greece to assist in the defense of Greece against Italian forces (and potential German intervention).

March 1941. German General Erwin Rommel and his Afrika Korps come to the assistance of their Italian allies in North Africa. By a surprise offensive, he soon puts the British on the defensive, forcing them back hundreds of miles.

April 1941. Germany invades Yugoslavia (where a pro-Nazi government has just been overthrown) and Greece. Both nations surrender within a month.

April 1941. America takes control of Greenland (from Nazi-occupied Denmark).

May 1941. British forces, driven out of Greece, retreat to the island of Crete. The Germans then launch an airborne assault on Crete and take the island.

May 1941. British naval forces chase the German battleship *Bismarck* across the North Atlantic and eventually sink it. The main Italian forces in Ethiopia and Somalia surrender to the British.

May 1941. The U.S. merchant ship *Robin Moore* is sunk by a German U-boat in the Atlantic. The Americans are getting nervous, but not nervous enough to make declaring war on Germany a popular issue.

May 1941. A pro-Nazi uprising in Iraq is put down by British forces.

June 1941. A British offensive in North Africa fails against the Afrika Korps and its Italian allies.

June 1941. Pro-German French ("Vichyite") and Arab forces in Syria are defeated by British and Free French forces.

June 1941. The Germans invade the Soviet Union, launching the largest military campaign in history. While this takes direct pressure off Great Britain (Hitler can't very well invade Great Britain while fighting the Soviet Union), there is fear that if the Germans win in the Soviet Union they will possess the largest empire of modern times. Worldwide, Communist parties and sympathizers, who have hitherto argued that the war is an "imperialist" one, suddenly begin claiming it's a "democratic" one, and the United States and everyone else should help the "democratic" Soviet Union.

July 1941. America freezes Japanese assets in the United States. Great Britain does the same.

Japan was still trying to conquer China and now occupied all of French Indochina. All previous protests and sanctions had not made any impression on the Japanese. The asset freeze, however, had the effect of prohibiting exports of British- and American-controlled oil to Japan (without government-issued permits). As Japan was entirely dependent on these oil imports to keep its industry and military going, the embargo would eventually cripple Japan's war effort, as well as its economy. The Japanese had a choice between getting out of China and avoiding the bad effects of the embargo, or going to war and hoping that would break the embargo. A rational decision would have been to give up China. But this was not a rational situation, and the Japanese decided on war.

July 1941. America occupies Iceland, a Danish possession heretofore occupied by British troops.

This was to assist the British, by freeing the British garrison for other duties, and to put American forces one step closer to a war footing.

August 1941. British and Soviet troops invade Iran to overthrow a pro-Nazi government.

The Iranians were seeking aid from the Germans not so much because they were keen on fascism, but because they wanted to get Great Britain out of the Persian Gulf. The Persian Gulf was a key route for sending military and economic aid to the Soviet Union, as well as a major source of oil.

September 1941. American warships begin protecting convoys going to Europe, escorting them halfway across the Atlantic. German U-boats proceed to attack these escorts, sinking one and damaging another in October. The United States issues "shoot on sight" orders to the U.S. Navy (directed mainly at German U-boats). In effect, a state of war now exists between the U.S. and German navies.

November 1941. A British offensive in North Africa has some success in driving the Axis forces back.

November 1941. Renewal is made for five years of the Anti-Comintern (anti-Communist) Pact of November 25, 1936, in Berlin, by Germany, Japan, Italy, Hungary, Spain, Manchukuo (a Japanese puppet state), Bulgaria, Croatia (an Italian puppet state), Denmark (under German control), Finland, Romania, Slovakia (a German puppet state), and, curiously, the Nationalist government in China (which fought local Communists throughout the 1930s). Many of these nations are induced to send troops to fight the Soviets.

November-December 1941. The Soviet Union begins a counteroffensive against the Germans, pushing them back on all fronts, notably away from the suburbs of Moscow.

This was the third major defeat the Germans had in the war, the other two being the Battle of Britain and their recent reversals in North Africa.

December 1941. The Japanese attack Pearl Harbor, the Philippines, and other U.S. territories. British and Dutch possessions are also attacked.

America is now in the war, somewhat to the relief of many Americans, who feared the consequences of an Axis victory. The unnerving series of events from the mid-1930s to the eve of Pearl Harbor had left few believing that the United States would not get involved in the war. And few believed that the coming battles would be easy.

MILITARY EXPENDITURES AND ESTABLISHMENTS IN PEACETIME, 1930

Each nation adopts a military policy suited to its priorities, traditions, strategies, and politics, given a particular international climate and the limitations of its treasury. For several centuries this created a situation in Europe where most of the major nations were always on a war footing.

Beginning in the eighteenth century, this profligate defense spending has continued into the twentieth century. But by 1930 there existed what perhaps was the only genuinely "peacetime" military balance in European history. There a prevailing sense that permanent peace was more or less attainable, and, in any case, "reasonable" men could avoid war through negotiations. So military budgets were slashed through the 1920s. And the onset of the Great Depression caused military establishments to be reduced even further. The horrors to come were unanticipated. Japan's aggression in China was a year away, Stalin had not consolidated his power in the Soviet Union, Hitler was still just another crackpot politician in Germany, and Mussolini was still content to make the trains run on time. So it seemed a peaceful world, and nations tailored their military establishments accordingly. A look at them is of some interest, considering what was to come.

Examining the character and quality of a nation's military establishment cannot be wholly limited to "bean counting," simply adding up the total forces and resources. There are several other ways in which the military resources of different nations can be examined. An unusual one is to compare per capita military expenditure (PCME—the total amount expended on defense divided by the number of people in the country) in various nations, their military participation ratio (MPR— the number of civilians per person in uniform), and their active forces per capita expenditure (AFPCE—the military budget divided by the number of men under arms).

National Military Resources

	PCME*	MPR†	AFPCE‡
Belgium	$13.5	277.9	$3,751.5
Czechoslovakia	1.5	121.9	183.0
France	5.0	129.7	648.5
Germany	2.0	638.3	1,276.5
Great Britain	6.5	313.2	2,036.0
Italy	3.0	212.8	638.5
Poland	3.0	115.5	467.5
Portugal	1.5	178.2	267.5
Spain	2.5	110.8	277.0

NOTES: Contemporary (i.e., 1930) dollars are used, which were considerably more valuable than current ones (by a factor of 9 to 10).

There was some difference in the efficiency with which different governments applied their defense funds. Nevertheless, the table shows the relative importance each nation placed on defense.

* PCME is per capita military expense (dollars per citizen).
† MPR is military participation ratio (citizens per soldier).
‡ AFPCE is active forces per capita expenditure (defense budget divided by number of troops).

This table refers to active metropolitan forces only, thereby excluding often enormous reserve forces (Belgium, 800,000; France, 4.5 million; Italy, 3.5 million; and so forth) that were, of course, supported by a part of the regular military expenditures. In addition, the figures exclude colonial forces, which were relatively modest, except for those of Great Britain. Note also that the Soviet Union is missing, reliable data being wholly unavailable (and the Communists had dispensed with modern bookkeeping anyway).

The AFPCE actually gives a better notion of the nature of a nation's military expenditures than does either the PCME or the MPR, since it suggests the proportion of investment in advanced technology. Belgium, for example, was at that time investing rather heavily in a complex system of frontier fortifications (France's Maginot Line was as yet still in the planning stage). Great Britain, of course, was putting its money into the Royal Navy, expending the maximum amounts possible on the new 10,000-ton, 8-inch-gunned "Heavy Cruisers" permitted under the 1922 Naval Disarmament Treaty. It was also investing in the Royal Air Force, which had been found rather useful for policing some colonial areas (especially Iraq). Germany, restricted by the 1919 treaty of Versailles to an army of 100,000 men and a navy of 30,000, was investing its money in higher pay, increased benefits, and better training, as well as superior equipment (such as the genuine light machine gun) within the limits of the treaty. The data given for Germany are the "official figures" and exclude expenditures on forbidden

Strength of the Armies

	Men*	Tanks	Artillery	Machine Guns	Divisions† Infantry	Cavalry	Pool‡
Austrian	30	0	90	420	3	0	0
Belgian	90	50	926	4,000	24	2	800
British	148	580	1,400	14,200	19	2	300
Czech	165	100	1,286	10,500	13	2	1,000
French	228	3,500	16,700	35,000	81	9	4,500
German	100	0	310	2,000	7	3	0
Hungarian	35	0	96	1,192	4	0	0
Italian	200	150	2,070	5,000	40	3	3,500
Japanese	230	40	3,000	21,000	34	0	1,800
Polish	150	350	2,400	10,600	33	7	3,200
Romanian	100	80	1,050	4,500	44	4	700
Soviet	563	250	4,500	26,500	71	13	9,200
Spanish	150	48	1,200	4,500	16	3	1,500
Swiss	2	0	548	7,118	6		700
U.S.	140	1,047	3,936	35,000	25	6	300
Yugoslav	108	20	800	4,000	17	2	3,500

*Men is the number of troops on active duty, in thousands.
† Reserve divisions have been included in the infantry and cavalry divisions (as some countries had separate brigades rather than divisions, these have been grouped into national divisions for our purposes).
‡ Pool is the number of trained men available for mobilization, in thousands (some estimates give the Germans about 150,000–200,000 "secret" reservists).

technologies such as tanks, submarines, aircraft, and poison gas, which were procured and tested covertly in several other countries, notably the Soviet Union, Sweden, and the Netherlands.

A more traditional look at the strengths of these armies (in the table on page 25) (and some others) can also be of value, of course.

It is interesting to note that in 1930 only the French Army had more tanks and artillery pieces than did the U.S. Army, but these were, of course, mostly obsolete World War I vehicles, notably Renault FT-17s. Austria, Hungary, and Germany were restricted by the World War I peace treaties and so could not own tanks, at least not officially. The figures in the table exclude colonial forces.

SOCIETAL MOTORIZATION, 1939

In an extremely perceptive observation made during the 1930s, Benito Mussolini remarked that Italy could not afford to have a motorized army. His reasoning was that Italy lacked not only the industrial base to produce such a force, but also a "motorized" population, people familiar with and skilled in using motor vehicles. He was right, up to a point. The general pattern of the war that followed demonstrated rather effectively that in any sustained conflict the more technically sophisticated society had an enormous advantage.

Motor Vehicles and Population, 1939

	Population in (millions)	Motor Vehicles in (millions)	P:MV*
France	42.0	1.8	23.3:1
Germany	75.0	2.0	37.5:1
Great Britain	48.0	1.5	32.0:1
Italy	39.0	0.3	130.0:1
United States	132.0	30.0	4.4:1

*P:MV is the number of people per motor vehicle.

There were about forty million motor vehicles in the world in 1939. The countries listed in the table accounted for nearly 90 percent of them. Indeed, the United States alone had 75 percent, which was also about its share of automotive production facilities. Note that the table suggests that Mussolini's conclusion concerning the relationship between a motorized army and a motorized society is erroneous. After all, Germany was much less motorized than France and yet produced the blitzkrieg armies that would overrun France in a month. However, while the French Army of 1940 was actually more completely motorized than the army of Germany, German success was based on the fact that it concentrated its motorized resources (trucks as well as tanks) in a relatively small number of divisions, permitting about 15 to 20 percent of the army to be completely motorized. The British Army was even more motorized than the French Army (the British troops sent to France in 1939–1940 were the first fully motorized forces in history, the only horses were those taken along for exercise and polo), but it too dispersed its motorized assets. It was the policy of concentrating motorized resources, coupled with its sizable prewar stockpile of motor vehicles, that sustained German efforts until attrition, particularly in the Soviet Union, began to destroy vehicles faster than their industrial base could replace them.

The U.S. experience in the war, however, confirmed Mussolini's observation. U.S. troops required far less training to become proficient drivers and mechanics than did those of any other nation, usually being familiar with motor vehicles long before they were drafted. In fact, U.S. troops were so motor-minded they quickly figured out that by carefully organizing all available motor vehicles, no one had to walk, even in an infantry division. This was a matter of considerable strategic consequence when the Third Army sprang across France in August and September 1944.

American automotive expertise had other interesting results. The average American unit in Europe actually tended to accumulate motor vehicles during the campaign. As the men advanced, captured enemy vehicles, and even abandoned U.S. vehicles, were quickly repaired and pressed into service. Some divisions eventually were very over strength in motor transport by the end of the war in Europe: The record apparently was held by the 83rd Infantry Division, which owned about 40 percent more motor vehicles than it was supposed to have.

THE BATTLE OF THE NUMBERS

While the French were eager to get involved in World War I (largely to recover the territory they had lost in the 1870 war with Germany), they were much less willing to go to war in the 1940s. Part of their fear came from the memory of how close the Germans came to winning World War I. But there were also numbers to consider, namely the number of young men France and Germany could put into uniform. France had been suffering from a declining birthrate since the early nineteenth century, while the fecund Germans were not. What this came down to was the number of young men available to be soldiers. In 1937, France had only 4.3 million men of military age, while the Germans had 8.3 million. Then, in 1938, with the annexation of Austria and the German-speaking parts of Czechoslovakia, Germany added 9 million more people to its population. This gave the Third Reich 11 million potential soldiers by 1940.

The French were not only outmatched in terms of people, but also with regard to defense spending. In 1932, France was spending 5.2 percent of its GNP on defense, compared to only 1.9 percent by Germany (which was constrained by the Versailles Treaty). But in 1935 Germany tore up the Versailles Treaty and began to rearm. While France and Great Britain dithered away their chance to intervene with relative ease, Germany began a massive arms buildup. By 1938, Germany was spending 17.2 percent of its GNP on defense, while France was spending only 8.6 percent. Alarmed at this situation, in 1939 France increased defense spending to 23 percent of its GNP. Germany more than matched that with 30 percent. Moreover, Germany's economy had boomed through the 1930s, becoming substantially larger than France's. To make matters worse, the French were spending a lot of money on fortifications and a navy, in neither of which did the Germans need to invest.

Outnumbered over two to one in potential troops and actual defense spending, the French did not view a war with Germany very optimistically. Their only hope was that in a long war Germany would begin to run out of key raw materials, such as tungsten and cobalt, that it had to obtain overseas. In World War I, the naval blockade of Germany had been successful, but it had been successful too late. Lack of raw materials did not become catastrophic in Germany until the Allies had won a brute-force military victory. The French were worried about a reprise, that the Germans would do a little better, well enough to defeat France.

THE FIRST ARMORED DIVISIONS

The division, a large (4,000–20,000 men), self-contained fighting force of all arms (infantry, artillery, cavalry, and so forth), capable of a considerable degree of independent operation, was introduced in the late eighteenth century and has ever since remained the principal tactical formation for large-scale, protracted ground combat. Although the creation of the first armored divisions was proposed as early as 1918, no units larger than brigades were actually activated until the 1930s, when international tensions began to rise. In that decade several countries created experimental armored divisions, testing a variety of organizational and equipment plans, known as tables of organization and equipment (T/O&Es). Every armored division T/O&E actually adopted between 1934 and 1939 is summarized in this table. All of these primordial armored divisions were essentially experimental since no one was sure how they would work in actual combat.

The First Armored Divisions, 1934–1939

	1934			1935	1938			1939	
Army	French	Soviet	German	British	French	German	Italian	Spanish	French
Type	DLM				DCR				DCR
Troops	10.4	10.0	12.0	12.0	6.5	11.5	6.5	8.0	6.5
Tanks	240	463	561	600	250	266	330	330	158
Battalions									
Tank	4	7	4	9	6	4	4	7	4
Infantry	3	4	3	2	5	4	3	3	2
Artillery	3.0	1.3	4.0	2.0	3.0	4.0	2.6	1.3	3.0
Reconnaissance	1.0	1.0	1.0	1.0	0	1.0	0.3	1.0	1.0
Engineer	1.0	0.3	0.3	0.3	0	1.0	0.3	0.3	1.0
Signal	0.6	1.0	0	0	0	1.0	0	0	0
Rating	10	7	10	8	7	12	6	7	8

NOTES: DLM is *Division Légère Méchanique* or Light Mechanized Division; DCR is *Division Cuirassée de Réserve* or Reserve Armored Division. Troops is the number of men in a division, in thousands. In addition to tanks, all of these formations had varying numbers of other armored fighting vehicles, ranging from armored cars to self-propelled artillery pieces. In Battalions, .3 indicates a company. Artillery includes antitank and antiaircraft battalions. In some armies, signals were subsumed in the engineers. Rating, an approximation of the fighting power of the division for purposes of comparing its relative capabilities, is a rough mathematical calculation of the relative fighting power of each division, combining manpower, equipment, and organizational and doctrinal factors.

Ultimately, the most important organizational fact about armored divisions is not the number of tanks on hand; indeed a division can have too many tanks. In order to operate with maximal effectiveness, the tanks have to be supported by other arms such as, infantry, artillery, engineers, and so forth. Experience has demonstrated that the critical factors in mechanized organization are

1. a rough parity among the numbers of tank, infantry, and artillery battalions, in the ratio 1:1:1, and

2. that all elements be equally mobile. This greatly enhances tactical flexibility and enables the division to hold the ground it takes, a task that tanks cannot do without infantry, as tanks are most effective attacking, not defending.

To further strengthen the ability of an armored division to perform its duties it ought to have a strong reconnaissance element able to seek out and secure information. Ideally, a reconnaissance battalion ought to be something of an armored division in miniature, with tank, artillery, and infantry elements enabling it to fight for information when necessary. Similarly, an armored division requires considerable support from engineer and signal troops, the former to facilitate overcoming natural and tactical obstacles, and the latter to keep the fast-moving elements of the division in constant communication. On this basis, it can be seen that most of the divisions formed in the prewar years were deficient in some form or another.

Surprisingly, it was the French and Soviets, not the Germans, who created the first armored divisions. However, while on paper the French *Division Légère Méchanique* was remarkably sound, the tactical and strategic doctrine for its employment was poor, limited to the notion of operating as a sort of mobile reserve for rapid counterattacks. The Soviet division was less technically balanced, but its tactical and strategic doctrine was fairly good, with the Soviets having come up with the idea of massing armor for penetration attacks. Unfortunately, Soviet expertise in mechanized operations would not survive the Great Purges of the late 1930s, as Stalin slaughtered most of the senior leadership of the Red Army. Thus it was the Germans who developed the well-balanced armored divisions with the doctrine to match. This produced the blitzkrieg (fast-moving tank and motorized infantry units smashing and overrunning enemy units). Among the other great powers, Italy alone had a reasonably sound idea of how mechanized operations ought to proceed and actually had some success with blitzkrieglike operations in the latter part of the Spanish Civil War, although it was handicapped by an inadequate industrial base, poor equipment, inferior training, and a generally disastrous military system. None of the other great powers came close to having a good idea about how to organize and employ armored forces.

It was the German 1938 pattern panzer (''armor'') division that opened the Second World War so impressively in Poland in September 1939 and carried much of the burden of the even more spectacular French campaign in May and June 1940. Despite this, the German panzer divisions were not the first to see combat. This distinction belongs to the two Spanish Republican *Divisiones de tanques y blindados*. These were, however, actually administrative rather than operational formations and saw no action as divisions, their elements being committed piecemeal in support of essentially infantry operations. The first whole armored division to enter combat was the Italian *131 Centauro*, which went into action during the brief Albanian campaign of early 1939.

Despite their relative tardiness in organizing armored divisions, and getting them into action, the Germans did much better with the new formations than did anyone else. This was because they were diligent in testing the panzer divisions. Between 1935 and 1938 they conducted extensive maneuvers which pointed out some flaws in their organization and doctrine. Their occupation of Austria in the spring of 1938 was conducted in anticipation of combat and revealed still more problems. As one German officer charitably put it, "Only thirty percent of the tanks broke down" during the road march to Vienna. The Germans were also forced to get fuel from local gas stations when their own supplies did not catch up with the thirsty tanks. Then came their occupation of the Sudetenland in the fall of 1938 and of the rest of Czechoslovakia the following spring. So by the late summer of 1939, as the panzer divisions concentrated for the invasion of Poland, they had accumulated an extraordinary amount of training and experience. This would pay off in the great blitzkrieg victories of 1939–1941.

THE BIRTH OF THE BLITZ, 1916–1933

The tank was born in the horrors of the First World War. In 1914 the European powers had marched off to war expecting that victory would be secured after a few months of intensive campaigning. Instead, the cumulative effects of the Industrial Revolution (mass armies, machine guns, quick-firing artillery, barbed wire, and the continuous production of supplies and munitions) led to the protracted agony of trench warfare. Try as they might, the tactical commanders could find no way to end this stalemate, which, beginning toward the end of 1914, pretty much lasted into early 1918. Repeated attempts to throw ever greater masses of men and material against even relatively lightly held trench lines yielded little more than endless casualty lists. Although many of those generals may have deserved the collective nickname "the Donkeys" for the stubborn determination with which they kept trying more of the same in the face of ever-mounting casualties, not all were so thickheaded. A few soldiers and thinkers put their minds to trying to come up with truly novel solutions, most of which were either wholly impractical (like body armor for the troops) or merely made matters worse (like poison gas). But one idea actually worked: the tank.

Developed at the suggestion of Winston Churchill, First Lord of the Admiralty during the early part of the war, the tank was so obvious a solution that the Italians, the French, and the Russians were working along essentially the same lines, and in fact, some years earlier an Austrian officer, Günther Burstyn, contemplating the future of war, had proposed precisely the same vehicle. The basic idea of the tank was quite simple, take a caterpillar track–laying vehicle (they were then being used in agriculture) and equip it with armor and weapons. With its tracks the vehicle (named a "tank," i.e., "cistern," for reasons of secrecy) could move across the muddy, shell-pocked, and trenched ground of "no-man's-land" readily, crushing obstacles like barbed wire. Its armor would permit it to ignore enemy machine-gun fire and its own weapons would allow it to deliver fire to the enemy. The tank was a device that would enable the infantry to break loose from the stalemate of the trenches. And it worked. The first serious test came in the Battle of Cambrai in 1917, when several hundred tanks in three British brigades attacked without preliminary artillery bombardment in support of six infantry divisions. The results were startling. In less than six days the Germans had been thrown back four miles, perhaps the most significant advance on the Western front since early 1915. However, the mechanical unreliability of the tanks, coupled with a shortage of infantry replacements and a series of skillful German counterattacks, forced the British to lose most of their gains over the next few weeks. But even the most dull-witted generals were impressed. As a result, the Allies more or less called a halt to offensive operations until the summer of 1918, when tanks (and a lot of American infantry) were available. Using their thousands of tanks and hundreds of thousands of American troops to spearhead a series of offensives in the summer and autumn of 1918, the Allies were able to secure an armistice on November 11. So the tank/infantry team had proven capable of winning the war.

There were some dissatisfied people, however, among them British Major General J.F.C. Fuller, a staff officer who had served with tanks

at Cambrai and elsewhere. Fuller believed that far from merely supporting infantry (i.e., helping them overcome local obstacles), tanks
could play a leading role in warfare. One of the officers charged with
planning Allied operations for 1919, Fuller envisioned tanks as having
a strategic role, not merely a tactical one. In Plan 1919, Fuller provided
for massed attacks by heavy tanks to spearhead an offensive, breaking
through the German lines. Thereupon light, faster tanks would pour
through the opening followed by infantrymen loaded into special transport tanks and trucks, which would be able to keep up with the light
tanks. These mobile forces would speed deep into the enemy's rear,
disrupting his lines of communication, supply, reinforcement, and retreat. Such an offensive would permit the Allies to encircle large
enemy-held areas at relatively little cost. Fuller's proposal aroused
considerable interest. Ferdinand Foch himself, the Allied generalis-
simo, expressed approval. But the war ended in 1918 and Fuller's plan
became an academic curiosity, soon forgotten, as the "war-winning"
combination of infantry supported by tanks became the doctrine.

But if the armies were convinced that the tank was but a tactical
supplement to the infantry, a number of military theoreticians continued to differ. During the 1920s and 1930s men such as Great Britain's
Fuller, B. H. Liddel Hart, and Guiford LeQ. Martel, France's Maxime
Weygand and Charles de Gaulle, America's Adna Chafee, Russia's
Mikail Tukachevsky, and Germany's Heinz Guderian wrote and lectured on how they saw tanks being used in a future war. While the
specific details of their ideas varied, all of these theorists saw tanks as
more than just a support weapon for infantry.

Despite all this theorization and not a little experimentation, it was
in Germany that the greatest success was obtained. Germany had been
prohibited from owning tanks by the Versailles Treaty in 1919. However, this did not prevent the German Army from experimenting with
tanks, making use of dummy vehicles (and a few real ones on secret
testing grounds in the Soviet Union). By the early 1930s Heinz Guderian, a relatively junior officer, had been put in charge of tank development. Acting independently, and inspired by the highly successful
"infiltration" tactics with which Germany had very nearly won World
War I in the spring of 1918, Guderian began to envision a role for the
tank much like the one J.F.C. Fuller had evolved, a combined arms
force capable of strategic employment. When Hitler came to power in
1933, he began to examine Germany's military establishment and
potential. Guderian was asked to demonstrate his ideas about the employment of tanks. Within a few days Guderian had cobbled to-

gether a reconnaissance detachment consisting of some motorcycle infantry, some light antitank guns, some armored cars, and a platoon of prototype Panzer I tanks and led them through their paces.

Hitler was impressed and the German panzer force was born.

SO WHY DID HE WEAR PISTOLS?

George S. Patton was the only American ever granted the title "Master of the Sword" by the French Army Cavalry School at Saumur. So expert a swordsman was he that as a junior officer Patton had represented the United States in the 1912 Olympics, finishing fifth in the decathlon. Later, he even designed the last saber ever issued to the U.S. cavalry, which is still in use for ceremonial occasions.

AN EDUCATED SOLDIER IS A SUPERIOR SOLDIER

The first British infantry battalion to report not a single illiterate man in its ranks was the 1st Gordon Highlanders, in 1933. This may not seem important, but was in fact overwhelmingly so. Long experience has demonstrated that the better educated a man is, the better a soldier he is likely to make. One reason for the superior performance of some armies in World War II (e.g., the German, American, and British) was the high proportion of literate men in the ranks, in contrast to most of the less successful armies (e.g., the Italian, Chinese, and to some extent even the Soviet), which had significant numbers of illiterate fighters.

ALL THE COLORS OF THE RAINBOW

In peacetime, armies and navies are supposed to consider possible threats and make plans accordingly. Of course such matters have to be kept secret, lest a journalistic leak lead to embarrassment or even an international incident. As a result, from quite early in the twentieth century the U.S. armed forces began referring to potential opponents, allies, locations, and objectives by various colors. Thus, while discussing a hypothetical operation, the brass could refer to War Plan Indigo, knowing that it was the plan for the occupation of Iceland in the event that Denmark fell under the control of an unfriendly power. Similarly, they could discuss our options if we had to assist Lemon in the event that it was attacked by Olive, or was allied with Red against Black, all the while confident that outsiders would be thoroughly confused by the cover names for the countries involved. This was the origin of the famous War Plan Orange, the scheme (actually a successive series of blueprints developed over some forty years) for war with Japan, designated Orange. Altogether there were more than twenty color plans. The list that follows indicates the countries and other places represented by the various colors as far as is known today.

Black: Germany
Blue: United States (as a belligerent)
Brown: Indonesia
Citron: Brazil
Crimson: Canada
Emerald: Ireland
Garnet: New Zealand
Gold: France
Gray: the Azores
Green: Mexico
Indigo: Iceland
Lemon: Portugal
Olive: Spain
Orange: Japan
Purple: Soviet Union
Red: Great Britain
Ruby: India
Scarlet: Australia
Silver: Italy
Tan: Cuba
Violet: China (intervention in an internal matter)
White: United States (domestic disorders, e.g., a Communist putsch)
Yellow: China (international conflict)

The origin of the colors is unclear. In some cases there is an obvious link, such as Great Britain and red (and variations of red for the Commonwealth), perhaps deriving from the reddish tint that has traditionally been used to indicate British territories on maps. Gray for the Azores probably comes from an old poem about Columbus that includes the line "Behind him lay the gray Azores." And yellow for China seems rooted in some blatant racism. But others are more obscure. Orange, for example, might refer to the color of the Japanese flag, and olive might refer to one of the principal products of Spain, but what was the connection of purple to Russia or indigo to Iceland?

Although the first version of War Plan Orange was developed quite early in the century, all versions envisioned a systematic island-hopping advance across the Pacific, so that the plan remained the principal guide for the conduct of the war in the Pacific.

Beginning in 1939 the army and navy began to develop a new series of war plans based on the assumption that the United States would participate in a multinational alliance against the Axis powers. War Plan Rainbow ran through five incarnations before the United States actually entered the war. Although Rainbow Five incorporated the final version of War Plan Orange, its basic assumption was the "Germany first" strategy, that is, that in the event of war with both Germany and Japan, the Allies would concentrate their efforts on defeating Germany first, as the more dangerous of the two.

YOU HAVE TO GET YOUR PRIORITIES RIGHT

In 1937 the British Army riding school at Weeden had a budget of £20,000 (about $1 million in 1994 dollars) for 38 students, more than £526 (about $26,000 in 1994 dollars) per pupil, while the Tank Corps School, with 550 students, had to make do with £46,000, or about £83 (about $4,100 in 1994 dollars) per pupil. This effectively demonstrated the priorities of the senior leadership of the British Army in maintaining tradition rather than preparing for war.

THE OHIO PLAN

The United States enacted the first peacetime military draft in its history on September 16, 1940. The intention was to train a sizable body of men as a deterrent to attack. Under the terms of the Selective Service Act (so named because it was not necessary to draft everyone) the president was authorized to draft up to 900,000 men between the ages of twenty and thirty-six for service not to exceed one year, with provision for extension to eighteen months in national emergencies. Registration began on October 16, 1940, and names were first drawn on October 29. As the first batch of selectees was inducted on November 25, men sometimes referred to their service as being on the OHIO plan, for Over the Hill In October. In the summer of 1941 it was proposed to amend the bill to extend the term of service to as long as thirty months. This was bitterly contested by a strange mélange of both right-wing and left-wing elements. Nevertheless, on August 18, 1941, the amendment was passed, squeaking through the House of Representatives by just one vote, a margin that helped convince Japanese military leaders that the United States lacked the will for war.

Without the Selective Service, the United States would have been even less prepared for war than was actually the case. Of course, this didn't help the poor fellows called up in 1940, for after Pearl Harbor everyone was in for the duration, most not getting out until mid-1945, and a few not until early 1946.

"*I* . . ."

In 1939 a newspaper subjected the speech patterns of the then principal world leaders to analysis regarding the use of the first person singular. The results were not surprising.

Adolf Hitler was wont to use *I* or the equivalent about once every 53 words, while his partner in crime, Benito Mussolini, used it about once every 83 words. In contrast, Franklin D. Roosevelt said *I* about once every 100 words. French Premier Édouard Daladier referred to himself in this fashion only once in every 234 words and British Prime Minister Neville Chamberlain only once in every 249 words, perhaps because they had so much to be modest about.

Since at the time this analysis was made Winston Churchill was an unemployed politician, he was omitted from the survey. However, in his "Blood, Toil, Tears, and Sweat" address to the House of Commons on May 13, 1940, he used the first person singular about once in every 35 words, thereby beating even Hitler in the egotism stakes.

WHAT DID YOU DO IN THE GREAT WAR, DADDY?

Whereas most of the senior officers and virtually all of the political leaders in World War I had seen little or no serious active military service prior to 1914, virtually all of the senior officers in World War II and many of the political leaders had served in the Great War. Their experiences are generally regarded as having greatly influenced the character of the war, for they were determined not to repeat the senseless slaughter they had witnessed.

HAROLD ALEXANDER, who commanded the Allied 15th Army Group in Italy, had been an officer in the Royal Guards.

TERRY DE LA MESA ALLEN, among the most famous U.S. infantry division commanders in World War II, was a cavalry officer serving with great distinction in the infantry in France.

WLADYLSAW ANDERS, who commanded the Polish Army Corps in Italy, enlisted in the Russian cavalry in 1914, joined the infant Polish Army after the Russian Revolution and later served as a senior staff officer in the Russo-Polish War of 1919–1921.

CLAUDE AUCKINLECK, who had a tough time at Rommel's hands in North Africa, had been an Indian Army infantry officer.

PIETRO BADOGLIO, who became the prime minister of Italy after the fall of Mussolini, had been an infantry officer, rising to command of a corps before ending the war as deputy chief of the General Staff.

FEODOR VON BOCK, who commanded various army groups early in the war, had been a Guards officer, winning the *Pour le mérite,* the highest decoration of Imperial Germany, equivalent to the Congressional Medal of Honor.

MARTIN BORMANN, Hitler's principal aide in 1944–1945, was an eighteen-year-old conscript in the artillery very late in the war but saw no active service.

OMAR BRADLEY, the principal American ground commander in northwestern Europe from D-day to the end of the war, spent the earlier war just as did his World War II boss, Eisenhower, training troops and trying to get overseas.

ALAN BROOKE, chief of the British Imperial General Staff for most of the war, had been an artillery officer.

SIMON BOLIVAR BUCKNER, killed in action commanding the U.S. Tenth Army on Okinawa, was an aviation instructor.

WILHELM CANARIS, who headed Hitler's intelligence service while plotting against him, began the war as an officer in Graf Spee's unfortunate squadron, being on the only ship to escape the German disaster in the Falkland Islands early in 1915. He returned to Germany, where he transferred to the intelligence service, working mostly in Spain, where he made many contacts that would eventually prove most useful.

CLAIRE CHENNAULT, commander of the Flying Tigers and the Fourteenth Air Force, was a schoolteacher in 1917, becoming a pilot after attending O.C.S., but saw no overseas service.

WINSTON CHURCHILL, beginning the war as First Lord of the Admiralty, spent some time commanding an infantry battalion on the Western front after the disastrous Gallipoli campaign and later became Secretary at War.

MARK CLARK, commander of the Fifth Army in Italy, served as an infantry officer with the AEF, being wounded as a battalion commander.

ANDREW CUNNINGHAM, the most distinguished British sea dog since Nelson, served in destroyers, rising to command the H.M.S. *Scorpion.*

WILLIAM "WILD BILL" DONOVAN, head of the OSS, was commander of New York's old "Fighting 69th" (165th Infantry) during World War I, garnering three wounds and a Congressional Medal of Honor in the process.

JAMES DOOLITTLE, who led the Tokyo raid in early 1942 and later commanded the Eighth Air Force, had been an enlisted flying instructor in the United States.

HUGH DOWDING, who lead Fighter Command during the Battle of Britain, was an artilleryman in 1914, later transferring to the Royal Flying Corps.

DWIGHT D. EISENHOWER, the Supreme Commander, ETO, was a 1915 graduate of West Point; a temporary infantry major by the end of the war, he was unable to get overseas.

JAMES FORRESTAL, undersecretary and later secretary of the navy, left a lucrative Wall Street law firm to serve as a naval aviator in World War I, winning a Navy Cross.

FRANCISCO FRANCO, the Caudillo of Spain, was a very young, very brave infantry officer in Morocco.

BERNARD FREYBURG, who commanded the New Zealand Division in North Africa and Italy, was a volunteer with Pancho Villa in Mexico when the war began. He soon enlisted in the

British Army and accumulated an heroic record, ending the war as a twenty-eight-year-old division commander with a Victoria Cross.

MAURICE GAMELIN, who bungled the defense of France in 1940, served as a staff officer throughout the war.

CHARLES DE GAULLE, leader of the Free French, began the war as a lieutenant in Henri Pétain's 33rd Infantry Regiment, becoming a prisoner of war at Verdun in 1916.

ROY GEIGER, one of the most distinguished U.S. Marine Corps commanders in the war, and the only Marine ever to command a field army (the Tenth, on Okinawa), was a Marine aviator and won a Navy Cross.

GEORGE VI, who proved an excellent king, had served as a junior officer in the Royal Navy during the earlier war and was under fire during the Battle of Jutland.

JOSEPH GOEBBELS, Hitler's propagandist, was physically unfit for military service because of a club foot and spent the war as a student; in postwar years he would sometimes attribute his limp to a war wound.

HERMANN GÖRING, head of the Luftwaffe and long Hitler's right-hand man, was a fighter ace (twenty-two kills) with the famed Flying Circus, which he commanded for a time, earning a *Pour le mérite,* Imperial Germany's highest decoration.

LORD GORT, who commanded the doomed BEF of 1939–1940, was an infantry officer and won a Victoria Cross.

HEINZ GUDERIAN, founder of Germany's panzer arm and for a time chief of the General Staff, began the war as a cavalry officer who later moved to staff.

WILLIAM F. HALSEY, the commander of the Third Fleet in the Pacific, skippered various destroyers in Europe during 1917–1918, winning a Navy Cross in the process.

THOMAS HART, who commanded the Asiatic Fleet in the dark days of 1941–1942 and later went on to the Senate, had enlisted during the Spanish-American War and had commanded a submarine squadron operating out of Ireland during World War I.

LOUIS B. HERSHEY, head of the Selective Service System, was a National Guard officer called to active duty in France in 1918.

RUDOLF HESS, one of Hitler's closest confidants early in the war, enlisted as a volunteer in 1914, rose to lieutenant in the *Stosstruppen* ("storm troopers," the elite assault troops), and ended the war as a pilot.

HEINRICH HIMMLER, head of the SS and Gestapo, was a young officer cadet in 1918, seeing no combat service.

ADOLF HITLER had been an infantry runner (a messenger delivering orders and reports across the battlefield on foot), winning an Iron Cross 1st Class and 2nd Class, plus several lesser decorations, while being twice wounded and once gassed; for a time he served in trenches directly opposite those held by the battalion commanded by Winston Churchill.

ALBERT KESSELRING, Luftwaffe marshal and one of the most tenacious defensive fighters in the war, was an artilleryman in 1914, later becoming a staff officer.

ERNEST J. KING, Chief of Naval Operations for most of the war, was chief of staff to the commander of the Atlantic Fleet throughout the war, earning a Navy Cross in the process.

IVAN STEPANOVICH KONEV, Soviet marshal and front commander, began World War I as a private in the Czar's army.

JEAN-MARIE DE LATTRE DE TASSIGNY, who commanded the French First Army in 1944–1945, served as a cavalry officer and was severely wounded by a saber during a mounted skirmish in 1914, probably the last notable soldier to have had such an experience.

RITTER VON LEEB, who commanded various German Army groups early in the war, was an artillery officer during 1914–1918.

DOUGLAS MACARTHUR, who commanded in the Philippines and southwest Pacific, was an infantry officer, ending the war as a brigadier general.

CARL GUSTAF EMIL VON MANNERHEIM, the Finnish Chief of Staff, was a Russian infantry officer in 1914, ending the war as a *Generalmajor* (brigadier general in U.S. terms).

ERICH VON MANSTEIN, distinguished tactician (if not human being) on the Eastern front, was a Guards officer.

MAO TSE-TUNG, leader of the Chinese Communists, was a recently discharged infantryman from Sun Yat-sen's revolutionary forces, working as a librarian.

GEORGE C. MARSHALL, the Chief of Staff and arguably the most distinguished American soldier of this century, served as a very effective staff officer in the AEF.

BERNARD LAW MONTGOMERY, Great Britain's most successful field commander, began the war as an infantry platoon leader, being severely wounded in 1914; later he served in various staff assignments and by 1918 he was a battalion commander.

LOUIS MOUNTBATTEN, who had a distinguished career in Combined Operations and later commanded the British Far Eastern theater, was a very young naval cadet, ending the war as a midshipman.

BENITO MUSSOLINI, *il Duce,* had been a sergeant of *Bersaglieri* with a distinguished record in the Italo-Austrian war, during which he was severely wounded.

CHESTER W. NIMITZ, commander of the Pacific theater, although a gunnery officer, was on the staff of the navy's submarine service.

GEORGE S. PATTON, commander of the Third Army, was a tank officer, rising to colonel.

FRIEDREICH PAULUS, who led the German Sixth Army in the disaster at Stalingrad, was an infantry and staff officer during the war.

HENRI PÉTAIN, the leader of Vichy France, began the war as a regimental commander and ended it as a marshal of France.

DUDLEY POUND, until his death in 1943 the First Sea Lord (Chief of Staff) of the Royal Navy, was flag captain to an admiral at Jutland.

JOACHIM VON RIBBENTROP, Hitler's foreign minister, served as a volunteer on the Eastern front for a time, winning an Iron Cross 1st Class, but later joined the foreign ministry, serving with the German military procurement mission to the United States.

KONSTANTIN KONSTANTINOVICH ROKOSSOVSKY, Soviet marshal and a critical player at Kursk, the greatest tank battle in history, was a private in the Czar's army, later joining the Bolsheviks.

ERWIN ROMMEL, the Desert Fox, had a notable career as an infantryman, particularly distinguishing himself during the Battle of Caporetto, for which he won a *Pour le mérite*.

FRANKLIN D. ROOSEVELT had been assistant secretary of the navy.

GERD VON RUNDSTEDT, Hitler's most consistently successful senior commander, was a staff officer throughout the war, ending it as a *Generalmajor*.

WILLIAM SLIM, who commanded in Burma for much of the war, rose from a private to a regular commission in the Indian Army during the previous war.

RAYMOND A. SPRUANCE, the victor of Midway and commander of the Fifth Fleet in the Pacific, commanded the destroyer *Aaron Ward*.

JOSEPH VISSARIONOVICH STALIN was a minor Bolshevik leader who spent much of the war serving time in a Czarist jail, until the Revolution.

KURT STUDENT, who conducted the successful airborne invasion of Crete, began World War I as a pilot, serving variously in the air and on staff until its end.

SEMYON KONSTANTINOVICH TIMOSHENKO, marshal of the Soviet Union and the only senior Russian officer to remain continuously in command from 1941 through 1945, served as an enlisted man in the Czar's cavalry before joining the Red Army in 1917, rising rapidly thereafter to high command during the civil war.

TITO, the Yugoslav partisan leader, began the war as an enlisted man in the Austro-Hungarian Army, being wounded several times before being captured in Russia in 1915; released by the October Revolution of 1917, he promptly joined the Red Army.

HARRY S TRUMAN, who became president on the death of FDR in 1945, was a very effective artillery captain with the AEF, reputedly the best mule skinner and best "cusser" in the army (a skill he acquired by deliberate practice and study).

ALEXANDER VANDEGRIFT, the most distinguished Marine commander of the war (Guadalcanal) and the first Marine to hold the rank of full general, was in the *Garde du Haiti* during World War I.

YAMAMOTO ISOROKU, Japan's most talented naval strategist, was a staff lieutenant commander for most of the war.

GEORGY KONSTANTINOVICH ZHUKOV, the most successful Soviet general of the war, served with distinction as an enlisted volunteer in the Czar's cavalry, before joining the Red Army.

It is interesting to note that Badoglio (1871–1956), Freyburg (1889–1963), MacArthur (1880–1964), Mannerheim (1867–1951), and Rundstedt (1875–1953) were the only men to serve as generals in both world wars. Badoglio ended the Great War as a lieutenant general, Freyburg (the youngest of the lot) as a major general, and MacArthur as a brigadier general, equivalent to Mannerheim and Rundstedt, who ranked as *Generalmajor.*

PRIORITIES IN PEACE, PRIORITIES IN WAR

During peacetime, armies can readily lose sight of what is and isn't important in wartime. For example, in 1935 British Field Marshal Sir Archibald Montgomery-Masingberd, the chief of the Imperial General Staff (IGS), proposed that any officer who became involved in a divorce should be dismissed from the service. This may seem odd, but after all, 1935 was a pretty peaceful year, and the Imperial General Staff had time to concern itself with trivialities such as social propriety, not having anything more important with which to occupy its time. What is more surprising is that in 1944, John Masters, an Indian Army brigadier, received an official communication from the IGS stating that, as he had been named as a correspondent in a divorce, he should forthwith resign from His Majesty's service. Masters, who later had a distinguished career as an author and screenwriter (*The Road Past Mandalay, Bhowani Junction,* and others), found the request odd, as he was at the time commanding a Gurkha brigade fighting the Japanese in the jungles of Burma. Fortunately for the war effort, Masters brought the memorandum to the attention of his superior, General William Slim, who took care of the matter in a blistering letter back to London.

THE CLASS THAT STARS FELL ON

Fully 61 of the 164 men in West Point's class of 1915 attained the rank of general, for a total of two generals of the army (five stars), two generals (four stars), seven lieutenant generals (three stars), and fifty lowly major generals (two stars) and brigadier generals (one star). This earned them the collective nickname "the class that stars fell on." Interestingly enough, the first man in the class to become a general was Luis Raul Esteves who was promoted to brigadier general in the Puerto Rican National Guard in 1939, some time before his subsequently more famous classmates Dwight D. Eisenhower and Omar Bradley.

THE SUPERIOR SOCIETY?

The homicide rate in prewar Nazi Germany was only 12.8 percent of that of the United States; an annual rate of 0.75 murders per 100,000 people as against 5.84, figures that, of course, exclude officially sanctioned killings.

ANTIWARMONGER?

Herbert Hoover's presidency (1929–1933) has the distinction of being the only one in American history during which not a single major combat ship was added to the navy. This is sometimes attributed to the fact that the president was a Quaker by religious persuasion, but was more accurately the result of the profound belief that perpetual peace had been attained in the 1920s, as a result of all the disarmament agreements and things like the Kellogg-Briand Pact, in which all the powers agreed to make nice and not make war "no more."

"PEACE IN OUR TIME"

In Munich on September 29, 1939, British Prime Minister Neville Chamberlain, French Premier Édouard Daladier, and Italian Duce Benito Mussolini, concocted a deal with German Führer Adolf Hitler that gave the German-inhabited Sudetenland region of Czechoslovakia to Germany. The statement from Chamberlain about the pact, made back at home after the conference, ". . . I believe it is peace for our time . . ." is the ultimate definition of appeasement in the face of aggression, of cowardice and "peace at any price" delusions. In retrospect, some historians, such as A.J.P. Taylor, have argued that had Great Britain and France stood up to Hitler, he would have backed down, or even been replaced by his own generals. Indeed, they continue, even if it had come to a fight, the democracies would have been strong enough to take on Germany in 1938. How accurate is this assessment?

In fact, quite the reverse is true. As unprepared as Great Britain and France were for war in late 1939, they were even more so a year earlier. Relatively speaking, however, Germany was readier in 1938. Also, the Allied military position in late 1938 was seriously flawed. The overall balance of ground forces, 65 to 70 German divisions to 80 to 85 British (7) and French (75) divisions, was on paper favorable to the Allies. But where Germany had five panzer divisions and six motorized divisions, the Allies between them had three light-armored divisions and as many motorized divisions. The situation in the air was even more imbalanced, for the Germans had about 2,850 first-line combat aircraft, while the Allies had only about 2,350 (the British had committed about 900, the French some 1,450). Moreover, virtually the entire French Air Force consisted of obsolete airplanes, and the Royal Air Force had only a few hundred modern aircraft, while the Germans had mostly first-line equipment.

By September 1939 the Allied situation had greatly improved. Although the ratio of German to Allied divisions was still roughly the same (80 German to 90 Allied), the situation in the air was considerably more favorable to the Allies, who had about 3,700 aircraft (the British 1,900, having introduced hundreds of Hurricanes and Spitfires, and the French, 1,800, having begun to bring their DeWoitine 520 into service), whereas the Germans had increased their strength to about 3,600. So the ratio of Allied to German forces on the ground went from about 1.12:1 to about 1.16:1, while that in the air went from about 0.82:1 to 1.03:1, a significant increase.

Of course, in 1938 the Allies would have been supported by Czechoslovakia. The Czechs had a considerable military force, some 16 divisions and 600 aircraft, and, moreover, had promises of support from the seemingly immensely powerful Soviet Union. This certainly sounds like the Allies missed the boat in 1938. But appearances can be deceiving. About a fifth of the Czech reservists were actually Germans, those very Sudetenlanders around whom the crisis revolved. Moreover, Czechoslovakia was surrounded by enemies, not only Germany, but Poland, Hungary, and Romania as well, all of whom would claim portions of Czechoslovakia as part of the spoils of the Munich summit. Arguably, had Chamberlain and Daladier stood up to Hitler at Munich, they might well have found Poland, with whom he had a nonaggression pact, allied with the Germans. Nor could the Soviet Union do very much. Russia nowhere bordered Czechoslovakia, so that its offers of assistance were predicated upon Poland or pro-German Romania to allow Soviet forces to cross its territory, hardly a viable proposition. As well, the Soviet armed forces were not nearly as capable as they appeared to the outside world. Stalin had no desire to take on the Germans. Yet.

Despite appearances, Chamberlain was no fool. He was quite aware that Hitler's ''No More Territorial Demands'' speech at the time of Munich was a fraud. He was also quite aware of the parlous state of British defenses. He had consulted his commanders and they had given him a precise assessment of the probabilities. When he asked what the chances were of defending Great Britain from an air assault in 1938, he was rightly told that they were not good. It would be at least a year before the Hurricanes and Spitfires would be available in great numbers, and the new mystery weapon, radio direction finding (later given the American name *radar*), on hand. Weighing the odds, Chamberlain backed down. Hitler was no fool either. When Mussolini, who had worked particularly hard to bring about the Munich Pact, boasted of his accomplishment, the führer roasted him. Hitler wanted it to come to a fight in 1938. A year later, when Hitler made his demands for a piece of Poland, Chamberlain again went to his military leaders to ask if there was a reasonable chance of defending Britain. By then there were hundreds of Hurricanes and Spitfires available, and the ''Chain Home'' radar net was in place. Chamberlain promptly issued an ultimatum, and Great Britain was shortly at war. Perhaps the most interesting commentary upon Chamberlain's role is that his replacement as prime minister, Winston Churchill, chose to keep him informed of every development in the war and sought his advice on matters of diplomacy. As a result, at the time of his death, during the Battle of Britain, Chamberlain had the satisfaction of knowing that Great Britain was besting the Nazi onslaught from the air.

2
THE WORLD
AT WAR

While many events were specific to one particular part of the war, there were many others that were more universal in nature. This was the first truly world war, with combat operations in virtually every time zone. The following items also tended to occur throughout the planet during the conflict.

HOW MANY PEOPLE DIED IN WORLD WAR II?

The war killed a lot more people than is commonly thought. We estimate the total death toll to be near a 100 million. However, the number of people who were killed in or died as a consequence of World War II cannot be determined with any absolute degree of accuracy. Traditional estimates range from a low of 30 million to a high of 55 million, yet with some merely cursory research of available information we readily arrived at a figure approaching 80 million.

   The figures published by some countries are very incomplete. For example, generally published figures for civilian losses in Hungary are about 200,000, yet about 90 percent of Hungary's 400,000 Jews perished in Hitler's death camps. Civilian deaths in the Soviet Union were actually higher than previously thought according to recently published documents from previously secret Soviet archives. And then there is the problem of losses in the Third World. The millions of civilians who

Deaths per Country

	Military (in thousands)	Civilians (in thousands)	Total (in thousands)
Allies			
Australia	37.6	2.5	40.1
Belgium	22.7	76.0	98.7
Brazil	1.5	1.0	2.5[a]
British Colonies	7	92.7	99.7[b]
Canada	42.7	1.0	43.7
China	1,400.0	20,000.0	21,400.0[c]
Czechoslovakia	6.6	315.0	321.6[a]
Denmark	6.4	1.0	7.4
France	245.0	350.0	595.0
Great Britain	403.0	92.7	495.7
Greece	88.3	325.0	413.3
India (Br.)	48.7	3,000.0	3,048.7
Indochina	0	2,000.0	2,000.0[a]
Luxembourg	0.1	1.0	1.1
Malaysia (Br.)	0	50.0	50.0[a]
Mexico	0.1	0	0.1[a]
Netherlands	13.7	236.0	249.7
Netherlands East Indies	0	100.0	100.0[a]
New Zealand	8.7	0	8.7
Norway	3.0	7.0	10.0
Philippines	40.0	100.0	140.0[a]
Poland	597.3	5,675.0	6,272.3
South Africa	8.5	0	8.5
Soviet Union	12,000.0	17,000.0	29,000.0[d]
United States	407.0	6.0	413.0
Yugoslavia	305.0	1,355.0	1,660.0
Allied Total	15,692.9	50,786.9	66,479.8
Axis			
Bulgaria	18.8	140.0	158.8
Finland	82.0	12.0	94.0
Germany	3,250.0	2,445.0	5,695.0[e]
Hungary	200.0	600.0	800.0[a]
Italy	380.0	152.9	532.9
Japan	2,565.9	672.0	3,237.9
Korea	10	250.0	260.0[f]
Romania	450.0	465.0	915.0
Axis Total	6,956.7	4,736.9	11,693.6
Grand Total	22,649.6	55,523.8	78,173.4

[a] Partially estimated figures.

[b] Territories not otherwise enumerated.

[c] Includes casualties from 1937 onward.

[d] Includes Latvia, Estonia, and Lithuania, and people shot by Stalin for various reasons, including having the misfortune to have become prisoners of war.

[e] Includes Austria.

[f] Korea was actually a Japanese colony during the war. Korean military dead are apparently included in Japanese military dead. Figures for civilians are a minimum as there was widespread hunger in Korea during the war.

starved to death in India and Indochina as a consequence of a global shipping shortage are not usually listed as victims of the war, but most certainly were.

There were also deaths, albeit small, due to military operations in Iran and Iraq, as well as from accidental air attacks on Switzerland and Sweden, as well as among neutral merchant seamen.

Nor do the figures include people in many countries killed during industrial accidents because of the increased work load for the war effort: About 300,000 Americans died in such mishaps during the war, some certainly war-related. And then there are the people who died after the war, often long after, from the lingering effects of wounds or privation, and from the civil disorders, insurrections, and anticolonial revolutions engendered by the war.

So it is not unreasonable to say that nearly a 100 million people perished as a result of World War II. This was about 5 percent of the planet's population at the time.

SLAUGHTER OF THE INNOCENTS

World War II was notable for the large number of civilians who were killed. Many of these were the "normal" deaths of civilians caught up in the fighting. Others were deliberate actions by nations to destroy civilian populations. Most notable of these were the Nazi programs to kill populations they considered subhuman (Jews, Slavs, Gypsies, etc.). Some nations suffered more than others in this slaughter of noncombatants, several losing more civilians than soldiers. The next table shows the nations suffering the most civilian losses, with their military casualties given by way of comparison.

NO QUARTER

The increasingly harsh conditions that Hitler's Reich imposed upon them through the 1930s convinced the Jews of Europe that the coming war would be particularly brutal for them. While the Nazi extermination program was run ruthlessly, efficiently, and deceptively, not all Jews went along with the deportations to the labor (death) camps. Many fought back, and fought with ruthless courage.

Some Jews were organized into regular military units, like the Jewish Battalion that fought alongside the British in North Africa

Slaughter of the Innocents,
Civilian Deaths per Country

	Civilian (in thousands)	Military (in thousands)	Total (in thousands)
China	20,000	1,400	21,400
Soviet Union	12,000	17,000	29,000
Poland	5,675	597	6,272
India (Br.)	3,000	49	3,049
Germany	2,445	3,250	5,695
Indochina	2,000	0	2,000
Yugoslavia	1,355	305	1,660
Japan	672	2,566	3,238
Hungary	600	200	800
Romania	465	450	915
France	350	245	595
Greece	325	88	413
Czechoslovakia	315	7	322
Netherlands	236	13	249
Italy	153	380	533
Bulgaria	140	19	159
Philippines (U.S.)	100	40	140
Netherlands East Indies	100	0	100
Great Britain	93	403	496
British Colonies	93	7	100
Belgium	76	23	99
Malaysia (Br.)	50	0	50
Finland	12	82	94

NOTES. This table omits areas, such as Thailand, and Burma, where there are no statistics available whatsoever. Note that Jews (about 6 million of whom perished) and Gypsies (about 500,000) have been included in the casualties of the nations in which they were residents, despite the fact that their fellow citizens often collaborated in their slaughter.

during 1942. Caught in an exposed position during a German offensive in June 1942, this unit came as close as a unit can to "fighting to the last man." By the end of July 1942, only forty-five of the battalion's approximately a thousand troops were still alive. Eventually a Jewish brigade went on to fight in Italy.

Equally grim losses were sustained by the Jewish partisan units formed in Poland and Russia in 1941–1944. Although about 6 million Jews were murdered by the Nazis, this represented only about 90 percent of the Jews the Germans tried to kill. The rest escaped. While some tried to lie low until the war was over, many of the escapees joined the resistance in whatever country they were in. The survival rate of these fighters was very low: Less than half lived to see the end of the war. In many guerrilla units, fewer than 10 percent survived. The harsh winters they spent in the forests of Eastern Europe were often more lethal than the Nazis.

The Germans did not consider partisans as soldiers and shot those taken prisoner. That wasn't the only problem. While the Jewish Battalion (and later Brigade) was trained, and many Jewish World War I veterans retained military skills, most of the partisans were young and inexperienced. Moreover, guerrilla warfare was quite different from the combat regular soldiers are accustomed to. Guerrillas, for example, had to kill informers to prevent the German secret police from finding the guerrilla hideouts or catching sympathizers in towns and villages. Although many Jewish resistance fighters served in all-Jewish units, they had to depend on the local people for support, and most of the locals were not Jewish. So if word got around that one of the villagers was passing information to the Germans, a few guerrillas would seek out the informer under cover of darkness and kill him or her. But even this grim business had its light side.

One young (and green) Jewish partisan operating in the Lvov area during 1943 was sent with a more experienced fighter to kill an informer in a nearby village. Sneaking up to the home of the informer in the middle of the night, the older man looked at the younger one and nodded toward the door of the informer's house. The young soldier, a city boy, walked over to the door and knocked. The older partisan looked on in disbelief and whispered loudly, "You don't knock, you break it down," and demonstrated by breaking in the door with the butt of his rifle. The door crashed open, the two dashed inside, shots were heard, and soon the two were fleeing into the woods.

The Germans took no prisoners when fighting the partisans, and neither did the partisans. It was a war with no quarter.

LEARNING HOW TO LOSE EFFICIENTLY

Three of the major participants in World War II, Germany, Russia, and Japan, began the war with an attitude that attacking all the time was the key to victory. But they had a curious omission in their bag of battle tricks. None of these nations bothered to teach its troops how to retreat. Going into the war, these countries were so dedicated to attacking that the troops were at a loss in situations where retreat was the more productive course of action. The Soviets were the first to learn this harsh lesson. When the Germans invaded the Soviet Union in June 1941, the Soviet troops they confronted had not been trained to retreat effectively. This meant that Russian troops faced with an overwhelming attack (as most of them were) fell apart, and what might have been a tenacious rearguard action turned into a rout. The German advance might have been slowed to a crawl if the Russians had practiced the stubborn delaying tactics they later adopted. But in 1941, their lack of defensive training was lethal to the Russians.

The Germans soon got their own lesson in defensive warfare. When their advance stalled in front of Moscow (and all along the front) in late 1941, the Russians gathered up whatever reserves they could and launched a counteroffensive. German combat training at that time paid little attention to defensive operations and now it was the Germans' turn to improvise. Even though the Soviet counteroffensive was hastily put together, it was in winter weather. The Russians were used to this, the Germans weren't. The combination of weather favoring the Russians and the Germans' lack of training in defensive operations made the Soviet attack a success.

The Germans and Russians went on to develop their own novel techniques for defending and retreating. The Russians would often strip most of their front line (over a thousand miles' worth) of all but a thin line of units, which were given meager supplies of ammunition and food. These troops would be well entrenched, and there would often be several lines of fortifications for the troops to fall back to if attacked. Then the Russians would concentrate as many troops as possible in a place or places for massive offensives. The Germans reacted to this by developing the clever (and risky) gambit of carefully observing the Russian preparations. As good as the Russians were at deception and camouflage, they were rarely able to hide the preparations for one of their big operations. The Germans knew that the Russians were not flexible enough to change their plans at the last moment. So, just before the Russians began their enormous artillery barrages, the Germans would move their troops from their positions to another line of fixed defenses farther back. The Russians would waste a lot of ammunition, and the Soviet troops would have to slog through the shot-up terrain until they bumped into the second line of untouched German fortifications. Russian losses in these "Where did the Fritzes go?" attacks were enormous. The Germans usually lost these battles anyway, but this technique slowed down the Russians and prolonged the war.

More than the Russians and Germans, the Japanese spurned defensive tactics and training. When in doubt, a Japanese commander would launch a straightahead charge, with sword drawn and shouts of "banzai" on everyone's lips. This made life easier for Allied troops in the long run, although the frequent desperate Japanese assaults were always unnerving. But these banzai charges were rarely successful. The Japanese never really came to grips with the concept of retreating, though they did develop formidable defensive bastions on the islands they suspected the Allies would invade. The Japanese were also good at "redeploying" (evacuating) troops from islands where they saw no chance of success. But both of these measures were seen as merely preliminaries for future offensives, which never materialized, unless you consider the desperate charges by the last survivors of some island garrison an "attack."

DEATH FROM ABOVE

World War II was the first conflict in which a substantial number of deaths were inflicted by aircraft. In some cases the numbers were enormous.

While no one was keeping records, at least several million or more civilian and military deaths can be attributed to air attacks. In addition, the British suffered 2,754 deaths from ballistic missiles (V-2s), a record that stood until the 1980s when Iraq and Iran rained Scud missiles (derived from the V-2 design) on each other's cities. Over 10,000 deaths resulted. Great Britain also suffered 6,184 deaths from German V-1 cruise missiles. This record still stands.

Civilian Deaths from Air Raids	
Japan	668,000
Germany	593,000
Great Britain	60,400

BOMBED OUT OF HOUSE AND HOME

More firepower was used in World War II than in any other conflict in history. Since the heaviest fighting was in heavily populated areas, one of the big losses (aside from the civilians themselves) were homes.

Many of the homes were centuries old, and often the loss of a family's home led to some of the residents dying of exposure. These are the countries that saw the greatest destruction of private homes.

Private Dwellings Destroyed	
Soviet Union	3,000,000
Japan	2,251,900
Poland	516,000
Great Britain	456,000
France	255,500
Germany	255,000
Netherlands	82,530

The figure for the Soviet Union is a conservative estimate. These other nations actually kept track of the destruction. For every home destroyed, there were two to four or more that were damaged to some extent (in Japan, destroyed homes were twice the number of those damaged because of the highly flammable nature of their construction material and the use of fire bombs). Naturally, there was equal (if not more) destruction to businesses and government structures. Not all of this was from aircraft attack; all those tanks and artillery generally tore up the landscape and anything that was built on it.

MUMBO JUMBO BEHIND THE HILL

A big U.S. Army advantage in ground combat was its innovative methods of controlling and coordinating artillery fire. This was no accident. Throughout the 1930s, American gunners improved their equipment and techniques to the point where the United States had the most effective artillery in the world. This success sprang from several sources:

- **Weapons.** America designed new guns after World War I and had them ready for mass production when World War II began. The standard 105mm howitzer was based on the German gun of the same caliber used in World War I, but the American version was much improved. Guns of other calibers were of equally high quality.

- **Mobility.** The decision was made to dispense entirely with horse-drawn guns, something most other armies did not do until after World War II. All U.S. artillery would be towed by trucks or be self-propelled (sort of like a tank, but without the armor and turret).

- **Fire Control.** This was the biggest breakthrough. A combination of advanced computing techniques (with mechanical computers) and lavish use of radios gave U.S. artillery the ability to be more flexible than that of any other nation. In the past, and for most nations during World War II, guns were aimed and fired according to a carefully prepared plan. This was acceptable if the enemy operated according to your expectations, but this was often not the case. Forward observers (FOs) had been used since World War I, but in that war they would call back instructions for only a few guns (usually a battery of four to six guns or a battalion of twelve to eighteen). The American innovation was to allow the FOs to call upon the fire of "all guns within range." U.S. artillery units practiced this constantly and this enabled their fire to be concentrated quickly, accurately, and massively. Even the Germans were impressed by this, but they were unable to duplicate the American techniques during the war.

- **Ammunition.** America was a manufacturing giant and millions of tons of artillery ammunition was produced and rapidly sent to the guns at the front using the equally numerous military trucks the United States turned out. Not only was American ammunition abundant, but it was of high quality, with a wide variety of specialized shells.

- **Aircraft.** Artillery units had their own single-engine aircraft (militarized Piper Cubs) to carry FOs aloft. From these heights, targets could be spotted and fire adjusted. Even fighter pilots could be impressed in an emergency to call in artillery fire. The widespread use of spotter aircraft ensured that there were few enemy targets that went unseen, and unhit.

To the enemy, American artillery seemed to be everywhere, all the time and in unbelievable quantity. And should the enemy launch an attack, every American gun within range would, as if by magic, begin firing on the advancing troops. The result was that both the Japanese and Germans were surprised, and usually pulverized, when they encountered the artillery support that accompanied U.S. ground units. The Germans thought this massive artillery support was somewhat "unfair" (if only because the Americans had it and they didn't), while the Japanese found yet another way to die nobly.

OPINION, PLEASE!

One of the little-known activities of the U.S. Army during World War II was its extensive use of opinion surveys. While the U.S. Army was being mobilized, several senior officers came up with the idea of collecting many of the professional sociologists and statisticians together in a special unit that would regularly survey the troops to gauge their attitudes. As a result, hundreds of surveys were taken of troops undergoing training in the United States and, later on, while they were in combat. After the war, Samuel Stouffer and several of his colleagues, all veterans of wartime survey duty, published much of the resulting material in a two-volume set, *The American Soldier,* which has become something of a classic and has gone through several editions.

The surveys revealed a great many things, some humorous, some tragic, some both. Some of the findings weren't all that shocking, others were:

- Enlisted men and officers had different, sometimes vastly different, attitudes about how effective, or how well run, their units were.

- Men who had been in combat wished their training had been more strenuous.

- Soldiers actually wanted more discipline and, in general, stronger leadership from their NCOs and officers.

- The troops were very astute in sizing up the effectiveness of their NCOs and officers.

- Combat veterans quickly sorted out the ins and outs of surviving on the battlefield, more so than the people in charge of training new recruits back in the United States.

- Veterans from the Pacific theater said that combat became more frightening as time went by, while those from the European theater said that it tended to become less so, albeit still very scary.

One of the surveys of American combat veterans who had fought in North Africa indicated that the average infantryman had a restricted, and somewhat inaccurate, view of what was trying to kill him. This was the first time U.S. troops came up against the Germans. When asked what the ''most feared'' weapon was, 48 percent of the troops surveyed said it was the German ''88mm artillery gun.'' When asked what the ''most dangerous'' weapon was, 62 percent of the GIs named the ''88.'' The Germans very rarely used their 88mm gun as artillery; it was primarily for antiaircraft and antitank work. In these roles, the ''88'' had acquired a fearsome reputation, and these U.S. troops assumed that anytime they were hit by German shell fire, it had to be the dreaded ''88.'' But the GIs had the percentages right. Artillery was the major cause of casualties among the infantry. The next most dangerous thing mentioned was mortars (17 percent), followed by the deadly German light machine guns (6 percent). Interestingly, none of the troops feared rifle fire, or considered it ''dangerous.'' This was also quite accurate. The most dangerous weapons were actually artillery (including mortars) and these accounted for over two thirds of all casualties.

These surveys were used by many senior officers to set policy. But they were also ignored by other officers who had their own firmly held visions of reality (for example, most commanders of black troops paid no attention to surveys explaining the causes of poor morale among their men, which consequently tended to remain poor). The surveys were, however, one of the remarkable innovations of World War II and their use continues to this day.

LIVE AND LET LIVE

It is common in wars for troops to arrange local truces and cease-fires with their opponents. Sometimes this occurs between nations when there are several countries on each side of a conflict. Such was the case in World War II when, in August 1943, Hungary and Great Britain reached an understanding that Allied aircraft flying over Hungary (to bomb other Axis targets) would not be fired upon. In return, the Allies would not bomb Hungary. Hungary was an uneasy ally of the Germans, and Hungarian troops had taken an awful beating on the Russian front in the previous year. This particular agreement was hammered out by British and Hungarian diplomats stationed in Turkey. The Germans were not amused when they found out. Germany took control of Hungary in March 1944, and this agreement came to an end, as the Germans were now in charge of the antiaircraft guns.

HOW TO REDUCE SUICIDES

Get involved in a war. A year after Great Britain entered World War II, the national suicide rate had gone down 15 percent. By 1941 it was down 30 percent from its 1939 level. By 1942 it was down to two thirds the prewar rate, and there it stayed until the end of the war. Suicide rates picked up markedly after peace returned. The same pattern was observed for divorces, which fell sharply during the war but rose substantially after the fighting ended and the troops (husbands) came home. No one is certain as to the reasons for these trends.

THE CIVILIANIZATION OF WAR

Approximately 95 percent of the casualties during World War I were military personnel, the remaining 5 percent being civilians. The comparable figures for World War II were about 33 percent soldiers to about 67 percent civilians.

"DON'T YOU KNOW THERE'S A WAR ON?"

Only once in nearly a century has bean soup not appeared on the menu of the Senate dining room in the Capitol. In Washington, on September 14, 1943, as a result of wartime shortages, the supply of white Michigan beans ran low. The ensuing senatorial uproar was sufficient to ensure that there were beans enough the next day, and on every subsequent day thereafter. In all nations, it was common for the senior leadership to avoid suffering the shortages most of their followers were enduring. On the other hand, American civilians suffered least of any nation's civilians in the war. While there was rationing of clothing, meat, shoes, and many other items, it was largely a cheerfully borne inconvenience, except in the matter of gasoline, which hurt the national romance with the automobile and was the most resented, and most evaded, restriction.

GREAT CONSPIRACIES, BETRAYALS, AND COVER-UPS THAT WEREN'T

Human nature and modern media being what they are, it's not surprising that people have a tendency to come up with theories about conspiracies, treachery, cover-ups, and other nefarious Machiavellian plottings, particularly in cases where unpleasant things occurred. World War II has come in for its share of such accusations.

THE PEARL HARBOR PLOT. The ultimate World War II conspiracy theory has it that President Roosevelt and sundry other national political and military leaders knew that the Japanese were about to attack Pearl Harbor, or even connived at arranging the attack in order to get the United States into the war and thereby save Great Britain's bacon. Variations on the theme are numerous, including an interesting one contending that Winston Churchill knew but refused to tell. Unfortunately, when all the information is examined, particularly the periodic "new" evidence (most of which turns out to be material of little relevance), the most charitable thing that can be said of the charges is "not proven." Indeed, some of the "proof" advanced in support of the conspiracy theory falls into the category of Elvis sightings, such as the charge that it was actually British airmen who conducted the attack from a secret air base on one of the other Hawaiian islands. The disaster at Pearl Harbor was the result of a lot of audacity and luck on the part of the Japanese and numerous blunders by many American political and military leaders, with no particular criminality involved. As historian Gordon Prange said, "There's enough blame for everyone."

THE SLAPTON SANDS COVER-UP. On the night of April 27, 1944, nine German E-boats (motor torpedo boats) attacked one of the convoys participating in a landing exercise off the Devon coast of England, sinking two LSTs and severely damaging another while killing over seven hundred American soldiers and sailors. Supreme Allied Headquarters promptly put a lid on the incident, classifying it as secret. This was because the Germans might be able to determine, from the extent of the exercise, the imminence of the Allied invasion, then scheduled for early May. Moreover, Devon is closer to Normandy than to the Pas de Calais (where the Allies wanted the Germans to think the invasion would be), its probable objective. D-Day came and went (with the units that had been at Slapton Sands suffering fewer casualties on June 6 than they had on April 27). From time to time various newspapers, writers, and television producers looking for some sensationalism have "discovered" evidence of a massive cover-up concerning the incident. There is even a locally built "monument" to the "cover-up" that serves as a tourist attraction. In fact, there was no cover-up.

Information about Slapton Sands was declassified shortly after
the war, and the incident is mentioned in numerous works,
including the army's official history of the Normandy operation
published in 1951, by which time no one was particularly
interested.

THE MT. SURIBACHI CONSPIRACY. Perhaps the most enduring
image to come out of the war is Associated Press photographer
Joe Rosenthal's shot of five Marines and a navy medical
corpsman raising Old Glory atop Iwo Jima's Mt. Suribachi on
February 23, 1945. This was actually the second flag raising that
morning. A platoon of forty men from the Twenty-eighth
Marines had reached the summit after fierce hand-to-hand
fighting, and at 10:20 A.M., three of the men raised a small
American flag on a piece of pipe. Realizing that the flag was too
small to be seen readily (and wanting to ensure that the
regiment retained the original flag), the officer in charge sent for
a larger one. Shortly afterward the battle ensign of *LST-779* was
brought up, fastened to a longer piece of pipe, and raised to the
cheers of many of the troops hotly engaged with the enemy. It
is this flag raising that was photographed by Rosenthal. Of late,
it has been claimed that this second flag raising was deliberately
staged as a "photo opportunity" by the Marine brass to garner
more prestige for the Corps, and ultimately a bigger share of the
postwar budget. Actually, the entire incident was unplanned.
Both flag raisings were made by the Marines on the spot,
several of whom did not even survive the subsequent combat.
The fact that there were two flag raisings can be found in all
detailed histories of the battle, and both flags are prominently
displayed in the Marine Corps Museum with photographs of
both flag raisings. Rosenthal's just happens to be the artistically
better of the two. Interestingly, several of the survivors of the
flag raising are still alive, but none appears to have been
consulted on the matter by those making the charges of "photo
opportunity."

THE BETRAYAL OF MARKET-GARDEN. Operation Market-Garden,
the "Bridge Too Far" attack that resulted in the decimation of
British and Polish airborne forces at Arnhem when they dropped
almost literally on top of two crack SS panzer divisions, was
one of the greatest disasters of the war. Rumors have long
circulated that the operation was betrayed by German

sympathizers in the Dutch Resistance. Actually, the Dutch underground had not been informed about the operation precisely because of fears that it had been ''penetrated'' by German intelligence. And in fact, if the British had heeded information that they received from the Dutch Resistance concerning German dispositions they would have been aware of the presence of the panzers.

FRANCOIS MITTERRAND WAS A VICHYITE. In 1941 Mitterrand requested and received a decoration from Marshal Pétain. This fact has several times been raised during French political campaigns, with the implication that Mitterrand was a collaborator during the war. Actually, Mitterrand, who held a position with Pétain's government as the supervisor of provisions for French troops held in German PW camps, was a clandestine agent for the Resistance. In fact, at the time that Pétain announced that he was decorating Mitterrand, the latter was taking part in a secret conference of Free French officials in London and had to hastily, and stealthily, make his way back to France.

TREACHERY AT DIEPPE. On August 19, 1942, some 6,100 Canadian, about 1,000 British, and several hundred American troops made a massive raid on the French coast near Dieppe. Resistance proved fierce, and by midday the attackers were forced to withdraw after suffering tremendous casualties, nearly 1,200 men being killed and 2,200 taken prisoner, while nearly 35 landing craft, 110 airplanes, and 30 tanks were lost, along with extensive damage to other vessels and aircraft. German losses were about 300 dead and 300 wounded, plus about 100 aircraft destroyed. Efforts have been made to depict the failure at Dieppe as a deliberate attempt by the British High Command to demonstrate the futility of a cross-Channel attack to the American high command, which was pressing for an early assault on German-occupied Europe. No evidence for such a cover-up can be found. Other theories put forth (especially in Canada, for obvious reasons) are that the raid was simply a publicity stunt by the British leadership and that it was a morale-building exercise for the hard-pressed Russians (who were constantly asking for a ''second front'' in the West). The raid continues to be a sore point with many Canadians, who feel that the British were being rather callous with the lives of "colonials." The failure of the Dieppe raid was due to a combination of inadequate preparations and prompt intervention by the Luftwaffe (fortunately noticeably absent on D-Day two years later), complicated by an unfortunate predawn encounter between one of the approaching convoys and some German coastal shipping, which alerted the defenders.

THE "OTHER LOSSES" COVER-UP. A recent book entitled *Other Losses* contends that after the war the Allies, and specifically Supreme Allied Commander Dwight D. Eisenhower, conspired to deliberately starve to death more than 700,000 German prisoners of war. The evidence for this is an "Other Losses" entry in Allied PW records followed by the number 700,000. The contention is that this innocuous-sounding entry covers up hundreds of thousands of men who died as a result of being denied proper rations during the winter of 1945–1946. Investigation has determined that about 90 percent of the men included in "Other Losses" were released from prisoner of war camps without formal discharge, being mostly old men and young boys dragooned into the German Army in the closing days of the war, and of no particular threat to anyone. The balance of the men covered in the "Other Losses" entry includes some 70,000 who died, many from wounds incurred before their capture or from typhus and other diseases contracted on the front, and some who were transferred to various countries to be dealt with as collaborators and war criminals. The evidence for this was available to the proponents of the conspiracy theory had they but looked for it.

HITLER PLOTTED STALIN'S PURGE. The purge of the Red Army in the mid-1930s, during which Stalin shot most of his higher-ranking commanders, is generally regarded as having been one of the causes of the disasters that plagued Soviet arms in the opening months of the German invasion. Several popular publications and writers have asserted that the purge was the result of a plot by German military intelligence to decapitate the Red Army. Supposedly, information was leaked to the Soviet secret police (NKGB) that implicated many of the leading Soviet generals in a conspiracy to overthrow Stalin. Despite extensive investigation, no evidence has ever been turned up to support this assertion, which appears to have been based on the imaginations of some German middle-ranking intelligence personnel who wanted to ingratiate themselves with their Allied interrogators after the war. In fact, of course, Stalin's paranoia was sufficient explanation for the purge, which, after all, involved all segments of Soviet society, not merely the Army.

WINSTON CHURCHILL'S STAND-IN. It has been asserted that Churchill did not make any of his famous radio addresses but rather used an actor. Actually, there is some truth to this, but not much. Most of Churchill's speeches before the House of Commons were recorded for later radio broadcast. However, his first speech as prime minister, the "Blood, Toil, Tears, and Sweat" address delivered to the House on May 13, 1940, was not recorded. Since Sir Winston was rather busy at the time, what with trying to form a government while the Netherlands was surrendering, Belgium being overrun, and the French armies being broken by the Nazi onslaught, an actor was asked to stand in for Churchill on the BBC. This was done once. All of Churchill's other radio broadcasts were either live or prerecorded.

THE HOLOCAUST NEVER HAPPENED. The evidence for the Holocaust is so overwhelming, including as it does not merely enormous numbers of survivors, but also equally large numbers of Allied troops who helped liberate the camps, and literally mountains of German documents, that proponents of the notion that it never happened must be viewed with considerable suspicion. The biggest source of disbelief of the Holocaust is sheer ignorance among many people (particularly Americans) about history in general, and World War II history in particular. American education in the past twenty years has deemphasized the study of history. The result is that many younger "educated" Americans are woefully ignorant about details of American, and world, history. You will find college-educated Americans who have only a vague idea of what World War II was. This is particularly true in the electronic media, where the "producers" (those who do the legwork of digging up material to be broadcast) are usually the products of this deficient education. What they don't know doesn't get broadcast, or gets sent over the air inaccurately.

BATTLEWAGONS AT WAR

By the onset of the Second World War the battleship had been the primary arbiter of sea power for over three centuries, during which time it had grown and evolved into a horrendously expensive, enormously powerful, yet surprisingly vulnerable weapon system. It had emerged from the First World War with its reputation largely intact. Of the scores of modern battleships that saw service in that war, only two were sunk, one by a mine (planted by a submarine) and the other by an internal explosion. The record of the two dozen or so battle cruisers, which toted battleship artillery but sacrificed armor protection for speed, was less impressive, four being lost in action, all to enemy gunfire.

This was rather surprising, since even the admirals of the age were perfectly aware that their ships could be sunk and had worried for years about their vulnerability to torpedoes, whether launched by surface vessels or submarines. Of course, a few aviation enthusiasts argued that the battleship was vulnerable to the airplane, but this was not a particularly convincing argument considering the capabilities of aircraft at the time. Even the famous sinking of the German prize *Ostfriesland* by U.S. Army bombers on July 21, 1921, was not considered a valid test, given that the trial had been rigged in favor of the airmen to begin with, and that they then cheated anyway (the test was conducted on a beautifully calm, clear day, with the ship anchored in open water, and the airmen coming in at such low levels that had the ship been shooting back none of them would have survived). More objective trials against other vessels, including far newer, albeit unfinished battleships whose completion was canceled by the disarmament treaties of the 1920s, provided some valuable clues as to the vulnerability of battleships.

During the 1920s and 1930s most navies still considered the battleship the principal arm of sea power. But the bigger ones (the Royal Navy, the Japanese Imperial Navy, and the U.S. Navy) also invested their money in aircraft carriers. This was partially out of the belief that the new weapon had potential. In addition, since the Washington and London naval disarmament treaties of 1922 and 1930 restricted the number of battleships (but not carriers), this made having some aircraft carriers around to provide billets for senior officers rather attractive.

These navies began to debate the ways in which the future of naval warfare would develop. Ultimately, they all came to assume that the battleship and the carrier were complementary to each other. In fleet actions, carrier aircraft would scout for the enemy and soften him up with air attacks. Then the battleships would go in to slug it out. And afterward the carrier aircraft would follow up victory by pursuing the fleeing enemy to sink damaged and disabled vessels, or cover defeat by serving as the rear guard, attacking the pursuing foe to slow him down.

Meanwhile, of course, bigger and better battleships were being built. Simply defined, a battleship is a very large (over 20,000 displacement tons), heavily armored warship toting eight or more very large guns (12-inch-caliber or greater). By the mid-1930s, when large-scale battleship construction was resumed, the ships and guns were growing very large, 35,000 tons and 14-inch guns being minimal. They were also growing faster. Earlier generations of battlewagons had been quite slow (about 20 to 22 knots), a problem that had fostered the development of the battle cruiser, basically a battleship in which armor protection was sacrificed for larger and more powerful engines, yielding higher speeds (about 30 knots). The battle cruiser had not worked out very well in combat since its thin armor made it particularly vulnerable in a slugfest, and by the late 1930s the surviving battle cruisers were even more obsolete than the older battleships. Then came World War II.

The aircraft carrier took awhile to establish itself as the primary warship, in fact, not until Pearl Harbor, when the war was already two years old in the Atlantic. But that didn't mean the battleship was a goner. In fact, battleships (whether the older, slower veterans of World War I or their new, speedier descendants) still played an important and varied role in the war. Battleships proved immensely valuable in helping to defend carriers (which are even more vulnerable than battleships, having virtually no armor, little organic offensive firepower, and carrying thousands of tons of highly inflammable aviation fuel) from air attacks while protecting themselves. (On one occasion the *South Dakota* shot down several dozen attacking aircraft in about five minutes.) And their heavy guns were extremely useful in covering amphibious landings all over the world, with not a few landings being made considerably easier by the support of battleship gunfire. During the protracted ground struggle for Okinawa, for example, U.S. battleships and large cruisers (sort of "junior achievement" battlewagons) expended 23,157 rounds of 16-inch, 14-inch, and 12-inch ammunition, a weight of metal of over 12,000 tons.

And surprisingly, battleships still occasionally managed to slug it out the old-fashioned way. In fact, there were more battleship-to-battleship engagements in the war (nine) than there were carrier-to-carrier battles (five).

1. *April 9, 1940.* The German battleships *Gneisenau* and *Scharnhorst* engaged the old British battle cruiser *Renown* in an indecisive action off Norway.

2. *July 3, 1940.* The World War I–vintage British battleships *Resolution* and *Valiant* with the 1920 battle cruiser *Hood,* the largest and fastest major warship in the world at the time, and some other ships, attacked the French fleet at Oran in Algeria, destroying the even older battleship *Bretagne,* severely damaging her sister *Provence,* and less seriously damaging the new *Dunkerque,* while the latter's sister *Strasbourg* managed to escape unscathed.

3. *July 9, 1940.* An Italian squadron including the reconstructed old battleships *Giulio Cesare* and *Conte di Cavour* was intercepted off Calabria by a British squadron including the older battleships *Warspite, Royal Sovereign,* and *Malaya* in an often intense action of about fifty minutes, during which the *Cesare* suffered serious damage by a shot from the *Warspite,* which holds the record for the longest-range artillery hit on the high seas in naval history, some 26,000 yards.

4. *May 24, 1941.* In a brief morning encounter with the new German battleship *Bismarck* and an escorting heavy cruiser in the Denmark Strait (between Greenland and Iceland), the even newer British battleship *Prince of Wales* was damaged and the battle cruiser *Hood* blew up leaving only three survivors. Later that afternoon the *Bismarck* and *Prince of Wales* briefly clashed again, without ill effects to either.

5. *May 27, 1941.* After a wide-ranging chase across the Atlantic, the *Bismarck,* slowed by several fortuitous aerial torpedo hits, was finally brought to bay by the new battleship *King George V* and the older *Rodney,* which in nearly three hours fired about 700 major-caliber rounds, not to mention hundreds of smaller stuff from two supporting heavy cruisers, reducing the battleship to a burning wreck which was finished off by several torpedoes.

6. *November 8, 1942.* The new battleship *Massachusetts* exchanged several hundred rounds of heavy-caliber shells with the partially completed French *Jean Bart* (she was still fitting out, tied up at a dock at Casablanca), with the latter being knocked out of action.

7. *November 14–15, 1942.* In a wild action that commenced shortly before midnight, a Japanese squadron including the *Kirishima* engaged the new *Washington* and *South Dakota*, with the latter taking considerable damage but the former pounding the modernized Japanese battle cruiser so badly that she had to be scuttled the next morning.

8. *December 26, 1943.* Off North Cape, the northernmost part of Europe, a British squadron including the new battleship *Duke of York* encountered the German *Scharnhorst*, resulting in the latter's sinking after a protracted slugfest.

9. *October 24–25, 1944.* A U.S. squadron including the refurbished old battleships *Mississippi, Maryland, West Virginia, Tennessee, California,* and *Pennsylvania* (all but the *Mississippi* veterans of Pearl Harbor), supported by numerous smaller warships, ambushed a Japanese force including the old battleships *Fuso* and *Yamashiro*, which was annihilated in an action so one-sided that the *Pennsylvania* never got to fire. This was the last time in history that battleships ever fired on each other.

On two occasions during the war battleships actually encountered aircraft carriers. This is meant literally. The first occurred off Norway on June 8, 1940, when the German battleships *Scharnhorst* and *Gneisenau* ran across the British carrier *Glorious*, sinking her after an hour's pounding. The second encounter between battleships and aircraft carriers occurred off Samar (in the Philippines) during the Battle of Leyte Gulf on October 25, 1944, when a Japanese squadron including the superbattleship *Yamato* and the older *Nagato, Haruna,* and *Kongo* blundered upon a clutch of U.S. Navy escort carriers. The running fight that ensued turned into a decisive victory for the Americans, when, despite losing three carriers and several destroyers to Japanese gunfire, they managed to drive off their attackers and protect the transports the Japanese were after.

One of the most unusual curiosities of battleship operations in World War II occurred during the last fight of the German *Bismarck* on May 27, 1941. For generations battleships had carried torpedo tubes, which had been used in action several times, but wholly without success. However, in the fight with the *Bismarck*, the *Rodney* fired several 24-inch "fish" at her foe and actually appears to have hit her once, thus gaining the distinction of being the only battleship ever to hit another vessel in combat with a torpedo.

Not so bad a record for an obsolete warship.

HITLER'S FOREIGN LEGION

The Waffen SS, the armed forces of the German Nazi party, filled the majority of their nearly forty combat divisions with non-Germans. Over half a million foreigners served in twenty-seven of these Waffen SS divisions (as well as in many smaller, independent units and as replacements for the horrendous losses SS divisions took). The radical racial purity message of the Nazi party got a bit garbled by the SS recruiters, as the largest single ethnic group enlisted was Slavic Ukrainians (100,000) followed by the "Aryan" Dutch (50,000). Three divisions were formed from among Bosnian Muslims and Croatian Christians and, like most non-German SS divisions, were used against partisans. So successful was this program that even the regular army regularly filled 20 percent of its divisions (after late 1943) with foreign "volunteers." These were usually Soviet prisoners of war who were given the choice between starving to death in PW camps or serving as combat support troops in German infantry divisions. Most of these foreigners in German uniforms, especially the Soviets, were killed or imprisoned by their countrymen after the war.

FIGHTING VICE AND HITLER

As a result of an antivice drive conducted by Mayor Fiorello La Guardia (who was also national director of civilian defense), the scrap from 3,252 slot and pinball machines confiscated in New York City during World War II was donated to the war effort, including 3,000 pounds of ball bearings.

WARTIME EXPEDIENT

As a wartime measure, the Macy's Thanksgiving Day parade was canceled in 1942, and the famous balloons were donated to the war effort, yielding 650 pounds of scrap rubber. The general shortage of raw materials because of wartime needs caused massive recycling and rationing efforts worldwide.

TOTAL WAR

At the end of World War II, Britain had 19 percent of its total male population, plus 2 percent of its total female population, under arms, in contrast to the United States, where the corresponding figures were 14 percent and less than 0.1 percent.

A VIRTUOUS FELLOW AT HEART

The leader of one World War II nation was in many ways a "new age" man before his time, neither smoking nor drinking alcoholic beverages, confining himself to a vitamin-enriched vegetarian diet, consulting his astrologer regularly, communing with the spiritual guardians of his people, and opposing animal experimentation and vivisection: Adolf Hitler.

PLOWSHARES INTO SWORDS

Enormous amounts of weapons and equipment were built during World War II. The United States was the most prodigious producer.

Production of Weapons and Equipment

	Worldwide	U.S.	% U.S.
Aircraft	542,000	283,000	52
Guns (all types)	49,300,000	17,500,000	35
Vehicles	5,100,000	2,470,000	48
Ships (tons)	79,000,000	54,000,000	68

In addition, the United States contributed enormous (and significant) amounts of industrial material to its allies, particularly Great Britain and Russia. This aid ranged from raw materials (ores, fuel, etc.) to industrial machinery, as well as substantial food and medicines. America provided the guns and the butter throughout the war.

By the end of the war the United States was accounting for something like 50 percent of the gross world product. At the beginning of the war, the United States was already the major industrial power in the world, accounting for nearly 30 percent of world product, despite the Great Depression. By 1945, every other major industrial power (including Great Britain) had some, or most, of its industries wrecked. The dominant economic position of the United States from 1945 until the 1970s, while nice for Americans, was not sustainable. Once the other industrial nations rebuilt their factories and infrastructure, the United States' share of gross world product fell back to a more "normal" 20 to 25 percent. This is still huge, for a nation containing less than 6 percent of the world's population.

BLOOD AND GOLD

The war was won with courage and determination, and the help of those nations who possessed sufficient resources to arm and supply their troops. National economies and wealth were at the base of each nation's military strength. Consider the money spent on armaments by each nation each year:

Approximate Annual Spending on Armaments
(in billions of 1994 dollars)

	1935–1938	1939	1940	1941	1942	1943	1944
United States	13.5	5.4	13.5	40.5	180	342.0	378.0
Canada	0	0	0	4.5	9	13.5	13.5
Great Britain	22.5	9.0	31.5	58.5	81	99.0	100.0
Soviet Union	72.0	30.0	45.0	76.0	104	125.0	144.0
Germany	108.0	31.0	54.0	54.0	77	124.0	153.0
Japan	18.0	4.5	9.0	18.0	27	42.0	54

One explanation for Germany's initial success in the war can be found in the figures for 1935–1938, when Hitler spent nearly as much as all the other powers indicated combined.

What kinds of armaments you bought, and how efficiently you spent the money, was also important. U.S. arms were more "expensive" than German arms because the United States paid its workers good wages while the Germans used millions of slave laborers—Jews, Poles, Czechs, Soviets, Italians, and so forth—who didn't get paid at all. The Soviet Union paid its workers but didn't give them much to buy, thus making the wages nearly worthless (to the workers). Some nations concentrated on different things. The United States spent over $300 billion (in 1994 dollars) on aircraft between 1941 and 1944. In that same period it spent nearly as much on ships, but only half as much on vehicles and only about $80 billion on guns and artillery. The Soviet Union spent little on ships, not nearly as much on aircraft, and a lot more on artillery and tanks. Even so, U.S. production dwarfed all others, no matter how much the workers were paid.

The United States came very close to matching its peak World War II defense spending in the late 1980s and the Soviet Union began regularly exceeding its peak World War II spending in the 1970s.

STRATEGIC RESOURCES

Mindful of the possibility of desperate shortages in materials critical to the war effort, in 1940 the British government moved to corner the market on what it considered its most precious strategic resource, establishing a worldwide monopoly on tea. At the height of the war Great Britain maintained stockpiles of about 150 million tons of the stuff, enough to brew up about 6 trillion cups. So critical was tea to the British war effort that only ammunition had a higher priority than tea for delivery to troops in action.

LEND-LEASE

During the war one of the most valuable items supplied by the United States to the Soviet Union under lend-lease was gold braid to decorate the uniforms of the Red Army.

Lend-lease was created because by early 1941 Great Britain and the other Allied countries were running out of money with which to purchase munitions and other assistance from the United States. As a result, President Roosevelt proposed an arrangement under which he would be authorized to "lend" military equipment and other materials to nations whose defense was considered vital to that of the United States. It was enacted as Public Law 1776 on March 11, 1941, over often hysterical ("This bill will guarantee that every fourth American boy is plowed under!") opposition from isolationist groups ranging from the German-American Bund to the Communist party, then still faithfully following the Moscow line of friendship with Hitler.

Lend-lease had an enormous impact on the war. Military equipment, foodstuff, and in some cases cash totaling nearly $51 billion of very uninflated 1940s money was dispensed to nearly forty-five countries (including the Soviet Union beginning within days of Hitler's invasion, to the praises of the suddenly interventionist American Communist party).

"Other Expenditures" includes materials not charged to the recipient nations, including goods lost in shipment, items consumed by U.S. forces, and administrative costs. In terms of 1994 dollars, the almost $51 billion spent during the war would be worth over $600 billion.

The range of materials covered by lend-lease was extraordinary. The Soviet Union, for example, received over 430,000 trucks, nearly 7,000 fighters, and over 340,000 field telephones, as well as samples

U.S. Lend-lease Aid

Country	Amount (in dollars)
Belgium	148,394,457.76
Bolivia	5,633,989.02
British Empire	31,267,240,530.63
Brazil	332,545,226.43
Chile	21,817,478.16
China	1,548,794,965.99
Colombia	7,809,732.58
Costa Rica	155,022.73
Cuba	5,739,133.33
Czechoslovakia	413,398.78
Dominican Republic	1,610,590.38
Ecuador	7,063,079.96
Egypt	1,019,169.14
El Salvador	892,358.28
Ethiopia	5,151,163.25
France	3,207,608,188.75
Greece	75,475,880.30
Guatemala	1,819,403.19
Haiti	1,449,096.40
Honduras	732,358.11
Iceland	4,795,027.90
Iran	4,795,092.50
Iraq	4,144.14
Liberia	6,408,240.13
Mexico	36,287,010.67
Netherlands	230,127,717.63
Nicaragua	872,841.73
Norway	51,524,124.36
Panama	83,555.92
Paraguay	1,933,302.00
Peru	18,525,771.19
Poland	16,934,163.60
Saudi Arabia	17,417,878.70
Soviet Union	11,260,343,603.02
Turkey	26,640,031.50
Uruguay	7,148,610.13
Venezuela	4,336,079.35
Yugoslavia	32,026,355.58
Payments to Nations	48,361,568,773.22
Other Expenditures	2,578,827,000.00
Grand Total	50,940,395,773.22

of unusual equipment such as the M-1 rifle, the T-10 heavy tank, and the B-17, not to mention that gold braid, which was found useful in raising the morale of Red Army officers (who wore it) and men (who saluted it).

Several countries provided the United States with what was termed "reverse lend-lease," goods and equipment not readily available, a category including everything from uranium ore to cheese. The total value of this was about $10 billion, leaving a deficit of about $41 billion. It is, however, worth recalling that virtually all the money involved was spent in the United States. And in any case, the balance may be considered to have been paid in blood at places like El Alamein and Stalingrad.

FIRST THINGS FIRST?

In 1943 Albert Speer, the German armaments minister, received, but wisely rejected, a request from the German Navy for the manufacture of fifty thousand ceremonial daggers, explaining to the offended *Krieges-marine* that the metal might serve the Reich's war effort more effectively if used for something besides ensuring that officers were properly uniformed. The German Navy's attitude was in sharp contrast to the more no-nonsense approach of the U.S. Army with regard to uniform details. While millions of men were being mobilized, the army realized that even small economies could yield immense savings. As a result, distinctive insignia (the small metallic badges worn on the shoulders to identify a soldier's regiment) were dispensed with during the war, with a consequent savings of over seventy-five tons of rare metals, paints, and enamels.

STEEL RAILS TO . . . ?

In June 1944 the German railway system employed over 1,500,000 people to operate an inventory of 988,000 freight cars, generating as many as 29,000 trains per day in support of the military, industrial, economic, and genocidal activities of the Reich.

OVER THERE

For millions of Americans, World War II was an unprecedented opportunity to travel. However, these were not tourists, but heavily armed soldiers, sailors, airmen, and Marines. As the U.S. armed forces increased from 1940 on, so did the number serving outside North America.

Throughout it all, U.S. population still increased. So, although there was a war going on, not everyone was spending all the time fighting.

Americans Abroad

	Total Military (in thousands)	Army	Percent in Navy	Marines	Number Overseas (in thousands)	Percent Overseas
1940	458	59	35	6	164	36
1941	1,801	81	16	3	281	16
1942	3,859	80	17	3	940	24
1943	9,045	77	19	4	2,494	28
1944	11,451	70	26	4	5,512	48
1945	12,123	68	28	4	7,447	61

NOTES: During World War II, the air force belonged to the army (as the army air forces [AAF]) and had a peak size of 2.4 million troops (20) percent of all troops, leaving the army proper [including ground forces and service forces, which also supported the AAF] with 48 percent). The navy buildup was not as swift as the army's because the navy first had to build ships. In 1940 an enormous shipbuilding program was begun and many of these vessels were completed and ready for crews in 1943 and 1944. Aircraft and tanks for the army could be built much more quickly.

The total number of men and women enrolled in the armed forces during the war was about 16.4 million, of which about 11.3 million were in the army, 4.2 million in the navy, 0.67 million in the Marines, and 0.24 million in the Coast Guard. The average member of the service spent 33 months in uniform, while the average overseas tour was about 16.2 months. Throughout it all, the population still increased. So, although there was a war going on, not everyone was spending all their time fighting.

TAKING A CHANCE

Americans going into the military during World War II knew there was a certain risk of getting killed or injured. Overall, of the 16.3 million men and women who served, 1.8 percent were killed in action (291,557), 0.7 percent died from other causes, such as accidents and disease (113,842), and 4.1 percent were wounded in combat and survived (679,846). Over half were injured by accident or disease during their service. This number is vague because of the wide range of noncombat dangers soldiers faced. The largest one was venereal diseases, which ranged from the merely inconvenient (gonorrhea) to the potentially fatal (syphilis). Overall, the troops had a one in fourteen chance of getting killed or seriously injured. This varied widely by type of service. About 40 percent of those serving were in essentially civilian jobs and never got near the fighting. The infantry suffered the greatest number of casualties and in many infantry units the chance of death or injury exceeded 50 percent. Aircraft crews were also at great risk, but their job was considered more glamorous and the living conditions were a lot better. The air corps contained a lot more volunteers than the infantry.

If you had to be in uniform during World War II, it was safest to be in the U.S. armed forces. On the other extreme, a citizen of the Soviet Union was a hundred times more likely than an American to die in the war. But this includes the massive Soviet civilian losses (of which the United States had very few). A Soviet man of military age was about thirty times more likely to die than his counterpart in America. Of all the major combatants, U.S. troops had the lowest rate of dead and injured.

BLOOD MONEY

U.S. troops were the highest paid during World War II, with enlisted personnel receiving (in 1994 dollars) an average of $750 a month and officers $2,200 a month. Troops in most other armies received token amounts, or rarely more than a few hundred dollars a month. Officers usually did much better, with many making about half what U.S. officers were paid. U.S. troops overseas were quick to note that not only were their dollars valuable, but so were the numerous goods they received as part of their normal rations. Cigarettes and candy were particularly valuable, as were the generally despised (by the soldiers) rations on which they often had to subsist. This led to the British referring to the relatively flush GIs as "oversexed, overpaid, and over here." Less well known is the phrase often said of the less-affluent British troops, "underpaid, undersexed, and under Eisenhower" (who was in command of all the Allied forces).

LITTER

Battlefields, especially after a battle, have never been particularly neat. Litter—bodies, weapons, sundry equipment—and, usually, looters abound. It was first noted during World War II that there always seemed to be a lot of paper lying about on the battlefield. Newspapers, forms, pages from field manuals, packaging, labels, tags, all sorts of paper. It was during World War II that bureaucracy (lots of paperwork) and mass literacy (most of the troops could read and write) met on the battlefield to add another element to the wreckage.

BEING YOUR OWN WORST ENEMY

While thousands of aircraft were lost in combat, the noncombat losses were substantial. Throughout the war, 40 to 45 percent of each month's German aircraft losses were due to accidents. Crashing on landing was very common, as were engine failures in flight. The Allies' record was better, but not by a whole lot. The Japanese were even worse off, frequently seeing over half a month's losses coming from noncombat causes. This figure became absurdly high toward the end of the war when no fuel was available to adequately train pilots. Many of the Japanese kamikaze pilots were so green they barely knew how to take off and land. If a training field became overcast while pilot trainees were in the air, the Japanese could expect to lose most of them as they tried to land in less than perfect conditions. Moreover, Japanese pilots generally disdained parachutes as not befitting a ''warrior,'' thus pilots in crippled aircraft died with their machines.

To many of the older pilots, who had flown twenty-five years earlier in World War I, the situation did not seem all that bad. In the 1914–1918 war, most of the planes and pilots lost were because of accidents. The early 1940s aircraft were much more reliable. But with so many new pilots often being forced to operate in bad weather or with insufficient ground crews, the accident rate was still substantial. It was worse than most people later (or even at the time) realized.

WHO WAS DEADLIER?

Allied troops invariably developed a grudging respect for the German troops they faced. Even during the last months of the war, German troops were still winning battlefield victories because of their better training and tactics. The Germans were better at the rifle-to-rifle level. But how much better? In the hundreds of World War II war games published in the past thirty years, the designers of these games had to deal with this situation in concrete terms. The historical games had to be able to accurately re-create the situations they dealt with and this meant calculating the degree to which the Germans were more competent in combat. However, there was no way the casual reader of World War II history could easily grasp this relationship until historian Trevor N. Dupuy came along. Dupuy's specialty was collecting information on hundreds of World War II battles. He organized the data and reduced it to easily understood values. Dupuy called his technique the Quantified Judgment Method, because he realized not all factors could be quantified and some professional judgment had to be used. This leaves a good deal of room for criticism but does not necessarily negate Dupuy's basic conclusions. What he came up with (published in several books on the subject) was the following relationship between the major combatants of World War II:

	Percentage of German Superiority over Their Opponents
Germans vs. Allies	26
Germans vs. Russians	58

	Percentage of Allied Superiority in the Pacific War
Allies vs. Japanese	30

Clearly, the Germans weren't supermen, but these values accurately portray their battlefield advantage throughout the war. Of course, this superiority declined during the war. In Russia, the German advantage in 1941 was often over 200 percent but steadily declined as the war went on, although the Germans were still more efficient at the end of the war than were their enemies.

There were considerable differences between the units of all armies. Among the Allies, the best divisions were about 50 percent better than the worst. Even among German units, the same relationship was found. This was usually the effect of a superior (or inferior) division commander.

It wasn't easy coming up with these values, as adjustments had to be made for a large number of combat variables. The current equipment levels had to be accounted for, as well as what each unit was doing. In particular, you had to take into consideration which unit was attacking and which was defending. The length and progress of the battle had to be noted, as well as each side's casualties. Overall, Dupuy's system stood up well to use in a wide variety of historical situations.

BOMBS OVER BROOKLYN (AND LOS ANGELES)

While the Allies dropped millions of tons of bombs on Germany and Japan, the Axis powers had little opportunity to return the favor. In particular, the United States was practically immune to such attacks. But not completely immune. The Japanese did make a few balloon bomb attacks on the West Coast, which caused several deaths. And both Germany and Japan did make long-range aircraft that could reach North America. Fortunately, they didn't make many of these aircraft, or a strenuous effort to bomb North America until near the end of the war.

In late 1942, a Japanese submarine modified to carry a single-engine reconnaissance plane (E14Y1 "Glenn") launched its aircraft off the coast of Oregon. Four 167-pound incendiary bombs were dropped in forests, but no major fire was started. Earlier in 1942, Japan put the first of its four-engine float planes, the H8K, into service. The H8K was a very large aircraft (124-foot wingspan, 92 feet long). Its defensive armament consisted of four 7.7mm and six 20mm machine guns. It had a range of 4,400 miles. It could carry over four tons of bombs and had a top speed of 289 miles per hour. Japanese admiral Kinsei did a little math and concluded that half a dozen H8Ks could fly to the California coast, land on the water, be refueled by submarines, bomb Los Angeles, and then fly back to Japanese-held territory. This plan was approved before the Battle of Midway and scaled back after the battle. Only three H8Ks were sent out to bomb Hawaii and bad weather forced them to drop their bombs blindly. Undiscouraged, the Japanese planned to take thirty H8Ks, refuel them from submarines off Baja California, and then fly across the country to bomb the Texas oil fields. Then, in cooperation with German U-boats (some of which would be tankers), the H8Ks would range up and down the east coast of the United States, making air raids on major cities, mainly for terror and propaganda value. The Germans were eager to cooperate and prepared the tanker subs needed to refuel the H8Ks. The deteriorating Japanese situation caused this plan to be shelved.

Meanwhile, the Germans were working on their own long-range bomber. In late 1942, the four-engine Me-264 took its first flight. This aircraft, the "Amerika Bomber," could carry two tons of bombs 9,500 miles. Total flying time was forty-five hours and it could fly from Europe to New York and back without landing. Like the Japanese, the Germans had other problems to distract them from late 1942 on. Their war with Russia was going badly, and it wasn't until early 1944 that the Germans decided to go forward with a bombing campaign against North America. Although a six-engine Ju-290 made a flight to New York City (where it took photographs of likely targets) and back, this aircraft was a transport/recon plane. Only forty-one Ju-290s were built. The Me-264 was designed as a bomber and with the introduction of the two-engine Me-262 fighter in 1944, the Germans converted the Me-264 from a propeller to a jet aircraft. This increased its speed from 373 to 500 miles per hour. At this speed, defensive armament and gunners could be dispensed with.

The Ju-290 flight to New York City did not go unnoticed. British code breakers learned about the flight, and the Me-264, from secret German messages. The British waited until September to tell the Americans, who promptly sent swarms of bombers to destroy the factory producing the Me-264. That was the end of that. But it could have turned out otherwise. The Me-264 first flew at the same time as the American B-29. By late 1944, B-29s were entering service in large numbers. The Me-264 could have done the same. However, the Germans were not able to spare the resources to build the Me-264. The B-29 project was more expensive than the Manhattan Project that created the atomic bomb. Even if the Germans had produced, say, a hundred Me-264s in 1944, they would have lost most of their French airfields by the middle of the year, and above all, the aircraft would not have been able to deliver enough bombs to make much difference. Certainly, it would have been uncomfortable for New Yorkers. But a few squadrons of P-51s stationed at New York area bases would have given the German bombers a very hard time. The Germans were aware of this and had made plans to send over Me-164s or Ju-290s each with two V-1 "buzz bombs" under their wings. The V-1 was a small pilotless jet aircraft that if launched a hundred miles off the coast could easily hit a target as large as New York City or Boston. Again, it would not have been a decisive weapon, but rather a terror tactic. The Nazis were great believers in terror. The Allied invasion of France in June 1944, however, upset all these plans. It was merely a matter of timing. Like so many things in World War II, this could have happened.

KILLER VEGETABLES AND THE FARTS FROM HELL

Aircraft crews discovered (the hard way) that gas in the intestines expanded several times over when they were flying at altitudes of 20,000 feet and up. This discovery was made because most World War II aircraft were not pressurized. The thinner air up there caused the higher pressure intestinal gas to expand, at great discomfort to the victim. At higher altitudes, the crews would wear oxygen masks and very warm clothing, but normally the lower air pressure was not a problem. Passing gas could be very painful, often debilitating, and sometimes fatal. With thousands of bombers and fighters flying at those altitudes, something had to be done. The solution, of course, was in the diet. Certain foods cause most of intestinal gas. Fliers solved the problem by removing from or reducing in their diets whenever possible beans, cabbage, corn, onions, and other foods that normally cause gas in humans.

STILL FLYING AFTER ALL THESE YEARS

Several World War II–era aircraft are still in use today, and one is a most unlikely candidate. The DC-3 (or C-47 or "Dakota" in military usage) continues to fly in commercial service into the 1990s. Over 1,000 DC-3s are still flying worldwide, mostly owned by small domestic carriers in the United States and by some Third World air transport companies. A state-of-the-art aircraft in the mid-1930s (during which only 500 were built), over 35,000 DC-3s were produced for use during World War II. The DC-3 was, in fact, the most widely manufactured aircraft of the war.

When Allied paratroopers jumped, it was usually from a DC-3 (which could carry twenty-eight troops, but over sixty people when squeezed in during emergencies). With a maximum range of 2,100 miles and a top speed of 185 miles per hour, the DC-3 was the common cargo carrier (up to 7,500 pounds) and general-purpose "flying truck." The Japanese were so impressed that they examined shot-down DC-3s and went on to produce their own version (under a prewar license) called the L2D. Rugged, versatile, and much beloved by its two- or three-man crews (who affectionately nicknamed it Flying Dumbo or Gooney Bird), the DC-3 is one old soldier of World War II that refuses to completely fade away. Some will still be in commercial service at the turn of the twenty-first century, carrying cargo and passengers in out of the way Third World countries.

The only other prewar aircraft that approaches the DC-3 in longevity is the Russian Po-2 biplane. First produced in 1920, simple, robust, and slow enough to efficiently continue its agricultural chores, it is used largely as a crop duster these days.

YES, BUT WHAT IS IT WORTH?

How do you compare different combat divisions in terms of their relative capability on the battlefield? Winston Churchill pointed out in his memoirs that the planning of military operations usually overlooked this consideration, until he began asking pointed questions on the subject. It seems the British staff officers had been counting all friendly and enemy divisions as if they were the same. Some allowance would be made for special types like tank and parachute divisions, but little attention was paid to the generally wide differences in capabilities between divisions in terms of quantity and quality of troops, weapons, equipment, training, and leadership, not to mention morale and experience. Under Churchill's prodding, the British staff officers began to look at these factors by 1944. The Germans had always taken into account many of these factors, as had the Russians. By D-Day, many U.S. staff officers had learned to collect all the information they could on enemy units and then translate enemy forces into "equivalent U.S. divisions." This was a very rough approximation, but it was better than equating a green 9,000-man German infantry division with a veteran 16,000-man U.S. infantry division. While the Germans were quite good at ranking friendly and enemy divisions according to their current combat worth, Adolf Hitler became less willing to accept these assessments as the German situation deteriorated. In Russia, home-grown techniques as well as ones borrowed from the Germans gave the Russian commanders a good grasp of which units were capable of what. The Russians continue to use these techniques for translating divisions from many different nations into numbers that mean something.

All of the analysis systems used in World War II, and since, had to show

- **How much damage a division could inflict.** This was a matter of how many weapons a unit had, how good the weapons were, and how well the troops could use them.

- **How much damage it could take.** This was mainly a matter of how many troops were in the unit, what kind of equipment the troops had (especially armored vehicles), how well supplied the unit was, and how well the unit's troops and leadership could cope with battlefield losses.

- **How mobile the unit was.** This was more than whether a unit had a lot of trucks and armored vehicles; equally important was how well the troops could use and maintain this equipment.

One of the better examples of this kind of analysis in action was seen during the Stalingrad campaign in late 1942. When the Russians attacked, they made their major effort against non-German troops. The Russians knew that the Italian, Hungarian, and Romanian divisions would crumble much more quickly than German divisions. This was an obvious insight, but the Russians carried it out in such detail that they bagged an entire German division and systematically eliminated it. The unit evaluation techniques used by the Russians at Stalingrad were employed for the rest of the war, but were often not noticed by most observers.

After the war, it was discovered (by examining records from both sides of battles) that of the same size and composition some units were twice as effective in combat than others. This was the case in all armies. The key factor here was leadership, a factor that was recognized during the war but not in a systematic way. Ironically, a method for accurately measuring divisions' effectiveness during wartime came from civilian researchers. The rise of historical war games, which began in the 1950s, produced a growing number of officers and civilians who possessed the skills needed to evaluate historical, as well as current, combat divisions. Turning divisions into numbers is still not an exact science, but it was practiced successfully during the 1991 Gulf War and is increasingly a standard part of the staff officers' toolbox worldwide.

OUTLINE DIVISIONAL ORDER OF BATTLE, 1930–1945

The principal unit for large-scale ground operations during World War II was the division. Divisions varied in size from about 4,500 men to as many as 20,000, depending upon their arm of service and nationality, but all were more or less self-contained combat formations of all arms (infantry, armor, artillery, support troops) capable of some degree of sustained independent operations. The principal differences among the numerous types of divisions (infantry, armor, parachute, marine, security, fortress, and so forth) were due to the specialized missions to which they were dedicated. In general, the Allied nations had fewer specialized types of divisions than did the Axis powers, which had serious occupation (of foreign territories) and internal security problems. This table summarizes the number of divisions available to each of the belligerent powers as of the beginning of the indicated year, regardless of location.

The figures for most countries are approximate. In some cases they include separate brigades, lumped together on the basis of three brigades per division. All types of divisions are included except training formations, depot divisions, and inactive militia and territorial units. No attempt has been made to modify the figures on the basis of actual

Available Divisions of the Power at War

	Eve*	1940	1941	1942	1943	1944	1945	End†
Australia	0	7	10	10	9	7	7	7
Bulgaria	12	14	14	16	23	29	29	20
Canada	0	1	3	5	8	6	6	6
China	(—	—	—	Above	300	—	—	—)
Finland	14	17	19	20	20	20	—	—
France	86	105	0	0	5	7	14	14
Germany	78	189	235	261	327	347	319	375
Great Britain	9	34	35	38	39	37	31	31
Hungary	6	7	10	16	19	22	33	30
India	3	5	10	14	16	16	18	18
Italy	66	73	64	89	86	2	9	10
Japan	36	36	39	73	84	100	145	197
New Zealand	0	1	1	2	2	1	1	1
Poland	43	2	2	2	2	5	5	5
Romania	11	28	33	31	33	32	24	24
South Africa	0	0	3	3	3	4	3	1
Soviet Union	194	200	220	250	350	400	488	491
United States								
Army	8	24	37	73	90	89	89	89
Marines	0	0	2	3	5	6	6	6

* September 1939.
† May 1945 for Germany and the other European powers; September 1945 for the United States, Japan, and China.

strength, degree of training, scales of equipment, or state of readiness. Japanese, German, and Soviet figures include "satellite" formations (for example, in January 1943 the German figure includes one Serbian-manned, eight Croatian-manned, and four Slovakian-manned divisions, not to mention the German divisions formed from troops of other nationalities). German figures include air force, navy, and Waffen SS ground divisions. British figures include three divisions comprised primarily of African personnel. Post-1939 figures for Poland include only formations raised in exile in the West, omitting units under Soviet control: one by January 1944, twelve by January 1945, and seventeen by the war's end. French figures after 1940 include only Free French units, omitting Vichy divisions, about sixteen by mid-1941, including those in colonies that later went over to the Free French. Italian figures post-1943 omit units of Mussolini's Italian Social Republic, four by January 1944 and six by January 1945. Romanian figures from January

1945 on reflect forces fighting under Allied control. In 1939–1940 the Netherlands had nine divisions (plus about three more in the East Indies), the Belgians twenty-two, and the Yugoslavs thirty-four, before being overrun by the Germans. Neither the Dutch nor the Belgians raised division-sized forces in exile. The Yugoslav partisans under Tito raised about twenty-four "divisions" (including one Italian-manned) from about mid-1943 onward, after Italy switched sides, opening up the Aegean to Allied shipping (and easier resupply of the Yugoslav forces).

GERMAN ARMY MOBILIZATION IN WORLD WAR II

The Versailles Treaty in 1919 prohibited Germany from having an army of more than 100,000 men, all restricted to long-term enlistments (twenty-five years for officers and twelve for other ranks). These troops were organized into seven infantry and three cavalry divisions which conformed to very rigid tables of organization prescribed by the treaty. The infantry divisions each controlled recruiting and training within their particular military district or *Wehrkreis*. There were in addition two superior commands (*Gruppenkommandos*) that were responsible for higher-level administration and training. Although the army was prohibited from having a general staff, an agency called the "Troop Office" (*Truppendienst*) covertly carried out general staff functions, among them conducting secret preparations for general mobilization of a much larger army on the day when Germany could openly rearm once more.

The basic army expansion plan was simple. When mobilization was proclaimed, each unit in the army would be filled up to 300 percent of official strength with new recruits and promptly divide itself in three. So each division would expand into three new divisions, each having a cadre of about one-third regular soldiers to train, season, and steady the new recruits, many of whom would already have had some training through various covert preparatory programs. As a result, Germany would be able to field about thirty divisions quickly. This was the plan in existence when Hitler came to power at the end of January 1933. And it was the plan with which Hitler was able to create the seemingly unstoppable Wehrmacht of 1939–1942.

The critical period for the expansion of the *Reichswehr* into the Wehrmacht was 1934–1935. During this period, while, for example, the old 1st Infantry Division was fissioning into the new 1st, 11th, and

21st Infantry Divisions, Germany was for a time without an effective army. Some astute diplomacy, coupled with a good deal of cowardice in France and Great Britain, enabled Hitler to squeak by without a military showdown, so that, with the addition of some armored divisions, by 1936 the Wehrmacht numbered forty divisions. Over the next few years as Hitler expanded Germany territorially, the army expanded further. What with the *Anschluss* with Austria (which brought in a half-dozen new divisions) and the annexation of the Sudetenland, by the end of 1938 Germany had fifty-one active divisions. Meanwhile, of course, as men were passed out of the active army and into the reserve, Germany's mobilization potential began to rise.

Of course, this mass army needed officers; fifty-one divisions required about 100,000 of them. There were about 4,000 available from the old *Reichswehr,* including medical personnel, and 1,000 or so from the former Austrian army, a pool obviously insufficient to meet the need. Recalling thousands of former World War I officers and commissioning many NCOs (after all, the *Reichswehr* had been highly selective) helped, but was still not enough. In the end, an efficient system of officer-training camps was established. All of this expansion of the army occurred at the same time that the navy was growing and the new air force (the Luftwaffe) was being created, which put further strains on Germany's manpower, not to mention the needs of Hitler's small but growing bodyguard, the Waffen SS. In order to regulate manpower management, on the eve of World War II Hitler fixed an annual allocation of personnel, with the army to get 66 percent of all new recruits (including about six thousand for the Waffen SS), the navy, 9 percent, and the air force, 25 percent.

Recruitment and training were the responsibility of the *Wehrkreis.* This system was extremely efficient. For example, Austria's six million inhabitants, who constituted a single *Wehrkreis,* yielded sixteen infantry divisions, a panzer division, seven Alpine divisions, and seven depot and reserve divisions in the course of the war, not to mention recruits for the air force and the navy. Divisions in the field received replacements from their *Wehrkreis* of origin and were often sent back home to recuperate their strength. The 26th Infantry Division, from the *XXI Wehrkreis* in the Rhineland, was more or less destroyed in combat nine times, each time being restored back to strength by fresh drafts from the Rhineland.

In addition to an efficient mobilization system, the German Army raised units by "waves." Each wave consisted of a number of newly raised or newly reorganized divisions, all of which were organized and equipped in precisely the same way. The idea was that in an army of literally hundreds of divisions all a senior commander had to know about an outfit was its wave, since that would tell him when it was raised, and hence how much training it had (older units having more than new ones), what its manpower and equipment allocations were, and how it was organized.

For example, 2nd Wave divisions were raised from reservists in August 1939, on a T/O&E (table of organization & equipment) similar to that of the prewar 1st Wave, with fewer light machine guns and no mortars. The 3rd Wave, raised at that time from the *Landwehr* (militia), was like the 1st Wave, with fewer engineers, signalmen, and other combat support elements. The 4th Wave, raised simultaneously from newly conscripted manpower, was like the 2nd but lacked a lot of combat support elements, and the 5th Wave, raised from older reservists during the Polish campaign (September-October 1939), had mostly Czech equipment. Waves contained from four to twenty-two divisions. The first thirty-two waves (divisions raised up to the autumn of 1944) were numbered, but the half dozen or so subsequent ones received glorious names, perhaps so that the men would not wonder what happened to the guys in the previous thirty-two waves. This was the system with which the German armed forces began World War II. Despite some obvious faults, it was logical and orderly. However, mounting casualties, the deteriorating strategic and political situation, and the peculiar internal political character of the Third Reich soon began to create problems.

Probably the biggest flaw in Germany's mobilization and manpower management arrangements was the desire of various leaders (both political and military) to build "private" armies for political purposes.

Heinrich Himmler's Waffen SS was the first and most obvious example of this. Originally a relatively small contingent of Nazi party troops earmarked as Hitler's personal bodyguards and triggermen, the Waffen SS soon expanded into a self-contained army approaching 10 percent of Germany's military manpower by late 1944, but including fully 25 percent of the panzer and mechanized divisions. So desperate did Himmler become for manpower that he secured a monopoly on recruitment of the *Volksdeutsch,* the numerous German residents, in other nations, and then began to recruit from "Germanic non-Germans" such as Swedes, Danes, and Dutchmen, then from "Non-Germanic Aryans" such as Frenchmen, Belgians, Spaniards, and Italians, and finally from the very "Untermenchen" themselves, the allegedly inferior Slavic Croatians, Bosnians, and Ukrainians, and African, Asian, and Indian prisoners of war, not to mention Arab volunteers. In fact, about the only people not consciously used were Jews and Gypsies, although some of them got in anyway, disguising themselves as Germans in order to hide among their enemies.

The Luftwaffe proved yet another drain on Germany's manpower. Hermann Göring very early established the notion that anything associated with the air was part of his air force, including not merely aircrews and base personnel, but also antiaircraft, parachute, and air base security troops, not to mention his own personal bodyguard. However, since the Luftwaffe eventually lost air superiority, it gradually came to have far more men than it needed. Adamantly opposed to transferring these troops to the army, Göring secured Hitler's permission to organize them into *Luftwaffefeldivisionen,* (air force field divisions). Fully twenty-two of these were raised. Commanded by erstwhile airmen, with no veteran cadres, virtually all of them disintegrated upon their first contact with the enemy, mostly in Russia. Of course, some air force units did perform well, the eleven parachute divisions and the "Hermann Göring Panzer-Parachute Division," which was the largest division ever committed to combat (so large, in fact, it was later split into two). But, as with the Waffen SS formations, these units were oversized, with more men (and better men) and more equipment than comparable regular army divisions.

This was an extremely inefficient use of manpower and equipment. Germany raised about 761 divisions during the war (about 670 army, 48 Waffen SS, 40 Luftwaffe, and 3 navy); the imprecision is due to the fact that a great many "divisions" were raised during the closing weeks of Hitler's Götterdämmerung, few of which had very many troops. About 110 of these were destroyed in action and fully 173, virtually all army, were disbanded due to severe losses. This was an enormous waste. New divisions consumed manpower and equipment that would have best been used to rebuild the cadres, however depleted, of old ones. The 22 *Luftwaffefeldivisionen* had sufficient manpower and equipment to have restored 100 regular army infantry divisions to full strength, considering "normal" losses. Imagine the possible beneficial effects of distributing among the regular army divisions the physically and intellectually superior personnel who composed the bulk of the manpower funneled into the air force and Waffen SS divisions, even allowing for the allegedly inferior qualities of the many "Untermenchen" which the latter contained.

BLOOD PRICE

By mid-1944, 35 percent of the men in the German Army had been wounded at least once, 11 percent at least twice, 6 percent three times, 2 percent four times, and 2 percent more than four times. During the war the average officer slot had to be refilled 9.2 times.

THE BLITZKRIEG: A QUICK LOOK

Blitzkrieg was an operational tactic that enabled the German armies to gain unprecedented successes in the field during the early years of World War II.

Although the word *blitzkrieg* ("lightning war," actually coined by a news correspondent, not by the Germans) instantly brings to mind Hitler's panzers smashing their way across Europe, the tank was only a cog in the intricate machinery of this new form of warfare. In fact, the tank was not the fundamental building block, but rather the internal combustion engine. Blitzkrieg was a doctrine for the employment of motorized combined armed forces, tanks in cooperation with reconnaissance troops, infantry, artillery, engineers, and logistical troops, plus ground attack aircraft.

The basic operational principle of blitzkrieg was *Einheit* ("unity") with all elements not merely cooperating in action but being integrated into combined armed combat teams at the lowest levels. Thus, a tank battalion of three or four companies might go into action accompanied by a company of engineer special-assault troops, two or three companies of infantry, some antiaircraft or antitank troops, and some signalmen. It would be supported by a couple of batteries of field artillery and a flight or two of dive-bombers, and covered by friendly fighters, all acting under the orders of the battalion commander. Integrated combat teams of engineers, infantrymen, and tanks would be formed at the platoon level to ensure that the strengths of each arm would help negate the weaknesses of the others.

Tactically, the engineers would remove obstacles, cover the advance with chemical smoke, and employ flamethrowers to permit the so-called combat elements to advance. The tanks would cover the advance of the infantry, protecting them from machine guns, while the infantry protected the tanks from antitank weapons. The antitank and antiaircraft troops took on enemy aircraft or tanks (flak guns having proven themselves very effective tank killers) while the artillery and dive-bombers dealt with particular tough obstacles while softening the enemy up, and the signalmen kept everyone working together.

Attacks were organized in echelons or waves. As soon as the first group of units secured its objective, the second and third would pass through to attain theirs. The idea was actually not so much to fight the enemy as to smash through his front and penetrate into his rear, where the true advantage of motorized and mechanized forces lay, in their superior mobility, permitting them to run rampant across the enemy's lines of supply, communication, and retreat, with the ultimate objective of cutting him off and forcing his surrender.

Strategically a blitzkrieg operation had several phases.

AUFMARSCH, movement to the enemy's front, something that could be done quite rapidly despite an apparent wide dispersal of forces, given that all of the attacking troops would be motorized.

GEFECHTSSTREIFEN, concentration against a narrow sector of the enemy's front, then

SCHWERPUNKT, center of gravity of the attack, to be made with great force, in contrast to the numerous feints that would be undertaken simultaneously with the principal attack.

EINBRUCH, penetration of the enemy front, which, if successful, would be followed up by additional forces in order to achieve

DURCHBURCH, breakthrough, permitting the mobile troops access to the enemy's rear, where they could employ

FLACHEN UND LÜKETAKTICK, the tactics of "space and gap," avoiding the enemy's reserves and strong points as much as possible, hitting him where he was least able to defend himself, in order to press on and secure control of his lines of communication while other troops undertook the

AUFROLLEN, rolling up, of the tattered ends of the pierced enemy front, mopping up strong points and widening the gap, so that additional forces (even nonmotorized forces) could move up to support the advancing spearheads in attaining

KEIL UND KESSEL, literally "wedge and pocket," the encirclement of the enemy.

Through all of this some simple rules had to be observed. The attacking forces had always to advance, avoiding the enemy's strength.

Success was to be sustained, failure abandoned. The object was not so much to fight the enemy as to cut him off and let him wither on the vine. These simple rules were first developed and practiced in the last two years of World War I. While the Allies had generally missed the import of these *Stosstruppen* (storm trooper) tactics, the Germans had remembered that it worked and had added motorization and tanks to the concept during the 1930s.

Blitzkrieg worked with remarkable success in Poland, in France, in the Balkans, in North Africa, and in the Soviet Union, at least for the first few years of the war. But the success of blitzkrieg depended as much upon the ineptitude of the enemy as upon the skill and capabilities of the German Army. The defender had to be surprised, he had to be intellectually and doctrinally inflexible, relatively immobile, inferior in antitank weaponry, lacking air superiority, and he had to fold up quickly as soon as his lines of communication were severed.

Without surprise, the enemy could make careful preparations to receive the attack. With intellectual and doctrinal flexibility he could react to developments as they happened, rather than after they happened. With mobility he could undertake blitzkrieglike counterattacks of his own. With equal or superior antitank capabilities he could chew up the attacking forces. With air superiority he could dominate the battlefield, severely punishing the attacking columns. And if he refused to surrender immediately upon encirclement he could tie down precious mobile resources, causing the offensive to lose its momentum. As the war went on, Germany's enemies learned. In the end it was the Allies, whose armies were increasingly more mobile and more lavishly equipped than those of Germany, who waged blitzkrieg, albeit not so spectacularly.

ODD DATUM

When properly deployed for an attack in "blunt wedge" formation, a German panzer battalion of seventy-five to ninety tanks occupied an area of from thirty to forty acres.

"FELDWEBEL SCHULTZ, THE BUTCHER"

Tradition has it that Napoleon said, "An army marches on its stomach." What filled the stomachs of Napoleon's armies most of the time was hardtack. Gustatory arrangements have come a long way since. In the twentieth century most countries try to give their brave boys a more varied and more nutritious diet. In addition to bakery units, by World War II most armies included self-contained mobile butchering (of animals, not people) detachments, which were able to process enormous numbers of rations daily.

This was the maximum daily processing capacity of the German Army's *Fleischzug,* which was fairly typical of these mobile butchering units, to provide rations (each ration being a half pound): 40,000 rations from 40 head of beef cattle, each head 1,000 pounds; or 24,000 rations from 80 pigs, each pig 300 pounds; or 19,000 rations from 240 sheep, each sheep 80 pounds.

Since the number of rations was half the total weight of the livestock, on average only about half of each animal was actually usable meat. Note that the most efficient source of meat was beef cattle. The work involved in killing and dressing cattle is considerably less than that involved in processing twice as many pigs or six times as many sheep, and the yield in rations is considerably greater. The ration yield from a single sheep is 8 percent, and that from a single pig only 30 percent, that from a single beef. Of course, in practical terms a typical butcher platoon might not be able to operate at maximum efficiency, having to process various numbers of beeves, pigs, and sheep simultaneously rather than concentrating on a single type of livestock. And, of course, sometimes they had to process horses. While figures for horses are not officially available, it appears that a single 1,200-pound draught horse would yield fewer rations than a beef of equivalent weight, as well as being more difficult to process, so that daily ration production would decline if horses had to be slaughtered. On the other hand, since an army reduced to eating its horses is probably already on short rations, the difference may not matter much, except to the horses.

Field bakeries were similarly efficient. The typical German field bakery company, with two mixers and seven ovens, could produce between 15,000 and 19,200 bread rations daily depending upon season and weather.

Incidentally, in case a butcher platoon or bakery company had to fight, it was equipped as light infantry with small arms and light machine guns, which were frequently put to use, particularly on the Eastern front.

DAILY CAUSES OF CASUALTIES IN GROUND COMBAT

Postwar analysis of the causes of casualties revealed some interesting patterns. Casualties as a proportion of troops actually in contact with the enemy varied depending upon the type and duration of an operation.

Daily Percentage of Casualties in Ground Combat

Type of Operation	First Day	Subsequent Days
Attack:		
Fortified Zone	18.7	9.8
Meeting Engagement	7.5	—
Position	11.5	6.1
Pursuit		4.3
Covering and Security		3.2
Defense		
Fortified Zone	4.9	—
Position	6.1	3.5
Mobile Defense	9.8	5.2
Inactive Zone (no attacking)		2.6
Reserve (Not in Contact with Enemy)		
Summer Weather		0.6
Winter Weather		1.0

These figures should not be considered absolutely hard and fast, as a number of factors may modify them. For example, seasoned troops will suffer fewer casualties than green ones. Likewise, attacks conducted with inferior force will incur greater casualties than those undertaken with overwhelming superiority, and fresh troops will suffer fewer losses than tired ones. In addition, the nationality of the troops has some effect, as doctrine, training, and even equipment will influence casualties. These figures are for U.S. troops in the ETO.

Note that the figures are relative, that is, each day's loss is proportional to the current strength of the formation. All figures include a daily allotment of noncombat casualties, equivalent to losses when a unit is out of contact with the enemy, in reserve.

One of the most critical factors in maintaining the effectiveness of an army in the field is being able to regulate the flow of replacements so that the momentum of operations can be sustained. The biggest losses are always among infantry, who normally constituted no more than a third of a division's strength. Thus, lengthy exposure to the enemy even in an inactive zone, where neither side is undertaking offensive operations, can rather quickly reduce a formation's combat effectiveness by attrition. Ten days of this sort of thing would reduce a division's strength by nearly a quarter, but its infantry by perhaps a third. Assaulting a fortified zone for a week would see a division reduced by about half, with its infantry suffering proportionately about 75 percent of that.

The type of formation involved would also affect casualty statistics, since the infantry suffers proportionately greater losses than any other arm. Thus, the average U.S. infantry division in the European theater suffered 7.3 casualties per day per thousand men on strength (500 to 600 a week), while armored divisions averaged only 4.8 casualties (300 to 400 a week).

The casualties themselves were subject to further predictability. For U.S. forces, on average, of every seven casualties, one was dead, either killed in action or mortally wounded, one was more or less permanently disabled by wounds, four were less seriously wounded, and one was a psychological casualty. (These figures are not greatly different from those reflecting casualties during the First World War.) What the United States experienced also demonstrated that on average for every 3 tanks destroyed four men were killed. The British had the same experience; in one of the major Normandy tank battles, they lost 126 tanks (manned by over six hundred men), but suffered only eighty-one dead.

THE LESS GLAMOROUS SIDE OF BLITZKRIEG

Blitzkrieg is a prodigious consumer of supplies, munitions, and fuel.

Consider the tank. A single World War II tank had perhaps thirty thousand separate parts, all more or less prone to breakage. Most tanks had an operational endurance of no more than about five hundred miles before needing an overhaul and needed at least routine maintenance, which required a couple of hours a day. All of the spectacular German blitzkrieg victories were attained with advances at less than five hundred miles. When the Germans tried to push their armor beyond that limit, as they did in Russia almost from the start, they ran into problems, as tanks began to break down with increasing frequency and greater seriousness. Not only did maintenance requirements hamper operations, but they also proved a drain on logistical support.

Mechanized armies require very extensive mobile workshops to repair worn vehicles, and these in turn require complex mobile warehousing services to supply all the parts the vehicles require and the tools needed to make the repairs. Such elaborate facilities are themselves a drain on resources, particularly so in the case of Germany, which had limited automotive production facilities. Of course, the mobile troops could not operate without such services, and they were useful in returning to use tanks and other vehicles that had been damaged in combat. Indeed, mobile repair shops were occasionally a critical factor in determining the success or failure of an operation. Most disabling damage to tanks can be repaired within a day or so and the tank returned to action. With a particularly efficient recovery and repair service it was sometimes possible to return upward of 80 percent of tank casualties to service.

Ammunition was also a critical logistical headache when waging blitzkrieg. The very nature of blitzkrieg operations caused ammunition expenditure to increase enormously. So supply columns had to be mobile as well, or the advancing spearheads would find themselves without the wherewithal to fight. A division's artillery could easily fire off about 300 tons of ammunition in an hour of heavy action. This is about 350 tons for transportation purposes, since the ammunition requires some packaging. Now consider that a panzer division would also have over 150 tanks, several scores of antitank and antiaircraft guns, and some thousands of machine guns, rifles, and carbines, all expending ammunition at similarly prodigious rates.

And then there's fuel, the greatest single logistical headache created by mechanized operations. Consider the fuel required to move a panzer division's worth of German tanks (about 160, of the average available types in 1941–1944) a hundred miles:

Year	Types of Tanks in a Division	Tons of Fuel Consumed (every 100 miles)
1941	Pz-II, Pz-III, Pz-IV, Pz-38	22.1
1942	Pz-III, Pz-IV	23.7
1943	Pz-III, Pz-IV, Pz V, Tiger	31.7
1944	Pz-IV, Pz-V, Tiger	35.8

And to this sizable amount, don't forget to add in a normal "waste allowance" of about 5 percent (refueling at the front can be an exciting and wasteful proposition) and the fuel required to move the fuel, itself sometimes considerable. In North Africa truck convoys from rear-area ports to Rommel's Italo-German panzer army consumed almost as much fuel as they delivered.

Of course, since you can't undertake blitzkrieg with tanks alone, you now have to consider the fuel requirements for the rest of the motor vehicles in the panzer division, all 2,600 of them.

GERMAN GENERAL OFFICER LOSSES

The German Army lost 136 generals in action during the Second World War, an extraordinary number for any army in modern times. From September 1939 to May 1945 the German Army lost a general on the

German Generals Killed or Mortally Wounded

Rank*	Number
Colonel General (General)	1
General (Lieutenant General)	19
Generalleutnant (Major General)	55
Generalmajor (Brigadier General)	61

* U.S. equivalent given in parentheses.

average of one every two weeks. And 110 division commanders were killed in action or died of wounds, about one every three weeks, plus 23 corps commanders, roughly one every fourteen weeks, and 3 army commanders, one every ninety-five weeks.

Although the precise cause of death is not known in all instances, air attack appears to have been the principal cause, accounting for about 32 percent of the deaths (Rommel himself was almost numbered among these when his staff car was strafed in July 1944). The second most frequent cause of combat death among the generals was artillery fire, about 14 percent, followed by small arms fire, about 13 percent.

All services counted together (army, navy, air force, and Waffen SS), there were approximately 3,000 generals and admirals in the German armed forces during the war. Of these, 84 were executed, 24 of them for "treason" by Hitler (the last one being Eva Braun's brother-in-law, Hermann Fegelein, who was shot on April 28, 1945, for trying to desert the *Fuhrerbunker*), and the rest by the Allies and West Germany as a result of convictions for war crimes.

GOOD-BYE OLD PAINT

The general utility of the horse in warfare began to decline in the mid-nineteenth century. The introduction of the rifle and then the machine gun made using horses on the battlefield highly dangerous. World War I, with its endless lines of trenches, doomed the cavalry as an effective tactical arm forever. But the horse still soldiered on in a number of ways, most notably for transport purposes. Horses actually saw more service during the Second World War than during the First. Indeed, despite the popular image of Polish lancers futilely charging German tanks (which never took place outside of the imagination of the German propaganda ministry), the horse cavalry made something of a comeback during the war, albeit not in its traditional roles. So unexpected was this development that it caught most armies by surprise.

The German Army, for example, began World War II with one cavalry division. This performed profitably during the Polish and French campaigns but was converted into the 24th Panzer Division early in the Russian campaign. Soon afterward, the peculiar circumstances of the Russian front prompted the Germans to raise new-mounted formations, which were found particularly effective in antipartisan operations and raids, notably in the frequent dense forests of western Russia. By the end of the war the Germans had seven horse cavalry divisions, mostly in the Waffen SS, largely comprised of non-German personnel, mostly Ukrainians and various Central Asians who preferred to fight against Stalin rather than for him. Italian horse cavalry units were also active with some success on the Russian front and even conducted what may have been the last successful charge in history: On the night of August 24, 1942, two squadrons of the Savoia Light Cavalry Regiment launched a flank attack that overran a Russian infantry battalion near Isbuschenski in the Ukraine. However, it was the Russians who made the most extensive use of cavalry, raising some fifty divisions during the war. Some of these were mated with armored units to form "cavalry-mechanized" groups, which proved useful in penetrations, exploitations, and raids. Several of them rendered valuable service during the Stalingrad offensive in November 1942. These units reached their zenith during the summer offensive of 1944. The Germans thought their flank was secure because of the vast Pripet Marshes, but the Russian horse cavalry attacked through the marshes, right into the flank of a very surprised German Army Group Center. Throughout the war, over half a million men served as mounted troopers in the Russian cavalry.

Even the United States, which had two regular and several National Guard cavalry divisions on the eve of the war, committed some horse cavalry units to operations overseas. The entire 2nd Cavalry Division, composed primarily of black personnel, was shipped to North Africa in 1943, where it patrolled the frontier between French and Spanish Morocco, lest Franco chose an inopportune time to intervene in the war. And the 112th Cavalry Regiment, a part of the Texas National Guard, served on horseback for a time on New Caledonia. Dismounted in May 1943, the 112th Cavalry was the last mounted U.S. formation to serve in a combat zone. Officially. However, during the Sicilian campaign the rugged nature of the terrain prompted the commander of the 3rd Infantry Division, Major General Lucian Truscott, an old horse soldier, to create a provisional mounted reconnaissance troop, a practice that was adopted by several other units during the Italian campaign.

Cavalry was also used by the Yugoslav partisans and rather extensively in China, by both the Chinese and Japanese. Even the U.S. Navy used mounted troops, raising a regiment from local manpower in Inner Mongolia, as a security force for navy weather stations, while the Coast Guard had mounted beach patrols along the U.S. East Coast in order to prevent German submarines from landing intelligence agents and saboteurs.

So the horse soldiered on with surprising effectiveness in an otherwise apparently mechanized war. But while its role in the cavalry was a distinguished one during the war, it was as a beast of burden that horses (and their kin donkeys and mules) really made their mark, for most of the armies had equine supply services and artillery for most of the war.

Consider the vaunted Wehrmacht, whose pride was the mechanized might of the panzers. When Hitler invaded Russia on June 22, 1941, the German Army had over 750,000 "hippotrain" (horse-drawn) guns and other vehicles, in contrast to only about 600,000 motor vehicles, including some 3,500 armored fighting vehicles. Aside from the operational limitations that the use of horses and mules imposed on the German Army, they also proved an enormous logistical burden. On average, to feed three horses doing useful work hauling howitzers and such required the services of two more horses to haul their weekly rations of feed and fodder. And since horses and mules are not as sturdy as cars and trucks, during the war on the Eastern front the German Army lost an average of 1,000 horses a day. About 75 percent of these losses were due to combat, 17 percent to heart failure brought on by overwork, and the balance, 8 percent, to diseases, exposure, and starvation. Replacing horses was a major problem. Nevertheless, since the Germans had an inadequate supply of motor vehicles, they continued to rely on horseflesh through the entire war. The total number of horses used by the German armed forces during the war is unknown, but losses appear to have totaled about 2.7 million, nearly double the 1.4 million that were lost in World War I. This includes animals killed for food: Unlike wrecked trucks, dead horses could be eaten, and this was done regularly by Germans and Russians alike.

Other powers used horses and mules for logistical purposes as well, but none so extensively as did the Germans, although the Russians probably came close. In fact, the Soviet Union did not fully motorize its military transportation until about 1960.

HORSEPOWER

Despite the fact that it was not technically a motorized formation, the U.S. infantry division possessed about 400,000 horsepower in its approximately 2,000 motor vehicles. In fact, the division was actually capable of "lifting" all of its personnel by motor vehicle for limited periods by piling troops on everything that could roll. Although this somewhat disrupted unit cohesion, it allowed for relatively rapid movement. This was one reason for the speed with which the Third Army drove across France in August and September 1944. Since there were also considerable numbers of motor vehicles in nondivisional truck units, during the closing weeks of the war in Europe the ratio of men to motor vehicles in the U.S. Army in Europe was 4.3 to 1, better than the 4.4 to 1 ratio in prewar American civilian life.

Although to a lesser extent, Allied forces were also quite well endowed with motor vehicles. From D-Day to the surrender of Germany, U.S. and Allied forces in northwestern Europe made use of approximately 970,000 motor vehicles. This enormous fleet of trucks, tanks, cars, tractors, and what have you consumed gasoline at a prodigious rate. The U.S. 1944 armored division drank about 74 tons of petroleum products a day. Daily Allied fuel consumption during the drive across France in August-September 1944 averaged 27 million gallons (nearly 100,000 tons).

Since most of the German Army moved at the rate of a walk, this was of enormous operational importance.

VD AND MILITARY NONEFFECTIVENESS IN WORLD WAR II

Venereal disease has long been recognized as a major cause of nonbattle-related military noneffectiveness in wartime. Throughout the Second World War the problem was of significant, but declining importance. During World War I the VD rate for men in the U.S. Army was quite high, about 87 cases per 1,000 men per year (higher than that prevailing in the French Army). During World War II the VD rate in the U.S. Army decreased markedly, to about 56 percent of that of the earlier war, due largely to an intensive educational program to alert the troops to the dangers of venereal infections, plus to the introduction of penicillin, and, not incidentally, to the fact that many troops campaigned in areas where there were few opportunities to contract VD (e.g., New Guinea). Despite this, VD cases still accounted for over a third of all infectious and parasitical disease cases among U.S. Army personnel in World War II.

It is interesting to note that in U.S. military operations since World War II (with the exception of the 1990–1991 Gulf War) the VD-caused noneffectiveness rate has actually increased. In fact, while the World War I rate was considered disastrous, that for the Korean War was much worse, and that for Vietnam worse still. The rate for the Gulf War was only a fraction of that for World War I—there are strong religious and social prohibitions against extramarital sex in Saudi Arabia. There was VD among U.S. troops in the Gulf, but the exact data was kept confidential for diplomatic reasons.

VD Cases per 1,000 Men per Year

	Number of Cases	Percent Ratio (to WWI)
World War I	87	100.0
World War II	49	56.3
Korean War	146	171.3
Vietnam War	325	373.6

CAUSES OF NONEFFECTIVENESS IN ARMIES

At any given moment during the war an average of 4.22 percent of U.S. Army personnel were classified as "noneffective." During operations in Europe in 1944–1945 the army experienced the loss of 101,698,977 man-days due to noneffectiveness.

Of course, these figures include long periods of relative inactivity. During periods of intensive combat, battle injuries could soar dramatically. For example, during the approximately fifty-five-day-long Normandy campaign (from D-Day to the end of July) about 80 percent of "noneffectives" among the British forces were the result of combat. In addition, relatively speaking, the ETO was a healthy theater, not being infested with interesting inflictions such as jungle rot, malaria, dengue

Noneffectiveness in the ETO

Cause	Lost Man-days	Percentage
Battle Injury	49,726,067	48.9
Disease	37,533,605	36.9
Other	14,439,305	14.2

fever, and other exotic tropical ailments. The British experience in Burma, one of two candidates for the distinction of being the least healthy theater of operations (the other being New Guinea), is interesting in this regard. For every man evacuated to the rear because of wounds in 1943, there were 120 evacuated for nonbattle-related conditions, mostly malaria and other even more gruesome tropical diseases, a figure that fell to 60 in 1944, due to aggressive preventive measures and the introduction of new medicines, and to 40 in 1945, which was better but still extraordinarily high.

If the whole U.S. Army is considered, including the several million troops who never left the United States or were stationed in other noncombat areas, the proportion of battle injuries as a cause of noneffectiveness drops to only 18 percent. Troops in places like Burma, New Guinea, and other tropical areas were, of course, subject to numerous interesting local diseases, which generally felled more men than did the enemy. In fact, even when there was no enemy around, tropical climes could be deadly. Attempts to build an air base at Ndeni in the Santa Cruz Islands were frustrated by a particularly virulent variety of malaria that killed so many engineer troops the place had to be abandoned. In addition, the accident rate in the ZI (zone of the interior, the forty-eight states) was extremely high. In 1943 alone fully five thousand people were killed in military-related aviation accidents.

THE GRADES OF THE IRON CROSS

The Iron Cross, the highest German decoration, was created by the king of Prussia in 1813, during the *Befreiungskrieg* ("War of Liberation") from Napoleon. Drawing its inspiration from France's Légion d'honneur, the new decoration could be awarded to officers and men for acts of heroism in battle and to senior commanders who won victories. As authorized, the Iron Cross was awarded during the campaigns of 1813–1814 and during the Waterloo campaign in 1815. It was not authorized for award during the Revolutionary War of 1848–1849, or for either of the Schleswig-Holstein Wars (1848–1850 and 1864), or the Seven Weeks' War with Austria (1866), apparently because these were at least partially civil wars rather than genuine foreign conflicts. The decoration was revived during the Franco-Prussian War (1870–1871), and again for the First World War (1914–1918) and the Second World War (1939–1945), during both of which it was given out rather liberally.

As originally conceived, the Iron Cross had only three grades, 2nd Class, 1st Class, and Grand Cross, and it remained thus until the Second World War. During the war Hitler, who had himself earned both a 2nd and a 1st Class on the Western Front during World War I, added five additional grades, primarily as a morale boosting measure. As a result, by the end of the Second World War there were eight grades to the honor.

Ascending Grades of the Iron Cross

2. *Eisernes Kreuz* (Iron Cross 2nd Class)
1. *Eisernes Kreuz* (Iron Cross 1st Class)
Ritter Kreuz (Knight's Cross)
Ritter Kreuz mit Eichenlaub (Knight's Cross with Oak Leaves)
Ritter Kreuz mit Eichenlaub und Schwertn (Knight's Cross with Oak Leaves and Swords)
Ritter Kreuz mit Eichenlaub, Schwertn, und Brillianten (Knight's Cross with Oak Leaves, Swords, and Diamonds)
Ritter Kreuz mit Goldaneneichenlaub, Schwerten, und Brillianten (Knight's Cross with Golden Oak Leaves, Swords, and Diamonds)
Gross Kreuz (Grand Cross)

The Grand Cross has been awarded only three times, twice to unquestionably deserving commanders, Marshals Gebhard von Blücher, who helped beat Napoleon at Waterloo, and Paul von Hindenburg, who led Germany's armies to striking victories on the Russian front in World War I, and once to the wholly undeserving Hermann Göring.

During the Second World War awards of the 1st Class and 2nd Class Iron Cross ran into the tens of thousands, and there were 7,377 awards of the Knight's Cross in its various versions.

Hitler also decorated twenty-nine women with the Iron Cross, of whom the most famous was Hanna Reitsch, Hitler's favorite woman pilot, who received both the 1st Class and 2nd Class for her services as a test pilot. Only one other woman received a 1st Class, the rest having to be satisfied with 2nd Class.

Although the Iron Cross has not been awarded since the end of the Second World War, a supply of them was struck in West Germany some years ago, so that recipients could trade in their swastika-bedecked Nazi-era decorations for a more traditional one.

DEADLY HEAT

In tropical areas, the heat was a significant danger. Among Allied troops operating in tropical areas (between 1942 and 1943), between 15 and 20 percent were victims of heat prostration (and similar afflictions). Of these, about 2 percent died.

IF YOU ARE INJURED . . .

Combat soldiers have two major fears: getting killed and getting wounded. If the latter, there are additional terrors regarding how soon, and how well, their injuries will be cared for. During World War II, great strides were made in the speed and effectiveness of caring for the wounded. The best equipped in this regard were the Western Allies, who provided the following procedure for combat injuries:

- Because medics were attached to every unit (down to the platoon level), injured troops were usually under a medic's care within ten to thirty minutes after being wounded. The medic would evaluate the wounds and apply first aid. This would often involve plasma, painkillers, and other battlefield medications. The medic filled out a tag describing the soldier's injuries and attached it to the wounded trooper. Stretcher-bearers then moved the soldier back to the battalion medical station, usually a thousand or so meters from the fighting. If the soldier's wounds were slight and he could still move under his own power, he made his own way back to the battalion medics, with or without the assistance of another soldier. If all this sounds pretty elaborate for what we generally consider the "chaos of the battlefield," it is. But a well-run military operation is a complex and carefully planned affair. The medics are well trained and the troop commanders place the medics and stretcher-bearers where it is thought they will be most needed. These preparations play a big role in keeping up the combat soldiers' morale. There is a natural tendency for troops to stop fighting and look after injured comrades, which reduces the efficiency of the unit and often leads to even more casualties. Effective frontline medical care also made for a more effective combat unit.

- Usually the injured soldier was at the battalion medical center within an hour of being injured. At this point the soldier was examined by the battalion surgeon (an M.D.) and more treatment was applied. While the medic's job was to get the injured soldier off the battlefield in one piece, the battalion surgeon began the cure. This involved "stabilizing" the patient. Sometimes this meant some surgery to stop bleeding and the application of more medications to prevent infection.

- If more medical attention was needed, within a few hours, the wounded soldier found himself at the division hospital, which was usually five to ten miles behind the front. This was, in fact, a mobile emergency room operating out of tents. Soldiers with wounds that would heal in a week or so were treated there and sent back to their units within ten days. More seriously injured troops received more treatment and were eventually evacuated to an army-level hospital, where they might take a month or more to recover. The most seriously injured were sent farther back or all the way to their home country for recovery and/or a medical discharge from the service (and continued treatment in military hospitals).

Most combat wounds were not serious. Flesh wounds, burns, broken bones, and sundry bumps and bruises were treated and eventually the soldier returned to duty. But even minor wounds could become deadly if not treated promptly.

HEAVY FIRE

What is "heavy artillery fire"? A lot of analysis was done during World War II to answer this question and the answer was "at least a ton and a half of shells per acre over three hours against a prepared enemy."

An acre is an area forty-eight by one hundred yards (about a football field). A ton and a half of shells translates into about ninety 105mm shells (one every three minutes) or thirty-five 155mm shells (one every five minutes). "A prepared enemy" is one who is dug in and thus relatively impervious to shell fire. The Germans in particular were quite good at digging shellproof field fortifications. These fortifications were usually quite spread out, with a defending battalion taking up an area of five hundred or more acres. This would require over seven hundred tons of ammunition to hit effectively. Troops will defend in depth, although an initial attack seeks only to grab the first of two or three lines of defenses.

Ideally, you would want to know exactly where each of the enemy defensive positions were. But a defending battalion would typically have over a hundred separate fighting positions, all well dug in and camouflaged and most not visible even to your frontline assault troops. Many of the frontline positions would be identified, and the guns would concentrate on those. Shells would be fired into identified targets behind the front (roads, likely assembly and supply storage areas). If you have thousands of tons of artillery shells available, you can demolish the first line of enemy defenses. But this requires hundreds of heavy-caliber (155mm-and higher) guns and ten or more tons of shells per acre. And, again, it must be delivered within a few hours, otherwise the enemy can shift reserves to block your breakthrough force. The World War I technique of continuous bombardment over several days was discredited before that war was over. The Russians tried this heavy-bombardment technique many times, but were not usually successful. The Germans learned to correctly read Russian preparations and then evacuate their first-line positions just before the Russian bombardment began. This wasted a lot of ammunition and got a lot more Russian troops killed as they slogged through the torn-up ground created by their own artillery and then ran into undamaged German fortifications. It was for this reason that the Russians used so much self-propelled artillery (and tanks) for direct fire. This was much more effective than bombardment by distant artillery. But direct fire put the self-propelled guns at great risk to German antitank guns and artillery. And there was still the problem of finding carefully hidden enemy positions.

The "ton and a half per acre in three hours" approach would work only if the attacking troops got into the enemy positions within a few minutes of the bombardment ending. The defending troops would quickly recover their composure once the bombardment ended. Indeed, enemy morale would actually improve quite a lot once they realized they had survived the three hours of shelling. The amount of shells you fired was not as important (as long as it was at least a ton and a half per acre) as long as it was delivered over no more than a three-hour period.

This technique was not the be-all and end-all of artillery techniques. In situations where the enemy was not well prepared, shorter bombardments were more useful. And rockets were very effective, because they could put a lot of shells on enemy troops immediately. Mortars and direct fire were useful for small-infantry-unit operations where you had to dig the enemy out of one position at a time. Attack from the air was also a useful substitute for artillery, and at Normandy masses of heavy bombers were used for one breakout operation. Gathering together enough bombers for this to be useful turned out to be more trouble, and expense, than it was worth. But those who went through this operation got a glimpse of what nuclear weapons might bring to the battlefield.

AIRBORNE, OVERLOADED, AND UNDERARMED

Starting from scratch, the United States created an airborne force during World War II. This eventually totaled five divisions (11th, 13th, 17th, 82nd, and 101st) plus several independent battalions. Only a third of the airborne troops came in by parachute; the rest were landed by glider. There was always a problem of how to arm these troops, as they were coming in by air and weight was at a premium. Moreover, these troops had practically no motor transportation. The infantry had to carry everything. The initial organization, established in 1942, was similar to regular infantry except that the paratroopers had fewer rifles (carbines were substituted) and fewer BARs (.30-caliber 20-pound Browning Automatic Rifles, which used a 20-round magazine) but more "light" machine guns (the .30-caliber 31-pound M1919A4, which required the use of a 14-pound tripod).

The regular infantry company (in 1944) had 193 men, 15 BARs, 2 M1919A4 machine guns, 1 .50-caliber machine gun, and 6 submachine guns. The infantry platoons had 41 men, 37 rifles, 1 carbine, and 3 BARs.

The parachute infantry company had 130 men, 12 M1919A6 machine guns (a 32-pound version that used a bipod rather than the tripod-mounted M1919A4 that weighed 45 pounds), 3 60mm mortars, and 3 bazookas. The parachute infantry platoon had 36 men, 2 M1919A6 machine guns, 1 60mm mortar, 1 sniper rifle, 1 bazooka, 22 rifles, and 14 carbines.

While this appeared to be heavier armament than that of the regular infantry, it was not the case. The regular infantry had more heavy weapons available from the battalion and regiment heavy-weapons units than did the paratroopers. The regular infantry regiment had 6 105mm howitzers, 9 57mm antitank guns, 55 .50-caliber machine guns, and many more .30-caliber machine guns. The regular infantry also had trucks and jeeps to haul all this stuff around, as well as ammunition. The paratroopers had a few jeeps (depending on what survived the glider landings) and not nearly as much ammunition.

Although the paratroopers were given more .30-caliber machine guns, they also had a lot of .30-caliber carbines. These weapons were a particular problem. Originally designed as a light weapon for support troops to carry around, the carbine fired what was essentially a pistol round. The carbine was more effective than a pistol, but that wasn't saying much. The standard U.S. pistol was .45 caliber and had more stopping power than the carbine round. Even the automatic carbine (the M2) wasn't much of an improvement. The additional machine guns were less than useful because they were so heavy.

At the end of 1944, the parachute infantry companies were reorganized and reequipped. Each new company had 176 men, 9 machine guns, 9 BARs, 3 bazookas, and 3 60mm mortars. Each parachute infantry platoon now had 49 men, 3 machine guns, 3 BARs, 1 60mm mortar, 1 bazooka, 39 rifles, and 10 carbines. The addition of the BARs was a big help, as were the lower number of carbines.

What was not done until Vietnam was to equip the parachute infantry with automatic rifles (the M-16) and lighter machine guns (the M-60). By 1944, the Germans already had weapons similar to what the U.S. troops wouldn't get until the 1960s. The Germans had the StG-44 assault rifle (the model for the AK-47) and the MG-42 (the model for the M-60).

THE FRENCH WAY . . .

During World War I, the biggest influence on U.S. Army organization was the French Army. U.S. troops frequently used French organization, tactics, and equipment. The American armies were sent to Europe in 1917 to ''save France,'' and the French were eager to assist them in any way they could. France provided most of the experienced instructors and a lot of the equipment. While the United States did not create a clone of the French Army, France was its major influence during World War I and for over a decade after.

Some of this influence carried over into World War II, with unfortunate results. For example, the infantry platoons were organized and equipped in an almost identical fashion to those of the 1940 French Army (the one the Germans rolled right over). Thus the U.S. infantry entered the war with squads that were too large for the squad leader to control in combat, with too little firepower (only automatic rifles, rather than machine guns), and without tactics capable of dealing with the better trained, organized, and equipped Germans. These deficiencies were noted by many senior U.S. Army commanders in 1940, but change came slowly until the United States was in the war. By then it was late 1941 and it wasn't until 1943 that a lot of the U.S. infantry units began to adopt (often unofficially) organizational, tactical, and equipment changes to better deal with the Germans and Japanese.

This attachment to French military practices was not so much because U.S. officers thought it was the best, but because coming out of World War I, it was all they had. As was the American custom, after World War I, the military was drastically cut back. There wasn't much money for defense in the 1920s and 1930s. Most of the military innovation during that period was directed at high-tech items (aircraft and tanks), not infantry matters.

WHAT'S MORE DANGEROUS THAN BEING AN INFANTRYMAN?

Being an American infantry replacement. The United States had what was probably the worst policy for replacing infantry casualties. Moreover, the policy was not officially recognized as deficient until after Vietnam. Going into World War II, it decided to use replacements like rounds of ammunition. When someone in a combat unit got killed or wounded, another man from the "replacement pool" would be immediately sent in to that unit. This was often done while the unit was still in combat. The results of this policy were disastrous for the unit, and usually fatal for the replacement. It was bad enough when done by the book. That is, the replacements came from the United States, where they had received several months of infantry training (in addition to the basic training all soldiers received). During the heavy fighting in France and Germany after D-Day, many of the replacements were not trained infantry, but men combed out of noncombat units and sent forward as replacements for the heavy infantry casualties.

Ironically, the brass would not have thought of sending untrained replacements to tank or artillery units, or at least they expected the replacements to receive some training before they were allowed to operate a tank or artillery piece. The official policy was that, since every soldier took basic training (which was oriented mainly toward infantry work), any soldier could be thrown into an infantry unit and immediately begin doing an infantryman's job. The result was just the opposite. Infantry work was far more complex and frightening than anything a tanker or artilleryman had to face. Most other armies recognized this, but not the U.S. Army. When infantry replacements were sent to a unit in combat, they often arrived at night (so they wouldn't be spotted, and shot at, by nearby enemy troops). Stumbling around in the dark, they would be led to a depleted squad (sometimes only three or four men remaining out of the original dozen). The veterans wanted nothing to do with the new soldiers and would often put them (if there was more than one, which was common) off by themselves someplace where they wouldn't endanger the veterans who knew just how dangerous combat could be. If the replacements survived their first night (and many didn't), their squad leader would try to size them up.

The squad leader was often new at his job, his predecessor often having been recently killed or wounded. These new squad leaders had combat experience but were not necessarily the best men for the job. In the midst of combat, the platoon leader would appoint the most likely private from the squad as the new squad leader and hope for the best. Thus the squad leader usually had no experience dealing with untrained replacements and, like the other veterans in the squad, wanted to avoid getting killed as a result of a mistake made by one of the greenhorns. In a defensive situation, this wasn't so bad. The new troops could be shown how to keep their heads down and briefed on the defense plan. If a new guy looked like he had his wits about him, one of the veterans might use him to help with digging and enhancing the field fortifications. After a day or so, some of the new guys might be entrusted to stand guard in one of the fighting positions. After a week or so of this "getting to know you" stuff, the replacements would be on their way to becoming trusted members of the squad. But often the replacements were sent in when the squad was involved in attacking or patrolling. And often the veterans had to take the new guys along because the entire squad had to move. Under these conditions, the replacements tended to die or get wounded quickly. If not that, then the new guys would collapse after a few days, from physical or mental strain, often both.

The preparation a soldier must have for infantry combat is extensive. Among other things, the trooper has to

Get used to the sound of rifle and shell fire.

Learn how to move in the combat zone without presenting a target.

Know the importance of taking care of weapons and equipment in a combat zone.

Know how to live in a combat zone without getting sick.

Know how to deal with night operations.

Stay physically fit.

Know how to use infantry weapons.

Too many of the replacements, especially those yanked out of non-combat units, lacked most of these skills. Moreover, those turned into infantry at the end of 1944 (especially to replace losses from the Battle of the Bulge in December) were shocked to discover that the war wasn't almost over and that the Germans still had plenty of fight left in them.

Many (but not all) commanders, at all levels, were soon aware of this problem. Although official army replacement policy did not change during the war, many commanders took their own steps to ease the problem. The simplest, and most effective, solution was just to not send replacements to units that were still in action, or at least not to units that were involved in an attack. When a battalion went on the defensive, or was pulled out of action for a few days, then replacements were sent in. Some commanders set up special training programs for replacements. This paid big dividends, and those units that had the most comprehensive training programs for replacements had the fewest problems with these new troops. Ideally, each division would have a training company that would give replacements a week or more of intense infantry training. When these new men were sent to their units, the platoon commander would have the squad leaders instruct the new troops on how that particular unit operated, introduce them to the veteran troops, and merge the replacements and veterans into a team. Unfortunately, these stopgap measures were not universally applied. Right up until the end of the war, replacements were being sent in with no preparations, and all too often became casualties before the veterans in their squad could even learn their names.

THE U.S. CAVALRY STANDS DOWN, AND IS REBORN

Among the many army units activated after Pearl Harbor were twenty-four horse cavalry regiments (another, the 26th Cavalry, was already fighting the Japanese in the Philippines). By the end of 1942, all of the regiments had been deactivated or converted to other arms. The survivors of the 26th Cavalry, of course, were marched off to Japanese prison camps. Six regiments converted to tank units. Four were converted to infantry. Two regiments were converted into light infantry for use in the Pacific. Sadly, the four segregated black regiments (the 9th and 10th Cavalry, the ''Buffalo Soldiers,'' plus two new regiments) were converted to service troops. Many of these regiments were already formed into the 1st and 2nd Cavalry Divisions. The 1st Cavalry Division converted to an infantry division. The 2nd Cavalry Division was a segregated black unit that was disbanded after it landed in North Africa.

The remaining eight regiments were turned into mechanized cavalry, or ''cavalry reconnaissance squadrons.'' An additional forty-seven recon squadrons were raised. Only forty-two of the fifty-five recon squadrons made it overseas. Armored divisions used fourteen of these squadrons, while the other twenty-eight were assigned to thirteen armored cavalry groups (later called regiments). The cavalry squadrons were one unit type that was heavily influenced by the German example. But the Americans did not go far enough, and were also influenced by the less-effective British reconnaissance techniques. The American ''cavalry squadron'' was actually a reconnaissance battalion of 743 men. Like the Germans, it had a lot of mobility and heavy weapons.

The U.S. squadron had six self-propelled howitzers, seventeen light tanks, twenty-six half-tracks, and most important, forty armored cars. There were also three 81mm and twenty-seven 60mm mortars as well as a lot of machine guns (both .30- and .50-caliber). But the German recon battalion was an even more imposing beast, with 1,140 men. The Germans did not have as much equipment in their battalion, having only twenty-five armored cars, two 81mm mortars, and two 75mm guns, for example. The Germans did have more machine guns and submachine guns. In general, the Germans had more infantry and better armored cars. This made a big difference. Mobile infantry was the key to effective reconnaissance and the U.S. battalion, in effect, had none. The American M-8 armored car was less mobile than the German model and no less vulnerable to tanks or other heavy weapons. The

Germans would quickly move to an area and get their infantry into action to scout around. American units would come into an area in their armored cars or jeeps and tended to stay in their vehicles rather than immediately going forward on foot to check out the area. The American vehicles were easier to detect than German infantry sneaking through the underbrush. American recon troops soon learned to hit the ground when near the enemy, but there were only twenty-nine men in a scout platoon, and nine of them were driving the three armored cars and six jeeps, and another nine were riding shotgun. That left only eleven men to go forward on foot. Often the platoon was under strength, which was a normal condition, and there would be even fewer foot scouts available. The Germans reorganized their recon battalion in 1944, but the changes were not that remarkable. Personnel strength was reduced to 945 and the number of armored cars cut. But thirteen assault guns were added, giving the unit a formidable antitank capability.

In addition to the Germans, the Americans had been influenced by the British, and the extensive British use of armored cars. After World War II, U.S. recon squadrons were reorganized again and got infantry and, eventually, helicopters. And got rid of the armored cars.

RED FLARE FOR GUNS, STAR CLUSTER FOR TANKS

Radio jamming got its start in World War II. It wasn't used very effectively in most cases because the technology wasn't available to easily shut down all frequencies, or to quickly identify and jam those that were being used. Most armies, however, understood the problems that successful jamming would present. The option, should jamming shut down one's radio network, was to resort to the technology of the previous war. Namely, flares. Flares, and other pyrotechnic signals, have been used by armed forces for centuries. Indeed, the first use of gunpowder was as a signal device. Gunpowder weapons came later. Flare use reached something of a golden age during World War I, mainly because flare technology was much more advanced than radio technology.

The problem with using flares in World War II was that the troop leaders had gotten used to the radio, and the radio's ability to allow long-winded discussions with other leaders on what to do next and how. While the military tries to rein in this chatter, the radio is still abused in even the most disciplined units. If one has to fall back on flares, there is a tendency to use too many flares too often. That problem aside, flares and colored-smoke grenades were still used in World War II, even without radio jamming occurring. Armies that could not afford a lot of radios, or smaller units that were not generally worth equipping with a radio, continued to use flares and smoke grenades. The use of flares and smoke grenades was also very common when cooperating with aircraft, as the planes often used radios not compatible with those used by ground units.

Flares and smoke grenades were used primarily for three tasks:

- **To Identify.** When units were maneuvering and, at a prearranged time, the commander wanted them to identify their position, each company in a battalion would fire off a different-colored flare so the battalion commander knew where each company was. Note that flares were usually fired out of pistols (called flare pistols, naturally) so they would gain some altitude before exploding into whatever color they were. While there were only a few colors of flares available (usually white, red, and green), two (each of a different color) would be fired in close succession to give the user more options.

- **To Warn.** Flares fired in a particular direction could, by their color and direction, indicate the presence of a particular type of enemy threat. A white flare might mean enemy artillery, green might indicate enemy infantry, and a star cluster (which explodes like fireworks into many other points of light) might indicate a really serious enemy threat, like tanks.

- **To Mark.** Different-colored-smoke grenades (whose smoke lingers far longer than a flare) can be used to mark the status of a particular piece of terrain. Green smoke can mean an area free of opposition, red smoke can mark a minefield, other colors can mark where friendly units are or are supposed to be. Smoke is particularly useful when working with friendly aircraft, as the smoke is easier to see from the air.

Now you know why new recruits are always tested for color blindness.

PASS ON THE GAS, USE THE HE (HIGH EXPLOSIVE)

Mortars were a very effective infantry weapon and most nations equipped their troops with 120mm mortars. This weapon was too heavy for the troops to carry with them, but it was lighter than regular artillery and as effective as the 105mm howitzers that provided most of the firepower. Oddly enough, the United States did not have a 120mm mortar, but a 107mm (4.2-inch) model that was designed just for delivering chemical shells. Since chemical weapons were not used during World War II (with a few minor exceptions), the 107mm mortars didn't have much to do except deliver smoke shells (also considered "chemical" weapons, even though they provided concealment for friendly troops rather than created casualties among the enemy).

By 1944, it was recognized that the 107mm mortars were useful as artillery and they were used as such. Each U.S. "chemical" battalion had thirty-two mortars and these were assigned to a Corps of two to four divisions. This was quite different from the practice of other nations, where regiments were given 120mm mortars. One benefit of the 107mm mortars was that the battalions were equipped with white phosphorus (WP) shells. The WP shell created a lot of smoke, but the burning phosphorus caused nasty casualties. The Germans made noises about illegal use of "chemical weapons" when they realized what WP could do, but this did not result in their use of chemical weapons in retaliation. Nor were they able to use many WP shells themselves because of raw material shortages.

As the war went on, it became the American practice to assign one mortar company (eight 4.2-inch mortars) to an infantry battalion but not all infantry battalions got mortars; preference was given to units involved in attacks. Most of the shells fired were "HE" (high explosive).

DEADLIER THAN A SPEEDING BULLET

Disease, while not the major cause of casualties it had been in pre-twentieth century wars, was still responsible for nearly half the 100 million deaths caused by World War II. Most of the deaths due to disease were among civilians, who were usually also suffering from starvation and exposure at the same time. For soldiers, the situation was somewhat better, as they were better organized and, obviously, trained to survive trying conditions.

Two diseases in particular caused much death and disability. The big killer was typhus, claiming over two million people, mostly in eastern Europe (where it has been a scourge for centuries). Typhus is generally spread by body lice. In peacetime, the lice can be kept at bay by clean clothing and regular bathing. In wartime, civilian refugees, prisoners, and troops in the field quickly get infested with the lice.

During World War I, German soldiers in Russia joked that it was more dangerous to shake a Russian soldier's hand than to be shot at by him. This "deadly handshake" was the result of the body lice problem that was worse among the Russians than the Germans. The most common victims of typhus were prisoners (PWs or concentration camp inmates, such as Anne Frank, who died of typhus a few weeks before the end of the war) and Soviet troops. But the Germans suffered also. There was a major typhus outbreak in the German Army in Russia during the winter of 1944–1945. There were nearly 90,000 cases, and a quarter of the victims died. It was worse in the concentration camps, with Bergen-Belsen suffering 80,000 typhus deaths during the first four months of 1945. There were outbreaks of typhus among Allied troops in Egypt, North Africa, and Italy in 1942 and 1943. But by applying three million doses of vaccine and tons of DDT, the Allies were spared major losses from the disease.

The next most common disease was malaria. While typhus was most active in the winter, malaria was a summer disease in temperate climates and a year-round affliction in tropical areas. A third of the planet's population is exposed to malaria regularly, and most of these people have some immunity to this mosquito-borne disease. Troops from malaria-free areas moving into areas with endemic malaria are at great risk. Fortunately, during the war, though, malaria was not particularly lethal. Because of extensive World War II experience with malaria, only 117 of the 58,000 dead in Vietnam were malaria victims. But those who had it were useless for combat duty. Moreover, there are many different strains of malaria. Some are quite lethal and resistant to treatment. For this reason, malaria was often a major problem during World War II in the Pacific and, for a while, in North Africa and Sicily, where, during the summer of 1943, the Allies had as many men out of action because of malaria as they did from battle wounds.

In Burma during 1943, it was much worse. For every man evacuated for wounds, 120 were sent out for disease (mostly malaria). Intense efforts to control malaria reduced this ratio to 60 in 1944 and 40 in 1945. Still, it shows how debilitating tropical diseases can be to troops from nontropical areas. The Japanese were in even worse shape because they did not have the enormous medical and logistical resources that the Allies did. As there is no cure for malaria, all you can do is issue medicines that suppress the disease, try to kill the mosquitoes (quite effective if you can regularly spray the area the troops are in), and evacuate the victims that are flat on their backs (some people respond better to malaria than others). The United States, with the best preventive measures, still found that half its casualties in the Pacific were from malaria and that throughout the Pacific campaign, each day 3 out of every 1,000 men would be out of action because of it.

Of the dozens of other diseases that "made war hell," the only other one of major proportions was epidemic hepatitis. This was not a big killer, only 2 in 1,000 victims would die, but those who got it would be out of action for at least two months and often up to a year. No one knows quite how this form of hepatitis spreads, but it is highly contagious. The Germans suffered much from hepatitis on the Russian front, with over 1 million cases reported. During September 1943 alone, 180,000 cases were reported. In many cases, over half the troops in a battalion would be laid low by the disease. The allies got off easy, with only 250,000 cases through the entire war.

NEITHER FISH NOR FOWL

Ranger battalions were the U.S. Army's version of the British commando units. The British developed the commando concept early in World War II. These were basically amphibious raiders, who went ashore in small groups, hit an enemy installation, and then departed as they had arrived, by sea. Unfortunately, the Americans lost sight of the British concept and allowed the Ranger units to develop into troops that were neither commandos nor regular infantry.

In 1942, the U.S. Army decided to form its own commandos and called them Rangers (after the backwoods raiders of Colonial America). During the summer of 1942, a group of U.S. volunteers (forty-five men and six officers) went off to train with the British commandos. These troops formed the training cadre for the 1st Ranger Battalion, which was ready for action by the end of 1942. This unit was used successfully in the U.S. invasion of North Africa. In their first combat, against French and Italian troops, they did well. But that's where the troubles began. Senior commanders did not grasp the essence of commando operations: Get them in against a target regular infantry can't handle and then get them out again. Commanders tended to use Rangers as elite infantry. This was what Rangers were, but this was not the way they were designed to be used.

The Rangers also adopted the British form of organization, which was shaped by the amphibious landing craft the commandos used on their raids. Since an assault landing craft (LCA) would hold 35 troops (or eight hundred pounds of equipment), the commando (and Ranger) platoon contained 32 men. Two platoons made up a company (which had a headquarters of 4 men) and six companies made up the battalion. The battalion headquarters and support troops came to 108 men, giving a total strength of 27 officers and 489 men. With this form of organization, the commandos (or Rangers) could be sent ashore in twelve to fifteen LCAs (small landing craft). It was in terms of equipment that the Rangers began to differ from the commandos.

The British equipped the commandos with light machine guns, submachine guns, and (in the battalion headquarters) light mortars and other heavy weapons as needed. British practice was to take only what was needed on a mission. Usually, the commandos used only the small arms and machine guns. The British realized that the commandos were raiders who were not being sent to duke it out in a sustained infantry fight. American commanders missed this point and loaded up the Rangers with heavier weapons. Instead of 20-pound automatic rifles (BARs), the Rangers got 45-pound machine guns (M1919A4s). Instead of 60mm mortars, the Rangers had to lug around 81mm mortars. The Rangers added bazookas, even though they kept the obsolete British antitank rifles. The commandos remained lean and mean, the Rangers continued to pile on the stuff to be carried. The Rangers also became less mean because there were too many of them and too many casualties that could not be replaced with qualified troops.

In early 1943, two more Ranger battalions were formed, from volunteers, in North Africa. Another two battalions were formed in the United States that year, and in early 1944, a sixth was formed in the Pacific. The Rangers were used to spearhead the amphibious assaults at Salerno in early 1943 and Anzio in January 1944. In between, the three Ranger battalions led assaults during the drive on Naples. In all of these campaigns, there was an increasing tendency to use the Rangers as very competent infantry (which they were). But this caused heavy casualties that could not be replaced by men of the same caliber. The quality of the Ranger units declined throughout 1943. When the Anzio invasion went in, the three Ranger battalions (1st, 3rd, and 4th) tangled with German mechanized forces, were virtually destroyed, and subsequently disbanded.

"Too heavy to move and too light to fight" is how many put it at the time. But the Rangers, and the higher commanders who used them, learned from the Anzio disaster. The remaining three Ranger battalions fought on throughout the war. The Rangers continued to be used as infantry, but not as much and not in situations where their lighter armament would prove troublesome. Rangers continued to train for, and occasionally pull off, commando-type operations. Two battalions fought from Normandy into Germany while the third did well in the Pacific.

Some have blamed many of the Rangers' problems on their first commander, Lieutenant Colonel (promoted from captain in two weeks after being given the job in 1942) William Darby. An artilleryman, Darby was held responsible for loading up the Rangers with a lot of heavy weapons that slowed them down. But it wasn't just Darby. The army didn't grasp the fact that commandos were specialists, to be held in reserve most of the time until they were needed to pull off some desperate mission.

CRASHING INTO COMBAT

One of the many failed experiments of World War II was the glider infantry. When airborne units were first raised, it was quickly realized that there would not be enough transport aircraft to deliver all the paratroopers that could be trained. Moreover, heavy weapons could not be delivered by parachute. Noting the Germans' use of gliders, the Allies began raising glider regiments. Only the three assigned to the 82nd and 101st Airborne Divisions (and those in British service) saw much action. With 1,600 troops, the glider regiments didn't have much more firepower than the parachute regiments. Gliders were able to put the regiment's four 37mm antitank guns (not much use against current German tanks) and eighteen 81mm mortars on the ground. Some jeeps could also be landed. Since the gliders literally crash-landed, casualties were higher than with the paratroopers. The gliders were, for the most part, lost during the landing process. There was also a spirited debate about what the glider pilots were to do once they had landed. The British formed their glider pilots into companies of infantry. The U.S. glider pilots, being of relatively higher NCO rank, were generally left at loose ends with the units they landed with.

THE COST OF THE MEDAL OF HONOR: AWARDS AND CASUALTY RATES

The Medal of Honor is the highest U.S. decoration for valor. Frequently awarded posthumously, it is traditionally granted for acts "above and beyond the call of duty" in the face of the enemy. A total

Medal of Honor Awards by Service Branch

	Total	Posthumous
Army/Air Force	294	134
Coast Guard	1	1
Marine Corps	81	51
Navy	57	32

of 433 were awarded during the war, of which over half were posthumous.

The relationship between the number of awards and casualty rates in the various branches of the service is interesting.

Service Branch	Deaths per Award
Army	
Air Force	861.0
Artillery	1,688.4
Cavalry	594.4
Engineers	1,665.5
Infantry	800.4
Medical Corps	1,124.0
Navy	
Navy	550.0
Coast Guard	811.0
Marines	368.9

These figures are based on the number of men in each branch who were killed in action, divided by the number of Medals of Honor that were awarded to members of that branch. (The figures were calculated in 1946, and are therefore not altogether valid, as a handful of men have been awarded the Medal of Honor since then in belated recognition of wartime heroism.) On this basis certain branches certainly appear to have garnered considerably more Medals of Honor than others. One may ask, of course, whether Marines were that much more extraordinarily courageous than were Army infantrymen. The answer lies in the nature of the Marine Corps' war in the Pacific, with repeated amphibious assaults against fanatical resistance, which offered greater opportunities for heroism "above and beyond the call of duty." Indeed, five of the navy's awards went to medical corpsmen serving with the Marines. However, other contrasts may be noted that are not so easily explained. Why were awards to navy personnel and cavalrymen more frequent than those to infantrymen, while those to airmen were almost as frequent as those to infantrymen? Part of the reason for this may be administrative.

There exist no universal criteria for awarding the Medal of Honor. Indeed, in World War II both services had separate administrative mechanisms for processing Medal of Honor recommendations, and today there are three such bureaucracies. This certainly helps explain some of the discrepancies. For example, one of the navy awards went to a diver working on the highly dangerous salvage of the ships sunk at Pearl Harbor; this was allowable under navy regulations.

One final point, it's not the Congressional Medal of Honor, but the Medal of Honor awarded by Congress. There's a difference, especially if you want to win a few bar bets.

AMERICAN WOMEN IN UNIFORM

Although about thirty-five hundred women were enrolled as nurses and three actually commissioned as medical officers in the Union and Confederate armies during the Civil War, women were first regularly enlisted in the U.S. armed forces early in the twentieth century. Shortly after the century began the Army Nurse Corps and the Navy Nurse Corps were founded. These were specialized, highly professional organizations. Initially, the women enrolled were actually not considered members of the armed forces. However, their status was regularized as that of officers before World War I.

It was during World War I that the notion of women in uniform began to be taken seriously. During the war nearly 50,000 American women served in some capacity. In addition to the Army Nurse Corps, which grew from 400 to 20,000 women, and the Navy Nurse Corps, which grew from 460 to 1,400, over 11,000 women were enrolled as ''Yeomanettes'' in the navy, thousands more served in the army, as clerical workers, switchboard operators, and the like, and there were even a few hundred ''Marinettes.'' Aside from the Nurse Corps, most of the women were not formally recognized as performing military duties despite the fact that they were in uniform, served more or less under military discipline, and often worked under the same conditions as did the male personnel beside whom they served. Not until years later were these women accorded the status of veterans. The AEF's

1,500 women telephone operators were designated that status only in the mid-1980s.

After World War I women were once again excluded from the service except in the two nurse corps. By 1939 there were barely a thousand women in uniform. Thereafter, as the nation began to expand its military forces, the number of women in uniform began to rise once more.

Initially, the armed forces were not enthusiastic about expanding the role of women in the service. However, as manpower became increasingly scarce, the idea of enrolling large numbers of women became increasingly attractive. In 1942 the enlistment of women began in earnest, under the slogan *Free a man to fight*. By the end of the war some 350,000 American women had served in uniform.

The Army. There were three distinct ways in which women could serve in the army, and over 200,000 served, including several thousand black women, who served in segregated units.

- Army Nurse Corps. Some 60,000 women served as officer nurses in all theaters.

- Women's Army Auxiliary Corps (WAAC). About 140,000 women were enrolled in a new separate emergency branch of the army. These women served in numerous ways, such as truck drivers, hospital orderlies, and aviation mechanics, in all theaters. Before the war ended this became the Women's Army Corps, a part of the regular establishment.

- Women Air Service Pilots (WASPs). Under the leadership of famed aviatrix Jacqueline Cochran, who had earlier served as a ferry pilot for the RAF, about 1,000 women were enrolled as pilots, ferrying aircraft of all types (including B-17s) throughout the United States and occasionally overseas as well.

The Navy. About 150,000 women served in the navy during the war (including the Marines and Coast Guard).

- Navy Nurse Corps. Some 14,000 women served.

- Women Accepted for Volunteer Emergency Service (WAVES). About 100,000 women served in a variety of duties, much as did their sisters in the WAAC. Several women served as air navigators, and as such became the first women permitted to serve in airplane crews. At the war's end, by which time the "Emergency" had been dropped from their title, WAVES made up 55 percent of the personnel at the Headquarters of the Department of the Navy.

Marine Corps. The Marines were the last service to enlist women, creating the Women's Reserve, which had no cute acronym, in 1943. About 23,000 women served. Although women Marines received more weapons training, their actual duties did not differ materially from those of their sisters in the other services.

Coast Guard. The SPARS (from the motto of the Coast Guard, *Semper paratus,* Latin for "Always prepared") enrolled a total of 13,000 women in the course of the war, who performed what was perhaps the broadest range of duties of any of the women in uniform, from radar operators to carpenter's mates, with some even serving afloat.

It is interesting to note that early in the war due to a peculiarity of naval regulations, women officers were supposed to be addressed as "Sir." This was universally ignored; "Ma'am" was the preferred form and eventually found its way into the regs.

The average age of women entering the service in the two nurse corps was twenty-five, that of women in the other branches, twenty-three and a half. As a group, the women in the service were better educated than their male counterparts, a surprising proportion of whom (nearly 20 percent) were found to be functionally illiterate. Army and navy nurses, of course, were all nursing school graduates. Of the other female personnel, 7 percent were college graduates, 15 percent more had some college, 41 percent more had completed high school, and 32 percent had some high school, while only 6 percent had never been to high school.

Most of the women who entered the service seem to have been from middle-class backgrounds. About a third had fathers who were managers or professionals, a considerably higher proportion than the nation's norm. Over 8 percent of the women did not feel that their families had been worse off than average during the Great Depression. Only 40 percent of them were from smalltown or rural backgrounds. About 67 percent of the women were Protestant, 5 percent Jewish, and

25 percent Catholic, the latter two groups being very overrepresented in proportion to their percentage of the American population as a whole.

Although most of the women in question were single, a few were married. About 86 percent of the WAACs were single upon enlistment, but about 7 percent of the single women married while in the service. Of married WAACs, about 30 percent had husbands who were not in the service. Of those whose husbands were in the service, 58 percent had husbands who were overseas during the war.

Unlike some of their sisters in the Soviet Army and in many of the European Resistance movements, American women did not actively engage in combat. However, except for the Resistance movements, uniformed women worldwide tended to be kept out of combat. Although the Soviets had many all-female combat units (including tank battalions) at the beginning of the war, these were quickly disbanded (the tank units) or sent to quiet sectors (the aircraft units) once the fighting got going in earnest. Many Soviet Army women were in danger. Thousands served in traffic control and air defense units, both of which exposed the women to enemy fire. Women were used in highly trained sniper units (where many won decorations for bravery). The Germans also used thousands of women in air defense units in Germany, and these outfits suffered heavy casualties toward the end of the war when Allied aircraft were numerous enough to go after flak positions.

The performance of American women in the armed forces during the war was outstanding, despite considerable harassment and ridicule. Not only did they serve in every theater, but many did so with distinction under fire, and a number earned the Bronze Star. Several women were taken prisoner, and a number were killed in the line of duty. So pleased were the brass with the performance of women that they proposed to draft as many as 1.5 million women if the war lasted into 1946. And when peace came, women more than held their own as personnel strength was reduced, so that there were proportionally far more women in uniform after the war than before.

WHO'S MORE IMPORTANT DEPENDS ON YOUR POINT OF VIEW

General Sir Frederick Browning, founder of Britain's airborne forces and their leader throughout World War II, was the husband of the distinguished author Daphne du Maurier (*The Birds*, *Rebecca*, and so forth).

CHANGED TO PROTECT THE INNOCENT

Shortly before the United States was dragged into World War II someone in the war department noted that the 45th Infantry Division, a National Guard outfit from New Mexico, had a rather unfortunate shoulder patch, considering current political trends. The "shoulder sleeve insignia" in question combined a certain ancient Native-American symbol with the traditional Spanish colors. This symbol was unfortunately identical to that used by a certain political movement just then immensely successful in Europe. As a result, the 45th Division's gold swastika on a red lozenge became a thunderbird on a red lozenge. Meanwhile, Native-American artists and artisans lined up to sign pledges that they would eschew the use of their ancient symbol, besmirched as it was by its modern associations. It might be noted that authentic copies of the original insignia are the most valuable of U.S. military patches.

MORALE BOOSTERS

During the Second World War over nine million free theater tickets were distributed to U.S. military personnel, nearly two thirds of whom had never before seen a live performance. Free theater tickets were only one way in which American society spontaneously responded to the need to help the boys in uniform. Communities ran volunteer programs for military personnel. For example, about 120 small towns in the sparsely populated region around North Platte, Nebraska, provided free refreshments for the literally hundreds of thousands of military personnel who passed through the town by rail, never once running out. Taking a lonely soldier home for Sunday dinner was common, as were USO clubs, picnics, pen pals, and much more. And then there were the "V-Girls" or "Victory Girls," who might be termed "war groupies," numerous young women willing to give their all for the boys in uniform.

AND JUSTICE FOR ALL?

During the Second World War there were an average of approximately 60 court-martial proceedings per day in the U.S. armed forces. In the ETO alone, there were 36,102 courts-martial. A total of 443 death sentences were passed, 255 for murder or rape and 188 for military

Executions for Crimes in the ETO

	Blacks	Others	Total
Desertion	0	1	1
Murder	22	6	28
Murder and Rape	8	4	12
Rape	25	4	29
Total	55	15	70

offenses, of which apparently only 70 were actually carried out, the balance being commuted to various lengthy prison terms.

Although black troops constituted only about 8 percent of military personnel, they constituted about 22 percent of the troops brought before courts-martial and received a majority of the death sentences. Moreover, black soldiers were four times more likely to actually be executed than were whites.

Approximately 40,000 men were officially classed as deserters during the war, of whom only 2,854 were tried by court-martial. Most of those convicted received prison terms, but 49 were sentenced to death, of whom only 1 was actually executed, twenty-five-year old Private Eddie Slovik, a habitual petty criminal who found his 4-F draft status turned into a 1-A in early 1944. Despite the legality of his sentence, Slovik's execution was apparently an attempt by the brass *pour encourager les autres* ("to encourage the others").

THERE MAY BE A PATTERN HERE

Although only 27 percent of the enlisted men in the U.S. Army during World War II admitted to having been occasional truants when they were in school, and only 5 percent admitted to having been chronic truants, fully 62 percent of men who went AWOL were found to have been chronic truants.

THE PAUSE THAT REFRESHES

It is estimated that during the war U.S. military personnel consumed about 10 billion wasp-waisted bottles of a certain soft drink. So popular was this beverage with the troops that the army brought along several complete bottling plants when it went to war, three being brought ashore in North Africa in late 1942–early 1943. In some remote outposts and on some ships far from home the precious fluid was so rare that bottles are known to have been stored in safes. Thus did Coca-Cola become another worldwide symbol of America.

RANK DOESN'T ALWAYS HAVE ITS PRIVILEGES

During World War II, Benjamin O. Davis, a brigadier general in the United States Army, could find only one restaurant in downtown Washington that was willing to serve him. This was probably because he happened to be black. For many years the only black officer in the army, Davis had a distinguished career stretching back to volunteer service in the Spanish-American War. His career was long and varied, and he often times displayed great courage in the face of racist harassment: While an ROTC instructor at Tuskegee Institute he had once stood in full uniform to confront a KKK march. Davis had actually retired on the eve of the war but was immediately reactivated. For a time he commanded a brigade of two black cavalry regiments, in which capacity he became the first black American officer to command whites, since black regiments had mostly white officers. However, all U.S. horse cavalry was disbanded in 1942. During World War II Davis held a roving commission as a sort of inspector general of black troops and as an adviser on black affairs to the War Department. Although immensely popular in the black community at the time, he has since been subject to unwarranted criticism as an Uncle Tom by people ignorant of his achievements.

Davis was one of nearly a million black men and women who served in the armed forces during the war. Blacks, who totaled about 10 percent of the population, constituted about 8 percent of the armed forces. However, restrictive policies and institutional discrimination kept them out of most combat jobs. Nevertheless, blacks served in every theater and in every branch, in a variety of duties. Over a third of the engineering troops who worked on the Burma Road and the Alcan (or "Alaska") Highway were black, as were most of the personnel of the famed "Red Ball Express," which sustained the army's drive across France in the summer of 1944.

Only about 3 percent of the armed forces combat personnel were black, comprising two divisions (the 92nd and 93rd), plus several independent regiments, battalions, and fighter squadrons. The experience of black troops was satisfactory, and often distinguished, but generally reported negatively. For example, when the 25th Regimental Combat Team first went into action in the Pacific there was some confusion in one company (a not unusual occurrence when a green unit enters combat for the first time) that was widely reported as panic in the ranks. Similar discriminatory treatment plagued reporting of the performance of black units throughout the war.

A number of artillery, tank, and tank-destroyer battalions performed yeoman service in the European theater, where the 332nd Fighter Group, commanded by Colonel Benjamin Davis, Jr., who had endured four years of silence at West Point before graduating in 1936, performed splendidly in numerous bomber escort missions and had the distinction of never having lost a single bomber to enemy interceptors. Toward the latter part of the campaign in Europe the army instituted the "Fifth Platoon" program, which added a black platoon to infantry companies in about a dozen white divisions, an experiment that was found quite satisfactory. In the heat of battle, many infantry companies had to be reorganized, and although it was an unofficial practice, black and white soldiers often served together in the same squads. There was never any problem, proving again that there are no atheists, or racists, in foxholes.

Black personnel also served in the navy and Marines, mostly in support roles, but with important combat-related duties as well, such as antiaircraft gunners, damage-control technicians, ammunition carriers, and occasionally emergency infantrymen. On ships, everyone has a combat job during battles, thus a black sailor might be a waiter in the officers' mess most of the time, but when general quarters sounded, he put on a steel helmet and manned a gun along with the white boys. In the Marines, every man was trained as an infantryman and was expected to turn out for that duty on short notice. Thus many desperate battles found black and white Marines fighting alongside each other.

The experience with black personnel in World War II was extremely important in the ultimate decision to end segregation in the armed forces, which was issued by President Truman less than a year after the elder Davis retired from the service. There was ample evidence that blacks and whites could serve in the same combat units without any problems. Even the most convinced racists had to accept the testimony of white combat veterans on this point and this eliminated what had long been the primary argument against putting blacks and whites in the same units (a practice that worked well during the American Revolution, but that's another story).

THE FIRST CASUALTY

Robert M. Losey, U.S. Army Air Force, was the first American serviceman killed in World War II. The air attaché at the American embassy in Finland, Captain Losey was killed during a Russian air raid on April 21, 1940. The first German serviceman killed in the war was a Lieutenant von Schmeling, a military adviser to the Nationalist Chinese who was killed in combat with the Japanese while commanding an infantry battalion of the 88th Division in the defense of Shanghai late in the summer of 1937.

MAJOR WARSHIP LOSSES IN THE SECOND WORLD WAR

The greatest sea war in history, World War II saw more warships sunk than any other.

	Aircraft Carriers	Light Aircraft Carriers	Escort Carriers	Battle-ships and Battle Cruisers	Heavy Cruisers	Light Cruisers	De-stroyers	De-stroyer Escorts	Sub-marines
Australia					1	2	4		
Brazil						1			
Canada			1				8	1	
China						2			
Denmark									9
Estonia									1
France				5	4	6	57	1	65
Germany				4	5	4	53		994
Great Britain	5		4	5	5	24	100	42	75
Greece						1	4	1	4
Italy				2	7	8	86	13	116
Japan	13	2	4	11	17	27	160	160	133
Latvia									2
Netherlands						3	11		15
Norway							5		2
Poland						1	3	1	2
Romania							4		2
Soviet Union				1		2	34		95
Sweden									1
United States	4	1	6	2	7	3	71	11	52
Yugoslavia						1	4		2

All warships lost during the war by the belligerents are included, regardless of what caused the loss, including accidents and the hazards of the sea. Neutrals' losses are included only in cases where they were caused by the actions of one of the belligerents. Ships sunk but subsequently raised and restored to active service have been omitted, as have all the numerous vessels smaller than submarines and destroyer escorts. Ships lost while still being built have not been included. Scuttled vessels are included (about 60 percent of French losses was due to scuttling, as were the Danish losses shown), as are those captured during hostilities (i.e., omitting those captured upon the surrender of various of the Axis powers). Note that since many captured vessels were put into service by their captors and subsequently lost, there would be some double counting if totals were taken (e.g., several Yugoslav destroyers were commissioned in the Italian Navy, one being lost and two being in turn captured by the Germans, who put them into service and subsequently lost them as well). British battleship figures include two battle cruisers. German heavy cruiser figures include three "pocket battleships." German and Greek figures omit two very obsolete battleships each. Norwegian figures omit four coast defense ships, sort of junior achievement battleships, while Danish figures omit two; Finland also lost a coast defense ship, as did the Netherlands and Siam.

Some idea of the losses among lesser ships may be gained by noting that the U.S. Navy lost 142 smaller warships, that is, motor torpedo boats, mine warfare vessels, Coast Guard cutters, sub chasers, and gunboats. Losses to seaplane and destroyer tenders, transports, tankers, and fleet auxiliaries totaled about 60 more. Losses to landing vessels and miscellaneous vessels (such as the floating dock *Dewey*, which was scuttled to prevent capture by the Japanese) are not included.

3

THE EUROPEAN WAR, 1939–1941

World War II got off to a poor start for the Allies. Nowhere was this more evident than in France during the 1940 campaign. But this was only the worst disaster. Other debacles were found in North Africa, the Balkans, and elsewhere. Despite all the bad news, there were rays of hope that foretold the eventual Allied victory.

THE MAGINOT LINE AND STRATEGIC PLANNING IN 1940

Often overlooked, fixed defenses had an important role in World War II. Of the many fortified positions that influenced the course of the war (from the Gustav Line in Italy to the numerous fortified islands in the Pacific) none was so extensive as France's Maginot Line. Nor have any been so misunderstood in the popular imagination.

The seeds of the Maginot Line were sown in the trench slaughter of World War I. After much debate, in the late 1920s the French began to develop an elaborate system of fortifications on their frontier with Germany. Named after a war minister who had lost an arm at Verdun, the Maginot Line was designed to prevent a direct German invasion of France by making such an attempt prohibitively costly in lives and time, permitting the French to husband their resources in the rear for a decisive counterstroke with mobile forces.

The basic concept was by no means as absurd as it would appear in retrospect. Among the greatest fortification experts in the world since the seventeenth century, the French were fully aware that their proposed new fortified zone (it was not a "line" at all) was not impregnable. But it would be so difficult to break that it would deter a German offensive into northeastern France. Unable to deliver a swift, decisive blow against it, the Germans would have to give up all thought of war with France, or accept a protracted war of attrition, or find an alternative way to carry on the war. It was this last that French policymakers perceived as the most likely eventuality, specifically a German thrust into Belgium. And such an undertaking by a revitalized Germany would inevitably bring Great Britain into the war on the side of France, a necessity given France's manpower inferiority vis-à-vis Germany's. So the principal function of the Maginot Line was to canalize a German offensive into Belgium, where it could be met by motorized French armies supported by British resources. This plan had the added (if unspoken) advantage of having the horrors of war visited upon Belgium rather than on France.

As built, the Maginot Line was a wonder to behold (as, indeed, its remains still are). It consisted of a loose belt of fortifications starting a few miles inside France. The defensive zone varied from five to ten miles in depth, liberally seasoned with sunken forts, redoubts, pillboxes, observation towers, tank traps, and other works. These works were designed to make maximum use of available ground, which already favored the defense, as northeastern France (Alsace and ,Lorraine) is rather mountainous, often heavily forested, and occasionally marshy. Most positions (which were all gastight) were mutually supporting, and all were capable of holding out independently for extended periods if necessary. In some of the more densely fortified areas the principal works were linked together by underground railroads to permit the rapid movement of reinforcements and munitions.

Actually only about eighty-seven miles of the Franco-German frontier were covered by permanent works, at the extraordinary cost of 80.5 million francs per mile (about $20 million in 1930s dollars and a quarter of a billion in today's dollars). These works covered the most vulnerable areas. Less vulnerable areas (such as the thirty-mile Sarre Gap) were to be protected in time of war by demolitions, waterlines (such as the Rhine itself), and inundations, covered by combat troops in field fortifications. Despite the enormous expenditure, over 7 billion francs (nearly $20 billion in today's dollars), the system was not fully complete by 1940, but sufficiently so to have precisely the deterrent effect for which the French had hoped.

There seems little doubt that the Maginot Line was more or less impenetrable from a frontal attack, at least at a price the Germans were willing to pay. Certainly German war planners proposed nothing more than demonstrations against the line in the event of war, preferring instead to go into Belgium, precisely as the French expected. French planning for the anticipated German offensive into Belgium presumed that the Germans would come more or less as they had in 1914, a massive wheeling drive across the northern Belgian plain and then southward into France. To meet this, the French allocated the best part of their army (about thirty divisions, including virtually all of their dozen motorized and light armored divisions) to their left flank, from whence, in company with the fully motorized British, they would boldly advance into Belgium in the event of a German invasion, to meet the enemy along the Dyle River, east of Brussels for a decisive battle.

In their initial planning for their 1940 offensive against France, the Germans actually came up with a plan that more or less was what the French expected of them, a holding action against the Maginot Line with a straightforward drive across the Belgian plain, taking advantage of the superior mobility and effectiveness of their seventeen armored and motorized divisions. The objective was to secure as much of the country as possible in anticipation of future offensives. Although this plan met with the approval of the General Staff, Hitler was dissatisfied. The führer wanted a quick win to maintain his popularity, and the plan suggested a protracted struggle. A relatively junior officer, Erich von Manstein, thereupon came up with a more complex, bolder, and riskier plan.

Under the new plan, a portion of the army, including some armored and motorized formations supported by airborne troops, would attack directly into Belgium and the Netherlands as a feint to draw Allied reserves northward. Meanwhile the bulk of the army would attack through the Ardennes, a rugged, heavily forested region covering most of Luxembourg plus adjacent portions of France and Belgium. The idea was to slice through the Allied forces, creating an enormous pocket in Belgium, perhaps winning the war in one grand offensive. This new plan appealed to Hitler's sense of grandeur, despite the risks which were considerable. Many years earlier Marshal Philippe Pétain, hero of World War I, had been asked about the possibilities of a German offensive in this very area, to which he replied, ''The Ardennes are impenetrable, if adequately defended.'' He was right, for the Ardennes are traversed by few roads, and those are narrow and easily blocked by light forces, provided there were enough of them.

When, on the morning of May 10, 1940, the French General Staff learned that the Germans had launched their long-anticipated offensive, one officer said to Chief of Staff Maurice Gamelin, "So it is the Dyle Plan, no?" Gamelin looked up and replied, "What else can we do?" And, indeed, everything went according to plan, the German plan.

At the first sign of the German offensive (the feint into the Netherlands and northern Belgium) the French and British leapt forward into Belgium. Elements of the French Seventh Army, on the extreme left, advanced something like 150 miles in the first forty-eight hours, one of the most impressive motor marches by a large force to that time. By nightfall on May 12 the Allied spearheads were well into the Netherlands and Belgium. And at that same moment the German main blow fell. Nearly a dozen armored and motorized divisions emerged from the Ardennes to fall upon second-line French forces near Sedan. The German movement had not only been undetected but virtually unimpeded, for the Ardennes had hardly been "adequately defended." Allied strength in the region consisted of two Belgian light infantry divisions and some French cavalry, who despite heroic efforts only managed to slow the Germans down by a few hours.

The French defenses at Sedan crumbled quickly under the extraordinary strength and violence of the German offensive. Within a day the Germans were across the Meuse and heading west through a fifty-mile gap they had torn in the French front. A few days more and the Germans were halfway across France despite often heroic attempts to impede them. And late on May 20 the Germans reached the English Channel near Abbeville, effectively pocketing nearly forty British, French, and Belgian divisions.

Then came the high drama of Dunkirk, the German offensive southward, the fall of Paris, and the surrender of France. And through it all the Maginot Line remained virtually unscathed. So the Maginot Line had worked, "worked" in the sense that it had canalized the German offensive into Belgium. Despite this "success" one somehow suspects that the French might have spent their money better elsewhere.

A LITTLE PROBLEM IN PROCUREMENT?

Fearing that a German invasion was imminent after the fall of Norway, in 1940 the Swedish Army mobilized, only to discover that the total available stockpile of antiaircraft ammunition was barely sufficient to sustain a simultaneous one minute's firing by all of the antiaircraft guns on hand.

PRETTY GOOD, NONETHELESS

The Royal Air Force defeated the Luftwaffe in the Battle of Britain (summer 1940) largely because of the radar warning system that allowed ground controllers to efficiently concentrate the outnumbered British fighters on individual groups of German bombers. As effective as this was, 69 percent of the British fighters sent to a specific location where the controllers thought the German bombers would be found nothing. The radars of that time were crude, and the information they provided was subject to misinterpretation or false alarms. Still, it was good enough.

A SHORT LIFE, BUT A GLORIOUS ONE

In an active career of only two hundred days during 1941, the H.M.S. *Prince of Wales*, Great Britain's newest battleship, commissioned on March 31, 1941, participated in the pursuit of the German battleship *Bismarck* in May, sustaining some damage in the process, carried Winston Churchill to the Atlantic Conference at Argentia Bay in Newfoundland in August, and was sunk in action by Japanese aircraft off Malaya on December 10.

FIGHTING OUTNUMBERED AND WINNING

What was most amazing about the German conquest of France in May 1940 was that the Germans were outnumbered. They had fewer troops, fewer tanks, fewer weapons of most kinds and were superior only in their number of aircraft. Yet within a month, the Germans defeated France, Belgium, the Netherlands, and the British forces sent to the Continent. Moreover, the Allies had had six months to prepare for this battle. War was declared in September 1939, when the Germans invaded Poland. At that point, most of the German Army was in Poland, while the French, Belgians, and Dutch began mobilizing on their borders with Germany. During this period, Great Britain sent eleven divisions and hundreds of aircraft. The rapid German victory in Poland shocked the Allies. In less than three weeks, the Germans had smashed the Polish armed forces. No one expected anything that fast. For that reason, as well as an excess of prudence, the Allies didn't invade western Germany in the fall of 1939, when the Allies outnumbered the nearby German troops several times over. The prudent Allies thought they would prevail anyway when the Germans attacked. After all, the Allies had numbers on their side. And surely they could put up a stiffer fight than the Poles had. The numbers were indeed impressive.

The Military Balance in the West
(May 10, 1940)

	Allies	Germans
Divisions	140	122
All Artillery	45,700	47,000
Tanks	4,000	3,200
Machine Guns	81,700	147,000
Aircraft	1,760	2,700
Artillery by type		
Antiaircraft guns	5,200	8,700
Antitank guns	8,800	12,800
Field Artillery	13,400	18,800
Mortars	18,300	6,700

The Allies were still thinking World War I, despite the swift German victory in Poland. Moreover, the Allied situation was, well, somewhat more complex than what the Poles faced. Aside from the fact that the Poles were outnumbered, Poland had no natural defenses and was surrounded by German territory on three sides. France had mountains in the southern half of its border with Germany. To make that area secure, France had built a massive line of well-armed concrete fortifications (the Maginot Line). In the north, it had neutral Belgium and the Netherlands. These two nations had mobilized a million men between them. But these troops were even less well trained and armed than the French. In World War I, the Germans had avoided the rough country in the south and come through the flat (like Poland) terrain of Belgium. The Allies expected a reprise in 1940, but could not convince the Belgians or Dutch to informally plan for such an eventuality. Of course, the German situation was not all that favorable either. But the Germans won quickly by taking advantage of the following factors the Allies did not pay much attention to.

- Warfare had changed since 1918. The Germans were aware of the changes, most of the Allied officers and troops were not. This meant that the Germans could do things that the Allied troops could not do. Most important, the Germans were able to take advantage of motorized units. This was a key element in the rapidity of the German victory. They massed over a dozen motorized divisions (most of them panzer units) in one place and literally punched a hole through the Allied line. This allowed them to reach the Channel and split the Allied forces. Motorization made this possible, but effective use of motorized units made it happen.

- The Germans had a better-trained army. This had been the case since the previous century and was no different in 1940. The Germans had had the best trained troops in 1918, even though they were defeated. In the next twenty years, they developed even better training methods. Not as quickly as with their masses of panzers, but a German infantry division would generally quickly win in a one-on-one battle with an Allied division. Even without several of their other advantages, the Germans could still have won because of their better-trained army.

- German weapons were not always superior, but they were always used more effectively than those of the Allies. The most glaring example was the tanks used by both sides. The Allies had more tanks. Moreover, Allied tanks generally had thicker armor and larger guns. But quantity and quality were less important than how you used them. Allied tanks were organized into only a few tank divisions (which were not used together), with the rest of the vehicles being in separate tank battalions that were scattered all over the place. This was classic 1918 thinking, and the Allies' 1940 tank doctrine was based on it. The Germans organized their tanks into ten panzer divisions, each with about three hundred tanks. They then used these divisions in panzer armies. And when faced with several German panzer divisions (over a thousand tanks), individual Allied divisions were blown apart. Also the Germans made better use of aircraft (they had more and of better quality too), artillery, and even machine guns.

- Better preparation was made by the Germans. Not only were the troops well trained, but so were the senior officers. They insisted on careful preparations for the 1940 campaign. The Germans also understood the need for better communications. They used a lot more radios on the front line. For example, all German tanks had radios, while many Allied tanks did not (a practice the Russians continued until the end of the war). German commanders were trained to take advantage of all these radios and, as a result, were more in touch with rapidly changing situations than were their Allied counterparts.

In one of those sublime ironies, the next nation to achieve victories of the type the Germans pulled off in 1940 were the Israelis. In 1948, 1956, and 1967 they fought outnumbered and won. They also did it with inferior weapons, but with superior training and preparation. The one time they stumbled was in 1973, when their weapons were better but their attitudes were not.

LET'S DO IT AGAIN

A year after the Germans conquered France in a six weeks' campaign, they invaded Russia. Interestingly, the Germans' casualty experience in the first six weeks of each campaign was remarkably similar.

German Casualty Experience in May 1940 and 1941

	In France	In Russia
German Divisions	122	134
German Troop Losses	155,000	213,000
Loss per Division	1,270	1,590
Enemy Divisions	140	183
Loss per Enemy Division	1,107	1,160

The big difference was that after Germany had been in France six weeks, their opponents were defeated. At that point, the Allies had suffered over half a million casualties (dead, prisoners, and missing) and were no longer capable of resisting. The Germans had won. Russia was different. In six weeks, the Germans inflicted nearly a million casualties (dead, missing, and prisoners) on the Russians. By the end of 1941, the Russians would suffer over four million such losses. But Russia was a lot bigger than France, with four times the population.

The Russians kept on fighting. Blitzkrieg worked in Russia, but it wasn't successful.

THE OTHER ROMMEL

German General Erwin Rommel was the famous Desert Fox and commander of the forces occupying France when D-Day arrived in June 1944. But there was another General Rommel in World War II. This one served Poland as an army commander. In fact, the Polish Major General Juliuz Rommel commanded the forces in Warsaw as the Poles made their last stand against the invading Germans in the second week of September 1939. The two Rommels are not known to have been related, although there may have been a connection in the distant past. The German Rommel was from a nonaristocrat family in Swabia, a poor area that experienced much emigration to America and other parts of Europe over the centuries.

POLISH TROOPS UNDER FOUR FLAGS

By the time World War II ended, Polish military units had served with four nations (Poland, France, Great Britain, and Russia). When Poland was invaded, first by Germany and then by Russia, in September 1939, the Polish armed forces were soundly defeated. But not destroyed. Of the 800,000 Polish troops on duty in 1939, 35,000 promptly fled to Hungary, 32,000 to Romania and 12,000 to Lithuania after their defeat. Nearly all the air force troops (9,000) escaped, most of them reaching France by early 1940. Three destroyers, and several smaller warships of the Polish Navy, escaped to Great Britain and promptly began serving with the Royal Navy.

By early 1940, over 100,000 Polish troops had found their way to France. The French planned to organize a Polish army of 72,000 men. Nearly all the personnel of the Polish 10th Mechanized Brigade had escaped there and was reformed with French equipment. Meanwhile, the Germans invaded on May 10. On May 30, the reformed Polish 10th Mechanized Brigade arrived in Paris, where it received some armored vehicles. The unit was later heavily engaged in the vicinity of Paris. Two infantry divisions (the 1st Grenadiers and the 2nd Light) were hastily put together. The former was destroyed manning the Maginot Line while the latter escaped into Switzerland. Two more infantry divisions (the 3rd and 4th) were still forming when the campaign in France ended. A brigade of mountain troops had been formed too and was sent to Norway in response to the German invasion there. Over 900 Polish pilots found their way to France, and 150 were able to join various Polish squadrons (flying French aircraft). Many of the remainder went on to Great Britain (joining the Royal Air Force).

The Polish pilots that went to Great Britain did somewhat better than their compatriots in the French Air Force. Five fighter and two bomber squadrons were formed with Polish pilots in time to participate in the Battle of Britain during the summer of 1940. By the end of the year, there were eight Polish fighter and four bomber squadrons in the Royal Air Force. Overall, the Polish pilots shot down more German aircraft per squadron than any others in British service.

By late 1940, 17,000 Polish troops had made their way to Great Britain, where the Polish government in exile had set up shop. These troops were formed into an armored division (the Polish Armored Corps). Several thousand Poles had found their way to French-controlled Syria in 1940 and were formed into an infantry brigade (the Carpathian Brigade). When France fell in the summer of 1940, the brigade moved to Palestine and went into British service. The unit fought in North Africa and eventually served as the cadre for the Polish Corps that was formed in late 1942. This unit was raised from the 115,000 Polish refugees (including some women and children) that the Russians allowed to exit via Iran, who then traveled to North Africa. Some 70,000 of these were forming into a Polish army within Russia in early 1942, but the Soviets decided this group was not sufficiently pro-Communist and agreed to let the British have them. By the summer of 1943, the British-equipped Polish II Corps (3rd Infantry Division, 4th Infantry Division, 2nd Armored Brigade, and corps troops) went into action during the battle for Italy. The Poles fought there until the end of the war.

Back in Great Britain, the Polish Armored Corps became the 1st Armored Division. In addition, the Polish Parachute Brigade was formed. In August 1944, the 1st Armored Division went to France and played a key role in trapping large numbers of German troops after the Allied breakout. The division then fought alongside the British as the Allies advanced into Germany.

Meanwhile, back in Russia, Stalin had second thoughts about forming a Polish army. In early 1943, the Kosciuszko Division was formed. Stalin was responding to the growth of the Home Army inside Poland. This partisan force, although it lacked many weapons, was controlled by the non-Communist, London-based Polish government in exile. Stalin wanted a Communist government in Poland after the war, and he would form his own Polish army to further that goal. By late 1943, the First Polish Army was formed in Russia. It had 44,000 Polish troops, but the officers were Russian (usually Polish-speaking and often of Polish extraction).

By 1944 the Home Army had 384,000 partisan fighters. The summer of that year, the Russians upped the ante and formed their own Communist government in exile for Poland. When the advancing Soviet armies crossed the old Polish border in July 1944, they claimed that their Polish government in exile was now in charge of the country. At the same time, the Germans were evacuating nearby Warsaw. The Polish government in London ordered its 48,000 partisans in the area to take over Warsaw. But then the advancing Soviet armies halted right outside the city, claiming that logistical problems (a common situation with the Russians) forced them to await supplies. This halt was viewed with some cynicism by the Poles, but the Russians had a case. Having just completed a long march, fighting all the way, the Russians were not in any shape to go right into city fighting. The Russians were not sure the Germans were just going to abandon Warsaw. When the Germans noted that the Russian armies had stopped, their evacuation of Warsaw was halted and combat units returned to fight the Home Army troops.

The Home Army held out until early October, receiving aid from Allied airdrops (flying out of Italy) and from the attempts by the Russian-controlled Poles to fight their way into Warsaw. The Soviets opened a major winter offensive in January and this allowed the First Polish Army (and its Russian officers) to enter the city on January 17. With Poland now largely under Russian control, more Poles were put in uniform. Eventually, there were two Polish armies containing 500,000 troops, led by 14,000 Russian officers. When the war ended, these troops were quickly demobilized and a smaller, more ''Communist'' army was formed. Many of the Poles who served in the West stayed there after the war. By 1952, Poland was completely under the control of the Communists and would stay that way until 1989.

There was, understandably, great bitterness among the Poles about how they were treated during and after the war. The Russians had stabbed them in the back in 1939, then conspired to impose communism on them after the war.

Poland, the immediate cause of World War II, suffered more than any other nation in that conflict. Some 20 percent of the population was killed and its economy was devastated. But in six years of hard fighting under Polish, French, British, and Russian colors, they managed to get the Germans out. It took another forty-four years to get the Russians out.

SAD BUT TRUE

Enemy action accounted for only 25 percent of the tanks lost by the British Army in France in 1940; all the rest were due to mechanical breakdown. On the other hand, this was a better record than that for French tanks, nearly half of which had to be abandoned for lack of fuel, French army policy limiting them to only a five hours' supply.

THE DIVISIONS OF THE "PHONY WAR," 1939–1940

The fall of Poland was brutally swift, and rather shocking. Then the war settled into a remarkable dull routine. Save at sea there was little action, and the term *Phony War* began to be heard. All that changed with a brutality and speed comparable to that seen in Poland when Hitler unleashed his armies in the West in the spring of 1940.

There were considerable differences among the armies that fought during the Phony War period, as can be seen by a comparison of the structure and strength of their divisions.

The Polish infantry division was a largely "leg" outfit, as were the comparable German and French infantry divisions. Capable enough in a traditional-style campaign, it could not keep up with the speed of a mechanized war. The results of the Polish campaign led all armies to make some changes in their armored division tables of organization, the British and French in an attempt to emulate the Germans, and the Germans in order to further refine their techniques. One important change instituted by the German Army was to take three "Light" divisions, sort of motorized cavalry formations, and convert them to light armored divisions through the addition of a panzer regiment of three battalions. In practice, of course, none of the German armored divisions actually conformed rigidly to the pattern indicated here. Omitted from the table are a number of formations, most notably cavalry divisions, of which the Germans had one with horses and the French several hermaphrodite (horse/mechanized) ones, as well as the German motorized cavalry divisions that

Principal Types and Strengths of Divisions During the "Phony War," 1939–1940

| | British | | French | | | German | | | Polish |
	Armored	Infantry	DCR	DLM	Infantry	Armored	Light Armored	Infantry	Infantry
Troops	10.5	13.9	6.5	10.4	16.9	15.0	14	17.2	16.5
Tanks	321	28	158	240	0	332	274	0	18
Battalions									
Tank	3	0	4	8	0	4	3	0	0
Infantry	1	9	3	2	9	2	5	9	10
Artillery	1.0	5.0	3.0	3.0	5.3	4.0	2.0	5.0	3.0
Reconnaissance	3	1	0	1	1	1	1	1	2
Engineer	1.0	1.0	0.3	1.0	0.6	1.0	1.0	1.0	1.0
Signal	0	0	0.3	0	0	0	1.0	1.0	1.0
Rating	12	11	8	10	8	17	15	10	8

NOTES: DCR is *Division Cuirassée de Réserve* or Reserve Armored Division; DLM is *Division Légère Méchanique* or Light Mechanized Division. All divisions with tank battalions are armored divisions of one flavor or another. Troops is the number of men in a division, in thousands. In addition to tanks, all of these formations had varying numbers of other armored fighting vehicles, ranging from armored cars to self-propelled artillery pieces. In Battalion, .3 indicates a company. Artillery includes antitank and antiaircraft battalions. In some armies, signals were subsumed in the engineers. Rating, an approximation of the fighting power of the division for purposes of comparing its relative capabilities, is a rough mathematical calculation of the relative fighting power of each division, combining manpower, equipment, and organizational and doctrinal factors.

served in Poland but were thereafter converted to panzers, and French fortress divisions. Note that since armored divisions are best at attacking, while infantry divisions do best at defending, the figures are not strictly comparable, except insofar as it was usually German armored divisions doing the attacking and Allied ones doing the defending.

THE STRATEGIC BALANCE, NORTHWESTERN EUROPE, MAY 1940

When the Germans undertook their spectacular offensive against France, Belgium, and the Netherlands on May 10, 1940, they were actually taking on enemies who collectively were their superiors in many material measures of military power.

Committed Divisions, May 1940

	Armored	Motorized	Infantry	Cavalry	Total
Belgian			21	2	23
British	1	15			16
Dutch		1	8		9
French	6	7	84	5	102
Polish			2		2
All Allies	7	23	115	7	152
German	10	7	118	1	136

These figures are for complete divisions active in France and adjacent areas as of the onset of the German offensive, or divisions that were brought in during the campaign. On May 10 there were about 140 Allied and 122 German divisions in the combat area, thereby omitting several divisions still in Great Britain, Germany, North Africa, and elsewhere. Also omitted are independent brigades (Belgian 5, British 5, Czechoslovakian 2, French 4, Dutch 2, Polish 1, and German 3). French figures include five "fortress" divisions, formations specialized for duty in fortified defensive areas, thereby lacking in organic transport and heavy artillery. It was against one of these (the 102nd) that the weight of the German offensive at Sedan first fell, it having been deployed to an unfortified sector!

Equipment, May 1940

	Machine Guns	Mortars	Antitank Guns	Field Artillery	Heavy Artillery	Antiaircraft Guns
Belgian	3,600	2,268	144	390	152	600
British	11,000	8,000	850	880	310	500
Dutch	3,400	144	88	192	242	182
French	63,700	8,000	7,800	8,265	3,931	3,921
Allied	81,700	18,412	8,882	9,727	4,635	5,203
German	147,400	6,796	12,830	15,696	2,900	8,700

As can be seen, the Allies actually had about 10 percent more divisions than the Germans, and nearly twice as many mobile divisions (armored, motorized, and cavalry). So the Germans were hardly superior in terms of the number of ground troops. They did, however, have some significant advantages in equipment.

These figures include all equipment committed during the campaign. Polish and Czech equipment is included with French. Allied figures include equipment in fortifications, which would not be available for field operations, and exclude about 90,000 French automatic rifles. Although in most categories the advantage tended to be with the Allies, the Germans were superior in precisely those areas that were most beneficial for the conduct of the fast-moving, violent assaults that characterized blitzkrieg; lots of relatively light weapons (field artillery, antitank guns, antiaircraft guns, and machine guns) to create an enormous volume of firepower. Moreover, most German equipment, in every category, was technically superior to that of the Allies, particularly their tanks.

THE TANKS, MAY 1940

Surprisingly, in many ways the Germans were very inferior to the Allies in tanks. They had only 3,227 tanks as opposed to 590 British and 3,437 French tanks, an Allied advantage of nearly 25 percent. However, sheer number of tanks was not necessarily the critical factor. The real issue was quality.

Tanks in Class 1 were fast, agile vehicles capable of making at least 25 miles an hour. Class 2 vehicles could do no better than about 18

Relative Mobility of Tanks, 1940

	British	French	Total	German
Class 1	334	921	1,255	3,227
Class 2	156	1,031	1,187	0
Class 3	100	1,485	1,585	0

miles an hour, while Class 3 tanks were at best able to do about 12 miles an hour, and that on roads. So while the Allies had about 25 percent more tanks, less than a third of their tanks were as nimble as the entire German tank pack. This advantage of agility had both tactical and strategic benefits. Tactically German tanks could maneuver with greater speed. Even a puny Panzer I (with two machine guns and barely a half inch of armor, but with a 25 mph road speed) could elude the heavily armed French Char B1 (with a 75mm and a 47mm cannon, several machine guns, and nearly three inches of armor, but with barely an 18 mph road speed). Strategically, the better engines of the German tanks gave them the speed without which blitzkrieg would have been impossible. Another element enhancing the effectiveness of the German armored forces was the fact that all German tanks had radios, making coordination much easier, while most Allied tanks lacked them. As if these advantages in tanks were not enough, there was the matter of organization.

Virtually all of the German tanks were concentrated in their tan panzer divisions. In contrast, the Allies dispersed their tanks. The French put most of their Class 3 tanks and about 300 Class 2 tanks in thirty-three separate tank battalions assigned to support infantry divisions at the front. As a result, their armored divisions (which were neither doctrinally nor organizationally uniform) shared about 700 Class 2 vehicles and most of the Class 1 vehicles, less about 220 which went to five semimechanized cavalry divisions. The British didn't do much better, putting all of their Class 2 vehicles and about a third of their Class 1 vehicles into their armored division and spreading the balance, 310 vehicles, into no fewer than three separate brigades and four independent cavalry regiments. So the British armored division had about 280 tanks and the French divisions averaged about 180 (three had 200 and three 158), while the German panzer divisions (which had even less organizational uniformity than did the French divisions, but nevertheless partook of a common doctrine) averaged about 325 tanks apiece. Thus the German tanks were far more concentrated than were those of their opponents. And the Germans didn't just keep all their tanks in their armored divisions. They went a step further and grouped seven panzer divisions into an armored corps, while the Allies distributed their armored divisions among three different field armies and the general reserve.

And, of course, the final elements in German success were their superior doctrine and training.

NO TWO ALIKE

The Germans had ten panzer (armored) divisions for their 1940 campaign, and no two of these divisions were organized in the same way. So much for German uniformity! In this case, the Germans were simply being practical. They were still sorting out the details of armored warfare. From their experience in the September 1939 campaign (where they used six panzer divisions), they quickly raised more for the May 1940 campaign in France. The unique organizations of the ten divisions looked like the chart on the next page.

In addition to the ten panzer divisions, the Germans raised seven motorized infantry (panzer grenadier) divisions. Actually, there weren't seven of these divisions, but rather independent regiments and brigades that equaled seven divisions. These units were as eclectic in their organization as the panzer divisions.

The Germans actually had a standard armored division organization in 1938, which was made up of 266 tanks (in four tank battalions), plus four infantry battalions, four artillery battalions, a recon battalion, an engineer battalion, and the usual support units. There was also a "light" division of 200 tanks (in three tank battalions) with five infantry battalions and otherwise like the armored division. What created all the organizational eclecticism was the rush to organize new divisions and the widely different interpretations of what an armored division should look like. Since an armored division didn't experience combat until 1939, the German High Command allowed the many different ideas to express themselves.

By 1941, with two armored campaigns under their belt, the Germans had adopted a more uniform organization for their panzer divisions. They added more infantry and artillery and cut the number of tanks in half (and increased the number of divisions to twenty-one). They also increased the number of panzer grenadier divisions to sixteen. Thus, with only thirty-seven motorized divisions (and ninety-

The Ten German Divisions, May 1940

	1	2	3	4	5	6	7	8	9	10
Total Tanks	332	332	338	416	380	274	274	274	285	332
Pz I	30	30	109	160	140	10	10	10	100	30
Pz II	100	100	122	107	110	40	40	40	75	100
Pz III	90	90	31	41	50	36	36	36	36	90
Pz IV	56	56	18	32	24	0	0	0	18	56
Pz 38	0	0	0	0	0	132	132	132	0	0
Armored Cars	56	56	56	56	56	56	56	56	56	56
Infantry Battalions	2	4	2	4	4	3	4	3	4	4
Artillery Battalions	3	3	2	2	2	2	2	2	2	2
Motorcycle Battalions	1	0	1	1	0	0	1	1	1	0
Engineer Battalions	0	0	0	0	1	0	0	0	1	0
Antitank Battalions	0	0	0	0	1	0	0	0	1	1

NOTES: Pz: *Panzerkampfwagen* ("armored combat vehicle").

Pz I: 1 6.6-ton tank with 13 millimeters of armor, a crew of two, and armed only with machine guns. This was a World War I–era concept that was being phased out even in 1939.

Pz II: an 11-ton tank with 30 millimeters of armor, a crew of three, and a 20mm gun. It was already obsolete in the late 1930s and being converted to a recon vehicle.

Pz III: a 21-ton tank with 30 millimeters of armor, a 37mm gun, and a crew of five. The first "modern" tank the Germans developed, it would continue in service (with more armor and a bigger gun) for two more years.

Pz IV: a 22-ton tank with 30 millimeters of armor, a 75mm gun, and a crew of five. It was a new tank that would serve to the end of the war (with more armor and more powerful guns). Note that most tanks in the 1990s weigh 40 to 65 tons, with 150 to 300 millimeters of armor, and a 100 to 120mm gun.

Pz 38: a 10.5-ton tank with 25 millimeters of armor, a 37mm gun, and a crew of four. A Czech design, it was built in Czech factories the Germans controlled. It was good but eventually converted to an assault gun (the turret removed and a larger gun installed).

seven infantry divisions with horse-drawn transport), the Germans invaded Russia. But that's another story.

A PROBLEM IN COMMAND

In late 1940 the Polish Army was reconstituted in Great Britain. Actually, this was the second time the Polish Army had been reconstituted, the first being in late 1939 and early 1940, when several Polish units were raised in France in a planned corps of four divisions. The manpower consisted of Poles who had been working abroad at the time of the German and Soviet conquest of their homeland in September and October 1939, and of men who had escaped from that debacle by way of Romania and Lithuania. These divisions had gone down in defeat with the collapse of France, in May and June 1940.

As a result, when it came time to re-create the Polish Army in Great Britain, there were severe manpower problems. However, enough men were soon collected together. They were prewar expatriates who had been unable or unwilling to go to France before her fall, men who had been engaged in specialized training in Great Britain at the time of the fall of France, and men who had managed to escape the French debacle, whether at Dunkirk or, as the Germans imposed their occupation regime, through Spain or by other means. The two latter groups, of course, were men with some military experience, and so could provide a cadre for the creation of larger units.

As the new army was being formed it transpired that there were too many officers and too few enlisted men. There were obvious reasons for this. After all, the men who were training in Great Britain at the time of the fall of France were mostly officers, and those most motivated to have escaped from German-occupied France were mostly officers as well. There was no way to employ most of these officers in their proper rank. Nor was it possible to reduce them in rank, a matter that would not only have been disastrous for morale but that was contrary to Polish military law. Eventually a novel solution was found, units consisting entirely of officers.

The all-officer units were organized precisely as were regular units. So a company conformed to the standard table of organization established for its particular arm of the service, save that instead of privates there were lieutenants, instead of noncommissioned officers there were captains, instead of lieutenants, there were majors, and instead of a captain there was a lieutenant colonel or a colonel. The new units had some problems, since officers had different privileges, rights, and obligations than did enlisted men, but they worked moderately well. Although this expedient may seem at first glance to have been rather silly, it was by no means a bad solution. It preserved the military skills of the officers in question, skills that would eventually be needed if the manpower problem could be resolved. And this proved to be the case. As time went on, increasing numbers of expatriate Poles, including many from the United States, made their way to Great Britain to enlist. And after Hitler invaded the Soviet Union, the Russians were eventually persuaded to release tens of thousands of Polish prisoners of war, mostly enlisted men, since Stalin had massacred the bulk of the Polish officers who had fallen into his hands in 1939.

As a result, the Polish Army in exile eventually rose to the equivalent of about a half-dozen divisions. Polish forces proved among the most effective in the Allied armies, serving with particular distinction in Italy, where it was Polish troops who made the final assault at Monte Cassino. So in the end, the Polish improvisation of officer-only companies proved a useful expedient.

As an aside, the Poles were not the only ones to have all-officer units. The Russians did this on purpose when they needed units that were of unquestioned reliability and competence. When the Soviets introduced mass conscription after World War I (prior to that, conscription had been very selective), they found themselves with a lot of well-trained officers, not many NCOs, and a lot of indifferent troops. Their occasional expedient for this situation was to form units made up solely of officers. This continued after the war, whenever they needed a unit that just had to get it right the first time, and was still occasionally resorted to right into the 1980s.

"NEVER HAVE SO MANY OWED SO MUCH TO SO FEW."

It was thus that Winston Churchill described the Battle of Britain, the "few" referring to the relative handful of fighter pilots in whose hands the fate of freedom rested for several critical weeks during the summer of 1940. Having overrun France in forty-three days, Hitler was seeking ways to bring his already successful war to a glorious end, by forcing Great Britain to conclude a peace. But the British refused to quit. So Hitler decided to invade Great Britain.

The invasion of Great Britain (Operation Sea Lion) entailed three battles: (1) with the Royal Air Force to gain command of the air, (2) with the Royal Navy to ensure command of the Channel, and (3) with the British Army, and the Home Guard, to write *finis* to the British Empire. And as history records, Hitler was unable to win even the first, and perhaps most critical, of these battles.

The Battle of Britain was the first strategically important air battle in history. Although the dates are somewhat arbitrary, from July 10 through October 31, 1940, as Great Britain stood alone (aside from some help from the Commonwealth), Hitler unleashed his henchman Reichsmarschall Hermann Göring's air force. In the end, the Royal Air Force triumphed over the Luftwaffe. On the British side the battle was fought by fewer than a thousand fighter pilots,

Churchill's "few." During the nearly three months of air combat, the British lost about 900 fighters (and a handful of bombers), the Germans over 1,700 aircraft of all types. There were a number of reasons for the British victory.

GERMAN STRATEGIC INDECISION. Hitler and Göring kept changing their objectives. At first they attempted to lure the RAF into one-sided air combats by means of aggressive patrols. Then they shifted to massive attacks on forward airfields, which were mostly of little strategic importance. Suddenly realizing that British radar defenses might be vulnerable, the Luftwaffe for a time attempted to knock out the "Chain Home" system, with only marginal success. Then they concentrated on the main airfields and fighter production facilities. Just as this strategy was beginning to hurt the RAF severely, luck intervened. In retaliation for an accidental German bombing raid on London, Churchill ordered the RAF Bomber Command to hit Berlin. Although the damage was slight, the corpulent *Reichsmarschall* (who had once said, "If Berlin is bombed my name is Meyer," generally regarded as a Jewish name in German), with Hitler's permission, shifted the weight of the Luftwaffe to terror-bombing of London. Although the destruction was great, it was by no means unbearable. And for every bomb that fell on London, one did not fall on the factories turning out Hurricanes and Spitfires.

THE STRATEGIC SITUATION. Although German bombers could reach most of Great Britain, they were forced to do so beyond the ranger of fighter escort. So the critical battle, that against the RAF Fighter Command, was fought in a relatively small area over southeastern England. Damaged British planes were frequently able to make emergency landings on roads and beaches and farms, while damaged German planes had to attempt the long flight back across the Channel to their bases in France and Belgium. Moreover, a British pilot who bailed out alit on British soil and soon returned to service; it was not unusual for an RAF pilot to be shot down in the morning and be back in the air in the afternoon. Downed German pilots quickly became prisoners of war.

THE PRODUCTION BATTLE. Although the Luftwaffe began the Battle of Britain with more airplanes, the British were producing

them at a faster rate: Between July and October the
Germans produced about 750 to 800 single-seat fighters, while
the British produced about 1,900, more than twice as
many.

100 OCTANE FUEL. At the start of the war both air forces used
87 octane fuel. But shortly before the formal beginning of the
Battle of Britain, the RAF began using 100 octane fuel, a richer
mixture that greatly enhanced the performance of Hurricanes
and Spitfires by about 20 to 25 percent. This, coupled with some
other technical improvements, such as the "constant speed"
propeller, led to somewhat higher speed and a much better rate
of climb. As both airplanes were already operationally equal to,
or in the Spitfire's case, superior to the standard German fighter,
the Messerschmitt Bf-109, this was a significant operational
advantage.

THE BATTLE OF FRANCE. Although Germany had overrun
France and northwestern Europe rather swiftly in the spring of
1940, its victory was by no means one-sided. The Luftwaffe had
committed about 1,000 first-line fighters to the campaign, while
the Allies between them had nearly as many. Allied losses were
heavy, including aircraft abandoned during the hasty Allied
retreat. These losses included about 65 Spitfires, 350 Hurricanes,
and 300 DeWoitine 520s (a very good French fighter quite
literally just coming off the assembly line during the battle). But
the Luftwaffe also took a beating, with nearly 500
Messerschmitt fighters lost, plus many bombers. Pilot losses on
both sides had also been serious. Moreover, in an inspired
moment, the RAF shipped German pilot prisoners to Great
Britain, thereby removing them from the war permanently.

RADAR. By the onset of the Battle of Britain a series of rather
conspicuous towers had been erected that provided considerable
warning as to the onset of major German air raids. Coupled with
a sophisticated centralized fighter direction system, this
permitted the Fighter Command to make maximum effective use
of its resources and allowed for a more reasoned response to
attacks. Although the Germans for a time attempted to knock
out the "Chain Home" system, they were only marginally
successful, and were not even aware of that because of effective
British deception measures.

So the British won the Battle of Britain, barely. Despite all their advantages it still came down to, as Air Marshal Hugh Dowding of Fighter Command said, British young men (aided by some Canadians, plus Poles, Czechs, and Frenchmen who had a special fervor their British comrades could not match) shooting down German young men in greater numbers than the latter could shoot down the former. As a result of the Battle of Britain, Hitler was forced to cancel Operation Sea Lion, in which neither his army nor his navy had much confidence anyway. He then had to find another way to win his war. It was a search that led directly to Russia on June 22, 1941.

"TOUT POUR LA FRANCE!"

The grandson of Alfred Dreyfus, the French Jewish staff officer whose conviction on a trumped-up espionage charge became a cause célèbre in the 1890s, died flying for France in the RAF during the Battle of Britain. Among other persons unwelcome in France who nevertheless served were the Count of Paris, the Bourbon claimant to the throne, and Prince Bonaparte, the heir to Napoleon. Legally barred from French soil, both served with considerable distinction in the Foreign Legion.

WHY NO BRITISH "88"?

One of the most feared German weapons of the war was the "88." Initially, the 88mm gun was an antiaircraft gun. This caliber was used for no other type of artillery. The Germans, in a manner that permeated all their military planning and operations, had foreseen the possibility of antiaircraft guns having to confront tanks. Thus they equipped the 88s with suitable sights for firing at ground targets, and a supply of armor-piercing shells. Despite popular belief that the Germans first used 88s against tanks in North Africa, the first use was during May 1940. A British armored counterattack against the Germans prompted the German commander to order up the 88s, which action promptly smashed the British attack. General Erwin Rommel is given credit for using the 88s in North Africa, and it was also Rommel who ordered the 88s into action earlier in the Battle for France.

The British had a weapon similar to the 88 (as did most armies; the United States had a 90mm antiaircraft gun). But the British 94mm antiaircraft gun was equipped solely to fire at aircraft. British officers and crews were trained to do nothing else. The Germans were trained to be flexible, and their equipment was designed to facilitate this. Contrary to a long popular opinion, it wasn't the Germans who were the thickheaded, "do it by the book," types. This attitude was much more common on the Allied side, with the British and Soviets being most prone to this kind of thinking.

By the way, the British did have an 88, as their famous 25-pounder field gun was actually an 88mm howitzer.

"NOW WHAT WOULD ARCH DO IN A CASE LIKE THIS . . . ?"

During his campaigns in North Africa in 1941–1943, Rommel carried with him a well-worn copy of the German translation of *Generals and Generalship*, written by Sir Archibald Wavell, one of his opponents.

DIDN'T HE NOTICE?

During the early part of the Second World War Hitler's private railroad train was named *Amerika*.

UNANTICIPATED LOSSES

Among the unheralded casualties of the Second World War must be numbered the approximately forty pedestrians who were struck by automobiles nightly in blacked-out London during the Blitz.

INAUSPICIOUS DEBUT

As the United States rearmed in 1940, the spectacle of the dreaded German panzers made it clear that it had to have a powerful tank to confront the Nazis with. The tank had to have thick armor and a powerful gun. The tank designers immediately ran into problems. European tanks had their turrets and chassis armor cast in large pieces. There was no U.S. foundry that could do castings of that size in quantity. So the tank designers improvised. The M-3 "Grant" tank had a 37mm gun in a small turret and a larger 75mm gun mounted in the body of the tank. The armor was riveted together. Put into production in 1941, many were sent (as lend-lease material) to the British troops in North Africa. There, the Allied troops appreciated the firepower of the 75mm gun (even if you had to turn the tank to turn the gun) but quickly noted the riveted armor tended to be lethal even if hit with a shell that did not penetrate. The rivets would pop off and slaughter the crew inside. The Grant was also too high, making it an easy target for the enemy. The forging problem was soon solved and a more conventional design, the M-4 Sherman, was put into mass production by 1942.

4

THE EASTERN FRONT, 1941–1945

If there was any one theater of World War II that was truly hell on earth, it was Russia. This was where most of the troops were, and where most of the troops died. Here was the scene of the biggest battles, grandest victories, and most dismal defeats. All by itself, the war in Russia killed more people than all of World War I. The war in Russia was different, not least because most non-Russians fail to realize how big and important the Russian front was.

WHO BEAT THE GERMANS?

A case can be made that the Soviets defeated the Germans in World War II, pretty much single-handedly. This has long been the official Soviet position. The numbers of troops involved, and the subsequent casualties, supports the Soviet position.

The Germans lost 2.2 million soldiers on the Eastern front, the Soviets some 12 million. As total German losses in the war were 3.7 million, most of the losses were inflicted by the Soviets. Of course, without the Western Allies, there would have been a lot more Germans in the Soviet Union, a lot more dead Soviets, and the possibility of a Soviet defeat. In 1944, only 40 percent of the German Army was in the Soviet Union because the Allies had invaded France and were advancing on Germany itself. More German troops were also tied down in

Midyear Manpower in the Soviet Theater

	Soviet (*in millions*)	German (*in millions*)	Percentage of Soviet
1941	5.0	3.3	84
1942	5.0	3.1	72
1943	6.2	2.9	78
1944	6.8	3.1	40

Italy and occupation duty throughout Europe. The Soviets have always insisted that they defeated Germany and that without the German invasion of Russia in 1941, the Germans could have taken Great Britain and the Middle East. This is one of the great "what if" situations in history. What prevented the originally planned German invasion of Great Britain in late 1940 was their inability to overcome the Royal Air Force. Even had this been accomplished, there was the Royal Navy to deal with.

Like Napoleon, the Germans had a much larger army than the British but couldn't muster the means to cross the Channel. It was unlikely, but possible, that Hitler would not invade the Soviet Union in 1941 (and continue going after Great Britain and the Middle East and its oil). The Germans and Soviets had signed a non-aggression pact in 1939. But the Germans knew that the Soviets were pouring troops into the border area. And the Soviets did plan to invade Germany once the Germans were preoccupied with an Allied counterattack. Even though America was not yet in the war, planning was already under way on the B-29 and B-36 bombers, designed to bomb Germany from North American bases. The first atomic bomb was meant to be dropped on Germany, not Japan. Germany was not likely to come out of World War II a victor, no matter what strange twists history might have taken.

Russia didn't defeat the Germans alone but paid the highest price of any of the Allies to share in the victory.

LESSONS MISLEARNED

Before Russia was invaded by Germany in 1941, it had some recent experience in four wars (in Spain, Manchuria, Poland, and Finland), and the opportunity to observe two others (in France and Poland). You'd think the Soviets would have learned something. No, they didn't.

The Spanish Civil War of 1936–1939 enabled the Soviets to pit a new "Soviet-style" army against German and Italian troops and weapons. The Spanish themselves were formidable opponents. However, new technologies and tactics were still in a state of flux. So was the Russians' ability to make sense of it all.

Spain. In the Spanish Civil War (1936 to 1939) the Soviets had plenty of opportunity to try out their new tanks and aircraft. The tank warfare was disappointing, as the fighting generally settled down to sieges and stalemates similar to World War I. The Russians blamed this on the terrain and the need to take cities. Moreover, airpower seemed to have gotten more powerful than it had been in the 1914–1918 war. The Russians decided to build a dedicated ground attack aircraft (the Il-2 Sturmovik, which performed well in World War II). With less conviction, they also formed armored divisions (although they called these three brigade units "corps").

Manchuria. From May to August 1939 the Russians fought a series of battles with the Japanese on the Manchurian border with Mongolia. The Russians used hundreds of tanks and decisively defeated the Japanese (whom they outnumbered about two to one). This gave the Russians some confidence in the use of massed armored units, although they attributed much of their success to the ineptness of the Japanese. There was some truth to this, as the Russians were generally successful in the all-infantry portions of these battles.

Poland. The Russians had signed an alliance with the Germans just before the Nazis invaded Poland in September 1939. This treaty allowed the Russians to also invade Poland and to incorporate part of it into the Soviet Union. The Russians waited until the middle of September before invading. Actually, the Russians did not expect the Germans to overrun Poland so quickly, so the Russian offensive was a hastily organized affair. Two Soviet armored corps led the way, and to put it charitably, it was not a pretty sight. The Russian units had not trained as hard as the German units and their advance was disorganized and haphazard. Had there been any substantial resistance, the Russians probably would have been stopped cold. The Soviets attributed the German success to the flat terrain and the ineptitude of the Poles. However, shortly thereafter, the Russian armored corps were disbanded and the tank battalions distributed among the infantry units.

Finland. In November 1939, the Russians invaded Finland. This was another disaster. But the Soviets piled on the greatly outnumbered Finns and by spring of 1940 had settled for an armistice (and most of the Finnish territory they were fighting for in the first place). From this conflict, the Soviets concluded that their training needed some improvement. It was "back to basics" time and much of the political and theoretical lectures that the troops had been receiving was replaced by constant field training. The authority of military officers was strengthened and the power of the political officers decreased. Many of the problems with leadership were a result of Stalin's paranoid purge of the officers corps in the late 1930s, but this was not discussed.

France. In May 1940, the Germans invaded France. The Russians expected a stalemate, but by June the German panzers had defeated the French. Also by June, Russia decided that maybe tank divisions were a good idea after all. The armored corps that had been disbanded the year before were now created anew. Officers were given still more authority, and the political commissars who normally looked over every unit leader's shoulder given still less. The Soviet air force was told that its primary mission was the direct support of ground forces (in recognition of the Luftwaffe's support for the German armored units). During the winter of 1940–1941 the Russian senior leadership conferred and decided that the coming war with Germany (in 1942 or 1943, they hoped) would be a war of attrition. General Georgy Zhukov, the commander of Khalkhin-Gol, insisted that "lightning war" would not be the key to victory. He knew, he had successfully practiced blitzkrieg against the Japanese. Zhukov correctly saw the coming war as a long battle of attrition and that blitzkrieg and armored divisions alone would not prevail. The Russian generals convinced themselves (with a little prompting from Stalin) that a future war would allow sufficient time to mobilize. At that point, the more massive Russian resources would smother the invader. But the generals knew that a surprise attack by the Germans was not unthinkable, especially since the Nazis had created a highly secretive police state that left even the formidable Russian spies in the dark much of the time.

*   *   *

No one really disagreed with all this, and no one was looking forward to a fight with the Germans. Stalin had the last word, and this is where the Russians got into the most trouble. Fearful of going to war with the Germans before the Soviet armed forces were ready, Stalin avoided doing anything that might antagonize Hitler. This, however, extended to ignoring early 1941 warnings that German divisions were massing on the Russian border. Stalin would not allow his divisions in western Russia to be put on alert or deployed more efficiently to withstand a surprise attack. Soviet propaganda to the Russian people caused the population to believe war would not come without warning.

When the German assault came, it was a shock to everyone but a few senior Russian generals. The Soviets had to begin their mobilization while the Germans were gobbling up huge amounts of the homeland. The lack of Russian armored divisions was less of a problem than many thought, as the Germans were much better at mobile warfare and would have quickly chewed up anyone's tank divisions. This had been amply demonstrated against French and British mechanized units in 1940. But the massive Russian reserves of trained manpower and weapons were decisive. For the first year of the war, the Russians beat back the Germans with hordes of infantry armed with rifles, machine guns, mortars, and artillery. It wasn't until 1943 that the Russians got into the armored warfare business to a significant degree. In the end, it was a war of attrition and the use of masses of unsophisticated infantry divisions that beat the Germans. The Russians had learned from the earlier wars, and suffered mainly from Stalin's unwillingness to practice what he preached.

GETTING THERE FIRST WITH THE MOST

It is generally accepted that the Germans invaded Russia while outnumbered. This is true in the general sense. The Red Army was larger than the German Army. But the rest of the Russian forces were thousands of miles away, scattered from the Urals to the Pacific Ocean. What counted was what was in western Russia.

The Axis forces included mostly Germans, but also several hundred thousand other Axis allies (mainly Romanian, plus Slovaks, Hungarians, and Finns). Russian forces were only those in Western Russia. To account for the rapid German victory, one must consider many other crucial factors. The most important one was manpower and quality. The former was somewhat fixed, the other could be changed. At the time of the invasion, the Germans had 7 million troops in uniform, the

Forces in Western Russia, June 1941

	Axis Forces	Soviet Forces
Troops	3,500,500	3,000,000
Tanks	3,300	12,000
Artillery	7,200	5,900
Aircraft	2,800	10,000

Soviet Union had only 4 million. The Germans arrived on Russia's borders with 3.5 million troops (with another million ready to follow up as replacements and reinforcements) against only 3 million in western Russia. The Germans had to move fast, because in overall manpower they were at a severe disadvantage. Germany had a population of 100 million they could draw troops from. But only 19 million were military-age males (eighteen to thirty-nine years old). The Soviet Union, with 199 million people at hand, had a military population of 41 million. The Germans also had Great Britain, and perhaps the United States, to worry about. The Russians were not involved in any other wars. If the Germans were going to win, it had to be in the first twelve months of the war, before Russia could begin mobilizing its more plentiful manpower.

The Soviet Union was prepared for just such an eventuality. It had been mass-producing weapons and training troops throughout the 1930s. Although many of the weapons were no longer the most modern, and the conscripts released through the 1930s had received little refresher training, the Soviet Union was a very regimented society. The Soviets had the capability to produce increasing numbers of trained and equipped troops.

Meanwhile, in the summer of 1941 the Germans were there first with the most. The Russians were in disarray even before the war began. Stalin had killed off most of the senior officers in a late 1930s purge. Most of the tanks and aircraft were obsolete and operated by ill-trained crews. Most divisions were undergoing some kind of reorganization. Worst of all, Stalin, and most Russians, did not believe the Germans would invade. Materially and mentally, the Russians weren't ready.

But there were more Russians than Germans.

Even though the Germans inflicted far more casualties, they were never able to increase their strength in the east. Germans got killed,

Manpower in Russia*

	Axis Troops (in millions)	Soviet Troops (in millions)
1941	3.4	3.0
1942	3.1	4.0
1943	3.5	5.5
1944	3.1	6.1

* In the summer of each year indicated.

too, and the Russians kept turning out far more trained troops and units than the Germans could.

Although the Germans got there first with the most, it wasn't quite enough.

MAJOR TANK LOSSES NEAR THE ARCTIC CIRCLE

One of the most expensive battles for the Allies cost them 5,000 tanks, 7,000 aircraft, and over 200,000 tons of other war material. This was all lost at sea in the holds of ships trying to reach Soviet ports in the far north of Russia, near the Arctic Circle. The 58 ships lost amount to 7.2 percent of the ships sent to the Soviet Union. This was a grim statistic, as overall merchant ship losses in the Atlantic war, 654, were only about 0.7 percent of sailings. But Russia had to be kept fighting, and the supplies had to get through. But more tanks were lost on the Murmansk run than in any single battle of the war. And all those tanks are still there, on the bottom of the ocean.

A PAPER VICTORY

The Russians made much of their heroic, and successful, efforts to evacuate over a thousand factories in the face of the German advance during the summer of 1941. This was not as crucial for the Russian war effort as is generally thought. Throughout the industrialization campaign of the 1930s, most new arms factories were built east of Moscow, in areas less likely to be overrun by an invader from the west. So, while the factory evacuation was helpful, the decision to build the new factories east of Moscow was crucial. On the issue of "factory evacuation," what the Soviets did win for many decades was a paper victory, by convincing the Western media that a minor victory was a major one. Score another one for the superior press release.

IMPROVING THE LEADERSHIP?

During the late 1930s Joseph Stalin, the dictator of Russia, purged about 67 percent of the generals in the Red Army: 3 of the 5 marshals of the Soviet Union, all 11 vice commissars of war, 75 of the 80 members of the Supreme War Council, 13 of 15 army commanders, 51 of 85 corps commanders, and 110 of 195 division and brigade commanders. This was one reason for the rather dismal performance of the Red Army in the opening months of the Second World War, as many good men were among those purged. Fortunately for Russia, Stalin did not actually kill all of the purged officers but merely sent many of them off to Siberia and other unpleasant places. As a result, after the debacle at the front in the summer of 1941, many of the survivors were released from the Gulag and sent to resume their commands.

WHAT WAS REALLY IMPORTANT?

The Western Allies supplied Russia with enormous quantities of aid during the war, over 100 billion 1994 dollars' worth. This material was most needed in 1941 and 1942, when the Germans had the Soviets on the ropes. The large amount of material was sent without much regard as to how useful it would be. It included a lot of equipment the British and Americans considered obsolete, but nonetheless the Russians were glad to have it. Several decades after the war, the Russian generals became more forthcoming on which items had really been the most useful. These were on one such list:

- **100 octane aviation fuel.** Production of this fuel, which was necessary for getting the most performance out of aircraft engines, required sophisticated equipment the Soviets were always short of. The Western Allies had this equipment to a much larger degree than did the Russians. Thus shipments of this fuel had a direct bearing on the success of Russian fighters against German aircraft.

- **Trucks.** The Russians built their own tanks, generally the most effective of the war (the ones they received from the West were usually obsolete even by Western standards and the Russians asked that no more be sent). Nearly the entire Soviet automotive industry was turned over to tank production, leaving it dependent on the superior military trucks delivered from America. U.S. military trucks were the best available during the war and the Russians took advantage of this.

- **Waterproof telephone wire.** This was another commodity that required high-quality manufacturing standards. Telephone wire is either waterproof or it isn't. Russian manufacturing standards were such that Russian-made wire always had a leak somewhere. The Western cable was much more reliable. As the Russians preferred wire communications to wireless (so the Germans couldn't listen in), this was a particularly valuable item for them.

- **Radios.** The Soviets didn't have much of an electronics industry, and as a result most of their tanks and airplanes lacked radios early in the war. Generally the senior officer's airplane or tank had a radio over which he could communicate with higher command, passing his own instructions on to his subordinates by means of hand signals. In combat this didn't work out very well, although as the war progressed most aircraft were at least equipped with receivers so the pilots could hear their orders. The United States supplied the Russians with some 340,000 radios, playing a major role in providing the Russian armed forces with modern communications.

ONE FOR THE GIRLS

The first woman to shoot down an enemy aircraft in aerial combat was Valeria Khomyakov, who downed a Ju-88 near Saratov in the Soviet Union while piloting a Yak-1 fighter of the Red Air Force's 586th Fighter Squadron early in 1942. Ms. Khomyakov was one of several hundred "girl" combat fliers in the Red Air Force.

The Soviets made a big deal out of having the world's only all-female aircraft units. There were three aircraft regiments (with thirty to forty aircraft each) with women pilots. One was a fighter regiment with Yak-1s that was used for air defense (and claimed thirty-eight German aircraft shot down). Another was a Pe-2 light bomber and the third

Po-2 night bombers. The last unit, called the Night Witches, was the most propagandized. The units were a mixed success. Most women pilots had a hard time handling the Pe-2, which required a fair amount of muscle power to fly. The Yak-1 was obsolete by 1942 and the Po-2 was a biplane which couldn't do much but nighttime harassment bombing. The three female regiments were relegated to quiet sectors after 1943, for on the main fronts the better German pilots were chewing up Russian aircraft at a rapid clip. But the women pilots posted to the quiet areas still had a good supply of German bombers and recon aircraft to shoot at. All three air regiments were disbanded in 1945.

THE FORTUNES OF WAR

The first German bomb to fall on Leningrad during World War II killed the only elephant in the city zoo.

WE'RE NOT ALL TURKEYS

The Soviets eventually defeated Germany, but did so at great cost. This was true in the air as well as the ground. The Soviets believed in quantity (which they could obtain more readily than quality). Several German aces racked up hundreds of kills on the Eastern front, while only a handful of Soviets got over fifty kills and none exceeded a hundred. Given the overall superiority of the German pilots throughout the war, the Russians developed several techniques that gave their pilots a better chance of surviving.

- Russian fighter formations tended to look like a swirling mob of aircraft. The Russians did this on purpose. Their pilots were instructed to fly every which way while the formation was moving in one direction. This made it difficult for the sharper Germans to get the drop on the Russians.

- Another technique was for the Russian aircraft to always fly at top speed. While this limited their range (because of the higher fuel consumption than at slower ''cruise'' speed), it made it difficult for a German aircraft to sneak up on them. Russian aircraft were faster than their German counterparts by the middle of the war and the Russians discovered that speed could be a life saver.

- As Russian aces emerged, they were collected together in "Guards" units. There weren't many of these outfits, but their existence made the Germans wary. Before engaging in combat, the Germans had to try to find out if the opposition was the "usual turkeys" (with whom you could take chances without much risk) or "Guards" (who had to be engaged with great care).

- The Russians had more fighters, producing 70,000 Yak, Mig, and Lavochkin aircraft during the war. The Germans produced only 30,000 Bf-109s and 20,000 FW-190s and increasingly these were needed for other theaters and the defense of Germany from Allied bombers. Nearly all Russian fighters were used against the Germans.

- When the Russians had a major operation coming up, they would achieve air superiority by flooding the skies with fighters. At other times, and in secondary parts of the front, they would let the Germans control the skies. This application of mass in the air was similar to how the Russians conducted ground warfare. Like their tank units, not every aircraft would have a radio. The leaders would have radios and the other aircraft in the unit were expected to watch and follow their leader. Simple, cheap, and effective.

PREFERRED BY RUSSIAN ACES

While over half the Soviet fighters produced were the speedy Yak-1, -3, and -9 models. Russian aces preferred the slower, more maneuverable, and more heavily armed Lavochkin 7 or 11. Most Soviet fighters were armed with one 20mm cannon and two 12.7mm (.50-caliber) machine guns. This was insufficient, or at least not as lethal as the generally heavier armament on German fighters. The Lavochkins carried three 20mm cannons, being more on a par with the Germans in the firepower department. The Soviet attitude was that fewer than 10 percent of their pilots would be aces (shoot down five or more aircraft) or even come close. Most pilots needed speed in order to stay out of trouble with the more proficient Germans. The Russian aces didn't need the extra speed of the Yak fighters; aces want to mix it up with the enemy, and in that case maneuverability and firepower are more important.

BIPLANES FOREVER

At the beginning of World War II, there were thousands of biplanes still in use. Most were quickly retired from combat duties. But the Russian Po-2 served throughout the war and for several decades thereafter. Production began in 1928 (over 35,000 were built, most of them during the war,) and continued into the 1950s. Po-2s were most famous for their exploits as night bombers, but were more frequently engaged in reconnaissance, artillery spotting, supplying partisans, and liaison duties. Some were equipped to carry injured soldiers (one stretcher and a medic). As a night bomber, the Po-2's primary function was to harass the Germans and prevent them from getting any sleep, and the Po-2 was quite successful in that role. The aircraft was slow (top speed of 90 miles an hour) but very agile. It had a range of only 470 km and a maximum altitude of 13,000 feet. Its armament consisted of a single 7.62mm machine gun (facing the rear), and it could carry a 600-pound bomb load. Weighing only 1.3 tons, it required less than 400 feet of open space for takeoff and less than 500 feet for landing. The original designation of the aircraft was U-2, which was changed to Po-2 during the war.

WORLD'S RECORD

From August 29 to October 8, 1942, the German 250th Infantry Division (the volunteer Spanish "Blue Division") marched (literally) from Suvalki in Poland to Vitebsk in the Soviet Union, a distance of some 1,000 kilometers, for an average daily rate of advance of about 25 kilometers, probably the greatest sustained marching effort in the Second World War. The division had a number of other distinctions to its credit. Continuously in action from its first entry into combat at Borisov on October 18, 1941, to the time it was withdrawn from the Leningrad front on January 15, 1943, to return to Spain, the division was involved in twenty-one major battles and hundreds of smaller ones, yet never lost an inch of ground.

On one occasion, resentful of German efforts to interfere in its pursuit of the local womenfolk, when the division was ordered to march in review for some German brass, the troops decorated their bayonets with inflated condoms.

The Blue Division was an interesting trick on the part of Spanish dictator Francisco Franco. The Spanish Civil War had only ended in

1939, and although Franco was considered a Fascist, he was much more of a Spanish nationalist and was more concerned with maintaining peace and quiet in Spain than getting involved in another war. The Blue Division was a way of getting the more determined prowar Spanish Fascists and anti-Communists out of the country, and out of Franco's hair. At the same time, the Blue Division was Francisco Franco's way of acceding to German pressures for him to enter the war. In what has been termed a "dazzling virtuoso performance," Franco repeatedly expressed his desire to join Germany, "with proper support," meaning guaranteed deliveries of arms, petroleum products, and other resources. These were, of course, precisely what Hitler was unable to supply, Franco apparently having been apprised of what to ask for by anti-Nazi Germans, among whom appears to have been Admiral Wilhelm Canaris, the chief of German military intelligence, whose acquaintance Franco (or one of his close advisers) had made during World War I, when Canaris was a German intelligence operative in Spain. Meanwhile Franco kept his options open with the West, turning a blind eye to Allied "escape lines" that helped fugitive prisoners of war to travel across Spain and issued passports to Sephardic Jews in some areas of Eastern Europe, enabling them to escape the Holocaust.

So tenacious was Franco in negotiation that after their one and only meeting together (Franco crossed the Spanish border to Hendaye in France, while Hitler traveled all the way from Paris) Hitler is supposed to have remarked that he would rather spend time with his dentist.

SNEAK, SMOTHER, AND PUNCH

There were three methods by which battlefield reconnaissance was obtained on the Russian front (and, to a large extent, in all theaters of the war). The "sneak" approach involved small groups (or even an individual) sneaking up on the enemy (or behind enemy lines), taking notes, and then getting back alive with the information. The Russians were particularly keen on this, as it made good use of the many agents and partisans they had behind the German lines, as well as the individual talents of exceptional scouts in frontline units. The major problem with this approach was that it was slow and the scouts were rarely able to take immediate advantage of opportunities they came across. Radio technology in World War II did not allow most scouts to carry a radio with them (one that had sufficient range to do the job). The "sneak" approach appealed to the Russians because they preferred to plan out elaborate operations in advance. The Germans were more prone to conjure up new plans on the spot.

The "smother" approach was one most often practiced by the Germans and the Western Allies. This involved lots of small, well-armed recon units fanning out to find out where the enemy strength was and to probe deep where there appeared to be no enemy at all. Armored cars were a favorite vehicle among the Germans and Western Allies. On the Russian front, the Germans found that infantry companies on bicycles were effective. The Americans had less success with jeeps mounting machine guns. The armored cars could take on infantry patrols that normally guarded parts of the front that were not occupied. This was common in Russia, where large areas of the front were virtually undefended, or defended lightly. When there was a major offensive, enemy and friendly units would get all mixed up and the side that had a better idea of who was where with what tended to come out of it victorious. It was usually the Germans who were most successful in these situations and it was their superior form of scouting that did it.

The "punch" approach was also much favored by the Germans. The "punching" was not done by the recon troops themselves, but rather by the heavier units the recon people would call in once a soft spot was found in the enemy line. What made this possible was superior leadership and tactics. The Germans were trained to take quick advantage of battlefield opportunities. Their recon units worked closely with tank and mechanized infantry units, thus allowing the German armored car scouts to rapidly bring in heavier units to overcome enemy troops in an area found to be lightly guarded. Later in the war, the Russians organized similar recon units but were less successful because their training and doctrine did not encourage independent thinking. Nevertheless, individual Russian units often got the hang of it and won some striking victories against the Germans using what were, essentially, German techniques.

The Americans organized "armored cavalry regiments" (consisting of three heavy recon battalions and supporting units) which had essentially the same doctrine as the Germans. These American units had some success in 1944 and 1945, especially once they got some practice in combat. General George Patton scared the Germans partially because of his use of aggressive reconnaissance with heavily armed recon units.

THE BIRTH OF MODERN WARFARE

In early 1943, German commanders on the Russian front realized that the techniques that had been so successful for the past four years were no longer working. They quickly developed new ways to fight, and what they came up with became the form of mechanized warfare that remained the standard for the rest of the twentieth century. From 1939 through late 1942, the classic blitzkrieg was the dominant form of warfare. This involved fast-moving tank and infantry formations, exploiting holes blasted in the enemy line, followed by a rampage through the enemy rear area, and the consequent collapse of the enemy's ability to resist. It was the Russians who came up with the antidote for this, and they did so with masses of cheap antitank weapons (towed, high-velocity guns) and multiple lines of defenses featuring well-dug-in antitank guns and infantry, supported by artillery and, for counterattacks, tank units. The Battle of Kursk, in the summer of 1943, confirmed what many German generals saw in early 1943. At Kursk, powerful German tank units wore themselves out assaulting Russian defenses. The Russian armored counterattack threw the Germans back hundreds of miles.

The new German tactic was twofold. First, it emphasized the increased importance of reconnaissance and the need to find lightly held portions of the enemy lines to advance through with armored forces. Second, more attention was paid to the complex procedure units had to use in defeating the new Russian defenses. What the Germans came up with was a complex interplay between infantry, armor, and artillery to methodically reduce the Russian-type defenses. In some respects, these new techniques were similar to what the Germans used late in World War I to break the fortified trench lines that had resisted all forms of attack for nearly three years. The critical point was that the two parts of the new tactic had to be used together. Neither would succeed alone. With effective antitank defense possible (and the Germans in North Africa had developed the same techniques for use against the British), tanks could no longer advance with impunity against enemy resistance. Tanks could still advance, but only as part of a well-trained combined arms team, and a lot more slowly than before. The mobility of mechanized forces became more important than ever. Neither side could construct tank-proof defenses everywhere, so warfare became a fast-moving chess match. Whoever got into the other's rear area first was usually the winner. With both sides now possessing roughly the same capabilities, the era of modern warfare began.

REINVENTING INFANTRY

World War II began with most infantry operating as they had in the closing days of World War I. Four years later, it became obvious that infantry operations had to go through another transformation, just as they had done in the last year of World War I. By the end of that war, it had finally been realized that infantry could not just charge ahead through enemy artillery and machine-gun fire. First the enemy had to be smashed with carefully, and quickly, placed artillery fire. The infantry could then advance around remaining enemy strongpoints and into the rear area. Tanks had been introduced late in World War I and became the principal offensive weapon early in World War II. Firepower had increased since World War I. The big German problem was that they were running out of infantry. The Germans ran out of troops first, but the Russians were in the same situation and were down to the dregs when the war ended. Both sides came to the same conclusions about resolving the shortage of infantry and using more firepower and fewer troops. For the Russians, this meant massive artillery bombardments against the German lines before the Russian infantry went into action. The Russians also massed tanks, moving these in front of and among the infantry to give the foot troops some additional protection. Russian infantry were given more personal firepower by increasing the number of machine guns and submachine guns (automatic pistols, small rifles firing pistol-type cartridges) in the infantry divisions. The growth of machine guns and submachine guns in Russian divisions was like this:

Weapons per 1,000 Men in Russian Divisional Organizations

	Submachine Guns	Machine Guns
May 1941	83	44
December 1942	234	69
June 1944	250	68

Russian infantry losses were still horrendous, but without these additional weapons, the casualties would have been worse, mainly because fewer Germans would have been killed and wounded. Mortars and guns were also increased, as well as the number of tanks and assault guns added to infantry divisions assigned to major attacks.

The Russians actually saw these changes before the war began. Their 1939 infantry division organization had no submachine guns and only forty-one machine guns per 1,000 troops. The disastrous war with the Finns in 1940 had something to do with this, but a lot of credit should go to a very bright bunch of senior Soviet officers (who had managed to survive Stalin's purges in the late 1930s).

At the beginning of the war in Russia, the Germans indisputably had the superior infantry, and it took a while before they noticed they had a problem with infantry losses beyond those caused by the strenuous conditions in Russia. German officers noted the higher proportion of submachine guns in Russian divisions (more than twice what the Germans had, until 1945, when the Germans closed the gap). The generals called for more firepower for the infantry, from submachine guns to mortars, artillery, assault guns, and tanks. But more critical was the shortage of good officers for the infantry. This was a problem in all armies. Even the Germans, who had the best infantry officers of any army, saw the need for better leadership in the infantry companies. The problem was made worse by the very high casualties in the infantry. Officers were lost even more quickly than troops because of the German practice of officers being up front most of the time. Since officers were the major force in raising the training level of the troops, the lack of enough officers put a greater burden on the NCOs and gradually caused the Germans' qualitative edge in infantry to decline. While the Russians never were able to match the infantry skills of the Germans, the Russians closed the gap as the war ground on and, until the end, had superior numbers.

The ultimate solution was to be found in the Panzergrenadier (motorized infantry) divisions. These units could carry all the additional weapons and ammunition the infantry needed to survive on the battlefield, and they had something of an armored punch of their own (usually in the form of armored assault guns, but occasionally in the form of some tanks). Perhaps most important, these motorized infantry units could keep up with the panzer (tanks) divisions and do those chores tanks weren't good at, like occupying ground, rooting enemy infantry out of fortifications and built-up areas, and beating off counterattacks. But Germany did not have the resources to form many of these. The German Army remained, until the end of the war, a largely horse-drawn army. By late 1944, far more submachine guns were added to German infantry divisions, as well as a higher proportion of mortars and assault guns. But it was not soon enough. The German infantry melted away in combat faster than it could be replaced or reformed.

THE MAN ON A HORSE

So lacking in motor transport was the German Army that, throughout the war, the vast majority of infantry battalion commanders were issued only a horse for transportation. Sometimes the battalion commanders would appropriate one of the dozen (usually less) trucks and motorcycles each battalion had to haul its heavy equipment. But this was often not possible, as it would mean something vital would have to be left behind. Infantry battalions were often spread over several square miles, and the battalion commander generally had to walk around. Horses died even more quickly than troops, especially on the Russian front.

THE BIRTH OF ROCK AND ROLL

In modern military slang, "rock and roll" means a unit of troops are all firing their assault rifles on full automatic. This produces an enormous amount of firepower, and few targets in the way escape undamaged. The modern assault rifle was first used in early 1944, when the Germans issued the MP-43 (the precursor of the SG-44, which in turn was the model for the Russian AK-47 and inspired the U.S. M-16) to several of their Russian front infantry battalions. This was a battlefield test to see how well the weapon would do under battlefield conditions. The Germans had already noted the Russian success with machine pistols (submachine guns). The major shortcoming of the machine pistol was that it was, in fact, a pistol with a longer barrel and a larger magazine (thirty or more rounds). Despite the longer barrel, the pistol cartridge lacked accuracy, even when fired from the hip in bursts of automatic fire. The pistol cartridge also lacked punch. Where a rifle bullet would kill a man, a pistol round would only wound. And the wounded soldier would often keep firing back. The assault rifle round (beginning with the MP-43/SG-44) was not quite as powerful as the standard rifle round, but more powerful than a pistol round. This made a big difference for the infantry, as the assault rifle could be fired at longer ranges with more accuracy and stopping power. The German units receiving the MP-43 for test purposes were given a lot of discretion on how to use the new weapon. Most battalions that got the MP-43 equipped entire platoons and companies with it. They soon found that in the attack, even twenty or thirty troops armed with the MP-43 were unstoppable against Russian infantry. The biggest problem the Germans had was giving the troops sufficient quantities of 30-round magazines. Initially, troops were sent in with six or seven magazines. Experience soon demonstrated that a dozen magazines per man was more effective. Even though the troops did a lot of their firing semi-automatically (one shot per pull of the trigger), even this was more effective because of the 30-round magazine. And the fact that full automatic fire could be had at the flick of a switch made the troops a lot bolder.

Up until this time, most of the firepower in a German squad came from one (or perhaps two) light machine guns (the MG-42). If the machine gun was knocked out of action, all the troops had left were their bolt-action rifles. Against Russians armed with machine pistols, or at night where the enemy could not be clearly seen, this was not enough.

While this new weapon didn't win the war for the Germans, it did increase Allied casualties whenever it was encountered. Large quantities of the SG-44 (the improved MP-43) did not arrive until late 1944. It may not have changed the outcome of the war, but it did make Allied victory take longer, and at a higher cost.

CAN'T HAVE TOO MANY SCOUTS

By early 1943, German divisions in Russia devoted about 15 percent of their infantry to reconnaissance duties. By this time, the Germans officially recognized that combat on the Russian front was a special form of warfare and they reorganized their infantry divisions accordingly. The new divisions had six infantry battalions (organized into three regiments), and a seventh infantry battalion was organized and equipped to serve as the division reconnaissance battalion. Like most German infantry divisions, this one was not motorized. Most of the transport was horse-drawn, supplemented by some trucks. The recon battalion had hundreds of bicycles. These were quite useful, except during the spring when the copious mud slowed everything to a crawl. Because the Germans were not fanatical about reorganizing existing divisions when a new organization came into use, there was a great variety in the organization of divisions. One thing most of these divisions had in common was a large reconnaissance capability. The Germans believed in the importance of battlefield information and were willing to devote the resources needed to get it. German reconnaissance stressed mobility, flexibility, and aggressiveness. If a recon unit found an objective that was lightly defended, it would go ahead and take it and hand it over to the regular infantry later. Speed was a hallmark of all German operations and the Germans' use of reconnaissance in Russia was another example.

THE "OTHER" D-DAY

The Western Allies were quite proud of their amphibious invasion of France in June 1944. The Allies had 3 million heavily armed troops, a massive fleet, and air superiority. The Germans had 1 million less well equipped troops, no fleet to speak of, and, obviously, no control of the air. After ninety-nine days, the Germans had lost half of their million ground combat forces and were defending the borders of Germany itself. An astonishing victory? Yes. But there was another one in the east. On June 22 (the third anniversary of the German invasion), 2.5 million Soviet troops crashed on to the 700,000 Germans making up Army Group Center. The Germans lost 400,000 troops and thirty divisions in five weeks and the Soviet troops ended up in the suburbs of Warsaw. As its name implies, this Army Group Center was at the center of the German forces on the Russian front. Earlier that year, the Russians had retaken the Ukraine, while the German forces in the north largely held their ground. This put Army Group Center in a delicate position, as its lines now formed a bulge, surrounded on three sides by Soviet forces. Throughout 1944 the Soviets were on the offensive. In places, they advanced over a thousand miles against sometimes stiff resistance. But the destruction of Army Group Center was the high point of the Soviet offensive. In many respects, it was as important as D-Day, for it demolished once and for all any doubts that the Russians could consistently beat the Germans at their own blitzkrieg game. The Army Group Center battle was a debacle from which the Germans never recovered, even though more than a million additional Russian troops would die before the Third Reich was finally destroyed.

YOU'LL HAVE TO WALK

The German Army, much like its Russian opponent, depended on horses more than trucks for transportation. While the horses allowed the troops to drag their heavy weapons and artillery along with them as they trudged across the battlefield, the trucks were needed to speed supplies, and troops, to areas where enemy troops (especially mechanized ones) were breaking through. Truck losses were heavy for the Germans. They never had enough trucks and they worked them hard, to the point that those unarmored vehicles often found themselves under fire. The worst period for German truck drivers was the first eight months of 1944. Between the battles in Russia and the Allied invasion of France in June, the Germans lost 109,000 trucks. This was 39 percent of what the German armed forces had and equal to their entire production during 1943. The losses were not only due to battle damage, but also to a chronic lack of spare parts. Moreover, the Germans looted several hundred thousand vehicles from occupied territories, further complicating their parts problems. Some units had over twenty different vehicle types, and many of the non-German vehicles were no longer produced. This further complicated the parts shortage, causing many basically sound vehicles to be abandoned because of the lack of common parts.

GENERAL MUD

Only one mechanized foreign army has operated in Russia and it was a sobering experience. The Russians have always relied on "General Mud" and "Marshal Winter" to assist their armed forces in repelling the enemy. The spring mud was particularly difficult. Russia had few hard-surfaced roads; most were dirt tracks. During the spring rains (and melting of the winter snow) these dirt roads turned into deep mud. The Russians were accustomed to dealing with the problem, although even they tended to just not travel until the mud dried out. Horse-drawn vehicles were specially designed (lightweight and with the axle high off the ground) to better traverse the mud and Russian drivers knew from experience where the mud was shallow (and more trafficable). The Germans got quite a shock during the spring of 1942, and by 1943 had stolen all the Russian horse-drawn vehicles they could find. German motor vehicles were another matter, and an ingenious solution was devised. The rear wheels of trucks were replaced with a track-laying mechanism (like on a bulldozer). This was similar to the armored "half-track" personnel carriers the Germans and Americans used in large quantities for their mechanized infantry. The German half-track trucks accounted for one third of their truck production in 1943.

THE FIRST, AND WORST, PARATROOPERS

The Soviet Union formed the first parachute units in the early 1930s. As with many aspects of modern military technology, the Soviets took the lead and the rest of the world followed. But the Soviets lacked the ability to make airborne forces work effectively, something Germany and the Western Allies were only marginally better at. Moreover, although in the 1930s new military technologies (tanks, aircraft carriers, dive-bombers) abounded, no one knew who would, or could, make what work.

By 1932, after several years of planning, the Soviets had a thousand paratroopers and were enthusiastically working out the technical details of airborne operations. After that, the strength of Russian paratroop forces took off.

Year	Number of Paratroopers
1932	1,000
1933	8,000
1934	10,000
1935	10,000
1936	10,000
1937	12,000
1938	18,000
1939	30,000
1940	50,000
1941	55,000

By 1934 the Soviets had standardized their paratrooper organization. The basic unit was a brigade, which contained 3,000 to 3,500 men (four 450- to 550-man infantry battalions, a recon company, artillery battalion, and support units). The Soviets pioneered the use of gliders, and the airborne brigades had combinations of parachute and glider battalions (usually two of each). Gliders allowed the landing of light tanks and artillery. Such a "two and two" brigade would have eleven light tanks, seventeen pieces of artillery (four 75mm guns, the rest being combinations of mortars and antiaircraft and antitank guns). The brigade would have sixty to seventy trucks.

While Russian paratroopers had trained hard and performed well in maneuvers, they had yet to enter combat as paratroopers. In 1939, one brigade fought (as ground troops) against the Japanese in Mongolia. In 1940, two brigades fought (again, as ground troops) against the Finns.

The closest the paratroopers came to an airborne combat operation was in 1940, when three brigades were dropped ahead of ground troops during the Russian reoccupation of the Romanian province of Bessarabia. There was no opposition during this operation, so it was basically another training exercise.

In late 1940, airborne divisions (called "corps") were formed, each with three brigades (3,000 men) plus support units (a light tank battalion, artillery battalion, and antitank-battalion). A full-strength airborne corps had 10,500 men. Five existed (although they lacked much equipment) when the Germans invaded Russia in 1941. Since the Germans had quickly attained air superiority, and the situation on the ground was desperate, the five airborne corps were sent into battle as regular infantry. This, in effect, destroyed the airborne force the Russians had so carefully built up over the previous nine years.

After two months of fighting the Germans, only two of the original five Russian airborne corps were still intact. Cadres from these two corps, plus survivors from the three that had all but disappeared, were used to form five more airborne corps. Many of these units subsequently participated in the 1941–1942 Russian winter offensive as ground troops. There were some air drops, but they were small and none had much effect on the ground fighting. Casualties, however, were heavy. During the summer of 1941, the ten airborne corps, and five independent brigades, were reorganized into regular infantry units and sent south to oppose the big German offensive that was approaching the Caucasus Mountains. That campaign resulted in the German defeat at Stalingrad. But even as Russian forces were massing for that battle, many paratroopers were pulled out of their infantry jobs at the end of 1942 and used to organize ten Guards Airborne Divisions (basically the same as the previous Airborne Corps). But the Germans began attacking again in the spring of 1943, and the paratroopers were once more sent in as ground troops, and most of them were lost.

Undismayed, the Russians formed another twenty airborne brigades, which they used to form another six airborne corps. Three of these brigades were used for the largest Russian airborne operation to date, and the first deliberate attempt to use parachutists to support a major operation. On September 23, 1943, the three brigades were dropped in the vicinity of Kanev to assist the crossing of the Dnieper River. The airborne assault was a failure. It was too hastily organized and the careful preparation required was simply not there. Moreover, most of the parachutists had never jumped out of an airplane before, although most had at least jumped in a parachute harness from a training tower. There were not enough transport aircraft, the pilots didn't have much experience, and the German flak was alert and effective. The drop was done at night, to avoid the risk of German fighters, but this just added to the muddle.

Stalin was not happy with this, the first real test of Russian airborne forces in their designed role. But then, their failure was not surprising. After the debacles in 1941, the Russians ruthlessly gathered whatever forces they could to stem the German advance. This meant paratroopers being thrown into ground battles as infantry. The persistent efforts to organize new airborne units represented a desire to maintain an airborne capability as well as the recognition that the paratroopers were more effective infantry. But the Soviet air force was never able to support airborne operations sufficiently to make them work. For the rest of the war, Soviet airborne forces were kept on the back burner. It wasn't until after the war that the parachute divisions again became well trained and equipped forces.

Ironically, a year after the Kanev operation, the Western Allies had their own airborne failure at Arnhem. Paratroopers were dropped on the flat terrain in the Netherlands, and the Germans responded aggressively. This was yet another airborne failure, and with three divisions and a brigade the largest airborne operation of the war. Learning from their mistakes, the next major Allied airborne operation occurred in March 1945, when an American and a British airborne division dropped in support for the crossing of the Rhine (at Wesel) by Montgomery's army group. This took place in daylight, with total air supremacy, and within range of 3,000 pieces of artillery. This was the last large paratrooper drop into combat in history. Smaller operations have been carried out, with mixed success. And by the way, the tale that Russian paratroopers jumped without chutes in the winter (to land in the snow) is based on the rare practice of having espionage agents jump from very low-flying and slow aircraft (to land in the snow). It's amazing how these tall tales change as they get passed around. Jumping without a chute is never practical.

AN AXIS OF TANK UNITS

Every nation in World War II quickly saw the value of armored forces and they all strived to field some armored units. Each of Germany's allies had a slightly different situation when it came to scraping together an armored force.

The Germans had quite a few allies, although most were relatively minor military powers who did not have the industrial capacity to produce tanks (or had the industrial facilities but could not secure production rights for German tanks from the Reich). Despite the constant German shortage of tanks, the Nazis supplied armored vehicles to their allies for political and, to a lesser extent, military reasons. These are the number of tanks sold to each of their allies throughout the war:

	1940	1941	1942	1943	1944	Total
Bulgaria	37	40		111		188
Finland				30	47	77
Hungary			158	85	185	428
Romania			48		214	262
Slovakia		21		78		99
Spain				54		54
Total	37	61	206	358	446	1,108

In addition to the tanks the Germans sold to their allies, captured enemy vehicles (usually obsolete models) were sometimes sold to these Nazi allies.

How each of Germany's allies fared in its efforts to create armored forces is described below, nation by nation.

Bulgaria had a few obsolete Italian and British tanks when the war began. More tanks were obtained from Germany, although initially most were second-rate, and secondhand, stuff. The Bulgarians never formed anything larger than an armored brigade, and their combat experience was limited to fighting Yugoslav partisans for the Germans and, after September 1944 when they switched sides, fighting against the Germans.

Croatia was a puppet state the Germans set up from a chunk of Yugoslavia populated largely by Croats. Local armed forces were organized and assisted the Germans in fighting Yugoslav partisans. The Germans gave the Croats several dozen light tanks (captured earlier from France and other nations). The Croats did not have any armored units as such and simply used their otherwise obsolete light tanks to support infantry operations against partisans.

The Finns had a few dozen British tanks early in the war and captured nearly two hundred more from the Russians. The remainder they bought from the Germans. The Finns didn't need many tanks, as their forces were generally on the defensive for most of the war. An armored division was formed but was used largely as a reserve against Russian armored attacks.

Hungary manufactured some of its own tanks, a Swedish light tank built under license. It also acquired some light tanks from Italy and built medium tanks (of mediocre performance) of its own design before it was occupied by the Germans in March 1944. The Hungarians sent two armored divisions into combat, but, as their equipment was largely light tanks, these units did not perform very well.

Italy built the tanks it needed for its own use. Many of the designs were second-rate and as a result Italian tank units usually got the worst of it. The Germans eventually gave the Italians permission to manufacture Panzer IVs, but that was in early 1943, by which time the Italians were just beginning to produce a decent tank of their own. And in any case, it was pretty much a matter of "too little, too late," for Italy would shortly drop out of the war.

Romania began the war with some French and Czech light tanks. New equipment came from the Germans and one armored division was formed. This unit (still with its German equipment) fought alongside Russian units when Romania switched sides in August 1944.

Slovakia was created when Germany dismembered Czechoslovakia in 1939. The Germans supplied their new client nation with generally obsolete tanks captured from earlier victims. The Slovaks formed a division-sized mechanized unit (the Fast Corps) which was largely destroyed in Russia.

Spain was sort of allied with Germany in the war but by 1943 was feeling secure enough to begin breaking its ties. In an attempt to bribe the Spanish into continuing to support Germany, Hitler authorized the sale of fifty-four Pz-IVs and four StuG-III assault guns. Although Franco used these and a battalion of Russian T-26 tanks captured during the Spanish Civil War to form an armored division, he continued distancing himself from Hitler. In the 1950s, Franco sold the obsolete Pz-IVs to Syria, and they were later captured by the Israelis in 1967.

WHAT "USA" MEANT TO A SLOVAK

The United States shipped thousands of tanks and other armored vehicles to the Soviet Union during the war. The Soviets took them off the ships and sent them right into action, after doing little more than painting a few slogans on them. This left the vehicles covered with serial numbers, shipping and inspection notes, and sundry other stenciled material (usually in white, against the army green the vehicles were painted). The numbers meant nothing to the Russian troops, and the written material even less as this stuff was in English and the

Russians used a different alphabet (Cyrillic). However, when the Russian units with their American tanks entered Eastern Europe, they encountered populations that did use the Roman alphabet. They still couldn't read the English inscriptions all over these Russian tanks, but they could guess. One popular "translation" (concocted by Communist political officers) of the "USA" found in many places on these tanks was *Ubiyat Sukensyna Adolfa* ("Kill that son of a bitch Adolf"). Most Russians, however, knew where the trucks really came from. But this was the era of Stalin, so most Russians kept their thoughts to themselves.

SAY IT BIG

If you've ever seen pictures of World War II Russian tanks, you may have noted many with large, white lettering (as large as three feet high) on the sides of the turrets. As these inscriptions are in Cyrillic (the Russian alphabet), most Westerners have no idea what these words mean. The lettering served the same purpose as a lot of the symbols painted on the noses of Allied aircraft. The Russians rarely used illustrations, preferring to spell out their messages. Typical inscriptions would say "On to Berlin," "Death to Fascists," "To the West," "Kill the Fascist Snakes," and similar warlike exhortations. Another common inscription was the name of the organization (school, factory, town) that had raised the money to "buy" that tank. Such sponsorship was common, and it served as another means to get everyone involved in the war effort (and take a lot of money out of circulation, as with the severe wartime rationing, there wasn't much to buy anyhow). Some tanks had more whimsical markings, such as the names of folk heroes, historical personalities, or mythical creatures. As the war went on, inscriptions denoting a tank's previous accomplishments, such as "Liberator of Kiev" began to appear. Oddly enough, one symbol that only rarely appeared on Soviet tanks was the red star. While standard on Soviet aircraft, official policy appears to have prohibited this symbol on armored vehicles.

NATURALLY

When the American Chief of Naval Operations, Admiral Ernest J. King, remarked upon the stirring courage of the Red Army, Stalin replied, "It takes a brave man not to be a hero in the Red Army."

A BAD YEAR

Nearly 80 percent of the males born in the Soviet Union in 1923 did not survive World War II. The war was also hard on the females born in that year, as many were unable to find husbands. In recognition of this situation, after the war the Soviet government urged men (married or not) to help these "war widows" to get pregnant so they could at least have children, even if their potential husbands had been killed during the war. Many of the elderly and impoverished Russian women seen in the wake of the Cold War are these same women born in the early 1920s, only to see their hopes for a family killed during World War II battles.

5

THE WAR IN THE WEST, 1941–1945

After France fell in 1940, most of the World War II fighting moved away from Western Europe until the Allies invaded France in June 1944. But all was not quiet in the area. Partisan activity grew steadily in France and other European countries. The fighting continued in nearby Africa, and in 1943 first Sicily and then Italy were invaded by Allied troops. For most Americans, the war in Western Europe is what they normally think of as World War II. That, and the island fighting in the Pacific.

LILI MARLENE

The most famous song of World War II, and the only one popular on both sides, was "Lili Marlene," a sentimental air in which a battle-weary soldier on some far-off front recalls a woman who used to meet him "underneath the lamppost, by the barracks gate."

"Lili Marlene" had its origin in a poem written in 1923 by Hans Leip, a World War I veteran who had in mind a number of women he had known during the kaiser's war. Several attempts were made to set the poem to music over the next few years, none of them very successful. Then in 1936 Norbert Schultze, a minor tunesmith, wrote new music. In 1939 the song was recorded by the Swedish-born singer Lala Anderson and it became moderately popular. Shortly after the occupation of Yugoslavia, a German armed forces radio station was established in Belgrade. One of the men assigned to the station had a close friend in the Afrika Korps who had been fond of the tune. So he played Lala Anderson's recording of "Lili Marlene" for his friend, airing it for the first time on the night of August 18, 1941. He soon made the song the signature of his musical program, playing it in full each night at 9:55, shortly before he went off the air.

German troops in North Africa picked up the song and were soon followed by their Italian comrades. It was not long before it became popular among British troops as well, since they too listened to Radio Belgrade, which played much better popular music than did BBC-influenced British military radio. The British passed on their enthusiasm for the tune to their American cousins during the Tunisian campaign, and it became even more popular after the German but decidedly anti-Nazi Marlene Dietrich recorded it, and even starred in a film based on it. Eventually translated into several different languages (there are English, French, Italian, Spanish, and even Hebrew versions), "Lili Marlene" retained its popularity among veterans, particularly German veterans, after the war. Leip and Schultze were still collecting royalties of about $4,000 a year into the early 1970s.

GOOD FOR YOU!

Although Iceland was a dependency of Denmark, its position in the North Atlantic preserved it from Nazi occupation when the Germans overran its motherland in early 1940. The Icelanders invited the British, and later the Americans, in to help them defend themselves. Otherwise, life went on more or less as before. Finally, in 1944 the Icelanders decided to go their own way and declared their independence. In distant Copenhagen, King Christian X, then under house arrest for his support of resistance to the Nazi occupiers, sent a telegram of congratulations to his rebellious subjects.

HIS ONLY ERROR?

The only nation against which Germany issued a formal declaration of war was the United States, on December 11, 1941. Hitler did this because he hoped that his show of Axis solidarity would induce the Japanese to reciprocate and declare war on the Soviet Union. This would force the Russians to fight on two fronts at one of the most critical junctures of the war, when Hitler's panzers were being driven back from the gates of Moscow by the first successful Soviet offensive of the war. The Japanese, however, had already had a taste of Russian abilities in their unofficial clashes with the Red Army at Nomonhan and elsewhere along the Manchurian-Siberian frontier before the war. As a result, they failed to return the favor (although they strung the Nazis along for some time, not coming right out and saying so). Hitler also believed that the United States would eventually enter the war anyway, and that the sooner Germany could unleash its submarines against the vulnerable North Atlantic shipping lanes, the better. The United States was already sending enormous quantities of war materials to Great Britain and, as long as the United States was technically neutral, German U-boats could not be used to their full effectiveness (as in right off the U.S. coast).

THE KAISER DIES HAPPY

German Kaiser Wilhelm II, who ordered Germany into World War I, fled to exile in the Netherlands in late 1918. Bitter about subsequent events in Germany, the kaiser viewed Hitler as a political thug. A man not noted for noble qualities, the kaiser did show a touch of class early in World War II. When the Nazi armies were overrunning the Netherlands in May 1940, the British government offered him asylum. The erstwhile kaiser replied by saying that he could not, in their moment of need, abandon the Dutch people, who had provided him shelter in his moment of need. Despite this, the kaiser congratulated Hitler after France fell. The führer was less than impressed and ordered that no honors be rendered to the former monarch, nearly sacking a general who had posted guards around the kaiser's modest house in Doorn in 1940. On June 4, 1941, the kaiser died, perhaps content in the knowledge that Germany was triumphant everywhere, or perhaps annoyed that the thugs who succeeded him had accomplished what he had not. Many members of the royal family continued to take a dim view of the Nazis (as did much of the old German nobility). However, a number of aristocrats served Hitler willingly. The kaiser's eldest grandson, and second heir to the throne of Germany, was killed in action during the Polish campaign in 1939. His funeral touched off a monarchist demonstration in Berlin, whereupon Hitler banned all members of the former royal families of Germany from service at the front. Despite this, one of the kaiser's other grandsons was an enthusiastic Nazi and became a general in the Waffen SS.

THE SECOND FRONTS

When the Germans invaded Russia in June 1941, they instantly created the alliance that would defeat them. Even though the United States didn't declare war for another six months, Great Britain almost immediately used U.S. economic aid to support Russia, and the United States soon began direct lend-lease shipments. But what the Soviets really wanted was for the Western Allies to engage more German ground forces. In 1941, over 80 percent of the German divisions were rampaging through Russia. The Soviets wanted a "second front." What they had in mind did not take place until June 1944, with the D-Day invasion. But in the meantime the Western Allies (Great Britain, the United States, Canada, sundry governments in exile, and others) managed to distract the Germans in several ways. The net result was a considerable easing of the pressure on the Soviets. Consider the location of German combat divisions each June during the war. The Soviets screamed the loudest for a second front in 1942, when the Germans went on another of their summer romps across the steppes. America was still mobilizing in that year, and

Location of German Combat Divisions*

	1941	1942	1943	1944
Soviet Union	134/32	171/34	179/28	157/30
France†	38/0	27/3	42/8	56/11
Norway‡	13/0	16.5/0.5	16.5/0.5	16/0
Denmark	1.0/0	1.0/0	2.0/0	3.5/1.5
Balkans	7/0	8/1	17/1	20/4
Italy	0/0	0/0	0/0	22/6
Africa	2/2	3/3	0/0	0/0
Total	195.0/34.0	226.5/41.5	256.5/37.5	274.5/52.5

* For June of each year indicated, divisions here are: total divisions/motorized divisions. The motorized divisions were mostly armored units; some were "motorized infantry" with fewer tanks than an armored division.
†Includes Belgium and the Netherlands.
‡Includes a few divisions that were in Finland.

Percentage of German Forces in the Soviet Union

	1941	1942	1943	1944
Divisions	67/94	75/82	60/75	57/57
Troops	84	74	72	40
Aircraft	64	65	42	45

Great Britain was already showing signs of strain going into its third year of war. But the Russians hung on. The Stalingrad campaign at the end of 1942 stopped the Germans. El Alamein and an Anglo-American amphibious invasion of North Africa in late 1942 ended German expansion in that theater. In May 1943 Italian and German forces in Africa were destroyed (costing Germany six motorized divisions). Then the Allies landed in Sicily, and later that year Italy surrendered, so the Germans had to rush divisions in to hold Italy and take over occupation duties from Italian troops in southern France, Greece, and Yugoslavia. While many German divisions were left in Russia, most of the replacements and reinforcements began going to Italy, the Balkans, and the south of France. The loss of Italy had indeed opened up another front in late 1943. Two dozen divisions that could have been in Russia were instead fighting Allied troops (in Italy) and Yugoslav or Greek partisans (in the Balkans). But the drying up of new men and material for the divisions in the Soviet Union was even more helpful to the Soviets. Many German divisions became mere skeletons. The growing Allied bombing of Germany also diverted aircraft replacements from the Soviet front to the air war over Germany itself. As a result, the Soviets were increasingly able to obtain air superiority. Right until the end, the German pilots and aircraft were better. But the Russians proved once again that "quantity has a quality all its own."

One of the less-heralded "second fronts" was Norway. Throughout the war the Germans were keenly aware of the long coastline Norway possessed and its vulnerability to an amphibious invasion. The Allies played on this fear, letting slip, from time to time, little tidbits about possible Norwegian adventures. This tied up a significant number of divisions throughout the war. In fact, the various operations of the Western Allies provided several "second fronts" that together led to a gradual shrinking of the portion of German forces facing the Russians.

GUERRILLAS IN ARMOR

The Yugoslav partisans, among their other distinctions, maintained some armored forces throughout their four-year battle for liberation. Guerrillas rarely operated tanks. For one thing, they had a hard time obtaining them. Moreover, tanks require a lot of maintenance, supply, and other support. Guerrillas keep moving and customarily travel light. But the Yugoslavs had two things going for them. First, for the initial two years of their war, the major occupation force consisted of Italians. Not very eager to battle partisans, the Italians often followed a "live and let live" policy. This allowed the partisans sufficient leeway to maintain those tanks they captured from the Italians.

Neither the Italians, nor later the Germans, sent much armor to Yugoslavia and most of what was used were light tanks captured earlier from the French. Italians also used their own light tanks, knowing these were not of much use against heavier British and Russian models in other areas where Italian units were in combat. By 1944, the partisans had over fifty captured tanks in running condition, organized into several "battalions." Later that year, the British supplied the partisans with a battalion of fifty-six light tanks and twenty-four armored cars. The crews for these vehicles were trained in Italy and landed (with their vehicles) in Yugoslavia in November 1944. The battalion then fought its way inland. The Russians equipped a partisan tank brigade (sixty-five T-34s) which then went to Yugoslavia and fought alongside other partisan units. Thus when the Germans finally evacuated Yugoslavia, they had to do so in great haste lest they be trapped by guerrilla armored units.

AIRPLANES KILLING AIRPLANES

During the air campaign against Germany the final (and for much of the war the only) line of defense of heavy bombers against interceptors was their own machine guns (and, to a lesser extent, those of nearby fighter escorts). In the course of operations against targets in Europe the Eighth Air Force (bombers and fighter escorts), which flew out of Great Britain, expended 76.9 million rounds of .50-caliber machine-gun ammunition plus nearly 0.7 million rounds of .30-caliber ammo, to account for 6,098 enemy aircraft, a ratio of about 12,700 rounds per kill. The Fifteenth Air Force, flying from Italy, expended about 30 million rounds of .50-caliber ammunition, downing 2,110 enemy aircraft, or about one for every 14,200 rounds fired. This may seem like a tremendous waste of ammunition, but the German antiaircraft gunners opposing the bombers were getting only about one kill for every 12,000 rounds fired, and that quite often with the vaunted 88mm antiaircraft gun. In any event, the target was moving fast and trying hard not to get hit. The bomber gunners, in particular, did not have a wide field of fire, as the bombers generally flew straight and level. The fighters would flash by, and the gunners would let loose with as many rounds as they could in the scant few seconds the enemy was in view.

THE DESERT WAR

The protracted duel between the Axis forces and the Allies in the deserts of Libya and Egypt has generally been regarded as the last "gentlemanly" war. It was as bloody and brutal as any war, but there was a distinct lack of atrocities of the sort that characterized the conduct of war in the other theaters, even Western Europe. It began when a large, but almost wholly nonmotorized, Italian army advanced into Egypt in September 1940. Rather quickly outrunning their supplies, the Italians settled into a series of fortified camps some miles inside Egypt. And there they remained. In early December, Sir Richard O'Connor, with the British 7th Armored Division and an infantry division in support, undertook a bold offensive. Taking advantage of the Italians' lack of mobility, and the fact that their fortified positions were not mutually supportable, he quickly overran the forward Italian formations and then proceeded westward. Despite often heroic resistance, press releases to the contrary notwithstanding, the relatively immobile Italians were incapable of coping with the fully motorized British, Indian, and Australian divisions with which O'Connor conducted his offensive. As a result, within about two months the Italians' position in North Africa was at best precarious and they had been driven about halfway into Libya. But then the offensive was halted in February 1941 for political reasons, the Allied troops being needed in Greece.

This coincided with the arrival in North Africa of Erwin Rommel, one of Hitler's protégés (he had for a time commanded the führer's SS bodyguard), a panzer officer with a fine record from France in 1940. Collecting what he could find at hand, portions of a German division and some Italian motorized formations, Rommel undertook his own offensive in late March 1941. Aided by the fact that his opponents had dispersed their troops all over eastern Libya, and the fortuitous capture of O'Connor, Rommel threw the British back even faster than they had driven out the Italians, and with relatively slender forces at that. But he proved unable to take the fortified city of Tobruk. Between late April and mid-November a lot of seesaw fighting took place along the Libyan-Egyptian frontier. Rommel, his army increased to several German and Italian armored and motorized divisions, plus several "semi-motorized" Italian formations, tried to invest Tobruk and beat off British attempts to relieve the place at the same time. He was mostly successful. But in November a greatly reinforced British army chased him all the way back to his starting position.

Barely a month later, Rommel, reinforced, and benefiting from the fact that the Japanese had just jumped on the British Empire at the other end of the world, undertook a new offensive, which in two weeks (January 21–February 4, 1942) brought him rapidly back to the vicinity of Tobruk. There, in front of the city, the British had constructed an elaborate defensive system, the Gazala Line. And there the exhausted Italo-German troops settled in for a long stalemate. In late May, aware that the British buildup was exceeding his own, Rommel received permission to resume the offensive. In a spectacular series of battles, Rommel outflanked, and then broke into the British position, nearly trapping several divisions (which escaped without most of their heavy equipment). The Battle of Gazala lasted from May 26 to June 13, 1942; Tobruk fell on June 21. During the next nine days the Italo-German forces advanced over two hundred miles to a place called El Alamein. It was there, on a front of about thirty miles which ran from the Mediterranean to the Qatarra Depression, a large, virtually impassable salt marsh, that British Commander Sir Claude Auchinleck chose to make a stand. In a series of desperate mobile battles during early July the exhausted German and Italian mechanized forces were halted by the British. Both sides settled into what can only be termed a World War II version of World War I: extensive wired-in field fortifications.

In late August and early September Rommel again tried to break the British defenses. But a combination of Axis bad luck, British Ultra-intelligence, Auchinleck's excellent planning, and a new British commander, Bernard Law Montgomery, resulted in a severe defeat in the Battle of Alam El Halfa. As the cautious Montgomery decided not to attempt an immediate offensive of his own, both armies camped out on the El Alamein Line for nearly two months.

On October 23, 1942, Montgomery's British Eighth Army began the Battle of El Alamein. In the face of greatly superior forces, the Axis troops held him for a week. Then, on November 2, the British broke

The Divisions of the Desert War, 1940–1942

	British			German			Italian		
	Armored 40	Armored 42A	Armored 42B	Infantry	Armored	Motorized	Infantry	Motorized	Armored
Troops	10.8	13.2	14.2	17.5	14.4	13.9	10.6	12.5	8.6
Tanks	342	230	186	0	163	48	5	48	189
Battalions									
Tank	6	3	3	0	2	1	0	1	3
Infantry	3	3	3	10	6	6	9	9	4
Artillery	2.0	1.6	4.0	5.0	6.0	5.0	5.0	5.0	9.0
Reconnaissance	1	1	1	1	1	1	0	1	1
Engineer	1.0	2.5	1.0	1.0	1.0	1.0	1.0	1.0	1.0
Signal	0	1.0	1	1	1	1	0	1	0
Rating	11	12	14	9	20	14	8	13	10

NOTES: Troops is the number of men in a division, in thousands. In addition to tanks, all of these formations had varying numbers of other armored fighting vehicles, ranging from armored cars to self-propelled artillery pieces. In Battalion, .3 indicates a company. Artillery includes antitank and antiaircraft battalions. In some armies, signals were subsumed in the engineers. Rating, an approximation of the fighting power of the division for purposes of comparing its relative capabilities, is a rough mathematical calculation of the relative fighting power of each division, combining manpower, equipment, and organizational and doctrinal factors.

through. Despite heroic efforts to restore the line, by November 5 Rommel's forces were in full retreat, and thousands of transportless troops, German and Italian alike, had to be abandoned to their fate in their fortified positions. The retreat was masterfully conducted. With the Anglo-American landings in northwest Africa on November 8, it was clear that the desert war was over.

The formations indicated in the table are the primary ones involved in the desert campaign. On the Axis side they omit the wholly nonmotorized Italian formations that were defeated in late 1940, and several unique formations (e.g., the German 164th Light Division and the Italian Folgore Parachute Division) that were involved. Their repeated defeats at Rommel's hands forced the British to several times reorganize their armored divisions. The German divisions in the campaign were organized and equipped rather differently than were comparable outfits in other theaters: Rommel had a tendency to "mix and match" elements from his divisions anyway, so there were at times no firm divisional structures. Italian divisions underwent some changes as well but on the whole tended to get better during the campaign, due partially to improvements in equipment and partially to increasing skill derived from greater experience. By the way, the rather impressive-looking artillery contingent of the Italian armored division actually represents the presence of several rather small specialized battalions: The total number of pieces of artillery, whether field, antitank, or antiair, was only seventy-four, counting everything from 47mm antitank guns on up (albeit excluding A/T pieces on tanks), proportionally about the same as that for a British or German division.

STATISTIC

It is estimated that during World War II the average Berlin apartment yielded 12.7 cubic meters of rubble after being bombed.

LOTTA METAL UP THERE

Allied bombers approaching their target knew they would eventually hit a "wall" of flak (from a German word meaning "antiaircraft fire"). Since early in the war, most antiaircraft units followed the practice of firing "barrages" of heavy (75mm and larger) shells with timer-equipped fuses that would cause explosions at a specified altitude. A network of observers sent reports to a command post, and there the speed, direction, and altitude of the bombers was calculated. Further calculations determined when the guns should fire, for how long, and at what altitude they should set their shells to explode. The gunners simply cranked the guns to the required angle and direction, set the fuses, and fired the number of rounds they were ordered to. They could usually hear the bombers, but as many of the raids were at night, they could not always see them. Searchlights were also used, but these were to assist the night fighters, which, naturally, operated away from their own barrages. The Germans, in particular, continually refined this barrage technique, especially the use of heavier-caliber (120mm–150mm) guns. Even so, throughout the war, it took several thousand shells to score one hit and the heavy Allied bombers needed many hits to bring them down. Over 12,000 heavy bombers were brought down during the war, so you can imagine the number of shells that were fired.

COMPARATIVE TONNAGE

World War II was very much the "golden age" of aerial bombing. Between 1939 and 1945, Allied forces dropped an average of 47,700 tons of bombs each month. Bombing activity was slow at first. The bombing campaign didn't really get going until 1943, with 1944 being the peak year. It wasn't until Vietnam that the bombing in another war came even close. This was largely due to a new generation of aircraft that could carry more bombs faster, farther, and with a smaller crew. Korea did not even come close to World War II in terms of tonnage. For the most part, the bombers in the Korean War were of World War II vintage. Over 50,000 heavy bombers were built by the Allies during World War II. But although 12,000 were shot down during the war, most of the surviving aircraft were destroyed or simply abandoned to rot after it. So there weren't many left to fight the Korean War in 1950–1953. When Vietnam came along, the new generation of aircraft was much more efficient than their World War II ancestors. The B-17 carried 4 tons of bombs, the B-52 carried over 30 tons. Even the F-4 Phantom fighter bomber could carry more than a B-17, travel nearly as far, move three times faster, and had a crew of two versus eleven for the B-17.

Tonnage of Bombs Dropped

		Monthly Average	Total
World War I	(1914–1918)	17	870*
World War II	(1939–1945)	47,700	3,435,000
Korean War	(1950–1953)	12,800	460,000
Vietnam War	(1964–1973)	44,000	4,225,000
Gulf War	(1991)	40,400	80,000

---

* Figure is approximate.

AH, THERE YOU ARE

Old, or sometimes relatively new, habits die hard. During World War I it was found useful to equip aircraft machine guns with tracer rounds. These are bullets with a colored pyrotechnic material added to the hollow base of the projectile. These left a colorful trail behind the bullet (like some fireworks) and let the pilot know where the bullets were going. Usually, every fifth bullet in the machine gun's ammunition belt would be a tracer round.

Initially, some aircraft units carried this custom over into World War II. It didn't work so well in that war. For one thing, the aircraft were now larger, faster, and had enclosed cockpits. This made tracers a liability, and it took awhile for pilots using them to catch on. Tracers became a liability in World War II because the distance between the firing aircraft and the target had increased. This was largely because not only were the aircraft larger and faster than the World War I biplanes, they were simply not as agile. World War II aircraft also tended to use longer-range weapons (13mm and 20mm rather than 7.7mm machine guns). This made longer-range shooting more practical. At these longer ranges, the hollow-base tracer bullets had different flight characteristics, with the tracer rounds going one way and the nontracer rounds going another. Since 20 percent or less of the bullets fired were tracers, the pilot was concentrating on getting only a few of his bullets on the target.

Another problem arose because pilots were now flying in enclosed cockpits. (Some aircraft flew with the cockpit enclosure partially open, but these were mainly slower, and older, single-engine bombers.) To World War II fighter pilots flying in a sealed environment the engine was much noisier. The end result was that while World War I pilots in open cockpits could hear enemy bullets going by (a sharp "crack" sound is made when a bullet goes by, the result of the bullet breaking the sound barrier), World War II pilots could not. Unless the enemy was firing tracers. When a pilot saw tracers going by, he knew that he was being shot at and would promptly take evasive action. Since most air-to-air kills were the result of surprising the enemy (shooting at someone who did not see you), the use of tracers let your target know he was a target.

Some units were also in the habit of putting ten or twenty tracer bullets all together near the end of the machine gun's ammunition belt. This would let the pilot know that he was almost out of ammunition. But the enemy soon got wise to this and they also knew when a pilot was nearly out of ammo. This is not the kind of information you want to share with the enemy.

Before World War II, there was not enough air-to-air combat for all air forces to become aware of the problems with tracers. Training did not involve pilots shooting at each other with live ammunition. Thus it wasn't until a year or so into World War II that most air forces became aware that tracers had turned from an asset to a liability. Units that dropped tracers from their ammunition supply saw their kills increase 50 to 100 percent, while their own losses declined.

THE BIGGEST BATTLE, AROUND THE CLOCK, UP THERE

One of the largest, longest, and most violent and destructive campaigns of World War II hardly gets noticed. The British and American air war against Germany pitted 1.5 million Allied troops and 69,000 aircraft against 2.2 million German troops (plus 2 million civilians repairing the damage) and 61,000 Nazi aircraft. While these air attacks against Germany began in 1939, they didn't really get going big time until 1943, when the "Strategic Bombing Offensive" got going. The four-engine strategic bombers dropped 1.5 million tons of bombs, while all other combat aircraft (single- and two-engine) dropped another 1.1 million tons.

There were actually two bombing campaigns going on against German factories, cities, transportation, and armed forces. The British had a peak of 718,628 pilots and ground crew who dropped 1.2 million tons of bombs, mostly at night. The Americans had a peak of 619,020 troops supporting the dropping of 1.5 million tons of bombs, mostly in daylight: this was about 75 percent of total bomb tonnage dropped by U.S. Army Air Force worldwide in the entire war. Losses were heavy, as 159,000 airmen became casualties (about evenly split between British Commonwealth and American). Aircraft losses were enormous, with 21,914 bombers lost (11,965 British) and 18,465 fighters (10,045 British). The bombers flew 1.5 million sorties and had a loss rate of 15 per 1,000 sorties. The fighters flew 2.7 million sorties, for a loss rate of 7 per 1,000 sorties. It was actually worse than it appears for the bombers, as many that survived their missions would still be shot up and have dead and wounded crew on board. Most of these missions were flown out of Great Britain. Half the bomb tonnage was dropped on Germany, with another 22 percent landing on France. Aircraft based in Italy accounted for most of the bombs delivered to Italy (14 percent), Austria, Hungary, the Balkans (7 percent), and sundry other locations (the remaining 7 percent).

The major reason the bombing campaign does not get much attention in history books is because the action was widely spread out, generally took place in enemy territory, and in many cases, had no appreciable effect on the conduct of the war. While the air power advocates preached that the bombing campaign would be decisive, this was not the case. But the bombing did make a major contribution to Allied victory and hurt the Germans quite a bit. The big problem the bomber generals had from the start was what to bomb. There were so many targets, and it took a little trial and error before they found out which targets would cause the most grief for the Germans. Overall, however, these were the target "systems" hit throughout the war and the percentage of the bombs that fell on them:

INDUSTRIAL AREAS: 36.4 percent, factories, for the most part (about two thirds). Nearly 24 percent of this went specifically after oil, chemical, and rubber targets. Some 4 percent was devoted to aircraft factories.

TRANSPORTATION: 36.3 percent, mainly railroads, especially marshaling and repair yards, bridges, tunnels, and locomotives; also bridges and tunnels for roads. About 12 percent of this (4.2 percent of all bombs) was for naval and water transportation (canal traffic).

MILITARY TARGETS: 11.1 percent, units themselves, as well as their equipment and any structures they were using.

AIRFIELDS and air force installations: 6.9 percent.

V-1 ("buzz bombs") and V-2 (from which the Scud missile was derived) launching sites: 0.2 percent.

ALL OTHER TARGETS: 6.3 percent.

When the bombing campaign got started in 1943, it was thought that hitting key factories would deprive German industry of vital components (such as ball bearings) that would render many other factories useless. It didn't work out that way, as the Germans were able to shift production faster than the bombers could trace and bomb the new plants. In early 1944 it was decided to attack transportation. Partially, this was in support of the upcoming D-Day invasion of France. In the course of the year the Allies discovered that hitting transportation had widespread effects. Not only were German combat units unable to move quickly to the front, but factories were unable to ship finished goods and components. The earlier bombing had forced the Germans to disperse a lot of their industrial machinery and assembly operations to smaller (and often hidden or underground) locations. This made them more dependent on the railroads. The Allies thought the railroads were too extensive to be knocked out. This was true, up to a point. But by concentrating on shooting up locomotives (fighter pilots loved this) and bombing rail yards (where the scarce locomotives were repaired) the rail system was severely hurt. The loss of the Romanian oil fields in August 1944, combined with the difficulty in shipping fuel by rail, put a severe crimp in German mobility. This was something that the Allied ground troops noticed only gradually. But the German ground troops were slowed down, and overall, this made it easier for Allied troops, increased German casualties, and shortened the war.

Another side effect of the bombing campaign was the decline of the Luftwaffe (which, to the U.S. Army Air Force, was the principal objective of the bombing). Allied troops had less and less to fear from air attack as the war went on. This was because a larger percentage of Luftwaffe aircraft had to be reassigned to air defense over Germany. The percentage grew steadily as the war went on.

Losses against bomber formations were higher than those against ground units. The bombers were more heavily armed and, increas-

---

Percentage of Luftwaffe Aircraft Used Only Against Allied Bombers

June 1940	0
June 1941	7
June 1942	17
June 1943	21
June 1944	39
January 1945	50

Percentage of All Allied Bombs Dropped

1940	0.8
1941	2.0
1942	3.0
1943	12.8
1944	57.9
1945	23.5

ingly, had fighter escorts. By late 1944, it was rare for Allied troops to suffer air attacks by the Germans. The strategic bombing campaign was largely responsible for this. The Germans, however, did still get their licks in from time to time. Toward the end of the war, some Allied troops had the unnerving experience of being strafed by German jet aircraft. The German Me-262 was the first jet fighter bomber to enter wide service. It was often used for ground attack missions. It was so fast, and the firepower of its four automatic cannons so devastating, that the troops under fire usually had no time to fire back.

There were other subtle effects of the bombing. The British did most of their bombing at night (they didn't believe daylight bombing would work). Almost all American bombing was in daylight. Because bombing accuracy at night was low, the British hit large areas (like cities) rather than specific targets (like factories). Thus a German industrial area was hit during the day and then, quite often, again at night. This left the Germans without sleep and quite anxious and contributed to lower worker productivity. The loss of homes and loved ones and the expectation of being injured also had an effect on worker enthusiasm. But production went on anyway.

The biggest failure of the bombing campaign was to effectively explain just what its accomplishments were. This was understandable during the war, when even the bomber generals didn't know exactly what effect their efforts were having. In contrast, ground and naval campaigns move to different physical locations and occupy enemy territory. After a land or naval battle, you can immediately get a pretty good count of what was lost on both sides. Air campaigns lack these features, and as a result are still not accurately appreciated by the public, the other branches of the armed forces, or even many historians.

THE AIR EDGE

While the German Luftwaffe made quite a reputation for itself early in the war, it was severely outnumbered from 1942 on. This table tells the tale.

Allied and German Combat Aircraft Available in the European Theater

	British	U.S.	Soviet	ALLIED TOTAL	German	ALLIED RATIO
June 1942	9,500	—	2,100	11,600	3,700	3.1:1
December 1942	11,300	1,300	3,800	16,400	3,400	4.8:1
June 1943	12,700	5,000	5,600	23,300	4,600	5.1:1
December 1943	11,800	7,500	8,800	28,100	4,700	6.0:1
June 1944	13,200	11,800	14,700	39,700	4,600	8.6:1
December 1944	14,500	12,200	15,800	42,500	8,500	5.0:1

The big shift in numerical superiority came in 1942 as U.S. industrial strength entered the fray. The United States sent aircraft and industrial materials to Great Britain and Russia, enabling these two nations to increase their air strength. Germany made a major error in not putting its war production on a war footing until 1943. German aircraft production thus peaked in 1944, when it was too late. Worse, Great Britain and the United States began a major bombing campaign of Germany in 1943. This required increasing numbers of German aircraft to be dedicated to air defense instead of supporting the struggle with Russia. In 1944, half of all German combat aircraft were assigned to the defense of the air over Germany. Even with that degree of effort, the Germans were still vastly outnumbered in their own airspace. In the last six months of 1944, the Allies had an average of 3,000 aircraft (bombers and their fighter escorts) a day over Germany. In that same period, the Germans could put up only about 400 fighters. Worst of all, during 1944 the Germans lost the qualitative edge in the air. During that year, Allied aircraft quality generally matched that of German planes. Moreover, the worsening fuel situation prevented the Germans from providing adequate flying time for their new pilots. The combination was devastating, and in 1944 the Allies obtained air superiority over every area in which the Germans were fighting.

PASS THE GAS

The mighty B-17 bomber was designed to carry bombs, right? Not quite. When a B-17 took off on a typical mission it carried 4 tons of bombs, and 11 tons of fuel. There was also 1.3 tons of .50-caliber bullets for the machine guns. The crew and their personal equipment weighed in at about 1 ton or so.

LIFE-GIVING LIQUID

No factor contributed more to a new pilot's success in combat than the number of hours he spent flying before going into action. Germany's fortunes in the air began to change when it could no longer produce enough fuel to allow its pilot trainees sufficient time in the air. This was a trend that had been ongoing since 1942. In that year, and since 1939, new pilots got 240 hours of flying time before entering combat (British pilots received only 200 hours and Soviet pilots even less). But in late 1942, Germany reduced training time to 205 hours (while the British increased theirs to 240 hours, and the United States was providing 270 hours). In the summer of 1943, the British increased flying time to 335 hours and the United States went to 320 hours. At the same time, the Germans reduced it to 170 hours. A year later, the Germans were down to 110 hours, while the British were at 340 hours and the Americans at 360. Five hours of fighter training requires about a ton of fuel. As the war went on, the Germans had fewer tons of fuel for anything.

THE TALE OF THE TAPE

The performance of air forces is measured in the number of sorties, and the number of friendly and enemy losses per thousand sorties. (A sortie is one aircraft making one flight to perform its mission— bombing or fighter escort.) The Germans were decidedly superior in the beginning of the war, but as the Allies obtained more, and better, aircraft and pilots, the situation changed. Consider the numbers for two campaigns at the beginning of the war, and the two toward the end.

Campaign	Total Sorties		Kills per 1,000 Sorties		Losses per 1,000 Sorties	
	Allied	Axis	Allied	Axis	Allied	Axis
France 1940	4,480	21,000	28.6	12.5	58.5	6.1
Britain 1940	31,000	42,000	21.8	29.5	29.5	19.6
1944 Pre–D-Day	98,400	34,500	12.7	29.3	10.3	36.1
1944 Post–D-Day	203,357	31,833	17.3	16.2	2.5	110.6

NOTES: France 1940: the battle for France between May 10 and June 20, 1940. The Germans were attacking and the outnumbered and desperate Allies were throwing everything into the battle they could in a losing attempt to stop the blitzkrieg. This accounts for the high kill rate for the Allies, and the even higher loss rate. The Germans were intent on supporting their ground forces with strafing and bombing. But the German fighters were superior enough to keep the Axis loss rate down.

Britain 1940: the Battle of Britain between July 10 and October 31, 1940. Germany attempted to soften up Great Britain preparatory to launching an amphibious invasion. Both sides took, and inflicted, tremendous losses. The British couldn't afford to lose, and the Germans gave up when they realized that they would have to sacrifice their air force in order to obtain air superiority. In that respect, it was a near thing for the British.

1944 Pre–D-Day: the air campaign that softened up the Germans before the D-Day invasion (April 6 to June 5, 1944). The Allied objective was twofold in this campaign. First, the Allies wanted to cripple the transportation network in France. This meant destroying most of the bridges and shooting up all the locomotives and trucks they could find. The Germans made a major effort to prevent this but failed. German losses were high; Allied losses were replaceable. The second objective was to destroy German air power in France.

1944 Post–D-Day: the air support of the invasion (June 6 to September 5, 1944). The air campaign begun in April picked up steam after the landings in Normandy. The Germans had to scrape the bottom of the barrel in order to match their effort in the earlier campaign. It was not good enough. The Allies more than doubled the number of sorties they flew. The Germans had lost many of their experienced pilots in the first campaign and the replacements were less well trained (and were often rushed through training in order to man the larger number of aircraft the Germans were producing).

WELL, IT MUST MEAN SOMETHING

A truly odd bit of data emanating from the war was the fact that aces (those with five or more air-to-air kills) tended to have blue or light-colored eyes (over two thirds), were shorter than average, and (later on in life) had more daughters than sons. This may mean something, but to date no one has figured out what.

ACES AND TARGETS

One of the more unpleasant aspects of air warfare is that there were only two kinds of pilots, aces (who shot down five or more aircraft) and targets (pilots who got shot down). There was no middle ground. There was no "average" pilot. During the war, a new pilot, on average, had about a 7 percent chance of being shot down on his first encounter with the enemy. As he experienced more combat, his chances of survival increased. By his tenth combat, his chances of getting shot down were less than 1 percent and tended to stay there for the rest of his career. Only 5 percent of pilots shot down five or more aircraft. The rest, for the most part, served mainly to provide victims for the aces in air-to-air combat. Only about a half of all pilots ever shot down another aircraft, and only 10 percent of that august group obtained five kills and qualified as an ace. Fortunately, many fighter pilots were able to apply themselves usefully in ground attack missions.

No one has yet figured out exactly what skills a pilot needs in order to become an ace. Flying skill and lots of training will help a pilot avoid being shot down but won't make him an ace. The only way you find out is to put the pilots in harm's way and see who are the natural killers, and who are the targets.

ELECTRONIC WARFARE

While it is generally thought that electronic warfare is a "modern" development, most of the devices used today were first developed, and saw wide use, during World War II. The following list of Allied and German electronic warfare equipment put into use during the air war over Europe is, in effect, a history of the beginnings of modern electronic warfare. Note that before the war began, the Germans, British, and Americans had radar sets. The British use of radar in the Battle of Britain (summer 1940) was a key element in winning that campaign. The Germans had radar ("Freya") in place by 1940 (three years after the British) but didn't appreciate the possibilities. Although U.S. radar detected incoming Japanese aircraft at Pearl Harbor, that warning was ignored. In 1942, America made good use of radar aboard its warships in the Pacific. The Germans were the first to put radar on a warship, in 1937 (on the "pocket battleship" *Graf Spee,* whose equipment the British retrieved after the ship scuttled itself in Montevideo harbor in 1940).

If you have read anything about the extensive electronic warfare activity during the 1991 Gulf War, you will notice that many of the items used in that war got their baptism of fire over Germany in the early 1940s.

Date	User	Item	Function
February 1940	Germany	Knickebein	Airborne navigation using signals from ground transmitters. Essential for accurate night bombing.
June 1940	Germany	Wurzburg	Improved ground radar with a 40-km range. Could plot altitude and was used to control flak guns.
September 1940	Allies	Asperin	Jammers to block use of Kickebein.
September 1940	Germany	Freya	Improved ground radar with a 120-km range. Could not detect altitude but gave early warning of bomber approach.
October 1940	Germany	Wurzburg II	Pair of radars used, one to track bombers and another to track German interceptors. Deadly when used at night.
September 1941	Germany	Wurzburg Reise	Improved Wurzburg with a 65-km range.
February 1942	Germany	Lichtenstein	Airborne radar for night fighters. Range varied from 200 to 3,000 meters.
March 1942	Germany	Mammut	More powerful early-warning radar with a range of 330 kilometers. Could not plot altitude.
March 1942	Germany	Wassermann	More powerful early-warning radar with a range of 240 kilometers. Could plot altitude.
March 1942	Allies	Gee	Airborne navigation using signals from ground transmitters. At 600 kilometers from transmitters, aircraft knew location to within 10 kilometers.

Date	*User*	*Item*	*Function*
June 1942	Allies	Shaker	Gee-equipped "Pathfinder" aircraft drop bombs blind, to provide aiming points for other equipped night bombers following.
August 1942	Allies	Moonshine	Aircraft device that detected Freya signal and increased the strength of those bounced back, making aircraft look like a larger bomber formation. Caused the Germans to send interceptors after the wrong groups of bombers.
August 1942	Germany	Heinrich	Transmitters that jammed Gee signals, making Gee unusable by November 1942.
November 1942	Allies	Mandrel	Electronic jammer fitted in lead aircraft to jam Freya radar.
November 1942	Allies	Tinsel	Electronic jammer that disrupted ground-to-air communications (making German night fighters less effective). Also a device that amplified bombers' engine noise so as to confuse ground observers who tracked bomber formations by their engine noise.
December 1942	Allies	Oboe	430-km-range ground radar device that calculated a bomber's precise location and sent signal when bombs should be dropped. Used day and night.
January 1943	Allies	H2S	Ground-mapping airborne radar, could distinguish between water, cities, and rural areas. Not fully debugged until November 1943.
March 1943	Allies	Monica	Tail warning radar for night bombers. Would alert a crew when another aircraft was within 1,000 meters of its aircraft.

Date	User	Item	Function
March 1943	Allies	Boozer	Radar receiver ("Radar Warning Receiver" in modern parlance), alerted a crew when it was being detected by Wurzburg or Lichtenstein radar.
June 1943	Allies	Al Mk 9	Improved radar for night fighters (also known as SCR 720.)
June 1943	Allies	Serrate	Radar receiver for night fighters that detected German Lichtenstein airborne radar. Allowed Allied night fighter pilots to determine where German fighter was and engage it. Since all this usually took place above the clouds, there was enough star and moonlight to allow engagements.
July 1943	Allies	Window	Tinfoil strips, cut to the right length to cause German radar to see a "wall" of, well, tinfoil strips. Bundles of it were tossed out of Allied aircraft, and this, in effect, created an electronic smoke screen behind which anything could be happening. Also called "chaff."
August 1943	Allies	Special Tinsel	Updated jammers to deal with new German aircraft radios (designed to operate in spite of the original Tinsel jammers).
September 1943	Germany	Naxburg	Receivers that could detect Allied H2S ground-mapping radars over 300 kilometers away.
October 1943	Allies	ABC	Airborne transmitters that would jam new radios in German fighters and make it difficult for the fighters to get information from the German ground radar-and-control system.
October 1943	Allies	Corona	Special Tinsel jammers that, instead of jamming, sent out false instructions to German fighters.

Date	User	Item	Function
October 1943	Germany	SN-2	Night fighter radar that was immune to Window. Had a range of 400 to 6,000 meters.
November 1943	Germany	Wurzlaus	Modified Wurzburg radar that could sometimes differentiate between stationary tinfoil clouds and nearby aircraft that were, of course, moving.
November 1943	Germany	Nurnburg	Modified Wurzburg radar that gave an electronic sound to the operator as well as the blip on the radar screen. After some training, an operator could use his ears to tell the difference between the radar signal coming back from a chaff cloud and one coming back from moving aircraft.
November 1943	Germany	Flensburg	Airborne receiver that told pilots when they were detected by the Allied Monica tail radar. This alerted the night fighter pilot to be prepared for some resistance from the bomber he was stalking.
December 1943	Germany	Dartboard	Jamming German radio stations that were used to send coded messages to fighter pilots (whose normal radios were now frequently being jammed).
January 1944	Allies	Oboe 2	Oboe with a new type of radar signal.
January 1944	Germany	Naxos	Airborne receiver for Allied ground-mapping radar transmissions.
April 1944	Germany	Jagdschloss	Ground radar that could switch between four different frequencies and thus be more resistant to jamming. Range of 150 kilometers.
April 1944	Germany	Egon	Fighter control radio that was more resistant to jamming and enabled ground controllers and radars to continually guide fighters. Range of 200 kilometers.

Date	User	Item	Function
August 1944	Allies	Jostle	Airborne "barrage" jammer that jammed a large range of frequencies simultaneously.
September 1944	Allies	Window 2	New tinfoil length that would jam airborne SN-2 radar. Window had to be cut to the right length to jam a specific radar frequency.
October 1944	Allies	Serrate 4	New Serrate could detect and locate the new German SN-2 airborne radar.
December 1944	Allies	Perfectos	Germans were now using electronic ID (IFF, "Identify Friend or Foe") and Perfectos could trigger the IFF and use the subsequent ID signal to locate German fighters. The Allies used IFF starting in 1940, primarily to avoid having their returning bombers mistaken for enemy aircraft by Allied radar. It took the Germans several years to catch on to the advantages of IFF and develop their own.
December 1944	Allies	Micro-H	Alternative to Gee for use once the Germans discovered a way to jam the original Gee.

WHERE TO DROP IT?

The major problem the Allies had with their strategic bombing campaign against Germany was figuring out what to bomb. While there were thousands of heavy bombers available, Germany was still a big place and there were far more targets than bombs. It was realized at the beginning that some targets would have a larger impact on German war-making power than others. One target was dismissed early on: power plants. It was no secret that Germany had 8,200 electrical power plants, and an extensive system of high-capacity power transmission lines. Some Allied experts concluded that the German "power grid" was extensive enough that the Germans could repair damage more quickly than Allied bombers could cause it. Examination of the power grid after the war made it clear that such was not the case. More to the point, the elimination of a few large power plants would have done large damage to the Nazi war industry. The German power system was, in hindsight, the most vulnerable aspect of the German economy. If half of Germany's electricity supply was eliminated, it would not be able to produce enough weapons to keep the war going. This vulnerability was very real. For one thing, a few large plants provided crucial amounts of energy. Most of the power (82 percent) was provided by a few (400) plants. Worse yet (for the Germans) their power grid was not capable of quickly and efficiently shifting power from one part of the country to another. Some of the British and American experts consulted did catch this key aspect of the situation. The experts were expert enough but were overruled by military and political members of the committee that selected targets.

After the war was over it was discovered that the destruction of two plants just outside Berlin would have shut that city down. Most of German generating capacity (79 percent) was coal-fired, the remainder hydroelectric. The plants were difficult to build and repair, relatively fragile and easy to damage. Most plants could have been put out of action for up to three months with as little as twenty tons of bombs (a single B-17 carried two tons). Forty tons could have knocked the plant out for up to a year. The larger plants would have required more tonnage, but a hundred tons would have done it. This kind of effort might have required several hundred B-17 sorties (making allowances for bad weather, stiff opposition, and poor aim). Throughout the war, less than nine hundred tons were dropped on power plants. This was not enough to have had a noticeable effect. In any event, the Germans were always short of electric power during the war and local brownouts were common. Nor could they expand electrical power output. There wasn't enough fuel for more plants, and most of what the industry needed to build new ones was tied up in arms production.

If a hundred plants had been hit hard, and this would have required about 1 percent of all the bombs dropped on Europe, German industry would have collapsed from the loss of over half its electricity supply. If this had been done in 1943, the war would have probably ended up a year before it actually did. Several million lives would have been saved and the history of postwar Europe might have been quite different.

But then, maybe not. Yet the opportunity was there, if only it had been seized when it could have been in 1943.

THE PRICE OF CLEAN SHEETS

Aviators were always envied by the infantry because the fly-boys would go out on their mission, come back, take a shower, and then sleep between clean sheets. All that was true. Moreover, the big bombers would rarely go out more than a few times a week. But there was a price: your life. Of the 1.4 million bomber sorties, 1.5 percent ended up in the aircraft being lost. On average, two thirds of the crew was lost for each aircraft destroyed. While there were three or four wounded for every man killed in ground combat, there were about six killed for each man wounded among bomber crews. The loss rate among bombers was such that the number of missions per man had to be limited for morale reasons. The logic of this was simple: If crews had to serve indefinitely, they would almost certainly get killed. So the number of missions a man had to fly was set at a level that gave him about a 50 percent chance of surviving. Most infantrymen had better prospects than that. Moreover, bomber crews knew that there was little they could do to maximize their chance of surviving. They had to fly straight and level through flak, enemy fighters, and bad weather to reach their target. If hit before the bombs were dropped, their aircraft would often be blown apart by the bombs it carried. On the way back from a mission, they knew the enemy was fully informed of their presence and position and would be sending up fighters to bring them down. Bomber missions were from five to ten hours long and most of that time was spent within range of enemy weapons. Whereas an infantryman could always dig a deeper foxhole when under attack, the airman had no place to hide. Infantrymen coming under fire would "hit the ground," a phrase that took on a rather different meaning for a bomber crew.

In the first half of 1944, Allied aircrews in Europe had the following percentage of being killed in action (KIA) or missing in action (MIA), usually meaning dead, but sometimes being taken prisoner. It was worse in 1943 and got a lot better after the summer of 1944.

Tour of Duty	Percentage of KIA/MIA
Heavy Bombers (30 Missions)	71
Medium Bombers (50 missions, varied a bit)	48
Fighters (300 hours of combat flying)	24

Despite the odds, of which the men flying bombers were keenly aware, they flew on, over 100,000 of them to their deaths.

WHAT LONDON AND BAGHDAD HAVE IN COMMON

Aside from once being the capital of great empires, both London and Baghdad share another, rather dubious, distinction. Both are the only cities (in addition to Antwerp) to have been attacked by both ballistic and cruise missiles.

German V-1 cruise missiles were first launched against southeast England in June 1944. Some 9,200 were eventually fired at Great Britain, of which about 2,400 made it to their target (usually London). Most of the V-1s that didn't make it were shot down by flak or fighters. During the 1991 Gulf War, America fired over 200 Tomahawk cruise missiles at Baghdad. This was widely hailed as the first wartime use of cruise missiles, apparently by people who had forgotten about the "buzz-bomb" attacks on Great Britain in 1944. While the modern cruise missiles contain much more accurate guidance systems, the V-1, for its day, did the job and fit the description.

During the 1980s war with Iraq, Iran fired over 200 Scuds at Baghdad. London received rather more of a pounding. Starting in October 1944, about 350 V-2s were sent against southeast England. Some 2,700 people were killed by the V-2 attacks, another 19,000 were wounded. Damage to real estate was greater, with 123,000 buildings either receiving some damage or being destroyed.

The current ballistic and cruise missiles are direct descendants of the earlier German weapons. The Soviet Scud and American Corporal (the U.S. "Scud") were both developed using the V-2 as a model. Indeed, German scientists and technicians who worked on the V-2 also worked on the later Soviet and U.S. versions.

Development work on the V-1 cruise missile began in June 1942 and the first successful flight took place in December of that year. The V-1 was a simpler weapon than the V-2, but the German example inspired both the Soviets and Americans to develop postwar versions. The United States dropped cruise missile work in the 1960s in favor of ballistic missiles while the Russians continued development of cruise missiles. When the Americans realized how lethal cruise missiles could be on (and against ships), they began working on them. The earlier Russian cruise missiles could be seen as obvious knockoffs of the V-1, but the post-1960s U.S. weapons took full advantage of modern propulsion and guidance technology. The Tomahawk looks quite modern. The guidance system of the V-1 itself was quite crude. The missile had to be launched directly at the target, as the V-1 flew in a straight line, at a constant speed (about 300 to 400 miles an hour) and altitude

(3,000 to 4,000 feet). It used a simple pulse jet engine and plunged to the ground after it had gone a programmed distance. The Russian versions used more sophisticated guidance, including radar and other sensors, to seek out enemy ships. The modern U.S. cruise missile (the Tomahawk) uses sensors and a powerful microcomputer to scan the terrain below it and literally "followed the map" to its target. This allows for very high accuracy. Accuracy aside, the V-1 and the Tomahawk cruise missiles had the same mission: to hit enemy targets. Since the V-1 was aimed at urban areas (London) it usually hit something and did indeed cause considerable damage and loss of life. The V-1 attacks didn't stop until Allied troops overran the Channel coast sites from which the short-ranged V-1s were launched.

Work began on the V-2 in 1938 and the first successful launch was in October 1942. Unlike the V-1, which had to be launched from catapult-equipped concrete ramps, the V-2 was mobile. The trailer the missile was towed around on contained hydraulic jacks that put the missile into a vertical position. Its liquid fuel was then loaded, the inertial guidance system adjusted, and the missile launched. Between September 6, 1944, and March 27, 1945, the Germans launched 4,300 V-2s. Most were fired at targets on the Continent, the rest were aimed at England. By early 1944, the Germans were producing 300 V-2s a month in an underground missile factory in the Hartz Mountains. The V-2 was originally designed to hit military targets beyond artillery range and this was largely how it was used. Hundreds were fired at logistic facilities in Antwerp, and had some success in hurting Allied supply efforts. Against London, however, the V-2 was used as a terror weapon, and it had some success there. Because it was a ballistic missile, you couldn't hear it coming. There was no warning and no defense. All of a sudden there was an explosion. As Londoners soon learned, if you heard the explosion, you were safe. It wasn't until the 1970s that space satellites were developed that could detect the launch of a weapon like the V-2 or Scud. It wasn't until the 1980s that weapons were developed (like the Patriot system) that could intercept these missiles.

The terms *V-1* and *V-2* were not the official designations of these weapons. The *V* stood for Vergeltungswaffe ("vengeance weapon"). The official designations were FZG-76 (the V-1) and A-4 (the V-2A). Comparison with their modern descendants is instructive.

Most of the improvements in post–World War II ballistic (V-2) and cruise (V-1) missiles were to make them lighter, fly farther, and be more accurate. If you look at the missiles developed in the 1950s and

Characteristics of World War II and Modern Missiles

	FZG-76 (V-1)	Tomahawk AGM-104	A-4 (V-2)	Scud
Weight	4,850	3,000	28,380	13,500
Range	200	2,500	320	300
Warhead	1,874	1,000	2,200	2,000
Accuracy	12.0	.05	6.0	2.0

NOTES: Weight of the missile when launched, in pounds.

Range of the missile, in kilometers.

Warhead, which is largely explosive, in pounds. One bonus missiles have over bombs or artillery shells is the weight and mass of the missile structure, which add to the destruction when the missile hits something. The metal of the missile body turns into fast-moving, and often lethal, flying objects in the aftermath of the missile's impact.

Accuracy, in kilometers, is represented by the circular error probable, (CEP). What this means is that the missile has a 50 percent chance of landing within a circle whose diameter is the CEP. Thus the V-1 had a 50 percent chance of landing within six kilometers of where it was aimed at.

1960s, you can clearly see the ancestry. What Londoners experienced during the latter half of 1944 was only a portent of things to come.

THE D-DAY FORCE POOL: RESOURCES AVAILABLE FOR THE NORMANDY INVASION

The Normandy Invasion was the greatest military undertaking in history. While several other operations, notably on the Eastern Front, involved more troops, none involved so much risk to so many, nor the use of such massive naval and air forces. It was truly a "mighty endeavor."

The Allies had a total of forty-one divisions and twenty-six separate brigades or regiments available in Great Britain for operations on the continent. Most Allied divisions were more capable than their German counterparts. The only exceptions were the nine panzer divisions and the one panzer grenadier division (armored infantry), included in the table under armored divisions, and the three parachute divisions, included under infantry. The German paratroopers were much more heavily equipped than Allied airborne divisions, and in any case had no airborne training or capability. Actually, only twenty-six of the German divisions were capable of mobile operations: the panzers and panzer grenadiers, the parachute divisions, and thirteen of the infantry

Major Formations Available

	Divisions			Brigades			Equated
	Infantry	*Armored*	*Airborne*	*Infantry*	*Armored*	*Airborne*	*Total*
Belgian				1			0.3
British	10	3	2	7	7		19.6
Canadian	2	1			1		3.3
Czech				1			0.3
French							1.0
Dutch				1			0.3
Polish		1				1	1.3
U.S.	14	5	2		8		23.6
Allied Total	26	11	4	10	16	1	49.7
German	50	10		2			60.6

divisions, plus one parachute brigade (included under infantry). All Allied divisions were mobile or had sufficient trucks available to quickly make them mobile. Most of the Germans walked and had their heavy equipment hauled by horses and a few trucks.

It is interesting to note that Allied deception measures were so successful that the Germans overestimated the forces available in Great Britain for the invasion by about 40 percent, believing that there were 85 to 90 infantry and armored divisions plus 7 airborne divisions. On D-Day itself, for example, Lieutenant General George S. Patton's fictitious "First U.S. Army Group" had under command 11 notional divisions (7 U.S. and 4 British), plus 2.5 real divisions (1 British), plus the headquarters of the U.S. Ninth Army, a real outfit being held in reserve for later employment.

Aside from the 26 mobile outfits, all of the other German divisions were so-called static divisions, suitable for manning fixed defenses, but of limited mobility. Many of the troops in these static divisions were disabled to some degree (having been wounded on the Eastern front), or Russian PWs who volunteered to switch sides. Altogether Germany had about 285 divisions at this time, 164 (57.5 percent) were in Russia.

The Allies had an additional 11 divisions (1 Anglo-American airborne task force, 2 French armored divisions, and 3 U.S. and 5 French infantry divisions) available in Italy, Sicily, and North Africa for the follow-up landings in the south of France. These are not shown in the next table.

These figures represent the total number of combat aircraft available in the general theater of operations in the opening days of the campaign. On D-Day the Allies attained a sortie rate (number of times

Available Manpower

	Allies	Germans	Ratio
Ground Combatants	1,000,000	700,000	1.43:1
Combat Replacements	120,000	20,000	6.00:1
Other	1,756,000	780,000	2.25:1
Total	2,876,000	1,500,000	1.92:1

NOTES: Ground Combatants is the manpower available to engage in combat on the ground. Combat Replacements is the troops available to replace losses among the ground combatants. In the British Army these were called "Reinforcements," a more psychologically satisfactory term. Other is all other personnel, including service troops, airmen, and seamen directly involved in the operations.

Not shown is another figure of importance, the Replacement Rate, the number of replacements that each side could accumulate each month, over and above those on hand at the onset of the campaign. For the Allies this ran to about 55,000 men, about 90 percent of whom were American and the rest British, while for the Germans it ran to only about 6,000 men, a ratio of 9.16:1.

Available Ground Combat Equipment

	Allies	Germans	Ratio
Battle Tanks	5,500	1,400	3.93:1
Other AFV	2,000	800	2.50:1
Artillery	4,800	3,200	1.50:1

NOTES: Battle Tanks are the principal medium and heavy tanks, such as the Shermans, Tigers, and so forth.

Other AFV are the miscellaneous light tanks, such as the Stuart and Tetrarch, plus armored cars, assault guns, and the like.

Artillery includes guns, howitzers, and heavy mortars with the ground forces, but excludes the several hundred heavy naval guns carried on the 6 battleships, 2 monitors, 23 cruisers, and 73 destroyers that supported the landings, not to mention the numerous smaller vessels, such as rocket-firing landing craft and minesweepers. If the naval guns were included, as well as the superior fire control of the Allies and their more abundant supply of ammunition, the ratio would approach 3:1.

an aircraft took off) of 10,000, since many airplanes went on more than one mission, while the Germans were only able to commit a handful of aircraft (tradition says two), which made a strafing run across the beaches and surprisingly managed to get away unscathed despite overwhelming Allied superiority in the air. In the days following the landings the Allied sortie rate fell to about 5,000 a day, while the Germans

Available Combat Aircraft

	Bombers	Fighters	Total
Royal Air Force	624	2,172	2,796
U.S. Air Force	1,922	1,311	3,233
Allied Total	2,546	3,483	6,029
Germans	400	420	820
Ratio	6.4:1	8.3:1	7.4:1

were able to build theirs up to about 250. In addition to combat aircraft, the Allies committed 1,628 transport aircraft (1,166 U.S.) and 2,591 gliders (1,619 U.S.) to the airborne operations, and there were also available about 2,000 additional fighters and 1,000 bombers committed to other operations at the time. Note that British figures include Allied contingents (French, Polish, Czech, Dutch, and Norwegian) as well as Canadian and other Commonwealth squadrons.

THE FIRST RULE

In early 1943 Ruth Baldwin Gowan, an ace reporter for the Associated Press, arrived in North Africa. There were a number of people who objected to her presence, holding that women could not make good war correspondents. Such doubts were dispelled at the highest levels.

It seems that shortly after Ms. Gowan arrived in North Africa she chanced to run into George S. Patton, the ultimate no-nonsense soldier. After being introduced, Patton gave her the once-over. Then he asked, "What is the first law of war?"

Ms. Gowan replied quickly, "You kill him before he kills you."

"She stays," said a smiling Patton, much to the disappointment of those who expected him to send her packing with an earful of soldierly profanity.

Ms. Gowan was one of about 800 correspondents from all nations who covered the operations of the Western allies during the war, some of them spending literally years on the fighting fronts. Operation Overlord, which involved nearly 3 million military personnel, including naval, air, and ground forces, was covered by about 300 Allied reporters (180 U.S. and 120 Allied), or about 1 reporter for every 10,000 troops. Fewer than 50 reporters (including Ernest Hemingway) landed on D-Day, about 1 for every 3,100 men. In contrast, the 1991 Gulf War was covered by about 1,300 journalists on the Allied side, although only about 700,000 troops were involved, including those all over the theater of operations, about 1 reporter to every 540 troops.

WHAT PRICE GLORY?

In November 1942 the 3rd Infantry Division went ashore in North Africa. Over the next thirty months the division fought in Tunisia, Sicily, central Italy, Anzio, southern France, Alsace, and Germany. This experience made the 3rd one of the five hardest hit U.S. divisions (3rd, 4th, 9th, 36th, and 45th) in the war, which collectively ran through an average of 176 percent of their personnel during the European campaign. As a result, by the end of January 1945 one company in the division had just 2 men left of the 235 who had come ashore at Casablanca. One of them was Audie Murphy, who had risen from private to lieutenant while accumulating twenty-four decorations, including a Medal of Honor. The other man was a supply sergeant.

BUT NCOS ARE THE BACKBONE OF AN ARMY

At the outbreak of World War II the Italian Army had 53,000 officers, but only 40,000 NCOs. This was one reason for the relatively poor performance of the Italian Army in the opening phases of the war. In order to have his "Eight Million Bayonets," Mussolini had to sacrifice quality for quantity. Once the prewar army was subjected to some rigorous wartime experience it quickly got better, and some of the toughest fighting of the North African campaign was actually done by Italian troops, such as Bir El Gobi, Giarabub, the breaking of the British 7th Armored Division at El Alamein, and the defense of the Mareth Line. But it was those initial reverses that set the pattern of the press releases.

A WOMAN'S PLACE...

A Croix de guerre has recently been awarded posthumously to Collette Nirouet, a teenager who disguised herself as a man to join the French Army in World War II, during which she was killed in action.

FIREPOWER KILLS

During the opening barrage of the Battle of El Alamein on October 23, 1942, the artillery of the British Eighth Army fired some 530,000 rounds in twenty-four hours, for an average of 22,083.3 rounds per hour, or approximately 1 round every 2.8 minutes from each of the 1,030 guns and howitzers available.

NATIONAL BEST

The greatest opposed single day's advance in the history of the U.S. Army is probably the ninety-odd miles covered by the 3rd Armored Division as it drove across the Rhineland on March 28, 1945, under the able leadership of Major General Maurice Rose, one of the highest-ranking Jewish officers in the army, who was killed in action four days later while trying to avoid capture.

AND THE RHINE FLOWS HOME TO THE SEA

When the Allied armies finally reached the Rhine in the spring of 1945, many of the troops performed a little male ritual to express their contempt for all things German. It is not known how many men piddled in the Rhine. Among the many thousands who so indulged were the entire British Imperial General Staff, led by Winston Churchill himself (who reportedly did so with great relish, to the cheers of onlooking American troops, who had themselves just performed the little ceremony), and George S. Patton, who was photographed in the act.

MIX AND MATCH

During the war the U.S. Army maintained around 45 percent of its combat strength in nondivisional formations, independent combat units of battalion, regiment, and brigade size. In contrast, the Soviets never had more than about 20 percent of their combat strength in independent units and the Germans never more than about 10 percent. This was due to two policies adopted by the army at the urging of Lieutenant General Lesley J. McNair, who became the Chief of Army Ground Forces shortly before the war, and later became the highest-ranking U.S. officer ever killed in action, when the Eighth Air Force dropped some bombs "short" during the breakout from the Normandy beachhead. These policies were "modularization" and "pooling."

Modularization was a simple idea: All units of a particular type in the army should be organized in precisely the same way. So all battalions of 105mm howitzers or medium tanks or combat engineers had the same table of organization and equipment (T/O&E), training, and doctrine whether they formed part of a division or were independent. The idea was to facilitate command and control. A division commander blessed with a couple of extra battalions for a particular mission didn't have to wonder how they differed from those of the same type already under his command. This notion seems so reasonable as to be self-evident and to merit no particular comment. Yet it was by no means a universally held idea. The German Army often had three or four different T/O&Es for units with the same type of designation. There were, for example, three-battalion infantry regiments and two-battalion infantry regiments. And regiments of different "waves" usually not only differed organizationally, but also had very different weaponry.

Pooling developed as a corollary to modularization. The idea was to keep units "slender." Divisions were to have enough men and equipment to complete their primary mission, sustained combat with the enemy. Troops or equipment not likely to be constantly of use were not to be included in their T/O&E. For example, since divisions did not always need antitank or antiaircraft protection, they were not to have such formations as organic components. These would be pooled at corps and army levels and parceled out as needed. So a division likely to be engaged with enemy armor would be supplied with a tank destroyer battalion or two from the army pool. In this fashion, threatened units could be rapidly reinforced from the pool without having to strip such specialized formations away from other divisions. As an added benefit, this would economize on the army's resources, since specialized combat formations would never be idle because their parent divisions was not in need of them.

As a result of the pooling of specialized formations, the U.S. Army had an enormous wealth of nondivisional combat elements. At peak strength the army had 663 battalions of field artillery, enough for 165 divisions. There were so many nondivisional units that had they been organized into divisions the army would have had almost twice as many divisions as its peak wartime strength, 90.

The number of divisions active on each date is compared with the

U.S. Army Combat Power

	Active Divisions	Available Nondivisional Elements	
		Battalions	Equated Divisions
December 31, 1942	68	1,057	60
June 30, 1943	84	1,212	84
December 31, 1943	90	1,227	88
June 30, 1944	89	1,292	87
December 31, 1944	89	1,215	87
June 30, 1945	89	1,011	74

number of nondivisional combat battalions available, including infantry, armor, reconnaissance, combat engineers, artillery, antiaircraft, antitanks, and the like. Had these been formed into divisions, they would have almost doubled the number of divisions available to the army, and there would still have been some nondivisional combat elements, amounting to about 5 percent of the army's combat power. In fact, from time to time "divisions" actually were formed from units in the pool. For example, a division-sized "Airborne Task Force" was temporarily created for the invasion of southern France in the summer of 1944. Most of these ad hoc divisions were short-lived, but in one case such an improvisation became a permanent part of the army, when the Americal Division (later dubbed the 23rd) was formed in 1942 from some independent infantry regiments, artillery battalions, and other troops on New Caledonia (hence the name, "Americal," from "America" and "Caledonia").

On balance, modularization worked quite well, making it easier for commanding officers quickly to take over new units, permitting easy coordination of elements drawn from different commands, and facilitating logistical planning. However, the large pool of nondivisional units was not so successful. The army did, of course, need some separate combat units for use in missions that did not require whole divisions. But the notion that divisions could be "tailored" for particular operations by the hasty attachment of nondivisional elements proved much less successful. The problem was not so much with the artillery, which was trained to an extremely fine standard and could cooperate with anyone, but with the nondivisional tank, antitank, and antiaircraft units, which had actually to fight on the ground in cooperation with divisional elements. The pool concept did not allow formations to become acquainted with each other, making newly assigned units uncomfortable and sometimes inefficient during operations. Experience eventually showed that the best use for the pool was more or less to permanently assign ("marry") nondivisional units to particular divisions. As a result, it was fairly common during operations in Europe after D-Day for infantry divisions to have permanently attached to them a tank battalion (74 light and medium tanks), an antiaircraft battalion (32 40mm AA guns, which were often quite useful in ground combat), and usually a tank destroyer battalion as well (36 76mm guns) or a mortar battalion (32 4.2-inch mortars). With these, and additional less permanent attachments, U.S. infantry divisions often went into action at quite an overstrength, with 20,000 to 25,000 men not being unusual, where Russian divisions with attached troops ran to 12,000 or so men and German divisions only about 15,000. This gave the average American division a lot more hitting power than the average German division had, hitting power that was to be needed, considering that the Germans tended to be better tactically.

Some idea of the way a division could grow may be gained by looking at the 1st Infantry Division ("The Big Red 1") on three separate occasions (the dates are approximate) during the war.

Battalions in the 1st Division

		Infantry	Tank	Recon-naissance	Artillery	Anti-tank	Anti-aircraft	Engineer
December 1, 1944	Organic	9	0	0.3	4.0	0	0	1
	Assigned	0	1	0	0.3	1	1	0
	Attached	0	0	0	1.0	0	0	0
March 1, 1945	Organic	9	0	0.3	4.0	0	0	1
	Assigned	0	1	0	0.3	1	1	0
	Attached	0	0	1.0	3.0	0	0	2
April 1, 1945	Organic	9	0	0.3	4.0	0	0	1
	Assigned	0	1	0	0.3	1	1	0
	Attached	0	3	1.0	3.0	0	0	2

NOTES: Organic is the units "organic" to the division, that is, those in the T/O&E. Assigned is nondivisional units normally "assigned" to the division on a more or less permanent basis. Attached is nondivisional units "attached" to the division temporarily. 0.3 indicates a company.

It is interesting to note that on April 1, 1945, the 1st Infantry Division had most of an entire armored division attached, and certainly had more tanks (about 250 counting those in reconnaissance units) than did German panzer divisions at that same time.

POURING IT ON: AMMUNITION CONSUMPTION

The American way of war in the twentieth century substitutes the expenditure of material for that of men. For example, U.S. troops in northwestern Europe from D-Day to VE-Day expended over 1 billion rounds of ammunition, counting everything from pistol bullets to 240mm artillery rounds, plus odd stuff like hand grenades, bazooka rockets, and bangalore torpedoes. This came to roughly 3.3 million rounds per day and doesn't include air force and navy munitions expended in support of ground operations. One result of this willingness to expend ammunition rather than lives has been remarkably low casualty lists. Another was an enormous increase in the logistical support needed to sustain operations.

Typical Daily Ammunition Expenditure in Tons

Operation	Armored Division	Infantry Division	155mm Battalion
Attack	436–832	353–658	66–121
Defense	596–969	472–768	86–142
Pursuit	107	83	15
Delay/Retirement	321	256	51

NOTES: The range given for the attack and defense figures represents operations of varying intensity. It is interesting to note that ammunition expenditure was higher in defensive rather than offensive operations. These figures are based on the experience of the European theater, but those for the Pacific were not much different.

Although there was a battalion of twelve 155mm howitzers in each U.S. division, most 155mm battalions were independent, maintained in a pool at corps and even army level, to be assigned to the support of various divisions as needed. The standard U.S. artillery piece of the war was the 105mm howitzer, an extremely good weapon based on the German 105mm howitzer of World War I. There were initially thirty-six of these in a division (three battalions of twelve pieces), a figure that grew to fifty-four by the end of the war as a cannon company was added to each infantry regiment. These "regimental guns" were supposed to be used in direct support of the infantry, but in practice most divisions merely added them to divisional artillery as an ad hoc extra battalion. A single 105mm could expend about 50 rounds an hour, or about 1.8 tons. On this basis a single 105mm would run through its basic "unit of fire" (the amount of ammunition a weapon was expected to expend in one day) in only four hours. So units were actually consuming ammunition at rates greater than they were supposed to. This may have caused headaches for logisticians, but it was a comfort for the GIs up at the front. It was also one reason that only about half of the U.S. Army actually was engaged in inflicting direct harm on the enemy during the war. The other half was helping to keep the guns firing and bringing up the ammunition, spare parts, rations, fuel, and so forth.

GOING FOR THE GOLD

During Rommel's pursuit following the defeat of the British Eighth Army in the Battle of Gazala, the 33rd Reconnaissance Battalion of his Panzerarmee Afrika advanced 158.7 kilometers (about 100 miles) in twenty-four hours on June 26–27, 1942. This is apparently a world's record for a single day's advance against resistance. There have been swifter performances, but all were against an opponent who was offering no opposition.

A PENNY SAVED IS A PENNY EARNED

Mindful of the strain on the Exchequer, during World War II the British Army managed to save about £20 sterling (about $1,000 in 1994 dollars) per soldier by the simple expedient of not issuing reserve parachutes to its airborne troops. A useful side effect of this parsimony was that British paratroopers could carry more equipment into action. On the other hand, the British did supply their airborne forces with an item useful during the sometimes rough flights to their drop zones, special grease-proof paper bags officially called "Bags, Vomit, for Use of." So at least the airplanes could return from their missions relatively clean and the brave lads could go into action with unsoiled uniforms. Or at least those who made it to the ground in one piece.

"AND WE WON'T COME BACK 'TIL IT'S OVER OVER THERE"

As the U.S. Army pressed eastward across France in the late summer and early fall of 1944, it was crossing country familiar to many of the older men, "retreads" who had been with John J. Pershing in "the war to end all wars." And thereby hang some tales.

- The commanding officer of an infantry regiment was poring over a map with his staff when he chanced to note some familiar names. Turning to his operations officer he said, "Major, any chance we can go around that town? Back in Eighteen I made some pretty tall promises to a young lady there and I'd rather not run into her just now."

- A wartime cartoon showed a youngish GI with glasses, a rather pointy nose, and a cowlick being greeted in a small French village by a crowd of locals, many of whom had glasses, a rather pointy nose, and a cowlick. The caption reads "My Daddy told me about this place."

- A pillbox in Lorraine, in northeastern France, was taken by American troops twice, once in each world war. On one of the walls is written a doughboy's name and a date in late 1918. Just under it appears the same name, with a date in late 1944. Beneath that is scrawled "This is the last time I want to be in this damned bunker."

The line from George M. Cohan's 1917 song was prophetic, for it wasn't "over over there" in 1918. And perhaps because American troops have been "over there" for fifty years now in peace, it has not been necessary for that man or his son or his grandson to visit that bunker again in war.

MALTA: PIVOT OR PAWN

One of the most heavily bombed places in the war was Malta, the tiny (122 square miles) British-owned group of islands a few dozen miles south of Sicily, which was bombed an estimated 14,000 times from mid-1940 through mid-1943. Malta played an important role in the Mediterranean war. From Malta, British aircraft, warships, and submarines were able to impede Italian maritime traffic to North Africa, making support of Axis ground forces extremely costly. At times as much as a third of the supplies failed to get through, although the wartime average was only about 14 percent. The difference lay in the degree to which the Italian and German air forces were committed to the interdiction of Malta as a British base. The most decisive period of interdiction was from January through August 1942, when a massive commitment of Axis air power and Italian surface forces virtually eliminated offensive operations from Malta. The British made extraordinary efforts to sustain Malta on the premise that it guarded the "lifeline of the British Empire," the Mediterranean route from Great Britain to the Middle East and India. There was desperate fighting on the convoy routes to the island, with enormous losses. The three convoys that the British attempted to run through to Malta during this period totaled 35 merchant ships, of which 16 were sunk and 11 forced to turn back, 5 of them severely damaged, so that only 8 got through, of which 3 were sunk by air raids soon after reaching port: One convoy managed to get only a single ship into Malta. Of 169 warships escorting the three convoys, 14 were sunk, and 17 severely damaged. Even the United States lent a hand, risking the carrier *Wasp* twice in the spring of 1942 to ferry precious Spitfires to within flying distance of the beleaguered islands.

On both occasions, within days every one of the fighters had been rendered unserviceable. Yet despite these efforts, the situation of Malta steadily deteriorated. By late June 1942, the island was incapable of supporting offensive operations. During this period only about 6 percent of Axis supplies failed to reach North Africa. This massive interdiction effort was preparatory to an amphibious assault on Malta, dubbed Operation Hercules by the Germans and Operation C3 by the Italians.

The proposed Malta invasion was meticulously planned. In fact, it was the only case of genuine integrated planning by the Axis powers during the war. Not only did Italian and German staffs work together closely, but Japanese experts in amphibious warfare were consulted. The operation was to involve over 75,000 troops in over six divisions, some 1,300 aircraft, and about 200 tanks (including some superheavy KV-IIs captured in Russia), plus virtually all Axis warships in the Mediterranean. To oppose these, the British had no more than about 18,000 combat troops in four brigades, supported by about 12,000 naval and air base personnel, with a handful of aircraft, a few tanks, and whatever meager resources the Royal Navy might be able to commit, it being stretched extremely thin by the demands of a global war. The operation was to unfold in several acts:

1. **Amphibious Assault:** The Italian San Marco naval infantry regiment was to land on a beach on the south coast. This would be a feint to attract the attention of the one mobile brigade in the British garrison.

2. **Airborne Assault:** The Italian Folgore parachute division and a German division-sized parachute task force under Kurt Student, the conqueror of Crete, were to drop in the center of the island, occupying one of the many satellite airstrips the British had built.

3. **Air Landing:** The Italian La Spezia air-landing division would be flown onto the captured airstrip.

4. **Reserve Landing:** Three additional divisions, one of which could be air-landed, would be brought in, the others coming in over the beaches.

Since the Axis powers had extremely good intelligence as to British resources and dispositions on Malta (a lot of Maltese were pro-Italian, and over a score were hanged for their espionage efforts during the war), the plan seems to have had a reasonable chance of success.

But the operation was never undertaken. The primary reason for this was Rommel's impressive victory over the British at Gazala (May 26–June 13, 1942). In anticipation of his offensive, Rommel induced Hitler to "lend" him the X Fleigerkorps ("Tenth Air Corps"), the German component of the massive Axis air force just then pounding Malta into ruin. With the Gazala battle won, Rommel was supposed to return the Fleigerkorps. Instead, as the British retreated toward the Nile hotly pursued by German and Italian troops, Rommel convinced Hitler that Egypt (and the Suez Canal) were within his grasp. But Rommel's drive ended at El Alamein, where, in early July, the British Eighth Army made a stand. The air corps was never returned to Sicily; many of the Italian and German troops earmarked for the Malta operation ended up holding the El Alamein Line, and the interdiction of Malta came to an end. As a result, during the second half of 1942, while Rommel's troops clung desperately to the El Alamein position at the end of a very long logistical line, Axis maritime traffic to North Africa was once again subject to intensive attack, with material losses reaching more than 35 percent, while British convoys to Malta suffered not a single loss.

The struggle for Malta was enormously expensive. The Axis forces lost about 1,000 aircraft, and the British officially put their losses at 565, a figure that is probably conservative. Surprisingly, despite the fact that Malta was rather densely populated, civilian deaths were quite low, about 1,500. This can be attributed to an enormously successful program that developed an elaborate system of deep bomb shelters in the rocky heart of the island. On April 15, 1942, the entire island was awarded the George Cross, which still graces its flag.

Some analysts have suggested that "Hercules/C3" been undertaken the entire course of the war would have been changed. For example, with Malta in Axis hands

The Axis armies in North Africa would have been assured a steady flow of men and material.

The "lifeline of the British Empire" would have been severed.

The German drive on Suez might have succeeded.

The Arabs might well have risen in support of the Axis effort.

The British might have been driven from the Middle East.

The Soviets would have been forced to call off the Stalingrad operation to meet the possibility of a German threat through the Caucasus, possibly supported by Turkey.

The Axis powers might have won the war.

An interesting series of notions. But not sustainable by the facts. In reality, by early 1941 Great Britain's "lifeline" no longer ran through the Mediterranean but rather took the longer but much safer route around Africa. Moreover, had Rommel not had the air power earmarked for Malta, his victory at Gazala might well have been less decisive. Nor does it seem likely that, in the event of Suez falling into German hands, a threat to southern Russia could have been mounted, even with Turkish support, before the Stalingrad operation was under way: The Russo-Turkish frontier is no place for mechanized forces. And, of course, if one situation in the western desert had grown more critical in mid-1942, the United States had plans to commit significant ground forces there in support of the British. So Malta was a chimera for the Axis powers, and perhaps also for the British, who might well have been militarily better off without it, although the political cost of abandoning Malta would have been enormous.

WELL, IT SEEMED LIKE A GOOD IDEA

During the war, America raised 103 tank destroyer (TD) battalions. These were antitank units equipped with several different generations of self-propelled antitank guns. The idea was that if antitank guns were good (which they were, for protecting infantry from tanks), then self-propelled antitank guns (or tank destroyers) were better, for they could go looking for enemy tanks to kill. The concept didn't work as planned. As a result, a planned additional 119 battalions were not raised and the existing battalions had to search for a role on the battlefield.

The basic problem was that there were numerous antitank weapons in all other units. Enemy tanks, as fearsome and numerous as they might be, were vulnerable to a wide variety of weapons. Aircraft bombs and artillery shells could destroy, or damage, tanks. Antitank mines were widely used and accounted for nearly a quarter of all tanks destroyed. Every infantry (and most other) units had antitank guns or rocket launchers (bazookas). And then there was the widely held assumption that the best antitank weapon was another tank. For the Allies, this was a reasonable proposition, as the Germans generally had fewer tanks than did their opponents throughout the war. Germany and Italy produced 49,000 tanks and self propelled-guns in 1939–1945, while Great Britain, the United States, Canada, and the Soviet Union produced 227,000. Most of these were tanks and it's no surprise that German tanks were generally outnumbered by two to one or more in most campaigns. Even though the German tanks were often (but not always) superior technically and better employed due to superior training and leadership, Allied infantry could usually rely on some friendly tanks to take care of the German panzers. In effect, the tank destroyers were superfluous and generally seen by U.S. infantry commanders as another useful weapon, but not always for fighting enemy tanks.

When the tank destroyers first went into action in 1942, they found that their lightly armored self-propelled guns were too vulnerable to German tank fire. Moreover, some TDs carried a relatively weak gun (often not as powerful as those used by Allied tanks) that could not penetrate the frontal armor of German tanks. In 1943, more impressive self-propelled vehicles were produced. But these still had very thin armor and their crews often got into trouble trying to operate like tanks just because their tank destroyers looked like tanks. The first TDs were armored trucks (half-tracks, which usually served as armored personnel carriers for the infantry, with a gun mounted in the back). The next generation used a tank chassis with the turret replaced by a superstructure containing the antitank gun and crew. At this point, the TDs at least had better guns. The earlier vehicles had used artillery pieces or small-caliber (in effect, obsolete) guns.

There were also philosophical problems. The TDs were, from the beginning, organized as a separate branch (the "tank destroyer force"). In effect, their only mission was to do something that couldn't be done (because effective vehicles were not fielded until the end of the war, along with more efficient tactics) and didn't need to be done (because of the proliferation of other antitank weapons). Yet there was a tank destroyer bureaucracy, and those officers were more successful at office politics in Washington than the TD crews were against the Germans. Despite a constant stream of unfavorable reports from the front, the tank destroyer force continued to build new TDs and raise additional battalions until the middle of 1943. At that point, the original concept of forming TD brigades (with 3 to 4 TD battalions each) was dropped, and the popularity of the tank destroyer force began to wane.

Meanwhile, in the field, the troops found more useful things to do with their tank destroyers. The infantry found the TDs to be excellent assault guns, despite the fact that the TD crews were trained to lie in wait for targets. The infantry battalion commanders would order the TDs to move forward with (or often ahead of) the infantry. In this way, the TDs were expected to use their high-velocity guns to destroy enemy machine-gun positions and fortifications. There were never enough tanks for this duty (as far as the infantry was concerned) and the ground pounders felt less naked on the battlefield with a few lightly armored, but powerfully armed TDs in the vicinity. Using TDs as "assault guns" worked, after a fashion. The TDs were lightly armored and took a beating from enemy antitank weapons. If unfriendly tanks showed up, the TDs got creamed. This practice persisted because although the TDs belonged to separate TD battalions, they were sent in platoon- or company-size detachments to support infantry battalions. The infantry battalion commander (a lieutenant colonel) outranked the TD platoon (lieutenant) or company (captain) commander. So the TDs did what they were told to do, even if it wasn't what they were trained or equipped to do.

By the time of the D-Day invasion (June 1944) there were only seventy-eight TD battalions left, the rest having been disbanded before they even got overseas. Only sixty-eight were left by VE-Day, of which only five were in the Pacific, where they found employment blasting numerous Japanese fortifications. A few of the TD battalions had towed guns, and five of these were still around in 1945 (being used more as artillery than tank destroyers).

Tank destroyer battalions had 660 men, 36 TDs, and 39 other lightly armored vehicles for scouting and support (plus 82 trucks and jeeps). The tank destroyer concept, born in 1940 in reaction to the "masses of German tanks storming through France," had acquired a life of its own. While it was obvious by 1943 that the concept was a failure, the tank destroyer force did not disappear until after the war ended.

THE DARK SIDE OF AIRBORNE

Paratroopers were glamorous, perhaps the most glamorous fighting forces to come out of World War II. Unfortunately, using paratroopers (at least in the way they were supposed to be used in World War II) doesn't work, at least not at a price most generals are willing to pay. This is why they have not been used much, at least as parachutists, since World War II. The Soviets and the Germans were the big proponents of paratroopers in the 1930s. The Soviets, who pioneered the idea, were never able to get it to work. The Germans were more successful, at least in 1940 when they used small groups of parachutists to seize key (and sometimes heavily defended) objectives. In early 1941 the Germans used paratroopers (and air-landed troops brought in by aircraft and gliders) to capture the island of Crete from the British. This appeared to be a striking victory, as 42,000 British troops were defeated by 22,000 Germans, leading Hitler to boast ''The German soldier can do anything.'' However, Crete was a costly victory, with many of the German battalions no longer capable of combat after the battle was over. Although the Germans rebuilt their airborne force to 30,000 by early 1942, they never again attempted to pull off another Crete.

On Crete the Germans learned that paratroopers had a chance only if they were carefully trained and well led. In fact, the most effective paratroopers were commandos dropped from the air. Aside from their better training and the surprise gained from descending out of nowhere, everything else was against the paratroopers. While they confused the enemy by the suddenness of their descent, the paratroopers themselves were also scattered while landing. No one ever came up with a solution to this problem. Paratroopers also came down with light weapons, although larger and larger gliders were built to carry heavy weapons and even armored vehicles. But whatever could be landed from the air was never enough. In 1943 and 1945, the Allies conducted several large airborne assaults (Sicily, Normandy, southern France, Arnhem, and the Rhine). All of them were more or less successful, but only one of them, Normandy, was a success worth the cost. In virtually every other case the operation was either largely unnecessary or hideously expensive.

On the other hand, some smaller airborne operations proved rather successful. For example, small airdrops (a battalion or two) were used to capture several vital crossroads and airfields during operations in French North Africa in late 1942, to insert desperately needed American reinforcements into the beleaguered Salerno bridgehead in September 1943, and to capture Corregidor from the Japanese in early 1945. Germany's last two airdrops were to help capture the Aegean island of Leros after the Italian surrender in September 1943 (a success) and to disrupt Allied rear areas during the Battle of the Bulge in December 1944 (a failure). Other small airborne forces jumped into the Burmese jungles, carving out airstrips in remote areas behind the Japanese lines, allowing stronger forces to be flown in to support the opening of Great Britain's final successful recovery of the country. Although in the postwar period many armies retained parachute troops, the high cost of massive airborne operations led most of them to restructure their airborne forces as highly portable, elite infantry, in which role they have generally proven quite successful.

GERMAN OCCUPATION FORCES IN WORLD WAR II

The enormous territories that Germany conquered in the first two years of war had to be occupied, a task that constituted a considerable drain on German manpower.

	Population (in millions)	Area (in thousands of sq. km)	German Occupational Forces (in thousands)	Ratio of Germans to Local Populace	Per Sq. Km
Balkans	21.0	403.9	200	1:105	0.5:1
Belgium	8.0	30.4	100	1:80	3.3:1
Denmark	3.6	22.7	40	1:90	1.8:1
France	40.0	550.7	500	1:80	0.9:1
Netherlands	8.5	34.2	100	1:85	2.9:1
Norway	2.8	324.0	150	1:19	0.5:1

This table gives some idea of the forces that Germany used to occupy southern and western Europe. Figures for German troops are averages, as the actual number varied considerably from year to year. On average, however, the occupation of these areas required over a million men, roughly a seventh of Germany's peak mobilized manpower.

The surface area of the territories to be controlled was not as important as the number of inhabitants. So the size of the occupation force was essentially dictated by the population. The ratio of occupiers to local population was fairly constant in most areas, hovering around one German for every eighty to ninety locals. The exceptions can easily be explained. In the Balkans (Yugoslavia and Greece) German forces were supplemented by sizable Italian forces and by equally strong Croatian and Bosnian collaborationist contingents (about eight to ten divisions' worth). This increased the number of occupying troops to about the same as those in France. Despite these additional forces, the Balkans were the most restless area in the Nazi empire, and about 24,000 German troops died there during the war, plus many more Italians and pro-Axis locals (who also kept large parts of the Balkans relatively pro-German and quiet). In contrast, only about 12,000 Germans were killed during the North African campaign. On the other hand, Hitler's obsession with a possible Allied threat to Norway explains the excessively large force stationed there. This also explains the relative inactivity of the Norwegian Resistance when compared with that in other countries.

UPON REFLECTION

"In the ultimate, victory through excess was cheaper than defeat without waste."
—Geoffrey Perret, historian of the American military experience in World War II

Surprisingly, at the time, there were a lot of people who worried more about wasting money than wasting manpower. During operations in northwestern Europe after D-Day the U.S. Army found itself expending artillery ammunition at a prodigious rate. As a result, ammunition stocks began to dwindle dangerously and by October orders had to go out to curb shell usage. Patton's Third Army, for example, was for a time limited to a daily expenditure of seven rounds per artillery piece. Fortunately, the shell shortage eased pretty quickly, so that by November the gunners were once again expending ammunition at virtually unprecedented rates. For example, between November 9 and 22, 1944, XX Corps, part of the Third Army, then operating in Lorraine, expended nearly 140,000 rounds of artillery ammunition (counting only guns and howitzers of 105mm and larger), an average of 29 rounds per gun per day. This seems an impressive figure until one realizes that on November 8 alone, XII Corps, in the same army, had expended nearly 22,000 rounds in just three and a half hours! This only a few weeks after the Red Legs had been ordered to curb expenditure.

The shell shortage was caused by excessive zeal to curb "waste" in military spending.

The army's prewar planning envisioned undertaking major ground operations within a year of entering the war. With the consideration of its experience in World War I, and its study of ammunition expenditure by the various armies during the first two years of the war, the army therefore ordered enormous amounts of ammunition. But political, military, and logistical obstacles combined to postpone the landings in France from late 1942 to mid-1943, and finally to mid-1944. So during 1942 and 1943 the United States produced a great deal more ammunition than it needed. Prior to D-Day only about a dozen U.S. divisions were in contact with the enemy, counting the European and Pacific theaters together. Some congressional penny-pinchers took a look at all that money going to "waste" to buy ammunition, just lying around in stockpiles, and concluded that the cash could be better spent elsewhere. As a result, ammunition orders were cut. And soon after D-Day it began to become apparent that artillery ammunition was being expended faster than it was being produced. Production cuts were immediately rescinded, and the gunners were soon firing away at everything in sight again. Fortunately, by October 1944 the Germans were themselves in pretty bad shape, so immediate disaster was averted. But the shell shortage, combined with the fuel shortage that brought offensive operations to a virtual halt, gave the Germans some breathing room, enabling them to begin to regroup, with dire consequences in mid-December, when they undertook the Ardennes offensive.

So saving a few bucks probably cost a few lives.

A PUFF OF SMOKE, A FLASH OF LIGHT

Little details can often have fatal consequences. This century saw the widespread introduction of "flashless, smokeless" gunpowder for rifles. Although it cleared the air on the battlefield somewhat, it made it more difficult to see where enemy fire was coming from. But not all "flashless, smokeless" powder was equal. The type produced by the Germans created a smaller flash and less smoke that what U.S. troops were using. The Germans quickly noted this difference and trained their troops to quickly spot the distinctive flash of U.S. rifles and machine guns. This made it easier for the Germans to spot where the U.S. troops were firing from. This German trick was not fully realized until after the Normandy invasion of June 1944. However, it was too late to do anything about it. By then, many GIs died largely because their rifle fire was a bit too flashy and smoky.

TOO MUCH OF THIS, TOO LITTLE OF THAT

U.S. forces found themselves invading France in 1944 with an unbalanced army. There were too many antiaircraft, antitank, and support units and too little infantry. This wasn't stupidity at work, but history.

When the United States began rearming in 1940, it did so under the influence of the striking German blitzkrieg victories of that year in France and a year later in North Africa and Russia. The U.S. Army had to prepare to fight the seemingly invincible German armed forces and planned accordingly.

The most fearful German weapons in 1940–1941 were tanks and aircraft. Even though the U.S. Army Air Force planned to build hundreds of thousands of aircraft, the ground forces prepared to field 557 antiaircraft artillery battalions. Against German tanks, there were to be over a hundred thousand U.S. tanks (most in armored divisions), plus over 200 antitank battalions (most of them self-propelled) and 65 independent tank battalions.

In order to slow down German production of tanks and aircraft by bombing their factories, plans were made to produce over 50,000 heavy (four-engine) bombers, plus as many lighter bombers. All of these antitank and antiaircraft measures absorbed millions of the best recruits.

When the Allies finally came head to head with a large German army in 1944, they found out that wars were still fought with lots of infantry. The campaigns in North Africa (tank country) and Italy (mountain goat country) were deceptive. Italy did tie up a lot of Allied infantry, but the mountains also turned it into a bloody stalemate reminiscent of World War I. The 1944 battles in France and Germany gave the Western Allies a taste of what the Russians had been going through since 1941. Moreover, the Allies by 1944 had overwhelming air superiority and the Germans had (relatively) far fewer tanks than in their salad days of 1940 and 1941. But the Germans still had plenty of infantry.

The Allies had missed the fact that, ever since the last few years of World War I (1916–1918), the Germans had concentrated on improving the effectiveness of their infantry. While German tanks and aircraft had gotten all the attention it was the superb German infantry that had done most of the work. When the Allies came ashore at Normandy in June 1944, they quickly found out that the primary antidote for German infantry was Allied infantry and the Allies didn't have enough infantry. But the Allies did have a lot of antiaircraft, antitank, and artillery battalions. These units were quickly applied to supporting the hard-pressed infantry. The situation was so bad for the British that they had to break up existing divisions to provide infantry replacements. The Americans had an even worse problem with their infantry because of equipment and organizational, training, and "political" problems. Briefly, these American problems were

- **Equipment.** While much American equipment was first-rate, the infantryman's weapons left something to be desired. The soldier's rifle, the semiautomatic M1, was the best available anywhere at the beginning of the war. But by 1944 it had been outclassed by the German SG-44 (the AK-47 is essentially a copy of this weapon). Fortunately, the Germans began to arm their infantry with the SG-44 only in 1944 and by the end of the year most German troops were still using the Mauser 1898 bolt-action rifle. A larger problem was the machine guns the American GIs had. It was recognized during World War I that the machine guns supplied most of an infantry squad's firepower. The other troops in the squad protected the machine gunner and did the maneuvering and dirty work with grenades and, sometimes, rifle fire. The American squad had one or two Browning Automatic Rifles. A World War I weapon, the Browning was, in effect, a 20-pound .30-caliber (7.62mm) automatic rifle that had a 20-round box magazine. It had a heavier barrel than a bolt-action or semiautomatic (like the M1) rifle, but would still overheat if too many magazines of ammo were shot off in a few minutes. In defensive situations, the Browning was at a distinct disadvantage because of the overheating problem. On the attack, it was more in its element. The Germans solved all these problems with their MG-42, a fast-firing, 26-pound .31 caliber (7.92mm) machine gun. Most important, the MG-42 had a removable barrel. Thus in defensive situations where a lot of firepower was needed, an overheated barrel could be quickly replaced with a fresh one. The closest thing the Americans had to the MG-42 was the M1919 .30-caliber machine gun. This beast weighed 32 pounds, needed a 14-pound tripod, did not have a removable barrel, and fired more slowly than the MG-42. A 33-pound bipod version was developed for American paratroopers, but that was the only improvement made.

- **Organization.** The U.S. infantry squad was too large (twelve men) and had no internal subdivision. In combat, this was an unwieldy situation and the squad leader (a sergeant) and his assistant (a corporal) had a hard time running things. In combat, a leader could handle supervising no more than three or four other troops. Other nations solved the problem by having smaller squads or (like the U.S. Marines) organizing the squad into four-man "fire teams" (a technique formally adopted by the army after the war, and informally during the war). In addition to the unwieldy squad, there were many other minor flaws in the organization of U.S. infantry units (battalions and regiments). After a few months of combat, units tended to come up with their own solutions to many of these problems. But in the meantime, many needless casualties were taken.

- **Training.** This was the major weakness of the U.S. troops. The Germans paid much more attention to training. Not only for troops, but also for officers and NCOs. It's telling that the Germans put their NCOs through longer training than U.S. infantry officers got. It's not that U.S. infantry did not spend a lot of time training, the problem was that it didn't learn the things it needed to know. This was largely a communication problem. Even before the United States entered the war, U.S. officers observing the fighting in Europe and Asia were taking a lot of notes. But this information was rarely turned into useful training for the troops who would have to do the fighting. This was compounded by the turmoil created as the army strove to expand from 150,000 men in 1940 to over 7 million in 1944. By 1942, seventy-four divisions were in various stages of organization. Each of these divisions needed officers and NCOs, and these were usually obtained by taking them from other units that were in a more advanced state of training. The situation was tolerable because many of the World War I veterans were recalled to service and the National Guard was activated. But none of these men had any recent combat experience, and having had World War I service was actually something of a disadvantage because of the enormous changes that had taken place in warfare since 1918. The end result was that most of the troops entering Europe in 1943 and

1944 had to go through some very bloody OJT (on-the-job training).

- **Politics.** There were many "unions" calling for troops and equipment for their particular area of interest. Combat support units were particularly popular, so the army ended up with over two hundred engineer battalions, and a lot of other "support" units. All these support units were easier to raise, transport, and support than infantry divisions, and until U.S. units got involved in heavy ground fighting in 1943 (in Italy), there was no loud voice pointing out that infantry divisions did the work and you needed a lot of good ones to get the job done. Not that all of these support units were wasted. Infantry divisions were given various support units (and often made them a de facto permanent part of the division), resulting in the actual size of infantry divisions going from a nominal 15,700 troops to nearly 20,000. But the support troops were not up front during the infantry's work, and there was never enough infantry.

Not only were there insufficient infantry divisions available (only sixty-five in an army of eighty-eight divisions), but there were serious problems with replacing casualties. The shortage of infantry divisions meant nearly all divisions had to be kept in action all the time. The lesson learned from World War I was that when a division had taken a lot of casualties and spent so much time in action that the troops were getting punch-drunk, it was time to pull them out for a little rest. During this rest period, replacements would be brought in and the veterans would train them and get to know them. The U.S. practice was to send in replacements while units were under fire. This did not work, and most replacements quickly became casualties. Units became worn out due to the unrelenting time spent in action.

It got worse. Because of the many other "priority" demands on manpower, the best-educated and most capable recruits generally went everywhere except the infantry. The ground combat units had the last pick of the recruits. Because of the chaotic nature of the buildup, a lot of good-quality recruits ended up in the infantry. But generally the infantry was considered a dumping ground for recruits no one else wanted.

There were additional divisions available for service in Europe, at least in terms of trained and organized manpower. The bottleneck was shipping, as some half-dozen cargo ships were needed to get an infantry division from North America to Europe. Until late 1943, German U-boats were a very real danger, and not all of these ships could be expected to make it. After late 1943, the subs were much less of a problem. But there were never enough ships, and so many other things (like supplies for the strategic bomber offensive) had priority. By then (1944) it was too late. Moreover, by 1944 there were 172 independent infantry battalions (enough to form the core of another nineteen infantry divisions) floating around. Many had not even left the United States. But in 1944 the big manpower crunch had arrived and it was too late to form new divisions and get them into the fight before the end of the war. The infantry that did do the fighting suffered enormous casualties, with some divisions suffering 300 percent losses among their infantry. True, a lot of these were minor wounds and many infantrymen were wounded several times. But if you were one of those dogface soldiers, you couldn't help but agree that there had to be a better way. There was, but it wasn't implemented until long after World War II was over.

ALL THOSE DAMN MACHINE GUNS . . .

One thing all Allied infantrymen remembered when fighting the Germans was the almost constant machine-gun fire coming from the enemy. This was no coincidence, as the Germans had, since World War I, built their infantry tactics around the machine gun. This was a wise move. A single machine gun provided more firepower than a dozen troops firing rifles. Moreover, for World War II the Germans developed the MG-42 light machine gun. The German Army is still using it and the United States, in effect, cloned it as the M-60 in the 1960s. The MG-42 was light enough (26 pounds) that it could be carried by one man. A belt of 100 rounds weighed 6 pounds and the gunner would be accompanied by two or three other men carrying over a thousand additional rounds. Every infantry squad of ten men had an MG-42 and the two- or three-man machine-gun crew would always set up, find targets, and begin firing before the rest of the squad moved forward to the attack. In the defense, the rest of the squad was there mainly to defend, and find targets for, the machine gun. The platoon commander has his three-squad MG-42s to work with and was trained to ensure that enemy troops would rarely avoid walking into a wall of machine gun fire. The Germans put a lot of thought and energy into placing their machine guns in the best positions to inflict the maximum damage on the enemy while safeguarding the MG-42 crew. In effect, a German infantry squad was basically just one big machine-gun unit. While the MG-42 gunner blasted away, the other men in the squad spotted targets, provided protection, and of course, carried a lot of ammunition (several thousand rounds per squad was not unusual). As a consequence, German infantry units carried a lot more ammunition with them than did comparable American outfits. On the battlefield, firepower was king, and the Germans knew it.

Toward the end of the war, many German infantrymen turned in their 9-pound, bolt-action Mauser rifles for 11-pound fully automatic SG-44s (similar to the AK-47). At this point the infantry company was reorganized. There were now two "assault" platoons and one traditional rifle platoon in the company. The assault platoons had two eight-man squads armed with SG-44s and a machine-gun platoon with eight men and two machine guns (a third was carried as a spare, along with the reserve ammunition supply), but was often given to the machine-gun squad to form a third machine-gun team). The increase in firepower was considerable. The older organization for a platoon had three MG-42s (each averaging about 150 rounds fired a minute) and twenty rifles (10 rounds a minute), yielding firepower of 650 rounds a minute. The assault platoon had two MG-42s in action, plus fourteen SG-44s (80 rounds a minute) for 1,420 shots a minute. The MG-42s and SG-44s could also fire much more rapidly for a few minutes (before their barrels overheated), generating three or four times as much firepower in an emergency. The MG-42 was particularly noted for its buzz saw sound (1,200 rounds a minute), which sent a chill down the backs of Allied infantry that heard it up close and loud.

It's no wonder that Allied infantrymen, when they think back on their experiences fighting Germans, always remember "all those damn machine guns."

THE BLITZKRIEG

The first blitzkrieg of the war, in 1939, was as fast as this form of warfare ever got. As the war went on, the speed of the advancing troops slowed down. The table on the next page, for example, was the average daily advance of attacking troops throughout the war.

The Germans gave their blitzkrieg its first large-scale workout in 1939 against unprepared Poles. The terrain of Poland was generally flat and dry and this made for fast movement. The speed of the German

Year	Daily Advance in Kilometers
1939	22.5
1940	12.3
1941	15.3
1942	—
1943	—
1944	17.1
1945	14.4

offensive shocked the world. But 1940 saw the Germans slogging through the Ardennes forest in France, and the mountains of Yugoslavia, in addition to flatter terrain of the Netherlands, Belgium, and the rest of France, as well as the deserts of North Africa. The invasion of Russia in 1941 was also on flat terrain, but for the first time the Germans encountered the effects of vehicles breaking down after advancing too many days in a row without stopping for maintenance. In 1942 and 1943 it wasn't much different from 1941, although the Allied offensives in Italy were at a snail's pace because of the advance through the Italian mountains. The 1944 battles showed an increase in speed largely because of the Soviet advances in Russia. But things slowed down again in 1945 as the Germans became more adept at slowing down the blitzkrieg they had invented and was now being used against them.

OUT-BAZOOKED

One of the more notable American innovations of World War II was the portable antitank rocket launcher, which became popularly known as the bazooka. Unfortunately, the Germans promptly copied it and quickly produced models superior to the U.S. original. The first U.S. version (the M-9 2.36-inch or 60mm rocket launcher) weighed about 16 pounds and fired a 3.5-pound warhead about a hundred yards. If the warhead hit just right, it could penetrate about four inches of armor. While this was insufficient to penetrate the front armor of most German tanks, it would do the deed if fired at the side or rear of the vehicles. The bazooka was a clever combination of simplicity and high tech, relying on the detonation of a shaped charge. Upon hitting the tank this formed a small jet of superhot gas that literally melted its way through the armor. If the jet of hot gas penetrated the armor, it would fry the crew and start fires inside the tank. This often, but not always, put the tank out of action. If the hot gas hit the tank's ammunition, the bazooka operator was rewarded with a spectacular explosion. The bazooka itself was little more than a metal tube equipped with a crude aiming device. The principal shortcoming was that, while the rocket came out of one end, a highly visible blast of hot gas came out of the other. Thus the bazooka could not be fired in an enclosed space, at least not without injuring the operator.

The German copy of the bazooka was in wide use less than a year after the bazooka first appeared. First, the Germans simply cloned the bazooka. But they knew this concept could be executed more effectively and in 1943 they introduced the *Panzerfaust* (''Armor Fist''). This weapon had several advantages over the bazooka. For one thing, it could penetrate twice as much armor (eight inches), largely because its warhead weighed nearly twice as much as the bazooka's. This allowed it to pierce the armor of any Allied tank (particularly the Russian heavy tanks). More important, this greater penetration made the *Panzerfaust* still effective if the warhead hit the target at an angle. In such a situation, a shaped charge penetrates much less armor than its operational maximum. Thus the *Panzerfaust* was more likely to wipe out a tank than the bazooka. In addition, the 14-pound *Panzerfaust* was a one-shot weapon. This was actually an advantage, as they could be given out as needed, just like grenades and mines. Although the effective range was only 80 meters (20 percent less than the bazooka), this was not, in practice, a serious shortcoming. Rocket launchers were only reliably accurate at 50 meters or less.

The Germans used the *Panzerfaust* from 1943 until the end of the war. In 1944 they introduced an even more lethal version, the *Panzerfaust* 44. It weighed only a pound more than the earlier version, but could penetrate more than 50 percent as much armor (over twelve inches) and had an effective range of 200 meters. This weapon so impressed the Soviets that they produced their own version (the RPG-7 and later models), which continues in use to the present.

Sad to say, the U.S. Army has yet to produce a portable anti-tank weapon as effective as *Panzerfaust* 44. It's not for lack of trying, but that's another story.

POISON GAS ATTACKS IN WORLD WAR II

While chemical weapons were not used in combat during World War II, they were used in other ways. Japanese Lieutenant General Suri Hasimoto ordered his First Army to use poison gas against civilians in China (in Shansi Province) during 1939. The Germans and Japanese used prisoners to test the effects of existing and experimental chemicals. All nations used chemical weapons in tests (on volunteers) of their protective masks and clothing. While the Germans and Japanese caused thousands of deaths with their ''experiments,'' there were also hundreds of injuries and some fatalities in the more humane Allies' tests as well.

And then there were the accidents. Thousands of tons of various chemical agents were produced, and shipped to the front, by all nations. While no one wanted to use chemicals, no one wanted to be caught unprepared if the enemy decided to ''go chemical.'' One of the worst of these accidents occurred in 1943, when a German air raid on the Italian port of Bari managed to hit an Allied cargo ship carrying mustard gas. Few people in the harbor knew what the ship was carrying. Mustard gas is basically an oily substance that on contact with the skin (or lungs, if inhaled) begins to burn through the flesh. Very nasty stuff. It got into the water of the harbor and floated to the surface along with oil from the fuel tanks of the ships that were sunk. The survivors were hauled out of the water and wrapped in blankets, but they were still covered with oil and mustard gas. Hours later, many of these victims began to die in agony. It took a while before the medical personnel could figure out what was going on. But even more quickly, the security people made sure that everyone was sworn to secrecy. This incident did not become generally known until many years after the war.

Beyond accidents, there were also the methods by which the thousands of tons of German chemical weapons (including nerve gas, which the Nazis invented) were disposed of after the war. Most were dumped into the Baltic Sea, or deep lakes, or left in bunkers and deep mountain tunnels because no one was still around who knew the stuff was there. Fish are still dying, and in some parts of Germany you are cautioned to be careful nosing around in the many World War II–era tunnels that still exist. Similarly, Japanese chemical weapons were dumped into the Sea of Japan, where some remain.

Toward the end of the Pacific war the United States did consider the possibility of using poison gas in attacks on Japanese-held islands, such as Iwo Jima, where it was known that there were no civilians. On consideration, it was decided that the savings in American lives was not worth the bad press that was sure to result. This remains a highly debatable point. There was an occasion during the New Guinea campaign where it appeared that the Japanese had made a use of chemical weapons, but no retaliation in kind was made and there was never another such incident. The Japanese did, however, practice chemical and bacteriological warfare against the Chinese.

Use of bacteriological warfare was first suggested, then developed and eventually carried out by Lieutenant General Shiro Ishii, a physician in the Japanese Army. Ishii began promoting the idea in the 1930s. He ended up commanding the germ warfare centers in Manchuria during the 1930s, including the infamous Detachment 731 (outside of Harbin). Major General Masaji Kitano was his deputy. Over three thousand technicians and support personnel were assigned to Detachment 731. Four subdetachments were set up during the war in China. Over three thousand Chinese, Koreans, Russians, and Americans were killed during experiments by Detachment 731. PWs and detainees who tried to escape or otherwise caused trouble were sent to Detachment 731 as punishment, and the result was usually lethal, or at least quite painful, for the victim.

The principal weapon developed from all this was the "Plague Bomb" (containers of fleas infected with the plague that could be dropped from aircraft). Bombs were tested in central China (Nimpo) in 1940. There was no dramatic effect, if only because the plague was endemic to China, where people knew how to avoid contagion, and fleas needed a host (such as rats) in order to survive long enough to spread the disease. The Japanese tried infestation on the ground in July 1942 to halt the Chinese Army advance at Chekang. Again, there was no dramatic effect. The Japanese also planned to send high-altitude balloons carrying plague-infected rats to North America (where the plague already existed in parts of the western deserts). Detachment 731 conducted experiments on communicability in humans of many infectious diseases. It also conducted frostbite research and effects of cold on humans, using prisoners as test subjects.

When the Soviets invaded Manchuria in the summer of 1945, Ishii ordered Detachment 731 facilities destroyed, with over four hundred of the remaining prisoners executed. Much of the equipment was shipped to Korea. Ishii and his senior staff fled south into China but were captured in Nanking during September and turned over to U.S. forces. Ishii negotiated immunity from prosecution in return for his research material. He later lectured at American army bases in the United States in 1948, describing his experience with human testing of infectious organisms. Major General Kitano also struck a deal with the Americans and went on to become president of a Japanese drug company (Green Cross). He lived into the 1980s as a respected member of the Japanese medical community.

The Soviets captured many Japanese officers and M.D.s who participated in human experimentation and tried all as war criminals. Most were sentenced to twenty-five years hard labor and many were released in the 1950s.

PRACTICING MEDICINE

The Japanese were in the habit of keeping their army surgeons in practice by allowing them to use prisoners to test new surgical procedures or simply to improve their skills. The ''patients'' usually didn't survive the procedures. If they did, they were killed anyway, as the Japanese did not see any reason to practice postoperative skills. The slicing and cutting was usually done without anesthesia, as medicines were always in short supply and were saved for Japanese patients. This macabre form of medical training was common in China, but American and Allied prisoners were subjected to it on Guadalcanal and other battlefields. Given their attitude toward prisoners (''better suicide than capture''), the Japanese thought nothing of this procedure. After all, the more skillful their doctors were, the better they could treat wounded Japanese.

THE LUFTWAFFE LAND ARMY

Empire building is a nearly universal phenomenon and never has it taken a stranger turn than in Nazi Germany during World War II when the Luftwaffe, the German Air Force, decided to field its own ground combat forces. Eventually, over two million troops served in the Luftwaffe ground forces. How this came about is a bizarre tale. At the beginning of the war, the only Luftwaffe troops who fought on the ground were the antiaircraft (''flak'') forces, which eventually made up over half the Luftwaffe ground forces, and a parachute battalion. In many nations, the army controls antiaircraft weapons and parachute forces. But the Luftwaffe was led by a World War I ace fighter pilot and close ally of Adolf Hitler, Hermann Göring. With all this influence, Göring was able to get about half the flak forces (those defending Germany itself) under his control. A similar application of influence got the first parachute battalion turned into a Luftwaffe unit. The army didn't fight this empire building too strenuously, as the parachute forces were small and operating flak units inside Germany was a job the army could easily give up. But by late 1942, during the Stalingrad campaign, there was a growing manpower crisis. The enormous losses (a million troops in the twelve months through March 1943, mostly in Russia) had to be replaced and reinforcements obtained. The army proposed taking excess personnel from the Luftwaffe. Göring responded by offering to scrounge up several hundred thousand men to form twenty-two infantry divisions, which would remain under Luftwaffe control. Göring had more influence than the army generals and got his way. Getting the manpower was one thing, finding experienced infantry officers and NCOs, as well as equipment, was something Göring could not handle. The divisions were raised and sent into action starting in early 1943. The Luftwaffe divisions ended up having about half the heavy weapons (artillery and mortars) as army infantry divisions. Only in machine guns did they approach the army level (being only about 15 percent short). But the lack of experienced leaders was the most serious shortcoming. The results speak for themselves. By mid-1943, four of the twenty-two hastily raised Luftwaffe divisions had been destroyed. In the second half of 1943, another three disappeared in combat. In the first six months of 1944, four more went and in the last half of 1944, seven more ceased to exist. By early 1945, only four of these divisions remained. The remnants of the destroyed divisions were usually absorbed by the army, although some became replacements for the Luftwaffe's growing airborne forces. The Luftwaffe divisions were destroyed at a much higher rate than the regular Wehrmacht divisions.

The parachute troops got off to a better, and more gradual, start. The original battalion was not used in the 1939 Polish campaign because Hitler wanted to use it as a "secret weapon" (commandos) in the 1940 battle with France. By then, the battalion had been expanded to 4,500 troops organized into the 7th Air Division. Companies of parachutists were used to good effect as commandos in Norway and Denmark. Most of the 7th Division was sent into the Netherlands, where it succeeded in quickly taking forts, bridges, and other key targets. These airborne attacks shocked the Allies, as nothing like this had ever been accomplished before. The army was still involved at this point, having raised the 22nd Air Landing Division, a unit whose equipment would fit into air transports, capable of landing at airfields recently captured by the parachutists. However, the 22nd Division did have to operate under Luftwaffe control.

In early 1941 came the paratroopers' Pyrrhic victory. The Germans invaded the Balkans in early 1941 and drove out hastily arriving British reinforcements. The British withdrew to the island of Crete. The Royal

Navy still controlled the waters around Crete, but Luftwaffe fighters and bombers controlled the air. The Germans decided to take Crete with airborne forces. The battle began on May 20. Parachute troops were dropped on the three main airfields. On the 22nd, the army's 5th Mountain Division (whose equipment was also light enough to come in by air) then landed on the captured airfields, in some cases while they were still under British fire. After two weeks of hard fighting, the 23,000 German invaders had defeated the 42,000 Allied defenders (16,500 of whom were evacuated, the rest either dead or captured). The Germans lost 4,000 men, 80 percent of them parachutists. In effect, nearly half the parachute infantry had been put out of action in one battle. While the Allies were astonished, the Germans began to reconsider the use of parachute assaults. However, the need for good-quality infantry led to the Luftwaffe's raising more parachute units in 1943. In that year, three divisions were created, followed by another six in 1944 and two more in early 1945. Most of these troops did not get parachute training because the Germans were losing air superiority and couldn't afford to build enough air transports anyway. But since it was prestigious to be a parachute trooper, and only volunteers (for the most part) were accepted, the original parachute troops were able to train thousands of additional troops. It was this need to draw on the original parachute troops in order to train and staff the new parachute divisions that was responsible for the Luftwaffe's twenty-two ordinary infantry divisions receiving such poor training and leadership. The experienced paratroopers were too busy training their own to help the new Luftwaffe's infantry units. Over a quarter of a million troops served in the parachute forces. Most of the eight parachute divisions, which were really excellent motorized infantry outfits, served in the west (Italy and France), where the Allies knew they were going to have problems whenever they ran into them.

In addition to the parachute units, there was one Luftwaffe division that was strange even by German standards. This was the "Fallshirmjägerpanzerdivision Hermann Göring" ("The Hermann Göring Armored Parachute Division"). This outfit began as an infantry battalion and flak regiment, organized as Göring's personal bodyguard. In 1940 these units reorganized into the "Panzergrenadier (motorized infantry) Regiment General Göring." The unit was soon expanded to brigade size, and then division size ("Panzerdivision Hermann Göring") in 1942. In early 1943, most of the division was destroyed as the Allies threw the Germans out of North Africa. The unit was quickly rebuilt into the largest division (19,000 troops) in the German armed forces.

More important, Göring saw to it that ample replacements were always at hand, so that his division was always up to strength, and indeed kept growing. German divisions generally fought on until they were half strength or less before receiving a lot of replacements. The Göring division was basically organized like a regular army panzer division, only with more and better equipment. Plus, a flak regiment (4,300 men and 250 antiaircraft guns of various calibers) was added. At the end of 1944 the division was split into two divisions (one armored, one mechanized infantry) and became "Panzerkorps Hermann Göring." If the war had gone on much longer, the unit might have turned into an army. As it was, over 100,000 troops served in the division throughout its various incarnations.

Over half the Luftwaffe ground troops were in the flak units. At its peak (in late 1944) nearly a million troops (including thousands of women) were assigned to serve over 20,000 Luftwaffe-controlled antiaircraft guns and searchlights. The remaining guns were in army units and on navy ships. While these guns were principally for defending Germany (and German-occupied areas) from air attack, this task grew in scope and importance as the Allies used increasing numbers of long-range fighters and bombers. The total number of flak guns grew enormously during the war:

Increase in German Antiaircraft Artillery ("Flak")

	1939	1940	1941	1942	1943	1944
Heavy Guns*	2,600	3,164	3,888	4,772	8,520	10,600
Light Guns†	6,700	8,290	9,020	10,700	17,500	19,360
Total	10,300	11,454	12,908	15,472	26,020	29,960
Searchlights	2,988	3,450	3,905	4,650	5,200	7,500
% Under Luftwaffe Control	50	61	54	64	74	70

* Mostly 88mm, with some larger.
† Mostly 20mm, but also included 37mm and 50mm models.

As Allied forces began advancing (1943) these rear-area flak units often found themselves on the front lines. The Germans had foreseen this possibility and the guns were built, and the crews trained, to deal with ground targets. This came as a painful shock to advancing Allied units. The flak guns were designed to fire quickly and quite accurately. Against ground targets they were devastating. Noting that, many flak units were motorized (like the one in the Hermann Göring Division) and used as a mobile reserve. Nothing could stop an enemy breakthrough quite like the concentrated fire of several hundred flak guns. Allied tank crews always lived in fear of encountering an 88mm gun.

Aside from being quite a curiosity, the Luftwaffe ground forces were quite wasteful and, in general, reduced overall German combat power. While the flak units were organized and used in a fairly reasonable manner, the other Luftwaffe ground units were inefficiently organized and used. For that we can be grateful.

BIG DOG ON A SHORT LEASH

As impressive as Germany's army forces appeared throughout World War II, they had an embarrassing little secret: They were always on the verge of running out of fuel. The only major oil fields the Germans had access to were in Romania, and these supplied, on average, about 45 percent of all German petroleum. Most of the rest came from converting coal to petroleum (an expensive process that requires complex facilities). When the Romanian oil fields were lost to the Russians in August 1944, the German fuel situation became critical. Training that required the use of fuel (tanks and aircraft, in particular) was severely curtailed. This resulted in pilots and tank crews that were not very skillful. Actually, this process had been going on since 1943, when Russians began to make big gains in the east. These Russian advances cost the Germans lots of fuel, which was either destroyed by the Russians or consumed by retreating German units. But aircraft and tanks were the biggest consumers of fuel. Production of these vehicles, and the training of their crews, grew enormously from 1943 on. Armored vehicle production doubled in 1943 and grew another 50 percent in 1944. Aircraft production went up over 50 percent in 1943 and nearly doubled in 1944. But oil production didn't change much at all:

	Oil Produced *(in millions of tons)*	
	Germany	*United States*
1939	8.0	
1940	6.7	
1941	7.3	
1942	7.7	184
1943	8.9	200
1944	6.4	223

The Germans managed to keep on hand 800,000 to 1.2 million tons of refined oil products through most of the war. But after Romania was lost, these stocks rapidly fell to under 400,000 tons by the end of 1944. Since units had to maintain stocks of fuel, and it took awhile to ship the fuel from the refineries to the front, over half the normal million-ton "reserve" was merely in transit. Thus in the last half of 1944, German units were operating from one fuel shipment to the next. The overwhelming Allied air superiority in this period made German fuel shipments prime targets. Frequently, German aircraft and tanks were brought to a halt simply because a fuel shipment had not arrived on time.

In addition to the lower quality of troops created by reduced training, German battle plans were heavily influenced by their fuel situation. The Germans often had to change their preferred plan to reduce fuel consumption. As it was, three quarters of the transport in their army was horse-drawn. But much vital equipment in army units could be moved only by truck.

As efficient as the Germans were on the battlefield, they would have been a lot more lethal if they always had a full tank of gas.

HIGH SCHOOL STORM TROOPERS

War brings out the worst in people, and in March 1945 the Germans brought out the fifteen-year-olds, armed them, and sent them to fight. During the previous year, the Germans had lost over a million troops. A year earlier, the art and music schools had been closed and their faculty and students sent to the front. By the end of the year, very few male teachers (of any subject) under the age of forty-five were left in the classroom. In the last month of the war, Allied units increasingly came up against teenage German soldiers. Ill-trained and poorly armed, the kids often put up a stiff, sometimes heroic resistance. The last photograph of Hitler shows him decorating some of his adolescent soldiers amid the ruins of Berlin. But teenage exuberance was no match for veteran soldiers and the adolescents died in droves. All that remains is photos of children as young as twelve surrendering, or dead.

THE BUCKET OF BLOOD

Some units, as well as individuals, have the bad luck to be in the wrong place at the wrong time. A classic case was the U.S. 28th Infantry Division. A Pennsylvania National Guard unit, its shoulder patch was a red keystone, which became known as "the bucket of blood" for the large number of casualties the division took during the November 1944, fighting on the German border. This battle was in the Hürtgen Forest, an area that became known as "bloody Hürtgen." After the Allied breakout from Normandy and romp across France, this was another of the increasing numbers of reverses the Allies encountered as they moved toward, and across, the German border. Allied supply lines were stretched to the limit, the troops and equipment were tired, and the Germans were bringing up reinforcements. The 28th Division got hit hard when it was unthinkingly sent into the Hürtgen Forest, a rugged, densely wooded region of no particular strategic importance, and ran into this German resistance. In the first week of November, the division was so shot up that it ceased to be capable of offensive operations. Several infantry battalions were nearly wiped out.

By the end of the month, the division was sent south to the relatively quite Ardennes area. But there, on December 16, the Germans launched their last major offensive of the war, the Battle of the Bulge. The 28th Division absorbed the full force of one of the two attacking panzer armies. Within a week, the 28th Division was broken into scattered remnants and it was over a month before it was capable of any battlefield operations. Overall, the division had 2,683 dead and 9,609 wounded in its nine months of combat (from its landing in France until the end of the war).

That wasn't so bad; other divisions had higher losses. The 4th Infantry Division, which came ashore on D-Day and spent eleven months in combat, had 4,834 dead and 17,371 wounded. While the 4th Division averaged 2,019 casualties a month, the 28th Division averaged only 1,366 a month. What mangled the 28th Division (and many other units during the war) was things like getting hit with two catastrophic battles within the space of six weeks. One of these scrapes (Hürtgen Forest) should not have been fought at all, but for an extraordinary series of command failures all the way up to Omar Bradley. All the American infantry divisions fighting in Europe in 1944 and 1945 averaged 50 combat casualties a day (including 10 or 11 dead). It varied between 40 and 67 a day depending on the division. Most of these losses were among the division's 6,000 infantrymen (including up-front support troops like engineers and tank crews). Fifty a day for several months is easier to handle than several hundred a day for nearly a week.

BACK TO THE FUTURE

For the infantry, World War II wasn't much different from World War I, at least as far as one's chances of survival were concerned. On average, the casualty rate in a World War II infantry division assured that all a division's riflemen would be killed off in a year or two of combat. This was about the same as the loss rate in World War I. There were survivors in World War II infantry divisions, of course. Some troops were lucky and survived. Others got seriously wounded and were no longer fit for service. Yet others got promoted or transferred to a safer job. And then, there were those who were simply very skilled at battlefield survival which, combined with a bit of luck, enabled them to live to tell the tale.

BUSTING RAIL, EAST AND WEST

Both the Western Allies and the Russians recognized the importance of crippling German railroads behind armies they were about to attack. In the west, the Allies used several months of intense air activity to cripple the French railroads. With 4,000 bombers and 4,000 fighter bombers at their disposal for such work, the Allies had little trouble shutting down German railroad capability in France. In the months before D-Day, over 100,000 sorties were flown against these targets. All the bridges across the Seine were dropped (and kept down, with repeated attacks). Hundreds of locomotives and thousands of railcars were destroyed, as well as hundreds of roundhouses, water towers, and other support facilities. The Russians didn't have such lavish air power to support their big June 22 attack, but they did have something the Allies lacked: a large, well-equipped, and well-disciplined partisan force. In the twenty-four hours before the June 22 offensive, the partisans attempted 14,000 sabotage missions on the rail network supporting the German Army Group Center. The Germans had several divisions of troops in their rear area and they were usually able to prevent many of these attacks. In the entire month of May, there had been 22,000 attempts, of which only 15,000 succeeded. But 14,000 in twenty-four hours was too much for the Germans; 10,500 succeeded. Most of these attacks were nothing more than tearing up an isolated stretch of track. Under normal conditions, a repair crew could fix that in less than twenty-four hours. But with so much damage in such a short time (and followed the next day by a major attack), the rail system was paralyzed. Some attacks did involve gunfire or explosives. In these, 95 locomotives and nearly 2,000 railcars were destroyed. Dozens of key bridges or viaducts were brought down. Just as in France, the German rail system around Minsk never recovered and the entire territory was soon in Russian hands.

THEY ALSO SERVE

The Allies had a tough time breaking out of their Normandy beachhead. The Germans were formidable defensive fighters and the broken terrain of Normandy favored the defense. By the end of June, the Allied timetable was already behind schedule and the situation didn't look good. The losses on both sides were heavy, and the British were facing a manpower shortage. Moreover, the Germans still had sufficient tanks and motorized units to give any Allied units that did get rolling a rough time.

The Allies came up with an ingenious strategy to overcome these problems. The British forces, on the northern end of the beachhead (where the British landing beaches were), had more open terrain and were, of course, closer to Paris and the German rear area in general. The British proceeded to launch a series of armor attacks throughout July. This served several ends. By using a lot of tanks (five tank divisions with 2,134 medium and 473 light tanks and five tank brigades with 1,235 medium and 315 light tanks), they minimized personnel losses and forced the Germans to commit their scarce armor to either fight the British tanks or stand by to counterattack a possible British breakout. While the British used a lot of infantry, it was the 4,000 tanks sent into these battles that got the Germans' attention. While most of these tanks got hit or destroyed, the personnel losses were relatively low, as men are lost less frequently than tanks. Using infantry instead would have increased personnel losses by a factor of twenty or more. At the time, and to this day, many feel that the British simply failed in their attempts to grab all the glory by smashing through the German lines and leading the race for Paris. But at the time, it was known that any breakout could be seriously compromised by one or more intact German tank divisions. The Allied strategy was to keep the German tanks facing the British while the Americans prepared for a breakout on their front. If the British managed to break through, fine, but the Allies weren't putting all their eggs in one basket.

The American force could launch a breakout also. American armor was much less plentiful in Normandy, with five tank divisions (930 medium and 385 light tanks) and fourteen independent tank battalions (784 medium and 238 light tanks) plus twenty-two tank destroyer battalions (792 self-propelled antitank guns).

During July, three quarters of the German tanks were tied up with the British. The plan worked. On June 6, the Germans had nearly eight hundred tanks in the area, by the end of July they had less than a hundred.

The American breakout itself used yet another special tactic: carpet bombing. The German unit defending the breakout area was the much depleted Panzer Lehr Division. In a seven- by three-kilometer area this division had 2,200 well-fortified troops and 45 tanks. The Allies sent in 1,500 heavy (four-engine) bombers to lay down a "carpet" of bombs. Then 380 medium (two-engine) bombers went in, along with 550 fighter bombers, to hose the area down with a more precise application of firepower. Two American infantry divisions moved forward and cleared out the few German survivors. Behind them came over 1,200 armored vehicles in four U.S. armored divisions. Within a week the German line was broken and the road to Paris open. While the July fighting had cost the Allies 150,000 casualties, and the Germans 110,000, it was the special measures to deal with the German tanks that made the operation a success, and prevented the British from running out of infantry.

A DIVISIONAL SAMPLER OF THE WESTERN FRONT

Although the fighting in North Africa and in Italy from late 1943 to the fall of Rome on June 5, 1944, was strategically important, and often intense, it involved relatively few troops. The Western Allies got into the war big time on D-Day (June 6, 1944). Some idea of the difference in scale may be gained by noting that worldwide U.S. Army casualties in June 1944 were roughly double those of May. About two thirds of all U.S. divisions were committed to combat in northwestern and central Europe, to which were added most of the British and French divisions, and all of the Canadian divisions. The Allied divisions that landed in France faced a mixed bag of German units. The best were the panzers and the paratroopers, about 20 percent of the total formations encountered. Most of the rest were at best semimobile formations, frequently full of non-German personnel recruited in Eastern Europe and Russia.

Divisions in Western Europe, 1943–1945

	British			U.S.				German			
	Armored	Infantry	Airborne	Armored 42	Armored 43	Infantry	Airborne	Panzer 44	SS Panzer	Infantry	Parachute
Troops	14.9	17.8	12.1	14.6	10.9	15.5	11	14.7	17.2	12.8	16.0
Tanks	226	0	0	390	263	0	0	175	219	0	0
Battalions											
Tank	3	0	0	3	3	0	0	2	2	0	0
Infantry	4	9	9	6	3	9	9	4	6	6	9
Artillery	4	5	3	3	3	4	6	6	8	5	6
Reconnaissance	1.0	1.0	1.0	1.6	1.0	0.3	1.0	1.0	1.0	1.0	0.3
Engineer	1	1	1	1	1	1	1	1	1	1	1
Signal	1.0	1.0	0	1.0	1.0	0.3	1.0	1.0	1.0	1.0	1.0
Rating	15	12	7	20	17	12	8	20	25	11	14

NOTES: Panzer is armored division. Parachute is parachute division in name only. Troop is the number of men in a division, in thousands. In addition to tanks, all of these formations had varying numbers of other armored fighting vehicles, ranging from armored cars to self-propelled artillery pieces. In a battalion, .3 indicates a company. Artillery includes antitank and anti-aircraft battalions. In some armies, signals were subsumed in the engineers. Rating, an approximation of the fighting power of the division for purposes of comparing its relative capabilities, is a rough mathematical calculation of the relative fighting power of each division, combining manpower, equipment, and organizational and doctrinal factors.

This table gives some idea of the comparable combat power of the various Allied divisions, as measured against the principal German ones.

Canadian divisions were more or less on the British model, although with some differences that tended to make them stronger. Polish formations conformed rather closely to the British model but were more formidable in combat because the troops were, well, rather mad at the Germans. It was the Polish troops who stormed Monte Cassino, after all others had failed. Although during their initial operations in North Africa and Italy the French had made use of their preexisting divisional organization, they rather quickly adopted the American model, partially because it seemed superior and partially because they were mostly operating on the U.S. dole. The German formations are the most formidable: the panzers, the Fallschirmjägers ("paratroopers"), and the few remaining regular infantry divisions.

THE TRAFFIC DESERT

As a portent of things to come, the Allies established the tactic of creating "traffic deserts" up to a hundred miles behind the German front line during the Battle for France in 1944. Hundreds of fighters and two-engine bombers were assigned to these areas throughout the daylight hours. Any vehicles seen moving were attacked (including any railroad traffic that had survived the bombing attacks even deeper into the enemy rear). The Germans soon learned that to move a vehicle in daylight was to lose it. As a result, mechanized units had to move at night, meaning that they moved at less than half their normal speed. Vehicles attempting to move in daylight were invariably attacked. The targets found in daylight were often senior officers taking a chance making a high-speed dash in their staff cars. Erwin Rommel was one such victim, nearly being killed when his car was strafed by an Allied fighter.

"WHOSE SIDE IS GOD ON?"

"The Lord mighty in battle will go forth with our armies and His special providence will assist our battle."
—FIELD MARSHAL SIR BERNARD LAW MONTGOMERY, *Viscount Alamein*

Montgomery's rather impertinent prebattle prayer was actually a useful bit of theater, showing off his supreme confidence. Although perhaps not the greatest commander in history, his swaggering, histrionic, arrogant, overconfident manner came as a refreshing tonic to British troops long used to being beaten by the Germans in North Africa (although Commonwealth troops, particularly Canadians, did not like Monty's style at all). Monty's great personal rival, George S. Patton, was very much cut from the same cloth. His showy outfits, ivory-handled pistols, theatrical behavior, and vulgar, profane, and belligerent talk were at least partially intended to help shore up the confidence of his troops, who were, after all, pretty green when compared with the veterans of the Wehrmacht against whom they had to fight.

GETTING THERE IS HALF THE FUN

If all that was required to win the war was to move the troops overseas, it would have been over pretty quickly. The two largest ocean liners, the *Queen Mary* and *Queen Elizabeth,* alone were each capable of depositing about 15,000 men apiece in Europe several times a month, while the *Aquitania, Mauretania, New Amsterdam, West Point* (the former liner *Lafayette*), and *Ile de France* could land between 5,000 and 10,000 several times a month. In fact, in 175 trips during the war, these ships carried nearly 1 million men from North America to Europe, traveling at speeds too high for submarines to intercept them. However, moving men is only part of moving an army.

To begin with the troops had to be equipped. And not just with their personal equipment. Without their "fair share" of the fuel, spare parts, ammunition, and so forth, they wouldn't have been of much use against the enemy. So for each man—and woman—sent overseas, the United States shipped twelve tons by weight of arms, equipment, and supporting material. And every month thereafter that he was abroad he had to be supported by about a ton of rations, clothing, medicines, ammunition, spare parts, miscellaneous supplies, and mail. And of course merely getting the guys and goods overseas was not what was needed to win the war either. It was the movement of troops in organized formations, specifically divisions, that was important.

In the examples in the table on the next page it is assumed that each unit has all its necessary equipment, plus three units of fire (full ammunition loads for three days for each weapon). Figures for 1942–1943 assume sixty days' maintenance, including petroleum, oils, and lubri-

Shipping Tonnage Requirements (in thousands of tons)

	Method of Loading	Infantry Division	Armored Division	Infantry Regimental Combat Team
1942	Boxed	54.8	176.4	18.3
	Normal	101.2	222.2	34.7
	Combat	200.0	440.0	66.7
1943	Boxed	69.9	177.0	23.3
	Normal	100.4	212.6	33.5
	Combat	200.0	424.0	67.0
1945	Boxed	44.9	89.2	14.9
	Normal	100.9	160.0	33.6
	Combat	200.0	0	66.7

NOTES: The 1942 infantry division had about 15,500 men and 2,100 motor vehicles, the 1943 division about 14,250 men and 2,000 motor vehicles, and the 1945 division about 14,000 men and 2,100 vehicles.

The 1942 armored division, known as the "heavy" armored division, had nearly 15,000 men with nearly 400 tanks and more than 2,600 other motor vehicles and wheeled guns, while the 1944 "Combat Command" division had about 12,000 men and only about 265 tanks and around 2,400 other motor vehicles and wheeled guns, which accounts for the considerable drop in tonnage requirements between 1943 and 1945.

An infantry regimental combat team was approximately a third of an infantry division, organized for an independent mission.

cants (POLs); those for 1945 assume only thirty days' maintenance and POLs.

The shipping required to move a formation varied depending upon the way it was loaded:

Boxed loading was the most economical way to move cargo, in terms of conserving shipping capacity. Wheels were removed from vehicles and artillery, and whatever could be disassembled was (like light observation aircraft), with everything then being packaged for optimal stowage, saving a great deal of space. A further savings was gained because the ships were loaded to optimize space utilization and stability, with the heaviest stuff down near the bottom. Boxed loading was common when units were being shipped to England during the buildup for the invasion.

Normal loading meant that vehicles and artillery were stowed with their wheels on, but all efforts were made to optimize space utilization and the ship's stability, so the heaviest stuff went on the bottom.

Combat loading was the most costly means of moving military cargo. Equipment was stowed as much as possible to be ready for use on the basis of probability of need, rather than for optimal utilization of cargo capacity. So, for example, ammunition, which is quite heavy, was stowed on the top rather than bottom of the hold. In addition, combat-loaded vessels usually required considerable modification to their holds, passenger areas, and loading tackle, which tended to reduce even further their cargo capacity.

Actually the figures in the table are approximations, as different situations might require different arrangements. A division making an amphibious landing might easily use more cargo capacity, while one being off-loaded in one of the Mulberries (portable piers) on the Normandy beach, in anticipation of going into action in a day or two, would probably come closer to the figures in the table. As there were no combat-loaded movements of armored divisions in 1945, no figure has been given, but it would probably have been about twice that of normal loading. Note that the importance of combat loading was discovered the hard way, during the Guadalcanal landing of August 1942. There, the U.S. transports had to withdraw (because of Japanese attacks) before the ships were unloaded. A lot of cargo sailed away with the half-empty ships, and the cargo that did get unloaded was not the most vital stuff.

EVOLUTION OF THE U.S. INFANTRY DIVISION

Not until 1936 did the U.S. Army began to consider alternatives to its existing infantry divisional table of organization and equipment (T/O&E). Called a "square" division, this had two brigades each of two infantry regiments, for a total of twelve infantry battalions. Everyone had entered World War I with square divisions, but most powers had abandoned them by 1916, due partially to strains on manpower and partially to the fact that the newer "triangular" formation (with three infantry regiments or brigades for a total of nine infantry battalions) was more flexible in combat. The United States, however, had entered the Great War late and with its own notions about how it should be fought. The standard U.S. infantry division in World War I was a brawny outfit of some 28,000 men, organized into twelve battalions of infantry, three of machine gunners, and nine of artillery. Although the experience of war, and mounting casualties, soon pared the U.S. division down to about 24,000 men, it was still at least twice as large as the contemporary British, French, and German divisions.

Indeed, Allied commanders occasionally treated U.S. division commanders as if they were corps commanders as a result. When the war ended, the peacetime army made only minor changes in its divisional T/O&E.

All immediate postwar military planning was based on one or another major variant of the square division. Through the 1920s and early 1930s, as military techniques and technology evolved, the United States clung to its obsolete T/O&E, rather than spend money on modernization. The army fell increasingly behind the state of the art. However, in the early 1930s some thought began to be given to modernization. The divisional T/O&E soon came in for serious scrutiny. There was no question of retaining the square division, but considerable controversy as to how to structure the proposed new triangular formation. Finally, on August 13, 1936, an experimental T/O&E was approved for field test purposes. In maneuvers against a square division the new formation proved significantly superior, being both more maneuverable and easier to command, with an increase in firepower at a considerable savings in manpower. As a result the army was committed to the new model division, defined as "a general-purpose organization needed for open warfare in theaters permitting the use of motor transport."

Putting the new triangular pattern into practice proved difficult. The army only had six active divisions, none up to strength, but there were about twenty in the National Guard. Attempting any changes in the National Guard was political dynamite (local politicians controlled the Guard in the peacetime and looked at any changes suggested by the regular army as an attempt to seize control of the Guard). As a result, the pace of conversion was not rapid. In a way this was beneficial, for it allowed the Army Ground Forces (a new overall command structure designed to unify thinking on tactics and organization) to carefully refine the proposed T/O&E. Not until June 1, 1941, six months before Pearl Harbor, was a T/O&E for the new triangular division officially approved. And even after Pearl Harbor many National Guard formations were still based on the old square model: New York's 27th Infantry Division actually sailed for Hawaii in early 1942 as a square division.

The T/O&E for the new triangular divisions was not static. As the army acquired experience from both maneuvers and combat, the organizational details were refined. Despite this, the basic concept was essentially sound and, with relatively minor changes in detail, remained in force through the mid-1950s.

Changes in division manpower and weapons allocations were rooted in technical developments, the growth in firepower, and the

T/O&E Manpower Allotments

	August 1936 (experimental)	June 1941 (official)	August 1942 (official)	July 1943 (official)	January 1945 (official)	June 1945 (proposed)
Total	13,552	15,216	15,514	14,253	14,017	16,502
HQ Company	271	165	313	268	270	275
Infantry Regiment	2,472	3,340	3,333	3,118	3,068	3,562
Infantry Regiment	2,472	3,340	3,333	3,118	3,068	3,562
Infantry Regiment	2,472	3,340	3,333	3,118	3,068	3,562
Artillery	2,529	2,656	2,479	2,160	2,111	2,273
Reconnaissance Troop	210	147	201	155	149	149
Tank Battalion	—	—	—	—	—	664
Engineer Battalion	518	634	745	647	620	621
Signal Company*	203	261	322	226	239	306
Medical Battalion†	525	520	504	465	443	467
Supply and Maintenance Troops	1,880	813	951	978	981	1,061

* The Signal Company was reorganized as a battalion in the proposed March 1945 T/O&E.
† Medical personnel assigned to other elements are included therein.

increasing role of tanks. In addition, there was a desperate need to conserve manpower. By eliminating a single man from each infantry platoon the army could realize a manpower savings of nearly 100 men per division, some 10,000 men on an armywide basis. Similar small economies in the manpower of other elements could yield sufficient surplus personnel to allow the army to raise entire new divisions. Of course such changes often led to acrimonious disputes. Not every officer, for example, was sufficiently understanding as to want to lose a couple of clerks or drivers. Army Ground Forces usually won such disputes, but not always. The Medical Corps, for example, changed the composition of a stretcher-bearer team from two men to four, without informing Army Ground Forces. In that case, the unilateral change was allowed to pass, as resisting it would have looked bad in the press.

By the end of the war, the U.S. infantry division had pretty much proven itself. In fact, postwar changes were essentially merely refinements of the last wartime T/O&E, such as the addition of tank, anti-tank, and antiaircraft battalions. This merely formalized wartime practice, for it had been common to informally "marry" divisions to various separate battalions from the general pool. Note that equipment allocations were usually exceeded in the field, when units would

T/O&E Equipment Allotments

	August 1936 (experimental)	June 1941 (official)	August 1942 (official)	July 1943 (official)	January 1945 (official)	June 1945 (proposed)
Rifles and Machine Guns						
.30 Rifles/Carbines	6,284	6,942	6,233	6,518	6,349	7,223
.30 Automatic Rifles	314	375	567	243	405	405
.30 Light Machine Guns	468	179	147	157	211	229
.50 Heavy Machine Guns	56	113	133	236	237	244
Mortars						
60mm	36	81	81	90	90	81
81mm	36	36	57	54	54	57
Armored/Tank Weapons						
2.36″ Bazookas	—	—	—	557	558	585
37mm Guns	—	60	109	—	—	—
57mm Guns	—	—	—	—	57	57
57mm Recoilless Rifles	—	—	—	—	—	81
75mm Guns	—	8	—	—	—	—
75mm Self-Propelled Guns	—	—	18	—	—	—
75mm Recoilless Rifles	—	—	—	—	—	57
90mm Guns	—	—	—	—	—	27
Field Artillery						
75mm Guns	24	—	—	—	—	—
105mm Howitzers	12	36	36	54	54	36
105mm Self-propelled Howitzers	—	—	6	—	—	27
155mm Howitzers	—	12	12	12	12	12
Tanks	—	—	—	—	—	75
Motor Vehicles	1,868	1,834	2,149	2,012	2,114	2,564

Note: Figures exclude pistols, submachine guns (which were issued as "emergency side arms" to tank crews and the like), and observation aircraft.

scrounge up additional equipment, often adopting overrun enemy material, including at times whole artillery batteries.

MAKING WAR PAY FOR ITSELF

Germany charged occupied territories for the privilege of being occupied. Up to the end of 1944 it appears that something like 55 billion reichsmarks were paid to Germany in compensation for occupation costs, not counting requisitions of goods or occasional "fines" levied on various communities for real or imagined acts of sabotage. In France alone these amounted to about 410 million francs in money, plus 2.8 million tons of wheat, about 800,000 tons of meat, and about 220 million eggs, as well as 750,000 horses and lots of other stuff. Not to mention literally tons of paintings, manuscripts, statues, rare coins, and so forth, among the 100,000 or so treasures that were looted by the Nazis in Europe. A lot of the loot has never been recovered.

GEORGE S. PATTON SLAPS A PRIVATE, TWICE

One of the most notorious untoward incidents in American military history took place during the Sicilian campaign, the "Patton Slapping Affair." There were, in fact, two such incidents which occurred only a few days apart. On August 3, 1943, Lieutenant General George S. Patton, Jr., wandered into the 15th Evacuation Hospital while on the way back to his command post after visiting the hard-pressed 1st Infantry Division on the line near Troina. As he toured the facility, he chanced upon a man who had no visible injury. Patton stopped and asked him why he was in the hospital. The reply, "I just can't take it," sent Patton into a rage. As he himself described it, "I gave him the devil, slapped his face with my gloves, and kicked him out of the hospital." Although the matter was hushed up, people in higher places were apprised of the details.

About a week later, Patton dropped in on the 93rd Evacuation Hospital. He came upon an unwounded young soldier sitting on a bed, sobbing to himself. The general inquired as to what was the matter. "It's my nerves," replied the young man. "What did you say?" asked Patton, in a voice described by some witnesses as a scream. "It's my nerves," came the reply once more, "I can't stand the shelling." At that, the general lost all control. Shouting at the man, he screamed, "Goddamn coward, you yellow son of a bitch," and slapped him hard across the face. Hospital personnel and the general's aides rushed him out of the place before anything more serious occurred, but this time there was no hushing up the matter. The incident caused an outcry in the United States, which ardent Pattonophiles attributed to "Communists." Patton was forced to make a public apology. Worse yet, at the end of the campaign he found himself essentially unemployed for nearly a year.

Patton's fans argue that his behavior was correct, while his foes suggest that it reveals deep-seated emotional problems. Actually, neither is a very accurate assessment. The two soldiers were obviously suffering from combat fatigue. Although it has not been publicly suggested, Patton himself probably had a mild case of combat stress (although he was a rough SOB even at the best of times). Patton was no stranger to combat, or its results. He had seen men's nerves crack under the stress of combat. He explained his behavior as an attempt to jar the soldier back to reality. What Patton did was, in fact, one of the techniques that other armies discovered useful in helping a soldier recover from combat fatigue. The other European armies had considerable experience with combat fatigue (then called shell shock) during World War I. It was found that the best treatment for most cases was to keep the soldier near the front and under military discipline. In effect, put the soldier on "light duty" in a quiet area of the combat zone and give him time to sort himself out. Sometimes this treatment would involve a combat-experienced NCO talking bluntly with the injured soldier. Slapping was not advised, but getting the soldier treated and back into action was. General Patton might have known instinctively what should be done, but few American generals paid much attention to the problem.

The real problem was caused by serious flaws in U.S. military policy. Despite lip service paid to the importance of unit cohesion and regimental pride, the army's manpower management policies since the beginning of this century considered men interchangeable parts. The first man Patton slapped had been under fire barely a week when he cracked from the strain. A replacement, he had been shifted from replacement depot to replacement depot, brought to the front as a spare part for a depleted unit, put in among seasoned troops with little time to forge links to his new organization, and immediately sent into action. Little wonder that he had collapsed. The second man was a combat veteran who had been with his outfit from the landings in North Africa in November 1942. He had been pretty much under fire constantly since then and was suffering from an undiagnosed case of malaria in the bargain. Army policy was that a man in combat stayed there unless he completely lost his composure. This despite evidence that troops under fire for stretches of four or more months at a time were particularly prone to serious psychological problems. Patton himself was in this very category, being often under fire and having to shoulder the burdens of command as well. Further complicating matters was the army's attitude toward "psycho" cases.

To begin with, during the induction process the Army attempted to "weed out" men deemed likely to succumb to battle fatigue. As a result, fully 10 percent of men rejected for service were classed as "psychologically unsuitable." Since the resulting personnel were therefore considered much less prone to battle fatigue, the army tended to ignore early indications of potential problems. The army then bungled the treatment of the men who were suffering from battle fatigue. Apparently on the assumption that psychological disorders were contagious, the policy was to immediately evacuate battle fatigue cases as far to the rear as possible, in the process cutting these men off from their buddies and plunking them down among perfect strangers in the psychological wards of evacuation hospitals.

In complete contrast was the policy of the German Army. There was no such thing as a "replacement" in the German Army. Units were allowed to remain in combat without replenishment of losses. When an outfit was reduced beyond a certain point it was pulled out of the front for a rest. New men, recruited from the same area as the original division, and recuperated wounded from the unit, were then used to bring it up to strength again. While in a rest area the new men got to know the old ones, so that they felt they were part of a team. Thus, when the unit went back into action everyone worked together. In addition, the Germans viewed combat fatigue as a kind of wound, to be treated as close to the front as possible. Considerate, compassionate care was mixed with reminders that the man was a soldier and had comrades who were expecting him to return to the front as soon as possible, for they needed his help. In the end, the German policy was far more successful in restoring men to duty than the U.S. policy, which actually discouraged recovery and deepened existing disorders. Curiously, the Germans had adopted their policy after studying the American practice in the First World War, a policy that was created by psychologists and psychiatrists. However, between the wars the U.S. Army decided that it knew more about combat stress than the "head shrinkers" and overruled their proposals to continue the earlier practice, with the result that a seventh of U.S. combat casualties were psychological, the highest rate among the major powers. Interestingly, the British Army rejected only about 2.5 percent of inductees for psychological reasons, and yet had a much lower rate of casualties from combat fatigue.

SAGE ADVICE

"It would be unwise to assume we can defeat Germany by outproducing her. . . . Wars are won by sound strategy implemented by well-trained forces which are adequately and effectively equipped."

—Brigadier General Leonard T. Gerow, head of the War Plans Division of the General Staff, 1941

Gerow, who after D-Day went on to become the very able commander of V Corps and later of the Fifteenth Army in northwestern Europe, was making a particularly sage observation. It was true, of course, that the Allies were perfectly capable of outproducing the Axis powers. But production did not automatically mean victory in the field, as the experience of the war showed. In fact, Allied war production was consistently higher than Axis production for virtually the entire war. Yet the Axis forces consistently outfought often overequipped and underprepared Allied forces, particularly for the first two or three years of the war.

THE COST OF WAR

The campaign in France, Belgium, the Netherlands, and Germany from D-Day (June 6, 1944) through VE-Day (May 8, 1945) cost the Western Allied armies 766,294 casualties (including some 200,000 dead), of whom about 60 percent were Americans, out of a total of 5,412,219 troops landed, for a casualty rate of 14.2 percent, or roughly 1 in 7. There were also at least 50,000 Allied civilians killed during the campaign.

THE COSTLIEST CAMPAIGN

The American strategic bombardment campaign against Germany in World War II cost approximately $43 billion (nearly $0.5 trillion in 1994 dollars). The Eighth and Fifteenth Air Forces lost 8,237 bombers and 3,924 fighters during the campaign. About 29,000 airmen were killed and 44,000 wounded. The number of dead amounted to about 10 percent of total U.S. personnel killed in action and was greater than that suffered by the army in the Normandy campaign (about 16,000) or the Battle of the Bulge (about 19,000). Roughly equal to the number of U.S. Navy dead, the losses among aircrew actually exceeded total Marine Corps deaths (about 20,000) for the entire war. Overall, your chances of surviving the war were better in the Marine Corps than as a member of a bomber crew.

British aircraft losses during the campaign were 8,325 bombers and over 10,000 fighters. Aircrew casualties (including many from Commonwealth nations) totaled 64,000 men, killed, wounded, and missing.

Aside from material damage inflicted on German industry and infrastructure, the strategic bombing campaign tied down about a million German troops in antiaircraft defense and about half of the Luftwaffe's total fighter strength even before D-Day, assets that were desperately needed elsewhere, particularly in Russia. German attempts to stop the bombers also crippled their fighter force because of the heavy losses in the air. Some 600,000 Germans were killed during the strategic bombardment campaign.

In a very real sense the strategic air campaign against Germany constituted a "second front."

EVERYTHING IS A WEAPON

In 1943 all 4.4 million parts of scissors produced in occupied Europe were requisitioned for the use of the German armed forces. The Germans also requisitioned some 6.2 million stamp pads to help them keep all their paperwork in proper order. It's worth noting that the strength of the German armed forces at the time was only about 7 million.

THE CONVOY SYSTEM

A convoy is a group of ships traveling together for mutual protection. In World War I it had taken several years, enormous losses, and the imminence of defeat at the hands of Germany's U-boats (not to mention pressure from some historically hip insurance companies) to convince the British to adopt the convoy system. This was despite the fact that the British had used the convoy system to considerable advantage during the great sea wars of the seventeenth and eighteenth centuries. Almost as soon as they began using them in 1917, merchant shipping losses fell dramatically. Over 90 percent of British merchant ships lost in World War I were proceeding individually. As a result, as soon as the Second World War broke out, the Royal Navy instituted a convoy system. Based on careful prewar planning, an elaborate system of routes was established to link Great Britain with her overseas markets and suppliers. Convoys were given a code designation indicating their destination and number. Thus, "OG-12" was the twelfth convoy outward bound from Great Britain to Gibraltar. Occasional convoys were given unique designations, such as "WS" for "Winston Special," an emergency shipment of material from the United States that had been urgently requested by the prime minister.

There were normally two types of convoys: "fast" ones, which proceeded at 9 knots, and "slow" ones, which dawdled along at 7.5 knots. Although most merchant ships could do better (albeit not much better) than these speeds, it was necessary to maintain some reserve capacity for maneuvering in emergencies. In any case, since once submerged most U-boats made only 5 to 7.5 knots, even the "slow" convoys were relatively fast.

The most important of the convoy routes were those to North America, the "Arsenal of Democracy." It was across the North Atlantic (the most maltempered regularly traversed waters in the world) that convoys brought the food, vehicles, weapons, and ultimately the men that secured the Allied victory. The first HX convoy (from Halifax) sailed on September 16, 1939, to be followed by several hundred more in the course of the war. By 1942 a convoy was departing from Halifax every four or five days, and one left a British port for North America at about the same rate. A fast convoy could make the North Atlantic crossing in ten to fourteen days, depending upon final destination (Halifax, New York, and so forth), a slow one in thirteen to nineteen days.

The typical North Atlantic convoy consisted of forty-five to sixty merchant ships, formed into nine to twelve equal columns. In nine columns, a forty-five-ship convoy would have a front of about four and a depth of about one and a half nautical miles, occupying an area of only about six square miles. Merchant mariners, a notoriously individualistic bunch, found this uncomfortably close and straggling was not unusual, particularly early in the war. Nevertheless, dispersal was bad. The idea was to keep the convoy as close together as possible, for the more concentrated it was the safer it was. It's a big ocean, and a lot of ships all in one place are much more difficult to find than the same number of ships scattered all over the seas.

Convoys were under the command of an officer designated the commodore, regardless of his actual rank. Convoys comprised of mostly U.S. ships were usually under a naval reserve captain or rear admiral, often a merchant mariner himself. British convoys were usually under the command of a retired Royal Navy flag officer. The commodore displayed his broad pennant on one of the merchantmen. He was responsible for keeping the convoy together, ordering changes in course and speed, and coordinating the movements of the merchant ships with the escort commander, who was in command tactically.

Initially escorts were rather scarce. Early in the war many convoys sailed with only three or four escorts. Two or three of these were corvettes, slow, small, uncomfortable vessels of around a thousand tons, with perhaps one light gun, one antiaircraft gun, and a lot of depth charges. There might also be a frigate (a little larger, a little faster, a little better-armed, a little more comfortable) or a sloop (a little bit more of everything) or even a genuine destroyer. Escorts were assigned sectors around the perimeter of the convoy. At night or in thick fog they maintained station, since maneuvering in total darkness was dangerous. By day, however, the escorts were able to actively patrol their sectors. In either case, the escorts searched for U-boats using a combination of sonar ("Asdic" in British parlance) and lookouts, the former to detect submerged U-boats and the latter to watch for any that might approach on the surface. When the presence of a U-boat was ascertained (often because a ship had just been torpedoed) the nearest escort immediately went in pursuit. The idea was not so much to sink the U-boat as to spoil its day. By keeping it busy with depth charges, the escort allowed the convoy to get away. Early in the war, when escorts were in short supply, they were not allowed to pursue a U-boat for more than an hour. This was sufficient time for the convoy to get beyond the sub's reach, at least as long as it remained submerged. As escorts became more numerous they were deployed farther from the edges of the convoy, increasing the protective "envelope" around their charges. They were also given a freer hand in pursuing U-boats, which led to more kills. Eventually escorts became sufficiently numerous to permit them to operate in pairs, making U-boat hunting still easier, since it was more difficult for the U-boat skipper to outmaneuver or outthink two opponents. And while escorts were becoming more numerous they were also becoming bigger and better, and gradually the smaller, less-effective ships were replaced by destroyer escorts and destroyers.

Although traveling in a convoy was a lot safer than traveling singly, occasionally a convoy got hit, and hit badly. This occurred when the Germans began to institute "wolf pack" tactics, in which a U-boat that detected a convoy would not attack it immediately, but rather spread the word to its sisters, who would converge for a coordinated mass attack. Ten convoys were hit so badly they lost more than 50,000 gross registered tons.

Note that on three of the occasions two convoys were traveling together. Normally this was an advantage, as it created a smaller target, while concentrating the escorts, but in these cases the convoys just ran out of luck. While the losses to SC-71 and HC-79 were the greatest inflicted on a convoy by submarines, overall the worst hit convoy was PQ-17, bound for Murmansk in northern Russia, which had to cope

The Principal Atlantic Convoy Battles

	Convoy				Submarines	
	Code Designation	Number of Ships*	Ships Lost	(GRT†)	Number of Submarines‡	Submarines Lost
October 1940	SC-71	79	32	(154.6)	12	0
	HX-79					
September 1941	SC-42	70	18	(73.2)	19	2
July 1942	PQ-17	42	16	(102.3)	11	0
November 1942	SC-107	42	15	(82.8)	18	3
December 1942	ONS-154	45	19	(74.5)	19	1
March 1943	SC-121	119	16	(79.9)	37	2
	HX-228					
March 1943	SC-122	89	22	(146.6)	44	1
	HX-229					

* Number of ships includes escorts, usually about 10 to 15 percent of the total. Escorts are also included in the number of ships lost, but not in the GRT lost.
† GRT is gross registered tons, the standard method of defining a merchant ship's size. In thousands of tons.
‡ Submarine figures are for the number actually taking part in the attack. There were occasionally others in the vicinity helping to coordinate the attackers.

with German aircraft in addition to submarines. When the convoy, which had an escort of only six destroyers, was threatened with the intervention of major German surface units (a battleship, pocket battleship, and heavy cruiser, with escorts) it was ordered to disperse, with the result that it lost twenty-two of its thirty-six merchantmen, with about two thirds of the cargo originally laded.

March 1943 was the turning point in the Battle of the Atlantic. Several favorable developments came together at the same time, all with dire consequences for the U-boats. The number of escorts finally began to become adequate, antisubmarine escort carrier hunter/killer groups began roaming the Atlantic (they didn't kill very many submarines but they certainly kept the U-boats away from the happiest hunting grounds), new technologies such as Huff-Duff began to come along, and Ultra intercepts of German coded communications became more frequent. Sinkings declined precipitously. The Battle of the Atlantic was won. But ships continued to travel in convoys right up until the surrender of Germany.

Altogether 2,889 transoceanic convoys sailed to or from Great Britain alone during the war, for a total of 85,775 ships, of which only 654 were lost, 0.7 percent. There were also nearly 8,000 coastal convoys, involving some 175,000 vessels, of which only 248 were lost, 0.14 percent. There were also numerous convoys that proceeded from North America to other places, such as Africa, the Middle East, the Caribbean, South America, and even the Pacific, so that several hundred thousand voyages were made in convoys during the war, virtually all of them safely.

THE MOST EFFECTIVE ANTISUBMARINE WEAPON

Although U.S. Navy airships (blimps) accounted for only two submarines during the war, they managed to escort some 90,000 merchant vessels without losing a single one. The key to the effectiveness of the approximately 200 blimps that the United States used in the war was their ability to loiter in the vicinity of a convoy. Submarines had to approach convoys on the surface, since they were too slow to do so when submerged. Since blimps were relatively speedy (about 80 miles an hour) they could patrol large areas around a convoy easily. In fact, they were much better at this than were conventional aircraft, which were too fast.

Blimps were armed with a mixture of depth charges and bombs, but were otherwise virtually defenseless. Despite this, only one blimp is known to have been lost to enemy action, *K-74*, which was shot down by *U-134* on July 18, 1943, with the loss of one of her ten crewmen. A surprisingly successful weapon, the blimp. In the 1980s, the U.S. Navy proposed to reintroduce the blimp for antisubmarine warfare. This project was later scuttled by the end of the Cold War.

OOPS!

The destroyer U.S.S. *Borie* (DD-215) sank in heavy seas off the Azores on November 1, 1943, hours after she had sprung a severe leak when ramming the German submarine *U-405*, which also sank.

THE LARGEST FLEET IN WORLD WAR II

The largest fleet belonged to the U.S. Army, sort of. During World War II, the army had 111,000 ships under its control, the U.S. Navy, 75,000. The navy had 1,400 to 1,700 combat ships, depending upon how one classifies some types of vessels, while the army had none. The army fleet consisted mostly of transports and support ships. At its peak strength, the army controlled 17 million tons of shipping, the navy only 8 million tons. The army total included 88,000 amphibious assault craft and 8,500 barges. Most of the crews comprised of soldiers and civilians, the navy being reluctant to supply all the manpower for the army's fleet. It should not be surprising that the army controlled so many ships, as most of the amphibious operations in World War II were army operations. The army also had 1,665 large seagoing ships, 1,225 smaller (under 1,000 tons) seagoing ships, and 11,154 harbor craft (including tugs, mine planters, crash boats, fuel lighters, dredges, and so forth). This situation was not to the navy's liking. Before World War II, it was agreed that the navy would control everything that floated. But in the chaos accompanying the U.S. entry into World War II, this rule went overboard, and the army grabbed more and more ships. This was not simply empire building on the army's part; it knew that when the navy controlled shipping, army needs took a backseat to navy requirements.

When the navy realized that the army was "assembling a fleet" it made a lot of noise back in Washington. In an epic bit of wheeling and dealing, the army managed to keep its ships. However, the army was always taking a backseat to the navy when it came to getting the best stuff. The navy was not reluctant to leave the army with the oldest and least-seaworthy ships. The army didn't care. It grabbed everything it could. Since the navy had now washed its hands (in most cases) of the responsibility for providing sea transportation for the army, the army had a big incentive to grab all it could, any way it could. The army ended up with a lot of ships the navy would never have considered, including ferries, freshwater (Great Lakes) ships, and even some ships built of reinforced concrete (an effort to save steel that the navy wanted no part of). Most of the larger army ships were chartered "for the duration." This made the navy happy, as it knew these ships would be easily gotten rid of after the war.

Typical of the way the army operated was in the Pacific, where General MacArthur was told to "not worry about formalities and details" when he quickly assembled foreign and captured ships during the dark days of 1942. The army did get some specially built troop ships, although many soldiers went overseas in ships like former Alaskan fish-processing vessels. Apparently they never got the smell completely under control. The army also got a lot of specially designed smaller amphibious craft—because the army made more amphibious landings than the U.S. Marines, and it was the army that perfected the routines for rapidly getting supplies and equipment over recently conquered beaches (much to the navy's chagrin).

Just for the record, however (and to assuage the navy's pride), by the end of the war the fleet totaled 6 million tons of warships (1.1 million of battleships, 1.7 of carriers, 0.9 of cruisers, 1.7 of destroyers, and 0.6 of submarines) and about 7.2 tons of minor combatant, amphibious, auxiliary, and miscellaneous vessels, figures that the army couldn't come close to approaching.

THE BATTLE OF THE ATLANTIC, 1939–1945

Arguably the most critical campaign of the Second World War was that to keep the sea-lanes open from North America to Great Britain.

From virtually the first day of the war Germany unleashed its U-boat fleet in a campaign to strangle Great Britain economically by means of unrestricted submarine warfare, a strategy that had seemingly come close to securing victory during World War I. Ultimately, this strategy failed a second time, as new technologies (radar, sonar, Huff-Duff, escort carriers, and so forth) made life for the submarine even more precarious than it had been during the previous war. But it was somewhat close, as can be seen from the figures below.

The climax of the submarine war came in the first quarter of 1943. Through mid-March losses to submarines were running at about the same rate as in 1942, but thereafter, fell off markedly, while U-boat losses rose impressively. The figures are for global Al-

Ship and Submarine Losses

		Ships Sunk	Submarines
	Total	By Submarine	Lost
1939	222	114	9
1940	1,059	471	22
1941	1,299	432	35
1942	1,664	1,160	85
1943	597	377	237
1944	205	132	241
1945	105	56	153

lied and neutral losses in merchant ships, most of which occurred in the Atlantic and adjacent waters. The figures include losses in the Indian and Pacific oceans, which were relatively small, and some of which were inflicted by German and Italian forces. Merchantmen not sunk by submarine were mostly accounted for by aircraft, mines, and surface raiders.

The approximately 800 U-boats that Germany employed in the Atlantic (of about 1,175 completed) sank 2,640 ships totaling rather more than 13 million gross registered tons, for an average of about 3.3 ships or 15,000 GRT per submarine sent into action. In addition, 30 Italian submarines served in the Atlantic (27 having slipped through the Strait of Gibraltar to operate out of Bordeaux in late 1940, where they were shortly joined by 3 transferred around Africa from the Red Sea flotilla), sinking 135 ships totaling 842,000 GRT, an average of 4.5 ships, or about 28,000 GRT per submarine. The difference can be attributed largely to the fact that most of the Italian submarines in the Atlantic were lost or returned to Italy before March 1943, when the tide turned decisively against the submarine. Ten of the Italian submarines were lost in the Atlantic, 5 without a trace.

SUB SUNK! CAUSES OF U-BOAT LOSSES IN WORLD WAR II

The German Navy lost 746 submarines during the war. Of these, 514 were sunk by British Empire forces or Allied personnel operating under British command (Dutch, Polish, etc.), 165 by U.S. forces, 1 by the Cuban Navy, and 7 by Russian forces, plus 16 "shared" between U.S. and British imperial forces. The most successful subkillers were aircraft, followed by surface ships, with accidents coming in a distant third.

The jump in U-boat losses in 1943, when more U-boats were sunk than in the previous forty months of the war put together, was due largely to a combination of fortuitous circumstances:

- The perfection of Huff-Duff (High Frequency Direction Finding), which enabled Allied ships to locate German subs by their radio traffic, which was considerable. The highly effective German "wolf pack" tactics required the widely dispersed U-boats to frequently use their radios in order to form the deadly pack. During the war, the Allies attributed much of their success to

U-boat Losses

Sunk by	1939	1940	1941	1942	1943	1944	1945	Total
A/C	0	2	3	36	140	68	40	289
Ships	5	11	24	32	59	68	17	216
A/C and Ships	0	2	2	7	13	18	2	44
Bombs	0	0	0	0	2	24	36	62
Mines	3	2	0	3	1	9	7	25
Subs	1	2	1	2	4	5	3	18
Other	0	4	5	6	17	43	17	92
Total	9	23	35	86	236	235	122	746

NOTES: A/C is the losses credited to aircraft not engaged in strategic bombing attacks on submarine pens; these were mostly land-based aircraft, shipborne planes accounting for only about 15 percent (43 submarines). Ships includes losses inflicted by surface vessels of all types. A/C and ships refers to submarines killed through combined attacks of both. Bombs is the attempt to destroy submarines in their pens by strategic bomber raids, which were numerous but ineffective until late in the war. About two thirds of the mines that claimed submarines (16) were laid from aircraft. Other is losses to accidents (including *U-120*, which sank due to a malfunctioning underwater toilet, and *U-459*, which sank after an airplane she had shot down crashed on her deck), weather, ground fire, a small number of captures (including the *U-505*, which is now in Chicago), and other unknowns.

Huff-Duff as a cover for the ULTRA code breaking. This convinced the Germans, who knew a lot about direction-finding technology and how far it could be pushed. Allied Huff-Duff was never as good as the Allies claimed, but it was effective and useful.

• Improved radar and sonar. The Allies managed to stay one jump ahead of the Germans in this technical competition.

• Better air cover. Especially the introduction of escort carriers for ASW (anti-submarine warfare) work.

• More numerous escorts.

• And, of course, the Allies' increasing ability to read the German naval code, the "ULTRA Secret."

At the end of the war the German Navy had about 300 submarines in commission, of which over 200 were scuttled, so that only about 75 boats were captured intact. Several hundred submarines in various stages of completion were captured in shipyards.

WOODEN WALLS

Great Britain's most famous warship, the old wooden hundred-gun ship of the line H.M.S. *Victory*, launched in 1765, played a role, albeit a minor one, in the Second World War. On the night of March 10–11, 1941, during a German air attack on the Portsmouth naval base, a five hundred-pound bomb fell between the ship's hull and the drydock in which she rests on a permanent cradle. Although the bomb caused some damage to about 120 square feet of the hull, the ship proved surprisingly resilient. Presumably the incident was a mistake. Or perhaps the Germans had learned that from time to time senior British naval officers were wont to hold conferences aboard the old battleship, perhaps seeking inspiration from Nelson's ghost.

The *Victory* came out of her encounter with the Luftwaffe a lot better than did another old liner, the seventy-four gun H.M.S. *Wellesley*, launched in 1815, which was more or less demolished at dockside by a German bomb in 1941, thus gaining the distinction of being the last wooden ship of the line to be sunk by enemy action. The *Victory* and *Wellesley* were actually not the only ships of line to have a role in the war. The Royal Navy, ever mindful of the public purse, had for generations made use of old warships in a variety of ways, such as barracks, schools, and the like. During the war there were about a half dozen of the old "wooden walls" still in the service.

The Royal Navy was not the only one to make use of such historic relics. The flagship of the U.S. Navy, which wore Admiral Ernest J. King's flag during the war, was the U.S.S. *Constellation*, a sailing corvette "reconstructed" in 1855 from a frigate completed in 1796 (actually the navy cleverly used the reconstruction money to build a new ship, salvaging what it could of the old one). The famous Russian cruiser *Aurora* (1895), preserved at Leningrad after allegedly having fired the first shots of the Communist Revolution on November 7, 1917, served as an antiaircraft platform in Leningrad harbor, suffering considerable damage during the German siege. And in 1944 the famous old U.S. battleship *Oregon* (1896), veteran of the Spanish-American War, was saved from the scrapper's yard, loaded with ammunition, and towed to Guam, where she helped supply the newer battlewagons pounding the Japanese defenses: After the war she was lost in a typhoon while under tow to the United States.

MISS ME

The venerable Piper Cub (single-engine, two-seat civilian aircraft) went to war as an artillery spotter. While the pilot dodged enemy ground fire, the second man spotted targets for the artillery and radioed back the information. In April 1945, one such aircraft, called *Miss Me* spotted one of their German opposite numbers (a Fieseler Storch) and the Americans drew their .45-caliber pistols and dove on the Storch with guns blazing. Amazingly, they damaged the German aircraft, forcing it to land. The Piper Cub then landed and the Americans jumped out and took captive the startled Germans. Four more and the *Miss Me* pilot would have been an ace.

6

THE PACIFIC WAR, 1941–1945

The campaigns in the Pacific were unique even by World War II standards. Unique, and quite different. Most of the naval battles were in the Pacific, and there was a submarine campaign to match the one the Germans waged in the Atlantic. The Pacific fighting was as vicious as anything on the Russian front. Unlike those fighting in Europe, with its frigid winters, the Pacific troops had to endure endless, sweltering tropical weather. The Pacific war was different, and so were its "dirty little secrets."

QUICK WALK THROUGH HISTORY'S LARGEST NAVAL WAR

Japan's plan for the Pacific war was to destroy the Allied forces in the region, seize all of the Allied colonies and possessions, and then sue for peace on favorable terms. It was a desperate gamble, and the military phase actually worked. The Pacific war began with the Allies and Japan having a rough parity in naval forces (except for carriers), while Japan had a superiority in air and land forces.

The Pacific was not heavily garrisoned. The British did have a large force in Singapore, as did the United States in the Philippines. But the nearby Japanese forces were better trained and led and had superior air support. The initial Japanese attacks in December 1941 and January

Naval Forces in the Pacific, December 1941

	Japanese	U.S.	Allied*	Total Allied
Carriers†	10	3	—	3
Carrier Aircraft†	545	280	—	280
Battleships	11	9	2‡	11
Heavy Cruisers	18	13	1	14
Light Cruisers	17	11	10	21
Destroyers	104	80	20	100
Submarines	67	73	13	86

* The United States' allies were Great Britain, Australia, New Zealand, and the Netherlands. In addition, the United States had its Atlantic fleet, from which it quickly withdrew three carriers to even up the carrier ratio in the Pacific, as well as a number of battleships and other vessels.
† Figures for carriers exclude ships working up and escort carriers. Including these would raise the Japanese totals to 13 carriers with about 650 aircraft.
‡ Allied battleship figures include 1 battle cruiser.

1942 soon overwhelmed all resistance. What stopped the Japanese eventually was a lack of merchant shipping to move the troops and supplies forward. By that time, Japan had seized all the central Pacific islands, all of what is now called Indonesia, and all of Southeast Asia except for northern Burma and most of New Guinea and adjacent islands. In the space of six months, Japan's carriers attacked targets from the Hawaiian Islands to southern India, literally going halfway around the world in the process.

But in May, with more U.S. carriers in the Pacific, Japan began to lose carriers. First, a light carrier was lost in the Battle of the Coral Sea (and one heavy carrier damaged). A month later, four more heavy carriers were lost at Midway. That essentially evened up the carrier situation in the Pacific despite the United States' loss of two carriers, as it was pouring land-based aircraft into the theater and this restricted where a handful of Japanese carriers could operate with relative safety.

In August 1942, the United States landed a Marine division on Guadalcanal and seized an unfinished Japanese airfield. Meanwhile, to the northwest, the Japanese were continuing to fight over possession of New Guinea. The Guadalcanal battle, which lasted six months and resulted in a Japanese defeat, was but the first of a series of battles that took Allied troops right up the Solomon chain of islands, past Rabaul, across New Guinea, and on toward the Philippines by April 1944, although the New Guinea battle raged on into 1944. During 1942 there were a series of carrier battles that demonstrated U.S. capabilities in carrier warfare and further depleted Japan's hard-to-replace pool of carrier pilots (already weakened by the losses at Midway and service from land bases in the Solomons). In the summer of 1944, the rebuilt Japanese carrier force was destroyed once and for all in the Battle of the Philippine Sea (the "Great Marianas Turkey Shoot").

Meanwhile, two other fronts gave the Japanese even more trouble. In Burma, the Japanese offensive stalled by mid-1942. Noting that the Allies were building railroad, truck, and air routes into China, the Japanese eventually tried in 1943–1944 to push the British back into India. But the forces were more evenly matched now and the Japanese offensive failed. By early 1945, the Allies were on the offensive and eventually pushed the Japanese out of most of Burma. While Burma was a stalemate the Japanese could afford, the third prong of the Allied counteroffensive led right to Tokyo. In late 1943, the United States began the series of amphibious operations that would, by late 1944, seize islands within B-29 range of Japan.

In late 1944 the Philippines were retaken. In early 1945, islands even closer to Japan were taken and the bombing campaign against Japanese industry and population intensified.

By the summer of 1945, Japan was isolated and broken.

FIRST DEFEAT

The Japanese were much chagrined when they suffered their defeat at Midway. This was thought to be the first Japanese defeat of the war. It wasn't, as the Chinese defeated the Japanese at the Battle of Taier-chuang in March 1938. The Chinese began by attacking a Japanese garrison in the walled town of that name. After two weeks of fierce fighting, with heavy reinforcements used by both sides, 16,000 Japanese and 15,000 Chinese were dead, and the Chinese held the town. This was one of the few Chinese victories in their war against the Japanese, which began in 1931 and went on to the summer of 1945. This was the first Japanese battlefield defeat in several centuries. The Japanese later lost several more battles with the Chinese and were ultimately smashed by a Russian blitzkrieg on the Siberian-Mongolian frontier in 1938–1939 and later in the summer of 1945.

However, although the Imperial Army had, in fact, been bested several times before the Pacific war began, Midway was the first defeat ever, regardless of the size of the action, in the history of the Imperial

Navy, since its foundation in the mid-nineteenth century, and this may have been of considerable psychological importance.

IS THERE A PATTERN HERE?

When, in 1904, the Japanese began their war with Russia by a "sneak attack" on the Russian fleet at Port Arthur, the senior Russian officer in command was an Admiral Stark. When, thirty-seven years later, the Japanese began their war with the United States by a "sneak attack" on the American fleet at Pearl Harbor, the most senior U.S. officer was also an Admiral Stark (no relation). Even more strange, *stark* is a German word meaning "strong." Both Russia and America had many citizens of German extraction and in both countries many descendants of these immigrants had risen to become prominent government officials and military officers, like General Dwight D. Eisenhower and Admiral Chester W. Nimitz, for example, as well as Walter Kreuger and Robert L. Eichelberger. The latter two generals were responsible for most of General MacArthur's military success in the Pacific but were generally obscured by their boss's overwhelming press.

THE MOST DECISIVE BATTLE OF WORLD WAR II THAT YOU NEVER HEARD OF

In 1939 the Russians and Japanese fought a series of battles in Mongolia. The Japanese got the worst of it, and this had a major impact on later battles in World War II.

Called Khalkhin Gol (or Nomonhan), it was basically a border dispute in which the Japanese tested their army against the Russian forces. The Japanese failed the test, and as a result decided to leave the Russians alone during World War II. This had a considerable effect on the Russian battles with the Germans far to the west. In 1941, Russia had nearly forty divisions facing a dozen Japanese divisions in Manchuria, and most of these Russian units were quickly shipped west when the Germans invaded in June.

The Japanese, Germans, and Italians had signed a military alliance in 1936 (the Axis), but the terms were vague. The Germans hoped that the Japanese would attack Russian forces in Siberia if the Germans invaded Russia from the west. The outcome of Khalkhin Gol caused the Japanese to leave the Russians alone throughout World War II.

In the mid-1930s, Japan felt that it was militarily superior to the Russians. Having defeated the Russians on land and at sea in the 1904–1905 war, the Japanese believed they still held a military edge. Then came a series of border clashes. They were defeated in a division-sized battle in eastern Manchuria in 1938. They rationalized this defeat and spoiled for another round with the Russians. While the Japanese had some success in smaller border skirmishes, they had yet to defeat the Russians in a deliberate battle.

They sought to test their imagined advantage in May 1939, by forcibly redrawing the border between Japanese-held Manchuria and Russian-controlled Mongolia. A Japanese division advanced to the Khalkhin Gol (or Halha) river, and a reinforced Russian division threw them back. Undeterred, the Japanese planned a larger attack in July. This battle involved two major changes. The Japanese reinforced the division they had used in May by adding two tank regiments (seventy tanks) and a new infantry regiment. The Russians brought in General Georgy Zhukov (later to be the architect of the Russian defeat of the Germans) and a larger force (about three divisions, mostly motorized). Because the battlefield was five hundred miles from the nearest railroad, the Japanese thought the Russians incapable of reinforcing their forces so quickly and heavily. Despite their transportation problems, the Russians massed over three hundred tanks against the Japanese. In the air, both sides were more evenly matched.

The July battles were another disaster for the Japanese. Their initial attack on July 3 made some progress, but then the Russians attacked and forced the Japanese back. By July 14, both sides halted. At this point, the Japanese decided that artillery was the key and brought in heavy guns. The artillery duels during the last week of July went against the Japanese. The Russians were able to fire three times as many shells and had generally heavier guns.

In August, the Russians planned their own attack, an armored offensive that would settle this border dispute once and for all. Bringing up four divisions and five hundred tanks (as well as 24,000 tons of ammunition), the Russians moved forward against the two Japanese divisions on August 20. This was, in effect, the first real armored offensive of the twentieth century and was a smashing success. Within four days, the Japanese had been pushed back to what the Russians considered the real border. There the Russians halted, although they could have kept chasing the shattered Japanese. Events back in Europe (Germany was about to invade Poland) made further involvement in

Manchuria inadvisable. In September a cease-fire agreement was signed, thus ending the fighting.

As World War II battles go, Khalkhin Gol was not a big one. The Japanese committed two divisions, plus replacements, and suffered 18,000 casualties (out of 40,000 troops involved). The Russians suffered 14,000 casualties out of 70,000 troops sent in. Altogether, some one hundred tanks were lost and nearly two hundred aircraft.

The Japanese drew the correct conclusions from this three-month battle. They acknowledged that the Russians were superior and discarded their pre–Khalkhin Gol plan for assembling forty-five divisions in 1943 in order to drive the Russians back to the Ural Mountains. At the same time the battle was ending, the Nazi-Soviet treaty was announced. This caused the Japanese to renounce their 1936 treaty with the Germans. These diplomatic and battlefield defeats hurt Germany the most, as the lack of an active ally in the Far East enabled the Russians to concentrate their full strength against the Germans. Most of the forty Russian divisions facing the Japanese were sent west to defend Moscow in late 1941. These divisions made a big difference, especially to the German troops who got close enough to Moscow in late 1941 that they could see the spires of the Kremlin. It was as close as the Germans ever got.

One of the most curious things about Khalkhin Gol is that the rest of the world knew virtually nothing about it, or any of the other smaller Russo-Japanese clashes, until several years afterward. The Japanese naturally were not inclined to spread the word about their unpleasant experience and the Russians were obsessed with secrecy. The Germans remained blissfully unaware of Japanese reluctance to take on the Russians, and attacked the Soviet Union with the idea that the Japanese could eventually get involved. Had the word got out about Khalkhin Gol, the course of World War II might have been rather different.

MANY WAYS TO DIE

The Japanese saw death in battle somewhat differently than Western troops saw it. This can best be illustrated by the many terms they used for a soldier lost in battle. They had a term for "killed in action" (*senbotsu*) but they also had terms for the various ways one could be killed. Each of these was associated with varying degrees of military honor. All cultures recognize a concept of "honor" in military operations and the ways in which a soldier may be killed, but only the Japanese had the term *gyokusai,* which meant "to seek death rather than dishonor." While that sounds familiar, for the Japanese this would mean a soldier would rather be killed in a hopeless situation than surrender.

Japanese culture did not expect a soldier to waste his life uselessly in a hopeless situation, thus there was the term *tai-atari* (literally "body crashing," or ramming one's aircraft or ship into the enemy). Wounded soldiers would explode a grenade when enemy troops came near, thus performing a *jibaku* (self-destruction while also hurting the enemy). If all hope were lost and no enemy were around, there was always *jiketsu* (usually called "hara-kiri" in the West). This form of suicide was not to be confused with *jisatsu* (garden variety suicide).

THE WAR BETWEEN THE GENERALS AND ADMIRALS

The military leadership of the Pacific war was dominated by conflicts and competition between army generals and navy admirals. The Japanese armed forces were the most divided, with the army running the show in China and, from October 1941, with an army general running the government as well. But because Japan was an island nation, the navy could not be shunted aside. When the Western nations decided on the embargo, it was the navy that was able to do something (however ultimately hopeless) about it by attacking Pearl Harbor and leading the way in Japan's six-month blitzkrieg.

Admiral Isoroku Yamamoto, the commander of the Japanese Navy, had spent many years in America and knew that any military success against the United States would be short-lived. The less well traveled army generals were more prone to believing their own press releases. Throughout the war, the army and navy had avoided cooperation, preferring to fight with their own resources even if that meant fighting at a disadvantage. What cooperation there was between the army and navy was usually hammered out back at general headquarters in Tokyo. Even then, local commanders would frequently drag their heels when ordered to deal with people from the other service.

The American situation was very similar to that of the Japanese, with the army and navy constantly squabbling over who would be the supreme commander of the Allied forces in the Pacific war. To keep the peace among U.S. commanders, General MacArthur was given command of the "Southwest Pacific" (the Seventh Fleet and the Eighth and Sixth Armies) while Admiral Nimitz ran the other three theaters ("Central Pacific," "Northern Pacific" and "South Pacific," including the Third/Fifth Fleets, First Fleet, Tenth Army, and Marines). In effect, America fought two separate wars against Japan in the Pacific. The Solomons campaign was a navy operation (with some army divisions brought in when the navy ran out of Marines), while the New Guinea operation was almost wholly an army operation, with the navy occasionally lending a fleet for a few days. The navy ran the show for the drive through the central Pacific, and it was only when the Philippines were attacked that the army and navy forces had to come together on a large scale.

STRATEGY AND THE PACIFIC WAR

Strategy is the overall plan a nation has for winning a campaign or war. The United States and Japan had quite different strategies for winning in the Pacific. The original, prewar U.S. plan for a war with Japan (War Plan Orange) was to advance across the central Pacific to the Philippines (whether or not those islands were under attack). Most of the central Pacific islands were under Japanese control and many were known to be heavily fortified. The principal weapon would be the battleship, with the aircraft carrier used for scouting and support. Once the enemy battleships were found, the decisive battle would be fought, the United States would win, and it would be all over within about six months or so. By the late 1930s prescient naval officers were beginning to realize that War Plan Orange was unworkable, but it was not really formally replaced. They were right, of course. When the war came the Philippines were lost, along with nearly everything else west of Hawaii, and the battleships that were not sunk at Pearl Harbor were now acknowledged to be quite vulnerable to carrier aircraft. Forced to use Australia as the main forward base in the Pacific, the U.S. forces made their primary advance initially from the south, through New Guinea and on to the Philippines, which were reached after nearly three years of war. All this was supported by carrier and land-based aircraft. The U.S. Navy had built so many carriers and support ships by late 1943 that a second advance through the central Pacific was proposed. This was accomplished with massive carrier air power, huge amphibious operations, and admirals determined not to let the army run the show by itself.

The Japanese strategy was to seize as many islands as possible and fortify enough of them with so many ground troops and aircraft that the

Allies would not be able to get through to Japan. It didn't work. The keystone of Japanese strategy was economic resources. The Japanese home islands had few natural resources and nearly all the raw material for Japanese industry had to be imported. While China and Korea provided sufficient ores and food, the oil had to come from fields in Indonesia. It was to obtain access to this oil that Japan went to war with the United States, Great Britain, and the Netherlands. Japan's strategy was one of desperation, as the Indonesian oil fields could not produce sufficient oil for Japanese needs. More to the point, Japan could not produce sufficient tankers to get the oil from Indonesia to Japan. Allied submarines kept sinking Japanese tankers, and shipping in general. Many senior Japanese military leaders recognized the futility of the war but they carried out their orders anyway. Death before dishonor was more than just a catchphrase in the Japanese military.

RULES ARE RULES

During the dark days of 1942, Australian stevedores often (very often) refused to modify their union contracts in order to aid the war effort. Even when the Japanese were, it appeared, about to descend on Australia itself. In 1942, U.S. and Australian forces were fighting a desperate battle to the north in New Guinea. Lack of adequate rail and road systems in Australia forced heavy dependence on sea transport along the Australian coast. The Australian government was unable (because of growing war weariness among the population for a war they had been in since 1939) to abrogate the union contracts the stevedores insisted on maintaining. Among other things, these contracts allowed the laborers to refuse work when it was raining. Because they received double- and triple-time pay for weekend work, many stevedores would show up only on weekends so they got a week's pay for two days' work. Often, U.S. troops had to be put to work unloading ships and it was found that, on average, the troops could unload cargo two to three times more quickly than the Australian stevedores unloaded it. Moreover, the Australians often didn't show up when they were supposed to, producing absenteeism of close to 20 percent on occasion. When the Americans tried to automate the process (more cranes and forklifts), the civilian workers threatened, and then staged, a few strikes. These problems were not fully resolved until the shipping operations could be shifted to ports in New Guinea and the Philippines in 1943 and 1944.

STARVATION ISLAND

The Japanese soldiers on Guadalcanal came to call the place "Starvation Island" because of the difficulty their leaders had getting food delivered to the place. This was not a situation unique to the Japanese. Islands in general, and the Pacific islands in particular, were not bountiful sources of food for the soldiers that fought there.

The first case of starving soldiers on Pacific islands was found among American and Filipino troops in the Philippines. Much to the dismay of the Japanese invaders, the American and Filipino defenders didn't just roll over and quit. The fighting went on for over four months. The Japanese controlled the seas and attempts to run this blockade were generally unsuccessful. Most of the civilian crews of the blockade runners forced the ships back as they approached the Philippines, or the Japanese sank the supply ships. Three boats did get through, but it wasn't enough. Although the food wasn't completely gone by the time the Japanese military action beat down the defenders, there wasn't much left. American troops had been getting less than a third of the food required for several months (and some of their Filipino comrades even less).

The second case of "Starvation Island" was again an American situation. The Hawaiian Islands could not feed themselves. When the Japanese struck on December 7, 1941, the 42,000 U.S. troops in the islands had a sixty-day supply of food. The 420,000 civilians on Oahu were worse off, with less than a forty-day supply. Most of the food consumed on the islands was imported. While the islands contained much fertile land, most had been turned over to plantations growing crops like pineapples. There was a great fear that the Japanese would blockade the islands and starve them into submission, or invade first. The Japanese didn't come, although several divisions were trained for that task. It was the Japanese who next suffered from the "Starvation Island" syndrome and saw thousands of their troops starve to death on Pacific islands before the war was over.

A DISTINCTION OF SORTS

The U.S.S. *Laffey* (DD-724), an Allen M. Sumner class destroyer commissioned in early 1944, has the dubious distinction of being the object of the most intensive kamikaze attack ever. Early on April 16, 1945, *Laffey* was on radar picket duty off Okinawa. Beginning at 0827 she was subject to the attentions of about fifty Japanese aircraft for some eighty minutes. A number of the attackers were downed by friendly fighters flying combat air patrol. However, at least twenty-two of the enemy managed to get through to make attacks on the ship herself. Altogether, *Laffey* was hit by six kamikazes, plus a seventh that bounced off to explode in the sea hard by her port quarter. In addition she was struck by four bombs and strafed several times. Aside from the kamikazes that actually struck her, the *Laffey* managed to shoot down eight of the attacking aircraft. By the time the attack was over, at 0947, the ship had suffered thirty-one crewmen killed and seventy-two wounded, about a third of her complement. She was down at the stern and unable to steer due to a jammed rudder. Her fire control director was gone and her only working weapons were four 20mm antiaircraft guns (out of six 5-inch, twelve 40mm, and eleven 20mm). Despite her damage, the *Laffey* was ultimately repaired and returned to service. After many years of active duty, the *Laffey* was retired from the navy and is today preserved as a war memorial in Charleston, South Carolina.

CHERRY BLOSSOMS FROM HELL

As bad as the kamikaze aircraft attacks were, the Japanese developed even more effective weapons for this form of combat. Because the kamikaze program was under way only during the last year of the war, the Japanese did not have time to mass-produce specialized weapons for these attacks. One system that did get into production was the MXY7 Okha ("Cherry Blossom"), nicknamed the "Baka" (Fool) by American seamen. This was a small, rocket-powered aircraft that was launched from a bomber. The Okha was made of wood, consisted largely of a 2,600-pound warhead, and had a minuscule cockpit and very simple controls. But because of its shape and rocket propulsion it could dive into an American formation at over 500 miles an hour. This made it very difficult for U.S. interceptors or antiaircraft guns to catch it. Fortunately, the ill-trained pilots had trouble controlling the Okha and only a handful were ever launched. But if the Japanese had thought to use the kamikaze tactic earlier, and built a lot more of the Okha, the results of the kamikaze attacks would have been far worse.

STRATEGIC BOMBING IN THE PACIFIC

Until 1941, it was thought that attacks on the Japanese home islands would be by ship bombardment and carrier aircraft. The new B-17 bomber did not have the range to reach Japan from any nearby islands. Although the army had started building the longer range B-29 bomber in late 1940, it did not make its first flight until September 1942 (by which time the even larger and longer-ranged B-36 was already on the drawing board) and would not be available in large quantities until late 1944. After Pearl Harbor, it became obvious that the decades-old war plans for attacking the Japanese home islands would have to be scrapped because of the danger from Japanese land-based aircraft. The B-29, designed to attack European targets from North America (with 2.5-ton bomb loads) could also carry ten tons of bombs against targets 1,500 miles distant. This would make it ideal for use against Japan, flying from small islands in the central Pacific. What made this combination decisive was the development of incendiary bombs that would devastate Japan's highly flammable cities. Japanese war industry was different from Germany's. In Japan, thousands of small workshops in residential areas provided parts for factories. Unless you destroyed the workshops, the parts would be moved to new assembly sites. While a few B-29 raids were launched from India (against targets in Thailand) and from central China (against Japan), supporting these operations with fuel and bombs was quite expensive. Material for China-based B-29s had to be airlifted over the Himalayas. So it was the central Pacific islands that allowed the fuel and bombs to be brought in economically by ship for use in massive B-29 raids against Japan. In June 1944, the first B-29 raid was launched from recently captured Saipan Island. In November 1944, the first 100-plane raid was undertaken. From January until August 1945, 100- to 120-plane raids were launched every five days, with an occasional raid by as many as 600 aircraft. Japan's cities began to burn.

NO, NOT US, THE OTHER GUYS

Off Okinawa, one hard-pressed destroyer, deployed on "picket duty" to try to keep Japanese suicide aircraft from the carriers and transports, grew frustrated at Japanese pilots diving on them instead of continuing on (if they survived the fire of the picket line destroyers) to the larger warships and transports. Knowing that the Japanese were mainly looking to sink carriers, the destroyer erected a large sign proclaiming CARRIERS THIS WAY. It's doubtful that many of the Japanese saw the sign, could even read it, much less paid it much heed. The incident did spotlight the dangerous nature of this picket duty. Most of the ships sunk by these Japanese aircraft were destroyers.

ANOTHER FORM OF FRIENDLY FIRE

Most of the civilian casualties during the Pearl Harbor attack were the result of civilians being hit by antiaircraft bullets falling back to earth. The bullets from .50-caliber (half inch in diameter) machine guns were a principal cause, as these falling rounds could injure or kill no matter where they hit someone in their path. Considering the amount of antiaircraft fire that was expended during Allied attacks on Axis cities and Axis attacks on Allied cities, the casualty rate from "friendly" fire must have been enormous.

SIX WAS NOT ENOUGH

The highest-scoring Japanese fighter ace, Hiroyoshi Nishizawa, had an attitude toward combat typical of most Japanese soldiers, sailors, and airmen. During the summer of 1942, Nishizawa was engaged in an air battle over the Solomons. In the course of downing six American Wildcats, his aircraft was hit. Thinking he would not be able to make it back to base in his smoking aircraft, he decided to get one more American aircraft by ramming. But he could find no American aircraft nearby, so he limped homeward and barely made it back to a Japanese airfield. Many Japanese pilots in damaged aircraft did succeed in "getting one more American" by ramming. Nishizawa, with over eighty kills, eventually died while a passenger in a Japanese transport aircraft shot down by U.S. fighters. This was ironic in that Nishizawa always maintained that he would never be bested in combat. He was right.

FLYING TIGERS AS THEY REALLY WERE

Those who recognize the term *Flying Tigers*, remember it as a unit of volunteer U.S. pilots working for the Chinese in their struggle with Japan before Pearl Harbor. Not so. While there were American volunteer pilots recruited for service in China, the Flying Tigers first saw action in Burma, where they were caught in transit (to China) by the Japanese attacks in December 1941. In those battles, the Americans fought under British control and in a few months most were inducted into the U.S. Army Air Force and continued to serve in China as part of the newly activated U.S. Fourteenth Air Force. The Flying Tigers' name itself did not appear until after Pearl Harbor (in a *Time* magazine article in late December). The Walt Disney Studios promptly provided a suitable insignia.

Officially known as the American Volunteer Group (AVG), the organization had a curious history. The organizer and leader of the Flying Tigers was Claire Chennault. An able U.S. Army fighter pilot, he made himself unpopular with his theories (largely correct) of how to use fighters. Forced to retire in 1937 (at age forty-four), he cast about for something to do before (as he was sure would happen) America was at war with Germany and Japan and he would be able to get back into uniform. Through his contacts with aircraft manufacturers, he secured a contract to do a survey of the struggling Chinese Air Force and suggest changes that would provide better defense against the rampaging Japanese fighters and bombers. Chennault made an impression on the Chinese and was asked to gather the dozens of mercenary pilots into one unit, train them to act as a team, and give the Japanese a bloody nose. He was also put in charge of training new Chinese pilots. It was a tall order. The largely non-American mercenaries were an undisciplined lot and many did not have a mastery of English. The aircraft were an oddball collection of whatever the Chinese government had been able to buy. Russian, German, Italian, and American manufacturers were all trying to sell additional aircraft (and not always their best stuff). The Russians had their own group of "volunteer" pilots, but the Chinese weren't impressed by the Russians' skill, nor did they trust the Communists. This is understandable, as the Chinese Communists were trying to overthrow the non-Communist Chinese government (a temporary truce was in effect in order to oppose the Japanese).

The U.S. government was also concerned with the hammering the Chinese were getting from the Japanese Air Force. By late 1940 an agreement was made for the U.S. government to provide loans for the Chinese to buy the latest U.S. fighter aircraft, and for U.S. Army and Navy pilots to be recruited for the AVG. Officially, the U.S. government had nothing to do with the recruiting (although the recruiters were free to entice serving pilots to join the AVG). But Chennault and the Chinese didn't care about these technicalities. With the AVG, the Chinese would have trained and disciplined pilots flying modern aircraft. The pilots and aircraft reached Burma in late 1941, and it was in Burma that a training base was set up for the AVG pilots to perfect their teamwork before going north into China. Thus it was in Burma that the Flying Tigers got their first taste of combat, and after Pearl Harbor at that. The AVG moved to China in early 1942.

In July 1942, the Flying Tigers ceased to exist. Oh, many of the pilots were still flying in China. But they and their aircraft were no longer mercenaries but part of the army air force. In their seven months of existence, the 340 pilots and ground crew of the AVG claimed (and 68 pilots were paid bonuses of over $5,000—in 1994 dollars—per aircraft for) destroying 296 Japanese aircraft. The AVG lost 86 aircraft (only 12 in air-to-air combat), including accidents and 22 were captured when Japanese infantry overran one of their storage facilities in Burma. Twenty-two AVG pilots were killed, captured, or missing. Postwar examination of Japanese records indicates that the AVG actually destroyed 120 Japanese aircraft and killed 400 pilots and aircrew. Many of the Japanese aircraft destroyed were bombers, which had larger crews. Put another way, the Tigers destroyed 21 Japanese aircraft per thousand sorties, while losing only 2 of their own. Their Japanese opponents shot down 6 Tigers per thousand sorties while losing 64 aircraft. The Tigers flew six thousand sorties during this period, versus only two thousand for their Japanese opponents.

MUCH FOR LITTLE

Dropping a lot of bombs doesn't do much damage. This phenomenon was first encountered in a bombing campaign against enemy forces on U.S. territory. In June 1942, the Japanese occupied two of the Aleutian Islands off the coast of Alaska. They held these islands for fourteen months. But in those fourteen months, hundreds of American aircraft were brought forward and an intense bombing campaign was conducted. Some 7,300 attack sorties were flown and 4,300 tons of bombs were dropped (in addition to tons of machine-gun bullets during strafing runs). After the war, when Japanese records could be examined, it was discovered that only 450 Japanese troops were killed by all these raids (about 6 percent of the troops being attacked), or about one soldier for each ton of ammunition expended. Perhaps if more of the pilots had served in the ground forces, they would have realized how resourceful their targets could be.

THE ENEMY IS EASY . . .

The war in the Pacific was notable for the high number of aircraft destroyed by "noncombat causes." Overall, only 25 percent of the aircraft lost were due to enemy action. The others were destroyed by the weather, the difficulty of operating from aircraft carriers, hastily built airfields, and the insidious effect the tropical climate had on machines. These losses were higher in the Pacific than in other theaters because of these unique conditions. And sometimes it got worse. In the fourteen-month Aleutian Islands campaign in Alaska, 87 percent of the aircraft losses were to these noncombat causes. Although there was no tropical climate to worry about in Alaska, the arctic weather proved even more ruinous to an aircraft's life span.

IT LOOKS GOOD, IT IS GOOD

World War II aviators, particularly fighter pilots, were a dashing bunch. Aviator glasses (sunglasses) certainly added to their slick appearance. But the sunglasses weren't there just to sustain a striking image. For fighter pilots in particular, sunglasses were often a matter of life and death. Aircraft usually fought above the clouds, and when you turned into the sun you could be temporarily blinded. In the tropical Pacific the sunlight was even more intense. Early in the war, Allied pilots (at least those who didn't already know) learned the advantage of sunglasses. The aviator glasses were considered as important as a parachute, because if you had your shades, you would be less likely to need your chute.

NOT SO MUCH A NAVAL WAR, BUT AN AIR WAR

The Pacific war was truly the Air War, with virtually every type of Allied aircraft serving there. This included several prominent types that did not see service in Europe, such as the Corsair fighters and the B-29 heavy bomber, not to mention less well known types like the P-26, B-10, B-18, Wirraway, B-32, and others.

"IT'S SIMPLY NOT DONE"

During the Japanese attack on Hong Kong in December 1941, objections were raised by British officers when a platoon of Canadian infantry sought to take up certain defensive positions during the fighting for the Stanley Barracks, because enlisted men were prohibited from entering the officers mess there.

A PROBLEM IN THE RANKS?

To improve morale during the tedious New Guinea campaign of World War II, an Australian officer offered a fortnight's home leave to whichever company in his brigade won a camouflage contest. The result was an energetic competition, with the winners joyfully flying off for home. And upon arriving in Australia, the winning company, of the 39th Battalion, deserted to a man.

A GOOD WORKMAN NEVER BLAMES HIS TOOLS?

> "Lack of weapons is no excuse for defeat."
> —Lieutenant General Renya Mutaguchi, Commanding General, Japanese Fifteenth Army, 1944–1945

This extraordinary bit of wisdom was included in an order penned by the man who commanded the attackers in the disastrous Imphal-Kohima campaign, on the Indian-Burmese frontier in 1944. Mutaguchi's view was common to many (though not all) Japanese commanders. Yet while it is true that at times raw courage can win great victories against tremendous numerical and material odds (one has but to think of Soumoussalmi in 1939 or Sidi Barrani in 1940) that's not the way the smart money bets.

NIGHTMARE IN NEW GUINEA

While Guadalcanal is generally regarded as the pivotal land battle early in the Pacific war, it was actually only an extension of operations in New Guinea, which was the main campaign in the South Pacific. New Guinea, a tropical island north of Australia, was controlled by the Netherlands (the western half) and Australia (the rest). Smaller groups of islands extended to the northeast (the Bismarcks) and southeast (the Solomons). All three island groups were considered vital parts of the Japanese defensive system. New Guinea was the scene of some of the longest and toughest ground combat of the Pacific war. The Japanese landed on the north coast of New Guinea in early March 1942. The Australians (and later Americans) were on the south coast. Fighting first raged in the Owen Stanley Range that form the rugged spine of New Guinea. This fighting combined the worst aspects of jungle and mountain combat. By late 1942, the fighting was concentrated on Japanese positions on the north coast. This fighting continued into 1944 as the Japanese continued to reinforce their battered forces. New Guinea was something of a forgotten battle. Partially this was because of the way the media worked. New Guinea was almost wholly an army operation. No Marines and little action by the navy, both of whom tended to attract more press coverage. More than even Guadalcanal, New Guinea was a dreary, grinding jungle campaign, characterized by mud, heat, and disease. Indeed, during the Guadalcanal campaign, far more sailors at sea were killed than Marines on land. New Guinea was a tropical meat grinder of constant combat through steaming jungles and steep mountains. All the aircraft operated from primitive, often mud-soaked, airfields. While Guadalcanal was over in six months, New Guinea went on for years. In the eyes of the American public, New Guinea got old real quick. That attitude carried on in the public's memory even after the war.

Although the New Guinea fighting did more to cripple the Japanese armed forces, Guadalcanal still got a higher place in the pantheon of Pacific battles.

THE FEW, THE PROUD, THE RELATIVELY NEW

The U.S. Marines had six divisions in combat during World War II, literally an army-size force. Yet, until World War I, the Marines had always been a very small force and until 1911 were not organized into large combat units. Actually, the 1911 reorganization simply took all Marines not assigned to ships and various land stations and formed them into companies of 103 men (identical to U.S. Army companies of that time). These companies were then organized into battalions (three companies) or regiments (ten companies) as needed. In 1917, when America entered World War I, there were only 13,700 Marines. By the end of 1918 there were 75,000 and about a third of these got into combat in France. But after World War I, the Marines were once again reduced to their normal peacetime strength (about 17,700). In the 1920s, a regular Marine infantry regiment organization was developed. This was a small unit of only about 1,500 men. The Marine Corps stayed small until the 1930s, when the expansion began.

By Pearl Harbor the Marine Corps had two divisions active, albeit both only partially trained. These were bloodied during the Guadalcanal campaign. The Marines went on to create four more divisions, each built around a cadre of 40 percent or so of combat veterans. By war's end all six Marine divisions had seen extensive service. Over the fifty years since World War II, Marine Corps strength has never fallen below 150,000 troops. This, incidentally, was the size of the entire U.S. Army in 1940.

TELL IT TO THE MARINES

The U.S. Marines undertook some of the bloodiest amphibious assaults of the war. But their overall casualty rates were not as high as many army units that engaged in less intense combat over longer periods. For example, the highest casualty rate sustained by a Marine regiment in one battle was much less than 100 percent (the 29th Marine Regiment sustained 2,821 dead and wounded in eighty-two days of combat during the Okinawa campaign in 1945). By early 1945, forty-seven infantry regiments in nineteen army divisions had suffered at least 100 percent losses, and in some cases over 200 percent casualties. All of these regiments had been in action over three months, many for eight months or more. Marines tended to be in combat for short, intense, island assaults. The army regiments endured generally less concentrated combat but were at it for much longer periods. The record for number of days in combat for a U.S. division is held by the 2nd Infantry Division, with 305. No Marine division even came close.

THE CONCRETE GEDUNK CRUISER

Navy slang for ice cream was *gedunk* (a term that was often used to refer to other tooth-rotting pleasures). Aircraft carriers were large enough to provide crew amenities like an ice-cream shop. But to supply ice cream to the rest of the fleet, the navy took one of the concrete transports built early in the war (when there was a steel shortage) and turned it into a floating ice-cream factory. The ship itself was a turkey (most of the concrete ships were fobbed off on the army), but the gedunk cruiser could produce up to five thousand gallons of ice cream an hour, making her one of the most popular ships in the fleet.

MacARTHUR'S FAMILY TIES

Three prominent World War II leaders had a common ancestor, Sarah Barney Belcher, of Taunton, Massachusetts. As a result of this common ancestry, U.S. General Douglas MacArthur was an eighth cousin of British Prime Minister Winston Churchill and a sixth cousin of U.S. President Franklin D. Roosevelt.

THE ENEMY BELOW, ON LAND

Land mines were one of the more feared weapons in the Pacific. Mines were usually detected only when you stepped on them, and the victim lost a foot, leg, or life. Mines were most frequently used on landing beaches and around heavily fortified Japanese positions. While the Japanese used a lot of mines, they did not have a very wide or sophisticated selection to choose from, compared with the Germans, or even the Americans. The most common mine was the 12-pound, saucer-shaped Model 93. It was used against both personnel and vehicles, by varying the pressure device on the top of the mine to different degrees of sensitivity, from 7 to 250 pounds. More troublesome was the 107-pound, semi-spherical Model 96. This was used on land or under a few feet of water, where it might encounter landing craft. Containing 46 pounds of explosive, the Model 96 would destroy any vehicle and most small landing craft. Another Japanese specialty was the Model 99 armor-piercing mine. However, this mine had to be placed against the side of a vehicle (or the metal door of a bunker) by a soldier who activated it, after which it would explode in five to six seconds. It was not entirely effective against heavier U.S. tanks, and was often fatal to the user. The Model 99 weighed 3 pounds, contained 24 ounces of TNT, and had magnets on it to keep it attached to its intended target. The Japanese considered it a "grenade" and it was issued one per soldier when conditions warranted.

The Japanese frequently improvised mines, using artillery shells, some even made from Russian stocks captured in 1905. These were relatively simple and not very effective but could prove an annoyance to advancing Allied troops. One very odd antitank improvisation used relatively large-caliber naval shells (five-inch and up). A large hole was dug into which the shell was placed. A Japanese soldier armed with a hammer then crouched down beside the shell and the whole was covered over with brush. The idea was that when an Allied tank drove over his position, the soldier was supposed to strike the detonator with the hammer. It is not known if any Allied vehicles were destroyed in this fashion, but Allied infantrymen caught a lot of Japanese troops assigned to this duty and shot them before the hammer came down.

The United States made only limited use of mines in the Pacific war.

THE TWO INVASIONS OF THE PHILIPPINES

The Philippines had the grim distinction of suffering two major amphibious invasions during World War II. The Japanese put a lot more into defending the Philippines in late 1944 than the United States had in 1941. The United States had about 110,000 mostly untrained troops defending the islands in 1941. Japan had 350,000 troops as a garrison in 1944. The Japanese troops were also better trained, motivated, and equipped. Japan also had a larger air force and fleet to defend the islands. In turn, the United States went after the Philippines with far larger forces than Japan had used in 1941. During their invasion, the Japanese actually had fewer troops than the defending Americans. In 1941 the Japanese went straight for the main island of Luzon (containing the capital, Manila), while in 1944 the United States first landed on Leyte, in the east central part of the Philippines. In both cases, the area first invaded was dictated by the presence of friendly air bases. The 1941 Japanese invasion was staged out of Taiwan (Formosa), which was a few hundred miles north of Luzon. In 1944, the Allies came from the south because they had just established air bases on recently captured islands northwest of New Guinea. In 1944 the Japanese were under far more pressure than the Americans had been in 1941. For Japan, the Philippines were the Allied staging area for an invasion of the Japanese home islands. This brought out the Japanese air and naval forces in large numbers, which the United States proceeded to destroy. After that, a series of amphibious landings extending into early 1945 led to the capture of all the Philippine islands. By early March 1945, Manila was again in U.S. hands. Although fighting continued in remote areas until Japan surrendered, the Philippines were effectively liberated. MacArthur had kept his promise to the Philippine people and "returned."

MacARTHUR'S DISASTER

While General Douglas MacArthur is generally considered one of the most capable military leaders America ever produced, he had his failures. One of the most devastating was the manner in which he conducted the defense of the Philippines. In late 1941, the Philippines were defended by 25,000 U.S. and Filipino regular troops and 110,000 poorly trained Filipino reservists and conscripts. Using air bases on Taiwan (then called Formosa), the Japanese first established air superiority. The Japanese Navy then established naval supremacy. The Japanese Army then invaded with 50,000 troops and, after five months of hard fighting, conquered the islands.

Despite ample warning of a Japanese attack, MacArthur allowed his air force to be largely destroyed on the ground. Although the Japanese air bases were five hundred miles away, MacArthur did not order his aircraft dispersed nor did he take pains to resist the Japanese air attacks effectively. Although MacArthur had been in the Philippines for several years, he failed to take into account the low training levels of his Filipino troops when reacting to the actual Japanese invasion. Most of the Philippine Army's troops had less than a month's training on December 7, 1941. When the Japanese invaded, MacArthur, rather than implement the long-standing operational plan, which called for an immediate withdrawal to the rugged Bataan peninsula, decided to try to halt the Japanese in mobile operations on the north Luzon plain, with disastrous results.

Meanwhile, troop and supply movements were bungled before and during the land battles with the Japanese invasion force. When the surviving U.S. and Filipino troops finally did retreat to the Bataan peninsula, they did so short of ammunition, food, and spare parts that were available but had not been ordered moved in time. Overall, MacArthur performed in a decidedly lackluster manner, especially compared to his later accomplishments.

What prevented "MacArthur's Disaster" from becoming the "End of MacArthur's Career" was largely MacArthur's reputation, his skill at public relations, and the need for a presentable hero in the dark days of early 1942. MacArthur was one of the most famous American officers of the post–World War I period. He had been the head of the U.S. Army and had accepted the job of leading the infant Philippine

Army (which brought with it the title "Field Marshal") partially because the Japanese threat was recognized and everyone felt safer with someone of his caliber in charge out there (and he was also paid the modern equivalent of several million dollars).

Although many American military leaders back in the United States could see that MacArthur was screwing up big time in December 1941, the political leaders looked at the bright side. While British and Dutch forces were collapsing even more quickly in the Pacific, MacArthur's forces were still holding out through the spring of 1942. Although the American situation was hopeless in the Philippines, MacArthur was declared a hero, and evacuated just before his army had to surrender to the Japanese and march off to four years of captivity. This gave him a chance for a rematch, with better results later. Despite MacArthur's errors in 1941, Roosevelt recognized that he was a man of considerable military talent. MacArthur was one of those rare individuals who had a talent for commanding vast military forces and, most important, being able to select able subordinates. While MacArthur was always ready to draw attention to himself and his accomplishments, this also served a military purpose. The Americans saw in him a mighty warrior delivering a steady string of hammer blows to the enemy in the Pacific. To the Japanese, MacArthur appeared as an even more formidable opponent than he was. This last image served MacArthur well when he was put in charge of Japan after the war. The Japanese were awed by MacArthur's reputation and things got done more expeditiously and with less hassle as a result.

The treatment accorded MacArthur stands in marked contrast to that given to Australian Major General Gordon Bennett. The commander of the Australian 8th Division in Singapore, upon the British surrender, Bennett eluded capture and, after a remarkable series of adventures, made his way to Australia, where he publicly criticized the quality of British military leadership. Although there were many in Australia who were inclined to agree with him, enormous pressure was brought upon the Commonwealth's government by the British and Bennett was essentially disgraced.

THE CURIOUS WAR IN CHINA

Most Americans don't think of the war in China as part of the Pacific war. In fact, the fighting in China was much more intense and bloody than what Americans faced in the Pacific. Casualties in China were in the millions, both before and after Pearl Harbor. It was Japan's invasion of China (which began in 1931 or 1935 or 1937, depending on how one wishes to count various "incidents") that eventually got the United States into World War II in the first place. Japan had been making steady inroads in China and Korea since the 1880s. The Japanese generals running the show in China became more and more independent of the government back in Tokyo. Using subversion and threats, Japanese military leaders gained control over larger portions of China. Through the 1930s, over a million Japanese settlers moved into Manchuria. Yet the Japanese government never made any serious attempts to rein in their ambitious generals in China. In 1936 there was an attempted coup by junior army officers. Several senior civilian officials were assassinated in Tokyo before the coup was suppressed. Those junior officers wanted even more support for the Chinese war, and they got it.

In 1937, Japan began large-scale warfare against China. Attacking from enclaves in Manchuria and along the coast, the Japanese advanced into central China. Japan had 300,000 troops in China at the time, plus 150,000 Manchurian and Mongolians under Japanese officers. The Chinese had over 2 million troops under arms, but these were much less well equipped, trained, and led than the Japanese invaders. For two years the Japanese advanced deeper into China. But progress was slow and casualties mounted. In 1939 they decided to return to their earlier subversion and attrition tactics. This continued until 1944, when they again advanced to overrun U.S. airfields in central China (between May and November). As with the 1937 campaign, the 1944 operation was hampered by logistical problems and constant resistance from the Chinese population. Moreover, China had been receiving more military aid and training from the United States since 1941. The 1944 offensive exhausted Japanese forces in China and made them ripe for rapid defeat by the Russians in the summer of 1945.

Throughout the Pacific war, most of the Japanese Army was in China. While the Chinese troops were not active much of the time, many of Japan's best troops were thusly occupied rather than being sent against Allied troops in the Pacific or in Burma (although later in the war, Japan lacked the shipping to move many of those units anyway). So China's role, though generally neglected, was critical to the Allied victory.

TANKS THAT SWIM

It wasn't easy developing a practical tank that could swim ashore with the assault troops. It wasn't until late in 1944 that there was an effective amphibious tank. This vehicle wasn't designed as a tank, but as a cargo vehicle that eventually acquired armor and tank armament. In the beginning of the war, all that was on the drawing board were cargo-carrying vehicles that could swim. But, amphibious operations were very much a learn-by-doing effort.

When U.S. Marines first ran into heavily fortified Japanese beaches in late 1943, they realized that some heavy firepower had to go ashore with the first wave of troops. As useful as destroyers a thousand yards offshore were, it wasn't the same as having some heavy firepower right with the troops. The defenders' fortifications were usually well concealed and the Marines themselves didn't spot a lot of them until they were very close. Often that was too late. Machine guns would rip apart Marines before some way was found to destroy the dug-in enemy. There were also problems in getting across underwater obstacles (coral reefs and sandbars) and beaches torn up by naval gunfire. The Marines saw a solution in a tracked amphibious vehicle originally developed to get around the marshlands of Florida. By 1942 this vehicle was in service as LVT-1 (Landing Vehicle Tracked, nicknamed the "Alligator"). LVT-1s were a great success at carrying supplies quickly to shore, across coral reefs, and over the beach. During 1943, an improved (faster and sturdier) LVT-2 appeared. Some of these new LVTs had armor bolted on so that these vehicles could accompany troops into combat (and often carry the assault troops). By the end of 1943, better armor was added and some LVTs had a turret containing a 37mm gun. By 1944, the final combat version, the LVT(A)-4, was introduced, equipped with a turret and a 75mm howitzer (plus several machine guns). Although over 10,000 LVTs were produced during the war, less than 10 percent were "(A)" models that had been converted to tanks. Most LVTs were still used to get supplies ashore and inland quickly. The armored LVTs were organized into battalions, with 700 men and 75 LVT(A)s and 12 unarmed LVTs used as tractors. These amphibian tank battalions led the assault elements of an infantry division onto a defended beach while providing artillery and machine-gun support as well as protection from enemy fire. The LVT armor was thick enough to deflect only machine-gun fire and artillery fragments. But these were the principal killers during an amphibious assault. Especially in the Pacific (the

Japanese had pathetic antitank weaponry), the LVT(A) was generally the king of the beach.

The Marines organized three of these amphibian tank battalions and used all of them in the Pacific. The Army organized six, but only one saw action in the Pacific. The war ended before the others could be used in the Pacific or Europe (to support river-crossing operations).

The armored and armed LVT was only a makeshift tank. At sixteen tons, it was half the weight of a medium tank, but larger in size (26 feet long, 10.7 feet wide, and 11 feet high). Its road speed was about 17 miles an hour and in the water it did only 5 to 6 miles an hour. This water speed translated to only about 150 yards a minute. This made the ten (or more) minutes of swimming to a hostile shore a harrowing experience. Fortunately, the naval guns would be pounding the beaches until the LVTs were a few hundred yards out. Then the shipboard guns would direct their fire inland and the amphibian tanks would blast their way ashore against the surviving opposition. Right behind the amphibian tanks came the LVTs carrying the infantry and soon the two would be operating together.

The first LVTs were slow, capable of only twelve miles an hour and three to four in the water. LVTs used their tracks like little paddles in the water to provide propulsion. The 1944 models were faster, doing twenty miles an hour on land and five in the water.

Efforts to make existing tanks amphibious were not very successful. Several solutions to this problem were tried during the June 1944 invasion of France, and some (the British) were more successful than others (the Americans). But none were as effective as the armored LVT. To this day, descendants of the LVT continue to serve as the most effective amphibious armored vehicle.

THE MIGHTY DUKWS

The DUKW (pronounced "duck") was a standard U.S. Army 2.5-ton truck that could swim. Amphibious operations during World War II were different from earlier amphibious operations in that there were now motor vehicles (trucks and tanks) and a lot more weapons to play with. Special ships were developed that could deliver vehicles right onto the beach. What was missing was a way to move sufficient ammunition and fuel to keep all these vehicles and weapons functioning once they were off the beach. This problem was quickly noticed, and by the end of 1942 an elegant and simple solution had been arrived at.

A steel, flat-bottom boat hull was built that was large enough to have the mechanical parts of the 2.5-ton truck built into it. A small propeller was added aft to provide propulsion while floating. Sundry other adjustments were made and by 1943, hundreds of DUKWs were in service. Some ten thousand were built before the war ended and some served on into the early 1950s before being replaced by tracked LVT-type vehicles. The letters *DUKW* are the army equipment code describing an amphibious cargo vehicle with a six by six wheel arrangement and a 2.5-ton carrying capacity. A fully loaded DUKW weighed 8.8 tons and was 31 feet long, 8.3 feet wide, and 7.1 feet high. It could go as fast as forty-five miles an hour on roads, and about six miles an hour in the water. One tank of fuel would carry it 220 miles on roads and 50 miles in water. There was also a smaller version of the DUKW weighing 2 tons, but few were manufactured or used. DUKWs spent most of their time ferrying supplies and troops (up to twenty-five men) from ships offshore over the beach to locations inland. Many amphibious operations would not have been possible without DUKWs, as the troops put ashore would not be able to advance far from the beaches without the supplies ferried in by DUKWs.

IT NEVER HAPPENED, FOR DIPLOMATIC REASONS

In March 1943, a ship full of British commandos steamed into a port in Portuguese Goa (India). The commandos then assaulted and destroyed an interned German freighter that had been using a powerful radio transmitter to let nearby German submarines know the comings and goings of British merchant ships in the Indian Ocean. The operation was never officially acknowledged by the British government. The reason was diplomatic. Portugal, though neutral in World War II, was a hotbed of Allied and Axis spies. Many Portuguese officials were pliant, and their cooperation could often be bought. But a major British military operation on Portuguese territory would cause many Portuguese to be more pro-Axis and this would have harmed Allied espionage efforts. Thus middle-aged members of a paramilitary British social organization (the Calcutta Light Horse) were asked to volunteer for an unofficial mission. The volunteers were told that, for diplomatic reasons, they could receive no official recognition. If captured, they were to be considered free-lancers and acting on their own. The raid was a success, but largely due to some preliminary diplomacy. One volunteer visited the port before the raid and paid off a Portuguese official to throw a lavish party the night of the raid and invite the officers of the German and Italian ships in port. Arrangements were then made to make the town's brothels free for the entire week before the raid. These two tasks ensured that few of the officers and sailors were on the ship the commandos attacked.

Many of the volunteers and their uniformed trainers later spoke freely about it. A film was made about the operation (starring David Niven, himself a graduate of the Royal Military Academy at Sandhurst, with a distinguished war record). Yet the raid was never officially recognized. But that's how diplomacy works.

THE SHORT GUY IS IN CHARGE

Throughout history, in most armies the officers were generally taller than the troops. This was because the officers were usually recruited from the wealthier class. These folks could afford a better diet and, as a result, the officers tended to be taller than the less well fed troops. This was not the case in the Japanese Army. Officers had to pass through the dreaded Military Academy at Ichigaya. Here the day began at 5:30 A.M. and went on relentlessly until 10 P.M. (unless there was night training, in which case the cadets would simply lose a night's sleep). Most officers began their officer training at special military grammar and high schools. All stressed the same dedication to "spirit" rather than the mundane matters of flesh and blood. Physical training was a minor religion, and even in the winter, it was done bare-chested. Worst of all were the bland and skimpy rations. As a result, teenage cadets on average grew only half an inch in their adolescence and gained only about 3 pounds. The resulting officers were indeed a tough bunch, but their weight averaged 128 pounds and their height five feet four inches. Allied officers averaged nearly 30 pounds heavier and six inches taller. Postwar Japanese military officers are nearly as tall as other armies' officers, mainly because they now get fed better during training.

SPIRIT VERSUS BULLETS

American troops were shocked by the seeming fanaticism of the Japanese soldiers, sailors, and pilots they encountered. Early in the war, it simply appeared that the Japanese were better soldiers than prewar estimates had assumed. The rapid victories in Malaya and Burma gave rise to the long-lasting rumor that the Japanese were natural jungle fighters (quite false, few Japanese had ever seen a jungle until they joined the army). But when the Japanese began losing, it became apparent that something else was at work. This was first noticed on Guadalcanal. There it was observed that the Japanese frequently attacked in unfavorable situations, and they just kept on coming. When trapped, they would not surrender. When successful, they were quite vicious and ruthless. When an occasional Japanese prisoner was taken, he was quite docile. What to make of all this? As we now know, after competing with them economically for the last few decades, the Japanese are different. What serves the Japanese well in business—conformity, eagerness, dedication, and a never-say-die attitude—had a somewhat different impact on the battlefield. Japanese soldiers in World War II came from a culture that emphasized, and rewarded, conformity, obedience, and demonstrations of ''spirit.'' ''Spirit'' is a bit difficult to explain to non-Japanese. Basically, ''spirit'' was similar to religious faith combined with the group spirit of an athletic team. Japanese culture is also full of ritual, the same kind of ritual that plays such a large part in maintaining the faith of the believers in most religions. In this case the emperor was a combination of pope and God, with all of Japan being the sacred cathedral. While there were nonconformists and nonbelievers among the Japanese, they were smothered by the majority who did believe, or simply found it convenient to conform. Japanese soldiers were not emotionless robots. When not in action they would get drunk and chase the local women. But when fighting was at hand, they eagerly united to engage in what was, for them, a quasi-religious experience. Moreover, they had one advantage every general attempts to get: They were resigned to getting killed. War is a dangerous business, and those who are afraid of death are less useful on the battlefield. This is a difficult concept for civilians to understand. But even American troops would grasp this important concept on the battlefield. An American officer yelling at his men, ''Do you want to live forever?'' and then leading them off into a hail of enemy fire is but one example. Fortunately, the Japanese were not as well trained, led, or supported as the Marines. Japanese military doctrine, because it did not recognize surrender as a viable option, gave Japanese troops caught in an untenable situation little choice but to attack and die. Thus, the Japanese would simply form up and make a suicidal attack (the banzai charge) on the Americans. This was always an impressive display of spirit, but it was no protection from American bullets, bombs, and shells.

BUT I THOUGHT THE JAPANESE WON!

In the early 1950s, Great Britain launched a large, and ultimately successful, military operation against Communist guerrillas in Malaya. One of the units involved was a Gurkha battalion. The Gurkhas discovered another Gurkha, one who had been hiding out since the Japanese overran the area in 1941 and killed or captured all the other British troops. The poor fellow had gone into hiding and thought that the Japanese had won the war. But, ever loyal to his king (now replaced by Queen Elizabeth), he fought on.

JAPANESE MARINES

The first successful amphibious operations in the Pacific were all Japanese. Since 1932, Japan had been using specially trained amphibious troops. First along the Chinese coast, and then in 1941 against American, Dutch, and British territories in the Pacific. These troops were not, however, identical to the U.S. Marines. The Japanese called them Special Naval Landing Forces (SNLF) and they were developed in response to ship captains not wanting their crews depleted when sailors were sent ashore with rifles to take care of some navy-related mission (like guarding a port or seizing some lightly defended shore facility). Prior to 1932, this use of armed sailors had been the common practice in all navies (and still is in most fleets). The Japanese did not have a fleet in the eighteenth century and thus did not develop the European and American tradition of Marines. So in the early 1930s the Japanese began forming battalion-size (1,000 to 1,500 men) units called SNLF. These were manned by sailors and trained as infantry and commanded by naval officers. The early operations along the Chinese coast were largely unopposed, which is the way the Japanese preferred it. Although the Japanese developed small landing craft to get troops and vehicles ashore quickly, they never had the shore bombardment and logistical arrangements that typified American amphibious assaults. Japanese operations depended more on deception and surprise. This made sense, as the SNLF rarely operated in multibattalion assaults. The army performed larger amphibious landings, often putting several divisions ashore at once. But, like the SNLF, the army was not prepared to assault a fortified coast. The Japanese would always scout potential landing sites and choose those that were undefended. When the Japanese did run into opposition on the beach, they were often defeated. In contrast, the U.S. Marines have never been thrown off a beach. The Japanese perfected their tactics in the 1930s with numerous landings on the Chinese coasts. When they unleashed their multiple landings in December 1941 and early 1942 (Malaya, the Philippines, Indonesia, Guam, Wake, and so forth) they were almost always successful. But by the summer of 1942, the era of Japanese amphibious success was at an end. Their last amphibious assault was in August 1942, at Milne Bay, by the SNLF's 5th Kure. The Japanese were defeated by the Australian infantry battalion they encountered on landing. For the rest of the war the SNLF were most frequently found as do-or-die garrisons on dozens of Pacific islands. There they often died at the hands of real Marines, the USMC variety. Many others were bypassed, to die of starvation and disease or to linger on to surrender at the end of the war.

The SNLF were not all that great as infantry, it being noted by experienced U.S. troops that Japanese "Marines" were not as effective as Japanese Army infantry.

THE LITTLE GIANT

When Japan went to war with America in 1941, it was taking on an opponent with over ten times as much industrial production. The situation got only worse for the Japanese as the war went on. During the war years, the United States produced thirteen times as much steel and over two hundred times as much oil. America produced sixteen times as much merchant shipping and vastly outbuilt the Japanese in all categories of combat ships. This situation hides the fact that Japan had gone from an industrial nonentity in 1930 to a Little Giant in 1940. Japan concentrated on developing its industry during the 1930s and the results were startling:

	1930	*1940*
Trucks	500	48,000
Aircraft	400	5,000
Tons of Steel	1,800,000	6,800,000

During this period, nearly half a million tons of warships were produced, plus many older ships were upgraded. Merchant shipbuilding increased fivefold, with nearly half a million tons a year being produced by 1940. Vast quantities of munitions and other military equipment were manufactured and stockpiled. But for a nation with less than two thirds the population of the United States, this was not enough. Moreover, the growth of Japanese industry was largely to serve the growing armed forces. During the 1930s the size of the navy doubled, the army more than doubled, and the air force grew even more. In 1931, the government spent 29 percent of its budget on the military. By 1940, government income was sixteen times larger than in 1931, and 66 percent of it went to military expenditures.

Japan began the war as a Little Giant. Unfortunately, it was fighting the industrial equivalent of Godzilla, as America was the largest industrial power on the planet. And still is.

RUST, DUST, AND FATIGUE

Most of the fighting in the Pacific took place close to water, and sand. While this may have been rather picturesque, it was hell on the vehicles. Those who had to use and take care of the many trucks that were constantly hauling supplies and troops off the beach soon learned that the combination of salt water and fine sand drastically shortened the life of the normally robust army trucks everyone used. Among other depredations, the brake shoes wore out in ten days and the tires had to be replaced weekly if the vehicles were constantly on the beach. More than a month of use under these conditions would reduce many trucks to a state of uselessness. Even off the beach, the rigors of constantly being driven across the generally roadless island terrain drastically shortened a vehicle's normal useful life. By the end of the war, most supply officers accepted the fact that a truck with more than 25,000 miles on it was more trouble than it was worth in the combat zone. Of course, under peacetime conditions these same trucks were still useful after they'd hit the 100,000-mile mark. But in wartime, and on the Pacific islands, the rust, dust, and fatigue wore the trucks out a lot more quickly.

THE STENCH OF DEATH

In the Pacific campaign there were some unique problems with the dead. All theaters generated a lot of dead bodies. But the Pacific theater was unique in that there were more bodies created in a short period, it was always hot, the Japanese tended to keep sniping right to the end, and until late 1943, few senior commanders paid much attention to the situation. This led to morale problems, which forced many local commanders to improvise. Initially, the dead were often buried where they lay and this led to a higher proportion of unidentified dead or lost graves in the wilderness that most Pacific battlefields consisted of. It was impossible to erect permanent markers in the jungle, and subsequent construction activity often unearthed former anonymous remains.

None of this was done intentionally. The U.S. military had developed an efficient "Graves Registration" system during World War I. But after 1918 most of this knowledge was lost. Well, not all of it. Graves Registration units were raised early in the Second World War, but the first ones, and most of the subsequent ones, went to Europe. Even before Japan attacked Pearl Harbor, U.S. leaders had agreed that, once the United States was in the war, defeating Germany would be the priority. The Pacific was starved more for support units than for combat troops. Moreover, it was in the Pacific that U.S. troops first got into ground combat. Worse yet, these battles tended to be spread out all over the place. These early battles were often desperate, and the living naturally got priority over the dead. But dealing with the bodies could not be ignored. It had been learned in earlier wars that it was better for troops' morale to have the specially trained Graves Registration troops recover, identify, and bury both friendly and enemy dead.

When no Graves Registration troops were around, commanders took note of the morale problem and improvised. Some units simply asked around to find troops who had been morticians, and usually found some. These impromptu Graves Registration specialists were then assigned a few more troops and given the task of taking care of the dead. This wasn't easy. In the tropical climate, the bodies decomposed quickly. While the stench was bad enough, there were also health problems arising from unburied corpses. The Graves Registration troops tried to get to the bodies as quickly as possible, for taking fingerprints was one way to identify a corpse that had lost its ID tags ("dog tags"). A less certain method was to simply note physical features (height, hair color, tattoos, and scars). But all these methods (save an examination for dental work) became more difficult if the body had been allowed to rot. Their next step was to lay out cemeteries and supervise the digging of graves. Here's where a soldier with undertaker experience came in handy. Even if soldiers had to be hastily buried in a combat zone, a Graves Registration specialist knew what information to record, including a careful note of the location of the temporary grave.

By the time more Graves Registration units arrived in 1944, the problem was under control, at least for friendly dead. The Japanese corpses were another matter, for the enemy had a tendency to die to the last man. While this was less of a problem when they died in a bunker or cave (which was simply sealed), there were often thousands of Japanese dead piled up in front of American positions. Getting these bodies buried in a hurry was always a formidable chore. Moreover, the Japanese who were still alive continued to snipe at the Graves Registration troops while the bodies were being attended to. Another oddity of this situation was that the Geneva Convention stipulated that enemy and friendly dead were supposed to be given equal treatment. Basically, this was meant to obtain confirmation, for the next of kin, that their loved one had died and was not going to be eternally "missing in action." For the Japanese dead, final rites usually consisted of a final head count and then burial in a mass grave. For a nation so devoted to ancestor worship, this was particularly painful to the families of the Japanese dead. Indeed, to this day, Japanese still visit the most remote Pacific battlefields in generally vain attempts to locate the remains of their ancestors.

For Americans, who won the war, thousands of "missing in action" still remain in unmarked graves beneath the lush vegetation on Pacific islands.

WHERE DID THEY GO?

While the Japanese had a reputation for fighting to the last man, they were also quite capable of withdrawing from a hopeless situation. They often did this so cleverly that the Allies attacked where the Japanese last were anyway, still thinking the foe remained dug-in to receive the attack. This Japanese tactic became impossible after 1943, when the Allies had complete naval and air superiority and could prevent any attempt at evacuation. But in that year, the Japanese pulled two of their most notable disappearing acts. On Guadalcanal, where the fighting had been going on since August 1942, the Japanese decided to quit the island and evacuated their 10,000 surviving troops at night in February 1943. The Allied troops weren't sure the Japanese were gone until American troops reached the north end of the island and found evidence of the final evacuation. A more embarrassing example of this

Japanese tactic took place in May 1943, in the Aleutian Islands off Alaska. There the Japanese had been dug-in since June 1942. After a bitter struggle for Attu in May, the Allies prepared to take Kiska. In August a force of 35,000 U.S. and Canadian troops began coming ashore, after the usual intensive naval and air bombardment, only to discover that the Japanese had evacuated their 6,000 troops two weeks previously: This discovery was a painful one, as the navy lost a destroyer and 75 men to a Japanese mine, and the ground troops lost 21 of their number to "friendly fire."

JUNIOR ACHIEVEMENT

The youngest combatant in the U.S. armed forces during World War II (and probably the youngest since the Spanish-American War, if not the Civil War) was Calvin Graham (1930–1992) of Forth Worth, Texas. Early in 1942 the twelve-year-old Graham lied about his age and enlisted in the navy. He served in the battleship *South Dakota* during the Guadalcanal campaign. In one of the battles, he was wounded and his true age discovered. When the ship returned to the United States for repairs, Graham was given a one-way pass to his original recruiting station, which didn't know what to do with him. Meanwhile, since he did not return to his ship, he was classed as a deserter, arrested, and jailed. Released after he finally managed to convince the navy that he was only thirteen, Graham was promptly given a dishonorable discharge and denied disability benefits because he had enlisted under false premises. Graham, who later reenlisted for a time after attaining the proper age, was eventually the beneficiary of special legislation to restore pay and benefits lost upon his original discharge. Graham was one of several hundred boys under seventeen who are believed to have enlisted in the U.S. armed forces using forged birth certificates and similar documents.

By a curious coincidence, Graham's division officer while he was aboard the *South Dakota* was Sargent Shriver, who was later President John F. Kennedy's brother-in-law, and one of the ship's steersmen was a future teacher of one of the authors (A. A. Nofi) of this volume.

PSYCHOLOGICAL WARFARE?

One of the many secret projects undertaken by the United States during World War II was a psychological warfare proposal to strike a blow at Japanese morale by painting sacred Mount Fuji red, which was abandoned only after someone calculated how much paint and how many aircraft would be required for the project.

SURPRISE! DOUBLED!

Adolf Hitler's elation upon receiving word of the successful Japanese attack on Pearl Harbor soon turned to anger when he discovered that not one of his senior military advisers knew where the place was.

GENERAL HORNBLOWER?

From December 1941 to March 1942, 142 dispatches emanated from the headquarters of U.S. Army forces in the Far East, of which 109 (77 percent) included the name of only one person, the theater commander, General Douglas MacArthur, the only U.S. citizen to hold the rank of field marshal, created for him when he accepted the post of commanding general of the armed forces of the Commonwealth of the Philippines in 1935.

THE LUCKIEST SHIP . . .

One of the most extraordinarily lucky ships in history was the Japanese destroyer *Shigure*. A unit of the Shiratsuyu class, the *Shigure* was completed in 1935 and had a very distinguished record. Yet despite being in the thick of things from the start of the war, she led a charmed life, repeatedly going "in harm's way" yet never incurring any serious injury for virtually the entire war.

The *Shigure*'s battle honors read like a record of the principal actions of the war.

CORAL SEA (May 7–8, 1942): the *Shigure* served as an escort to the Japanese carriers, coming away without a scratch.

GUADALCANAL (October 14–15, 1942): She participated in the bombardment of the Marine beachhead, once more coming away without a scratch.

GUADALCANAL (November 14–15, 1942): Taking part in the wild night melee that saw two battleships and four destroyers tangle with a Japanese squadron consisting of a battleship, a heavy cruiser, two light cruisers, and several destroyers, resulting in a severe pasting to the Japanese, with the loss of the battleship *Kirishima*, the *Shigure* suffered no damage.

VELLA GULF (August 6–7, 1943): One of four destroyers ambushed by some American counterparts, she was the only one to survive, and without any damage.

VELLA LAVELLA (October 6–7, 1943): Part of a squadron of nine destroyers and a number of lighter vessels assigned to evacuate Japanese troops from Vella Lavella, the *Shigure* apparently absorbed no damage when six American destroyers attempted to intercept, coming off the worse for it. That "apparently" turned into an "almost" when, a few months later, it was discovered that a U.S. torpedo had hit one of the *Shigure*'s rudders but not detonated, leaving instead a rather neat twenty-one-inch hole.

EMPRESS AUGUSTA BAY (November 2, 1943): One of four cruisers and six destroyers attempting to disrupt the Allied landings at Cape Torokina on Bougainville, the *Shigure*, came off second best in a clash with four American cruisers and eight destroyers in an action called by the Japanese the Battle of Gazelle Bay, and suffered not at all.

BIAK (June 7, 1944): One of several Japanese ships that were engaged in a long-range stern chase by some U.S. destroyers, the *Shigure* was near-missed five times, with no significant damage.

PHILIPPINES SEA (June 19–21, 1944): Although she was one of the escorts for Carrier Task Force B, the *Shigure* came away from the battle with no damage.

SURIGAO STRAIT (October 25, 1944): The *Shigure* was the only ship in her squadron to survive, with only slight damage (she was hit by one eight-inch dud) despite tangling with a nest of U.S. PT boats and some cruisers while in the midst of the biggest shoot-'em-up of the Pacific war.

The *Shigure*'s luck ran out on January 24, 1945, when she took a torpedo from the U.S. submarine *Blackfin* while escorting a small convoy about 150 miles north of Singapore. She sank with great loss of life.

THE LIBERTY SHIP

Even before the U.S. entered the war, the navy began to consider the problem of maintaining an adequate supply of shipping in the face of a global war and the depredations of the German U-boats. The solution was to mass-produce merchant vessels to a standard design. Thus was born the Liberty Ship, based on a modified version of standard prewar Maritime Commission designs. Liberty ships, of which there were several versions (including a tanker model) were relatively large for their day, with a capacity of 10,000 to 14,000 GRT. This was about twice the size of the average prewar merchant ship. A comparable tanker was about 16,000 tons, roughly 60 percent larger than the normal American prewar tanker. Liberty ships were also relatively slow, being able to make only about ten knots. But they were easy to build, and lots of shortcuts were employed in their construction, such as electric welding rather than riveting; prefabrication of engines, superstructures, bows, and sterns; and assembly line production.

All of these techniques reduced construction time to such an extent that, at least for propaganda purposes, it was possible to assemble a ship in a few days. More normally several weeks were required, that itself being quite an accomplishment.

Construction of Liberty ships began before the United States entered the war, and the first, the *Patrick Henry,* was launched in September 1941. Altogether nearly six thousand Liberty ships were built, including some to the modified Victory ship design, which was faster (about fifteen knots), at a total cost of about $13 billion. Although several ships met with unfortunate accidents due to their hasty, sometimes overly hasty, construction and some design flaws (e.g., poorly welded seams parting in heavy seas, substandard materials leading to ruptured fuel lines, and so forth), they were an immensely valuable improvisation and greatly extended Allied shipping resources.

JUST ANOTHER FINE MYTH

During the defense of Singapore in 1941–1942, the five 15-inch naval guns available were (rumors to the contrary notwithstanding) capable of firing upon targets on the landward side of the island fortress. Unfortunately they were supplied only with armor-piercing ammunition, of dubious value against infantrymen in jungles.

<table>
<tr><td colspan="2" align="center">*Liberty and Victory Ship Construction*</td></tr>
</table>

Year	Number of Ships
1941	2*
1942	746
1943	2,242
1944	2,161
1945	500*

* Figure is approximate.

CHOW TIME

The average U.S. battleship had a crew of about 2,000 officers and men. Typical fortnight rations for a horde of this size ran to several tons of flour, about 2,400 pounds of lemons (lemon pie was quite popular in the navy), 1,700 pounds of cucumbers, 2,400 pounds of lettuce, 1,800 pounds of sweet potatoes, 1,800 pounds of tomatoes, 1,800 pounds of asparagus, 1,200 pounds of celery, 3,000 pounds of carrots, 3,800 pounds of oranges, 18,000 pounds of white potatoes, 1,500 pounds of smoked ham, 20,000 pounds of frozen beef, 4,000 pounds of frozen veal, 500 pounds of luncheon meat (better known as Spam), 1,000 pounds of frozen fish, 1,000 pounds of rhubarb, and about 37,000 eggs, not to mention several tons of ice cream (immensely popular in the navy and available only on the larger ships like carriers and battleships) and from 2 to 4 tons of coffee, which the alcohol-free U.S. navy consumed in endless gallons.

THE MOST DANGEROUS BRANCH OF THE SERVICE?

During the war about 16 percent of the personnel of the Japanese Imperial Navy became casualties, as did some 20 percent of the men in the Imperial Army, and more than 30 percent of those in the Imperial Merchant Marine.

FEEDING THE FIGHT: THE FLEET TRAIN

Long before the war broke out the U.S. Navy had devoted considerable attention to the logistical problems involved in supporting fleet operations in a theater as vast as the Pacific. In earlier wars the navy had mostly relied heavily on chartered civilian vessels for logistical support, as did all other navies. But that approach was not considered workable in the event of a protracted naval war in the Pacific. So it was intended that the navy acquire and operate ships crewed by naval personnel to meet the needs of the fleet. During the years of peace the navy did acquire some vessels for logistical support but much preferred spending its money on warships. In the event of a national emergency it intended to acquire vessels from the merchant marine, whether through purchase or hire, or through requisition of vessels subsidized by the U.S. Maritime Commission.

Meanwhile, the navy perfected several techniques that would stand it in good stead during the war. Perhaps the most important of these was underway refueling. Most navies used a method whereby a tanker passed cables over her stern to take a tow on the ship being refueled, and then passed a fuel line. This was a slow, clumsy procedure, which, since the tow had to be done at very low speed, exposed the ships to possible attack by submarines. The U.S. Navy decided to try doing it with the tanker and the ship to be refueled running alongside, at a fair speed, twelve to fifteen knots. Specialized equipment was developed to permit fuel lines to be passed between the ships and personnel were trained to play the lines so that as the ships moved they would remain relatively slack, in an elaborate ballet that surprised and impressed foreign naval officers. Not only was this method faster than the towing method, but it was possible to refuel two ships from one tanker simultaneously, an even greater saving in time. This method also permitted larger warships to top off the fuel tanks of smaller ones when necessary. Similar, though less spectacular advances were made in the transfer of stores between underway ships. So when the war came, the navy was ready. Well, almost ready.

The problem was that the navy didn't begin acquiring merchant ships for the fleet train until relatively late. As a result, when the war began the navy was forced to operate with relatively slender logistical support. However, the navy soon began acquiring ships, which were organized into special fleet-service squadrons, known as "servrons." These squadrons consisted of a number of ships of various types, loaded with stores, munitions, and fuel, plus repair ships and even hospital ships, with the necessary escorts. The idea was to form a single group of vessels that could provide for the logistical needs of a task force. In fact, a servron might be considered a logistical task force. Early versions were relatively small, but then, there were relatively few ships out there battling the Japanese. By early 1943, servrons were getting larger. For example, around the end of March 1943 Servron 8 consisted of about 62 ships, excluding escorts:

4 ammunition ships
6 provision ships
3 general cargo ships
1 general stores ship
3 hospital ships
45 tankers (with mostly fuel oil, but some aviation gas)

A year later Servron 8 consisted of some 430 ships, with warships (including 1 or 2 escort carriers, to provide extra security), and was operating in four divisions of 100 to 120 ships each. As the combat forces got larger, the servrons continued to grow. In 1944 the servrons were reorganized and specialized. One, for example, was assigned the job of supporting the air groups of the fast carrier task forces. It was provided with ships that served as floating warehouses for aircraft parts, aviation gas tankers, an aircraft repair ship, and several escort carriers ladened with replacement aircraft and pilots. Other servrons specialized in fueling the fleet, and still others in bringing up food and other stores. Two examples from the Marianas campaign (late spring 1944) are illustrative of this specialization:

TASK GROUP 52.7 (service and repair): 1 net tender (to keep submarines out of anchorages), 3 ocean tugs, 1 seaplane tender, 1 repair ship, 2 salvage vessels, 1 landing vessel repair ship, and 8 miscellaneous yard craft, plus escorts.

TASK GROUP 50.17 (fueling group): 24 oilers, 3 hospital ships, and 4 escort carriers (2 to supply aircraft to the fast carriers and 2 to carry Army Air Force P-47s which were subsequently flown to land bases). There were also 21 destroyers and destroyer escorts, and the whole task group was organized into 7 oiler groups, 1 hospital ship group, and 3 escort carrier groups.

The servron system had broad strategic implications. Early in the war, combat ships, and particularly carriers, had to return to a major base after each operation to replenish their ammunition and stores. With the servron system, on the eve of a major operation the carrier task forces could rendezvous with a servron. After stocking up on fuel, stores, spares, aircraft, and aircrew, the carriers could go into action.

During the operation, individual task forces, by mid-1944 usually of three or four carriers, could fall back as necessary to rendezvous with a servron and replenish while their sister task forces carried on the war. In this fashion operations could be conducted continuously, with task forces rotating into and out of action as necessary. The strategic benefits of this were tremendous, since it kept the Japanese continuously under pressure.

As efficient as they were, the navy's logistical arrangements were strained mightily in the latter part of the war. The enormous size of the forces operating afloat and ashore in the Pacific created so extraordinary a demand for fuel, munitions, rations, and all the other necessities of war that during the protracted operations off Okinawa and Japan itself in the spring and summer of 1945 there developed serious shortages of some supplies and rations became boring. Politics and pride aside, this logistical strain was one reason the U.S. Navy preferred not to have the Royal Navy participate in the final campaigns in the Pacific. The Royal Navy, however, managed to scrape together a fairly effective version of the servron for its own use, totaling ninety-two ships, of which seventeen were tankers and thirteen ammunition ships.

In contrast to the efficient, if ultimately very strained, arrangements of the U.S. Navy, the Japanese Navy had a wholly inadequate fleet train virtually from the start of the war. Even as late as the Marianas campaign, the total fleet train for the mobile fleet, which fought the Battle of the Philippine Sea, was two refueling groups, totaling six smallish tankers, escorted by as many destroyers. Most of the ships were taken up from the merchant marine, operated by their civilian crews, and pressed into service without any modifications to permit efficient replenishment at sea. As a result, the Japanese never really mastered underway refueling, a matter that greatly hampered operations.

BACK BY POPULAR DEMAND

In modern war the demands of ''propaganda'' or ''public information'' to keep the folks back home happy have often led to rather extraordinary claims of success on the part of one's armed forces. During the Pacific war a number of vessels achieved the distinction of having been claimed as sunk numerous times. The U.S. submarine *Tang* seems to hold a world's record, being reported as sunk by Japanese forces no fewer than twenty-five times before she really did succumb (because of a torpedo malfunction) in October 1944. The most frequently sunk American surface ship was "the Big E"; the carrier *Enterprise* was claimed sunk no fewer than six times, a record apparently matched by U.S. claims of having sunk the Japanese battleship *Haruna*, including the one that really happened, when U.S. carrier aircraft finally did her in at Kure on July 28, 1945.

SOME PLACES YOU DON'T PULL RANK

One of the most popular places on any U.S. navy vessel in the Pacific was the ice-cream ("gedunk") bar. There was an unwritten rule in the navy that a sailor had the right to eat as much ice cream as he wanted, in any combination. So the gedunk line was a busy place, as men waited patiently for their turn to whip up some fanciful concoction.

Naval historian Samuel Eliot Morison, himself a veteran of the Pacific war, once observed that British tars often joked about their American cousins' addiction to ice cream, claiming that their grog ration was a superior privilege, but always seemed to head straight for the gedunk bar whenever they were guests on an American vessel.

Anyway, the gedunk line was once the scene of an unusual confrontation. It seems that two freshly minted ensigns aboard the battleship *New Jersey*, the flagship of the Third Fleet, decided they wanted some ice cream. Unfortunately, the gedunk line was interminably long, with dozens of sailors waiting patiently for their turn at the ice-cream bar. Immensely conscious of their exalted rank, the two decided to jump to the head of the line.

When they tried to cut in at the head of the line, saying something like "Gangway for officers," there was grumbling in the ranks. Then a strong voice rose above those of the other men in line, calling out something like "Get back where you belong," albeit much less politely. Just as they were about to deliver a severe dressing-down to the insubordinate sailor who dared challenge their authority, a rather stocky, craggy-faced fellow stepped out to confront them. It was William F. Halsey, of considerably more exalted rank than they, being a full admiral and commander of the Third Fleet, who had been patiently waiting for his turn at the gedunk bar. The mortified ensigns learned a valuable lesson on officer/enlisted relations and "Bill" (never "Bull" except in the press) Halsey added still more luster to his already formidable reputation among the sailors of the fleet.

THE LAST WALTZ

The Battle of the Kommandorshi Islands on March 26, 1943, was the last daylight gun battle between major surface ships that did not involve aircraft or submarines. It was also the longest naval gun battle in this century. What's more, it ended when the Japanese, who were at the point of defeating the American force, suddenly withdrew because they mistakenly thought they were under attack by American aircraft. In a desperate effort to resupply their bases on Attu and Kiska in the Aleutian Islands (seized in June 1942), a Japanese convoy was dispatched consisting of four transports, escorted by two heavy and two light cruisers. This was intercepted by an American force of one heavy and one light cruiser and four destroyers. The battle came down to a long-range gunnery duel between the heavy cruisers. Although outgunned, the American cruisers outfought the Japanese for over three hours. Then, a few hits by Japanese shells in vital areas left the U.S. heavy cruiser *Salt Lake City* (nicknamed "the Swayback Maru" by her devoted crew) dead in the water. At this point, it looked like the Americans were finished, as the Japanese could now pound the U.S. heavy cruiser to pieces and then move in and crush the smaller enemy force. Fortunately, the overcast weather and the fact that the U.S. cruiser was running low on ammo saved the day. The *Salt Lake City* had to use high-explosive shells, as it had run out of armor-piercing ones. These shells, coming in through the overcast and exploding on the water like aircraft bombs, made the Japanese commander think that American aircraft had arrived and that he was now under air attack, especially since the dye used to color the explosion for observation purposes was of a different color from that used in the *Salt Lake City*'s armor-piercing shells. Both sides had called for aircraft support as soon as the battle had begun. But the changeable weather in those northern waters had prevented either side's aircraft from taking off. The Japanese commander didn't know the U.S. aircraft were not able to fly, but he knew their imminent arrival was always a possibility. Seeing what he thought were bombs, he ordered his ships and the convoy to turn back. The amazed, and relieved, American commander signaled his base that the Japanese had withdrawn and that he would bring in his damaged cruiser as soon as emergency repairs could be made. The U.S. commander was rightly hailed as a hero. The Japanese commander was relieved.

IRON-BOTTOM RECORDS

The series of nearly forty surface engagements in the waters between Guadalcanal and the Florida Islands in the Solomons ("Iron Bottom Sound") in 1942 set a number of records for the U.S. Navy. To begin with, Guadalcanal was the navy's first major amphibious operation since 1898. And the Battle of Savo Island (August 9) was the U.S. Navy's first fleet action since 1898 (and only about the fifth or so in its entire history), its first-ever night fleet engagement, its first-ever defeat in a fleet action, and its worst-ever defeat (after Pearl Harbor), when four heavy cruisers (one of them Australian) and a destroyer were sunk, 1,270 men killed, and 709 wounded in an action lasting little more than a half hour, with virtually no loss to the enemy.

The Battle of Cape Esperance (October 11–12) provided three firsts, the navy's first victory in a fleet action since 1898, its first victory in a night fleet action, and its first surface victory against a Japanese squadron. A month later a less fortunate "first" occurred, the first death of an American admiral in a fleet action, when Rear Admiral Norman Scott was killed on the bridge of his flagship in the opening moments of the First Naval Battle of Guadalcanal (November 12–13), followed within minutes by the death of Rear Admiral Dan Callaghan, the task force commander, the two men immediately becoming the first and second admirals ever to receive a posthumous Medal of Honor in a fleet action (one had been awarded to an admiral posthumously for Pearl Harbor, a very different kind of battle).

The Second Naval Battle of Guadalcanal saw four American battleship firsts. Very early on November 15 there occurred the first encounter between battleships in the Pacific war, when the *South Dakota* and *Washington* took on the *Kirishima*, which was also the first time U.S. battleships had ever encountered enemy battleships at sea (and only the second encounter between a U.S. and an enemy battleship ever, the first having occurred just a week earlier, on November 8, when the *Massachusetts* had put the partially completed French *Jean Bart* out of action at her dock at Casablanca). The action was also the occasion of the first (and last) time a U.S. battleship was hit by fire from an enemy battleship, the *South Dakota* taking a 14-inch round from the *Kirishima*, plus possibly a 5-incher. And a few minutes later occurred the first (and last) time a U.S. battlewagon "sank" an enemy battleship, when the *Washington* turned the *Kirishima* into a burning wreck, her first two broadsides scoring with nine 16-inch hits (a 50 percent hit rate), followed up by about forty 5-inch shells.

Most of these surface actions took place at night between August and November 1942. There were also two carrier battles and many minor surface actions, and many encounters between land-based aircraft and ships. Never before, or since, has the U.S. Navy engaged in such a furious round of surface combat. As hard fought as the ground fighting on Guadalcanal was, four times as many sailors as Marines and soldiers lost their lives in the naval battles fought in support of the ground and air forces on the island.

THE SECOND OFFENSIVE, AND WHY IT WAS IMPORTANT

The U.S. capture of Guadalcanal on August 7, 1942, is rightly considered the first offensive operation of the Pacific war. But ten days later, on August 17, 221 U.S. Marine "Raiders" landed on the Japanese-held island of Makin. The Marines came ashore from two submarines and within hours had destroyed a new seaplane reconnaissance base and killed the ninety-man Japanese garrison. The Marines lost 30 dead and 14 wounded. The island was quickly evacuated before Japanese reinforcements could arrive. The raid was mainly for propaganda purposes, although it did serve some military function. But the raid had an enormous impact on subsequent fighting in the Pacific. The Japanese were alarmed at the vulnerability of dozens of similar island bases throughout the Pacific. The decision was made to increase the garrisons of these islands and to build the fortifications that U.S. Marines became so intimate with for the rest of the war. This was not the only case in which the Japanese reacted strongly to a minor American operation. The Doolittle raid (April 18, when sixteen B-25 bombers flew from a carrier to bomb Japan) caused the Japanese to keep hundreds of combat aircraft in the home islands to prevent another attack.

NEAR MISSES IN THE JAVA SEA

One of the few ship-to-ship naval battles between Allied and Japanese forces during the initial Japanese expansion occurred in the Java Sea. On February 27, the ABDA (American-British-Dutch-Australian) force, five cruisers and nine destroyers commanded by a Dutch admiral, sallied forth to prevent further Japanese landings in what was then called the Netherlands East Indies (Indonesia). Over the next three days, most of this force was sunk by Japanese ships and aircraft; only slight damage was done to the Japanese. But it was only some bad luck that prevented the ABDA force from doing significant harm to the Japanese invasion force. The Japanese were fairly reckless in pushing their troop-laden transports forward. Several times the Allied warships came dangerously close to sinking these vulnerable transports. As it was, the presence of Allied warships in the area threw the tight Japanese schedule into a state of confusion. The reason the Japanese were moving so quickly was because they had to seize the oil fields and refineries on Sumatra before they could be destroyed. The Japanese oil situation was desperate and was the primary reason Japan went to war in the first place. As it turned out, the Japanese were luckier than the Allies. The oil facilities were rapidly evacuated without being destroyed. Had the ABDA force gotten a few of those Japanese transports, the Sumatra oil fields would have remained in Allied hands long enough to be destroyed. That done, Japan would have been out of fuel by 1944 and suffered severe oil shortages for over a year before that. Japanese resistance to the Allied advance would have been weaker. In short, a little bit of luck in the Java Sea during February 1942 would have changed the course of the war.

THE CENTRAL PACIFIC: SON OF PLAN ORANGE

From 1919 through the 1930s, as war with Japan became ever more likely, the U.S. Navy developed a series of plans to deal with this: War Plan Orange (with lots of variations). Basically, War Plan Orange called for an amphibious advance across the central Pacific and, eventually, the Japanese home islands. The planners eventually realized that the Philippines might be lost, thus one variant of the plan had the U.S. fleet doing pretty much what it did in 1943–1945 (advancing to the Philippines first, then to Japan). What War Plan Orange did not foresee was how much success the Japanese would actually achieve in the first six months of the war. The U.S. battleship fleet was largely wiped out. So in early 1942, General MacArthur was made commander of the remaining U.S. forces in the Pacific. Many thought that MacArthur was the logical commander for the war effort against Japan. But MacArthur was an army commander and the U.S. Navy had long seen the Pacific as its responsibility. The navy was also the driving force behind the War Plan Orange work. The admirals knew that starting in 1943 a flood of new warships would reach the Pacific and they didn't want to have a soldier running their show. The solution to this dispute was to have two commanders in the Pacific. MacArthur would lead a primarily army and air force advance toward the Philippines, while Admiral Chester W. Nimitz would lead a navy advance through the central Pacific islands toward the Philippines. The first landing of the central Pacific drive was in November 1943 at Tarawa in the Gilbert Islands. In February 1944, Kwajalein and several other islands in the Marshall Islands group were taken. Between June and August 1944, the islands in the Marianas were taken. These included Saipan, Tinian, and Guam, each of which soon became a base for B-29 raids against Japan. This campaign, along with MacArthur's drive northward from New Guinea, isolated the Caroline Islands and Japan's primary Pacific base at Truk.

MacArthur's operations were not part of War Plan Orange, which had assumed a unified command in the Pacific. His operations in New Guinea made sense, as this was where the Japanese were still trying to advance. The Guadalcanal operation, which was, for all practical purposes, in MacArthur's area of operations, was given to the navy because it had a Marine division handy, was willing to risk its remaining ships to support the Marines, and, basically, didn't have much else to do until all its new ships began arriving in mid-1943.

MacArthur would have preferred to head for the vital Japanese oil supplies in the Netherlands East Indies (particularly Borneo), and thence to the Philippines and Japan itself. This plan short-circuited the War Plan Orange approach entirely. The U.S. Navy would be relegated to keeping the Japanese fleet occupied in the central Pacific while MacArthur used hordes of land-based aircraft and amphibious shipping to move through the thicket of islands leading to the Japanese oil, the Philippines, and Japan. The navy's argument was that it could use a central Pacific drive to force the Japanese to split their forces. Maybe, but we'll never know for sure. Thus, in effect, War Plan Orange was carried out, with the addition of MacArthur's advance from New Guinea.

IT AIN'T RICE PUDDING

Give a sailor some rice and raisins during World War II, and he didn't think of rice pudding but rather of a powerful homemade whiskey called "tuba." This was potent stuff, usually concocted by shipfitters or other below-deck types with access to tools needed for putting a still together (and a place to hide it). Proof varied, but was usually high, and unpredictable. Other improvisations were common. For example, the advent of alcohol-fueled torpedoes was soon followed by the discovery that "torpedo juice" was drinkable.

Potable alcohol has been prohibited on U.S. Navy ships since a blue-nosed secretary of the navy banned it in 1914 (the last night of legal booze found the fleet lying off Veracruz, and saw parties of officers rowing from ship to ship in a heroic attempt to drink up every last drop before the midnight deadline). So the hardest stuff officially available on U.S. ships was coffee, of which endless gallons were consumed. Indeed, British officers often complained of caffeine overdoses after staff conferences on U.S. warships. This was one reason why when U.S. ships were operating in conjunction with British or other Allied vessels the staff conferences tended to be on the foreign ship. The Allies avoided caffeine jags and the Americans could be treated to some alcohol (in exchange, since the British were on tight rations for the entire war, the Americans always brought a few hams or some other items to donate to the officers' mess).

Some captains were more fanatical about eliminating tuba (and other such improvisations) than others. A few captains and even senior officers (like William Halsey) winked at minor violations of the ban. Some officers even went out of their way to circumvent it, procuring hard liquor for "medicinal" purposes and issuing it to their men on special occasions. There was also quite a lot of beer shipped to the fleet, and this was issued "off the ship" periodically. The sailors would literally take one of the ship's boats a few hundred yards from their vessel, consume their two cans of brew, and then come back so the next batch of men could do the same. However, on the whole, let's just say that a sailor was in a lot more trouble if he left his ship drunk than if he returned to it in that state.

THE FIRST CARRIER BATTLE, EVER

The Battle of the Coral Sea was the first battle between aircraft carriers. As such, it was the first naval battle in which neither side could see each other. All the fighting was done by aircraft. The battle, fought May 7–8, 1942, set the pattern for all the other 1942 carrier battles. The battle began with the Japanese attempting to land troops to establish another base in New Guinea. In this case the objective was Port Moresby, on the south coast of New Guinea (facing the north coast of Australia). In March, U.S. carrier aircraft had carried out a daring attack on Japanese ships landing troops on the north coast of New Guinea, flying over the supposedly too high Owen Stanley Range by taking advantage of favorable thermal to catch the Japanese completely off guard. The raid was only moderately successful, as the ships had already discharged their troops and cargoes. Had the U.S. carriers arrived a little earlier and caught the Japanese ships on the high seas, the Japanese landing would have been stopped. As a result of this raid, the Japanese decided to occupy the balance of New Guinea.

For the Port Moresby operation the Japanese decided to commit three carriers to ensure that the U.S. carriers were kept off their transports. As it turned out, the Japanese transports were spotted before they got very far toward their objective. Two U.S. carriers attempted to intercept the convoys and the two carrier forces had it out. When it was over, the United States had lost the carrier *Lexington,* a tanker, and a destroyer, while the Japanese had suffered the light carrier *Shoho* lost and the fleet carrier *Shokaku* damaged. But the United States won the battle. The Japanese invasion had been frustrated, making Coral Sea their first strategic reverse of the war. However, there was more to it than that.

Although the Americans could ill afford the loss of one of their carriers, the Japanese carrier fleet suffered more. Although the *Shoho* was a relatively minor vessel, damage would put the *Shokaku* out of action for months. Moreover, Japanese pilot losses had been so serious that the *Zuikaku,* the other fleet carrier present, was also put out of action. So as a result of Coral Sea, neither the *Shokaku* nor *Zuikaku* was able to participate in the Battle of Midway a month later, where their presence might well have turned the American victory into an American defeat.

Coral Sea also revealed bad habits of both navies. Japanese communication was sloppy, with admirals being in the habit of not passing on vital information. This was a trait the Japanese were never able to overcome throughout the war. Japanese admirals tended to fight as if they were the only Japanese force engaged and constantly missed opportunities to coordinate with other Japanese forces. The Japanese also lacked the rapid repair techniques the Americans had. While the heavily damaged *Yorktown* was repaired in time for the Battle of Midway, the less heavily damaged *Shokaku* was not ready until a week after Midway was over.

The major U.S. errors were largely due to inexperience. The Japanese had more experience in carrier operations and were able to more efficiently attack American carriers, expertly maneuvering their aircraft groups to search out and attack enemy ships. American officers closed this experience gap by the end of 1942.

PLANNING IN 3-D

There was a lot of innovation during World War II, and much of it didn't get all of the attention it deserved afterward. One example was the preparation of three-dimensional maps and physical models of enemy-held islands. These were used to assist the navy gunners and pilots to locate their assigned targets, and Marines and infantrymen to "see" up close what the ground would be like when they hit the beaches. Such maps and models were particularly popular with airmen, who were wont to "fly" their hands over them so that they could get a "feel" for the hills and valleys over which they would shortly be flying for real. By 1945, these relief maps and models had become a regular feature of island assaults. Even destroyers were supplied with them. This made sense, as destroyers often delivered vital fire support. Destroyers, because they drew less water, could get in closer and provide more immediate support with their five-inch (127mm) guns.

MYTHS OF MIDWAY

The Battle of Midway, the second carrier battle of 1942, was the most decisive of the war. But not for the reasons the Japanese thought it would be, even if they had captured the place. In fact, the Battle of Midway would have turned into the "Siege of Midway" if the Americans had not known what the enemy were up to or did not have forces available with which to ambush their opponents.

The Japanese decided to seize Midway Island in order to force the U.S. fleet to come out and do battle, so that it could then be decisively defeated. A base on Midway would provide an "unsinkable aircraft carrier" for the rest of the Japanese fleet to maneuver around while the smaller U.S. fleet was chopped to pieces. Midway was a massive operation, involving eight Japanese carriers plus numerous destroyers, cruisers, battleships, and submarines. The operation also involved landing Japanese troops on several undefended islands off Alaska as a diversion. The Japanese plan was to seize Midway quickly and then advance down the chain of islands the thousand or so miles to Hawaii, sinking any U.S. naval forces rushing out to the defense of Midway. But that was the Japanese way of thinking.

The U.S. Navy had other ideas. If the Japanese had seized Midway, the United States would have put it under siege with long-range aircraft and submarines. Midway was over two thousand miles from the Japanese home islands and quite isolated. It would have to be supplied by sea and the Japanese never fully grasped the problems of logistics in the Pacific war. A Japanese-held Midway would have turned into another of many Japanese logistics disasters. While the Japanese played down logistics, they played up the importance of "military honor." They felt the Americans would come out to defend Midway no matter what. The Americans felt otherwise.

Because the United States had broken many Japanese codes, it knew most of the Japanese plan and had all of its three available carriers in the Pacific stationed off Midway to ambush the Japanese. The U.S. force was lucky, the Japanese force was sloppy, and four Japanese carriers were sunk to the loss of only one U.S. carrier. The Japanese Navy never recovered from this because the United States could (and did) build new carriers much faster than Japan.

American admirals knew they would have to deal with the Japanese carriers eventually, especially the six heavy carriers. By June 1942, the United States had only three heavy carriers available for operations in the Pacific and would not receive the first of the two dozen new Essex class heavy carriers until after the new year. It had already resigned itself to fighting a defensive battle until then, emphasizing submarines and land-based aircraft. Midway was an opportunity the Americans could not pass up, but only because they had the drop on the Japanese. Without the advantage of having been privy to the coded Japanese messages, the United States would not have risked its three carriers against the Japanese. Midway would have fallen to the Japanese, but the effect of this success on the course of the war may actually have been relatively minimal.

NASTY SURPRISES

The first time a weapon is used in combat, there are usually some nasty surprises for the user, especially when both sides are using the new weapon. Such was the case with aircraft carriers at war. Until the Battle of the Coral Sea in May 1942, carrier-to-carrier combat was a purely theoretical notion. The Pearl Harbor attack was no different from many peacetime exercises in which the planes flew off the carrier to hit land targets. Indeed, before Pearl Harbor this had been done repeatedly in war by the Japanese against the Chinese, or by the British in the Mediterranean. A true carrier battle would have the two carriers trying to sink each other. What Coral Sea demonstrated was how vulnerable carriers were, and what limitations they had. In 1942, carriers simply could not be protected all that well from the effects of attacking aircraft. Determined pilots would get through and carriers would be hit. Carriers that were hit were more likely than other types of ships to sink. Carriers were not well armored and carried a lot of flammable material (aviation gas and bombs). Carriers normally had several thousand tons of highly flammable aviation fuel on board. Bombs were often lying about waiting to be loaded into aircraft. Other warships did not have aviation fuel (high-grade gasoline) and kept their munitions in well-protected magazines. The flight deck made a nice large target for dive-bombers. This also made carriers very vulnerable to surface attack. But this rarely happened, mainly because carriers required high speed in order to be able to launch their aircraft (carriers turned into the wind and increased speed to give launching aircraft sufficient lift to get off the relatively short flight deck) and were able to use this speed to outrun other surface ships. Attacking aircraft were another matter. No ship could outrun aircraft.

Carrier tactics were simple. The primary rule in carrier warfare is that, as at Christmas, it is better to give than to receive, only more so. To do this, you sent out a lot of bombers as scouts. Once the enemy carriers were spotted, more bombers were launched. The enemy generally did the same and both sides' carriers got hit. Even though fighters aboard the carriers were used mainly to protect the carrier itself, it was quickly (and painfully) discovered that intercepting fighters could not stop all attacking bombers. There were two kinds of bombers: those coming in low and carrying torpedoes, and those coming in high carrying bombs (dive-bombers). Bombs proved more lethal, as they would more likely set off secondary explosions from aviation fuel and bombs on the carrier. Torpedoes, however, had longer-term impact as they would usually slow the carrier down (and sometimes sink it). A slow carrier is at a severe disadvantage. It has a hard time launching aircraft (and sometimes cannot do it at all), which lowers the number of carrier-based interceptors in the air. A torpedoed carrier cannot as easily run away from enemy surface ships.

In 1942, the Japanese learned that their carriers were more vulnerable to bomb damage than were American carriers. The Americans were able to make their cargoes of aviation gas less vulnerable and generally had more effective damage control. This alone cost the Japanese several carriers. But these advantages were somewhat counterbalanced by more effective Japanese aircraft and torpedoes. U.S. torpedoes had to be dropped at a lower altitude and speed than Japanese torpedoes and this made U.S. torpedo bombers more vulnerable as they flew in low and slow against Japanese carriers. This, in turn, was somewhat mitigated by superior U.S. antiaircraft guns. Neither side had enough of these on their ships at the beginning of the war and for most of 1942 it was the carrier-borne fighters that were most effective in stopping attacking enemy aircraft. In this case, the advantage went to the Japanese, as their Zero fighter was the most efficient fighter in the theater during 1942. But if a carrier was set upon by torpedo bombers and dive-bombers, the interceptors were not always efficiently split between the two threats. Fighters going after torpedo bombers could not climb quickly enough to get to incoming dive-bombers. And even if the fighters went after dive-bombers first, they would still have a hard time getting down to the approaching torpedo bombers before the torpedoes were launched. To further complicate these situations, the groups of enemy bombers would come in at different times and from different directions. There was also the problem of friendly antiaircraft guns. In theory, the carrier's fighters were to go after enemy bombers outside of antiaircraft guns' range, but often fighters would continue to pursue incoming bombers and both enemy bombers and friendly fighters would get hit by them.

After 1942, carrier combat became moot. Japan lost most of its best carrier pilots in 1942 and never came close to replacing them. The United States built many more carriers and surrounded them with more efficient defenses.

HIDING BEHIND THE OUTHOUSE

The Japanese quickly learned that U.S. amphibious operations were accompanied by unprecedented quantities of naval gunfire support. In addition to the battleships (14-inch and 16-inch guns) and cruisers (12-inch, 8-inch, and 6-inch guns) there were a lot of destroyers (5-inch guns). The "hardest" (most-fortified) targets were assigned to the largest guns, which plastered them with quarter-ton, half-ton, and one-ton shells from comfortable ranges before the landing craft beached. The destroyers (which fired puny 55-pound rounds) came into their own only when the troops hit the beach. Then the destroyers, which could come close in, were on call for all sorts of direct fire support missions. During preliminary bombardments, destroyers were usually assigned low-priority targets. And thereby hangs a tale.

During the invasion of Guam in July 1944, one destroyer was assigned to fire on some Japanese latrines. The men on the destroyer were disappointed at being given so lowly an assignment, but all the other targets were covered by larger ships. However, unbeknownst to naval intelligence, the Japanese, thinking the Americans would not waste shells on latrines, stored much of their reserve ammunition in what looked like a latrine. The destroyer sailors, upon firing at their target, began wondering if they had been secretly issued some new, extremely powerful 5-inch shells. Each shell they fired at the latrines resulted in a huge explosion. Later it was confirmed that it wasn't the shells, but what the Japanese had hidden behind the outhouse.

Incidentally, the Japanese never caught on to the notion of camouflaging their latrines, which was why the destroyer was assigned to blast them in the first place. One result of this, aside from a lot of destroyed outhouses, was that it was relatively easy to estimate the number of Japanese troops in an area. One had merely to count the latrines and consult the standard Japanese Army regulations on the ratio of outhouses to troops.

THE SUPERWEAPON OF THE NAVAL WAR: THE SUBMARINE

While it is widely known that the submarine was crucial in destroying Japan's merchant marine during the Pacific war, it often overlooked that U.S. subs sank only 45 percent of enemy merchant shipping. Aircraft accounted for most of the rest. But submarines did account for 29 percent of all warship tonnage sunk. Both battleships and carriers were vulnerable to subs. The Japanese were most eager to send their submarines after warships and it was one of their subs that sank the carrier *Wasp* in 1942, at a time when the United States could ill afford any carrier losses. What is all the more remarkable is that on the U.S. side, all this carnage was caused by sub crews that composed less than 2 percent of all U.S. sailors.

Japan began the war with 67 subs, the United States with 56 in the Pacific plus almost as many in the Atlantic. Both sides built relatively large subs with the necessary long range to be able to operate over the vast spaces of the Pacific. But beyond that, the U.S. and Japanese submarine forces were quite different. The U.S. boats were of better quality, but the Japanese commanders were more effective in the early months of the war. U.S. subs were stuck with defective torpedoes for the first two years of the war, ineffective doctrine for the first year, and unaggressive skippers as well. The most significant difference was that Japanese doctrine had subs going after warships exclusively, while U.S. doctrine had the subs spending most of their time attacking enemy merchant shipping. The U.S. approach was ultimately more successful, sinking most Japanese merchant shipping and causing disastrous economic and logistical problems for the Japanese. The United States did suffer some losses from Japanese attacks on their warships, but these were not critical. Several capital ships (carriers and battleships) took torpedoes, but only the *Wasp* was sunk. U.S. shipbuilding was much more productive than Japan's and any losses to subs were quickly replaced. Subs were one area where Japan nearly matched U.S. production. But Japan was able to produce only 120 subs during the war, versus over 200 for the United States. While U.S. subs went after unprotected Japanese merchant ships, Japanese boats took a beating tangling with U.S. warships. Japan was also reluctant to spend much effort on anti-submarine warfare. In 1942, 1943, and 1944, the United States produced nearly 600 destroyers and destroyer escorts. This was over ten times what Japan produced. While most of these antisubmarine warfare ships went to fighting German U-Boats in the Atlantic, enough went to the Pacific to make life lethal for Japanese subs. Had the Japanese attacked U.S. merchant shipping, it would have made U.S. operations much more difficult.

Everything the United States needed to wage war had to come from North America by ship. And much of this supply was literally stored in ships (as floating warehouses) until used. It was difficult to protect the hundreds of merchant ships, and Japan would have had a good shot at one of the most vulnerable portions of the U.S. Pacific war effort.

WORSE THAN THE JAPANESE

Stalking U.S. sailors in the Pacific was another lethal enemy that did not speak Japanese. These were the typhoons ("cyclonic storms," or hurricanes) that regularly swept across the Pacific. On December 17, 1944, Task Force 38 was blindsided by a typhoon off the Philippines. Over eight hundred sailors were killed, three destroyers were sunk, and twenty other ships severely damaged, as were numerous aircraft. This was not the only time a task force got hit, simply one of the worst. One reason for the seriousness of this incident may be due to the fact that Admiral Halsey flew his flag from a battleship, which was much more stable in foul weather than a destroyer, particularly one that was low on fuel. Halsey was accused of underestimating the danger of this storm, some said because the rough seas didn't seem so rough to him as he stood on the bridge of his battleship.

The typhoon "nursery" (for those north of the equator in the Pacific) is between 155 and 165 degrees east longitude most of the year—which was smack in the middle of the central Pacific theater of operations. During January through March it's between 145 and 155 degrees. Just to complicate matters, some cyclonic storms form west of Japan in the Sea of Japan and farther north. A few even start overland in northeast Siberia and then gain typhoon strength as they move out over the water. Most of these "northern" typhoons don't get beyond storm strength (over thirty-four knots' wind), but some do. And for every typhoon, there are several storms that don't make it to typhoon strength. These can be almost as bad as a typhoon, and carrier operations were not possible during most storms, which made it easier for enemy submarines to get close to the carriers. Worse yet, because the Japanese held so many of the central Pacific islands, there was often insufficient information on where new storms were forming or where existing ones were heading. For this reason the U.S. Navy regularly used submarines to report the weather, and maintained weather stations in China, including several in the Gobi in Inner Mongolia, probably about as far from blue water (perhaps from any open water) as the navy has ever operated. The Japanese were not the only enemy ready to hit you while you weren't looking.

THE 1942 CARRIER RAIDS

Immediately after Pearl Harbor, there wasn't much the United States could do in the Pacific. The Japanese quickly seized most of the major Allied bases in the region and the shock of this rapid conquest left the Allies in need of some morale building. This needed morale boost came in the form of a series of raids by the U.S. carriers, including the two that had escaped destruction at Pearl Harbor. The Japanese cooperated by committing their dozen carriers to supporting ground operations and a largely unnecessary sortie into the Indian Ocean. They made no effort to follow up their success at Pearl Harbor by tracking down and destroying the numerically fewer U.S. Pacific carriers. After Pearl Harbor the United States quickly added the *Hornet* and *Yorktown* from the Atlantic to the three already in the Pacific, the *Enterprise, Lexington,* and *Saratoga.* However, on January 11, 1942, the *Saratoga* was torpedoed by a Japanese sub five hundred miles south of Hawaii, forcing her back to a West Coast shipyard for several months of repairs and modernization. Since the *Saratoga*'s pilots and aircraft were distributed among the other carriers, this gave the United States four fully staffed carriers for use against the Japanese.

Despite the risk of losing more carriers, a policy of raiding was adopted. The first two attempts involved Wake Island. In mid-December 1941 an attempt was made to aid the hard-pressed U.S. garrison there, and had it been successful it might have resulted in the first carrier-to-carrier battle ever. Then, in January 1942 an attempt was made to hit the newly installed Japanese garrison on the island. Both attempts failed through a combination of inexperience, excessive caution, and bad luck. In early February, however, the Marshall Islands were hit in the first successful raid. In late February, a raid on Rabaul (in the Bismarcks) was called off when a U.S. carrier there was spotted by Japanese recon aircraft. Early March saw a successful raid on Marcus Island, only one thousand miles from the Japanese home islands. In mid-March, two carriers hit Japanese forces landing on the north coast of New Guinea, in a daring raid over some of the highest mountains in the Pacific area. Then came the most spectacular raid of all, in mid-April, when sixteen army B-25 bombers launched from the *Hornet* bombed Tokyo. At this point the Japanese decided to try to make a decisive attempt to crush the U.S. Navy, resulting in the battles of the Coral Sea (May 7–8) and Midway (June 3–5). The two battles evened up the carrier situation in the Pacific, when the Japanese lost five carriers (*Shoho,* at Coral Sea and *Akagi, Kaga, Soryu,* and *Hiryu* in about five minutes at Midway) at a cost of two American carriers, (the *Lexington* and *Yorktown*). This ended the period of desperate carrier raids by the United States.

By allowing these raids, or at least not taking aggressive action to stop them, the Japanese enabled the American carriers to gain valuable experience. As with all their ships and sailors, the Japanese began the war better trained than their Allied counterparts. Without these raids, and their opportunity for relatively risk-free practice, the Battle of Midway might easily have gone the other way.

The one thing that could have stopped, or severely limited, these raids was a few Japanese bombers hitting the massive fuel supplies stored in aboveground tanks at Pearl Harbor. These could have been destroyed in the December 7 raid, but the Japanese didn't think such mundane targets important enough to hit.

CREDIT WHERE CREDIT IS DUE: NAVAL MINES

Naval mines made their first modern wartime appearance in the 1905 Russo-Japanese War. The Japanese got the worst of it then from the mines and suffered once more during World War II when it was mines, more than anything else, that completed the blockade of Japan and brought the Japanese to their knees.

Mines have never been considered a "warrior's weapon" and as a result are generally disdained by many naval commanders. The U.S. Navy overcame this aversion to mines and used them delivered by submarine and air in 1945 to completely shut down Japanese shipping. One reason that mines were so effective was that much of Japanese shipping was actually carried by very small vessels. Much of Japan's foodstuff was moved in small craft of eighty tons or less, which could easily run along coasts at night and hide in bays, rivers, and other inlets by day, where they could be camouflaged against U.S. aircraft. Mines made this a problematic proposition. As a result, Japan began running short of food. Had Japan not surrendered in August 1945, millions of Japanese would have starved or frozen to death by the end of the next winter.

GUADALCANAL: THE FIRST-THREE DIMENSIONAL BATTLE

Guadalcanal was not the biggest or the longest battle of the Pacific war. Its main claim to fame was not as "the turning point" in the Pacific war, but rather as history's first three-dimensional battle. For the first time in history, air, land, and air forces were combined as never before in one campaign.

It all began in May 1942, when the Japanese landed construction troops on Guadalcanal Island in order to build an airfield, which would enable them to interdict Allied supply convoys going to Australia and provide a springboard for further advances to the south. Recognizing the danger of this strategy, the United States decided to make Guadalcanal the site of the first Allied counteroffensive. In August, the U.S. 1st Marine Division made a (largely) unopposed landing on Guadalcanal and nearby Tulagi, cleared the Japanese troops away from the still uncompleted airfield, and quickly completed it. For the next six months, Japanese ground, naval, and air forces fought desperately to take the airfield back. Two carrier battles, half a dozen major and some thirty smaller naval surface battles, over a dozen land battles, and over a hundred air raids were conducted in that six-month period. The Japanese effort failed. Over 75 percent of the U.S. combat deaths were among sailors, as surface and carrier battles raged in and around the island. By early 1943, the Japanese had abandoned attempts to retake the airfield and left Guadalcanal. This was the first of many three-dimensional battles in the Pacific war. It was also the only one in which the Japanese had virtual parity in resources with the Allies, which is why it was such "a near run" thing.

WHO INVENTED MODERN AMPHIBIOUS WARFARE?

No one nation did. It was a joint innovation on the Allied side. The Royal Navy, the U.S. Marines, and the U.S. Army jointly developed modern amphibious warfare during the 1930s and early 1940s. The British (who had had an unfortunate experience at Gallipoli in 1915) developed many of the modern amphibious ships, the U.S. Marines developed amphibious combat tactics, while the U.S. Army's engineers developed most of the amphibious support techniques that allowed the troops to get ashore with enough supplies and equipment to stay there and advance. During the war the U.S. Army actually undertook more amphibious landings than anyone else, although the Marines carried out the most difficult amphibious operations, which is probably why many think the Marines "invented" modern amphibious warfare. The Marines were also better at getting their story to the public, which has a lot to do with their high profile in this area. This is not to slight the Japanese, who successfully used amphibious warfare in early 1942. The Japanese also developed some unique amphibious craft, but not in the same quality and quantity that the Allies did as the war went on.

LEARNING SURFACE COMBAT THE HARD WAY

Before Pearl Harbor, surface combat was expected to be the more decisive form of naval action between the United States and Japan. Pearl Harbor and the carrier battles in early 1942 quickly demonstrated that carriers, not surface combatants, ruled the waves. But after the battles of the Coral Sea, Midway, the eastern Solomons, and the Santa Cruz Islands depleted everyone's carrier fleets, most of the 1942–1943 naval battles were surface combats, occasionally influenced by the presence of aircraft. In fact, there were over a dozen major and scores of minor engagements between battleships, cruisers, and destroyers during the Pacific war. Most of these took place in the vicinity of Guadalcanal, when, in about six months (August 1942–February 1943), there occurred five major and about thirty smaller surface engagements. Aside from a number of surface actions in the Netherlands East Indies in early 1942 and in the Philippines in 1944, virtually all of the remaining surface engagements took place in the Solomon Islands northwest of Guadalcanal.

Before the war, the Japanese and the Americans had developed differing notions about surface combat. The Japanese, mindful of their probable numerical inferiority in a war with the United States, trained for night actions, stressed the use of torpedoes by both destroyers and cruisers, preferred putting their heavier ships in the van, and were willing to use multiple columns, permitting the tactical independence of different squadrons operating together. The U.S. Navy, in contrast, was fairly rigidly tied to the single-line-ahead formation, with destroyers at the van and rear and the heavier ships in the middle, all to operate under a single command.

When the two navies began to clash, it soon became apparent that the Japanese attitude was superior. For the surface battles that took place did not conform to the U.S. Navy's expectations. Because of the presence of land-based aircraft, surface battles were almost always at night. This was because whoever controlled the air in daylight had a tremendous combat advantage. In night surface combat, the Japanese initially had an advantage. They had trained hard for night surface combat during peacetime. They evolved more realistic tactics for night combat and drilled their ships' crews relentlessly in all types of weather, regardless of casualties. They had also developed superior optical equipment for range finding. U.S. sailors had received a more leisurely diet of daytime training exercises, marred by a contestlike atmosphere that resulted in training being conducted in the calmest possible weather so that no ship would have an unfair advantage. Moreover, unlike the United States, Japan had equipped its cruisers with torpedoes and many of its ships with torpedo reloads. The Japanese torpedoes were superior (larger and more reliable) to all other torpedoes in the world. The U.S. admirals had generally neglected the use of the torpedo in surface combat, omitting it entirely from most cruisers, for example, and not getting enough practice in coordinating torpedo-armed destroyers with heavier ships during maneuvers. So from the Java Sea battles (February 27–March 1, 1942) through the summer and fall battles around Guadalcanal, the Japanese were generally triumphant at night. U.S. sailors had to undergo the same grueling training process as the Japanese had before U.S. surface ships could meet the Japanese on equal terms. A lot of material changes in late 1942 helped, but it was the training that made the difference. Learning how to fight in combat is the hard way, learning during tough, realistic peacetime training is the easy way.

Meanwhile, the United States gradually acquired superior ships, improved damage-control techniques, and better communications methods. And it began to learn to use its torpedoes. The torpedo was actually the most effective weapon used in the night battles, accounting for most of the ships lost. As it turned out, U.S. destroyer men already knew how to make effective torpedo attacks but had usually been kept on a tight leash by task force commanders lacking destroyer experience. Given a chance to operate on their own they proved particularly effective in torpedo attacks, as at Balikpapan (January 23–24, 1942) or Cape Esperance (October 11–12, 1942). Despite this, it was not until mid-1943 that U.S. destroyers were routinely allowed to operate in conjunction with rather than in line with heavier ships.

Radar came along too. Surprisingly, initially it may have actually handicapped U.S. night-fighting abilities. The first radars were inefficient, temperamental, and not at all understood by most senior officers. Indeed, at times the presence of Japanese warships was first detected by lookouts, if it had not already been announced by the arrival of their shells, before they were detected by radar, at which point it was usually too late to do anything but die bravely. As radar improved and commanders who understood its capabilities and limitations (like Willis "Ching Chong" Lee) came along, things began to get better, and U.S. ships began to feel more comfortable in night actions.

However, even as the U.S. Navy improved, the Japanese remained formidable opponents. At Kula Gulf (July 4–5, 1943) and Kolombangara (July 12–13, 1943) they gave better than they received, despite all the U.S. advantages. But gradually their edge was lost, and in the last important surface actions of the war on anything like even terms, Vella Lavella (August 6–7, 1943) and Empress Augusta Bay (November 2, 1943), they came off second best.

SAILORS DO IT FASTER

Within seven minutes after the first Japanese attack on Pearl Harbor, nearly all navy shipboard antiaircraft guns were manned and in action. The U.S. Army had thirty-one antiaircraft batteries at Pearl Harbor and only four got into action during the attack. There is some mitigation for the soldiers' slow performance. Sailors live (on the ship) near their guns, soldiers live in barracks some distance away from their weapons and ammunition. Sailors have a well-practiced drill (''General Quarters'') wherein all hands drop what they are doing and rush topside to their battle stations. It made a difference. Moreover, both soldiers and sailors had to take special measures to get at the ammunition, which is kept under lock and key in peacetime. The soldiers had to find tools to break the locks on the magazines. The sailors had many damage-control tools (designed for breaking and entering) with which to remove the locks on their ammunition containers.

UNCLE SAM'S U-BOAT WAR AGAINST JAPAN

The decisive weapon in the war against Japan was the submarine. Japan lost a total of about 9 million gross registered tons of shipping

Causes of Total Japanese Merchant Shipping Tonnage Loss

	Percentage of Loss	Tonnage Lost (in millions)
Submarines	55	5.3*
Carrier Aircraft	22	2.0
Other Aircraft	11	1.0
Mines	5.4	0.5
Surface Vessels	3.3	0.3
Miscellaneous†	4.3	0.4

* Figure is approximate.
† Includes the ''hazards of the sea,'' accidents, land-based artillery fire, and several commando raids. About 1.5 million GRT (16.1 percent) were lost in the first eighteen months of the war. Allied boats accounted for about 2 percent of Japanese tonnage losses to submarines (about 106,000 GRT). Approximately 23 percent of Japanese merchant ship losses to carrier aircraft after July 1945 were lost to British carrier aircraft. About half of the other air losses were attributable to land-based naval aircraft, and about 12 percent were inflicted by British, Commonwealth, and Dutch aircraft (about 120,000 GRT). In contrast to Japanese losses, note that Italy and Germany lost about 2 million tons each of merchant fleets, totaling about 3.5 million tons each in 1939, wartime construction accounting for the rest of their wartime losses.

Thousands of Tons Shipping Lost by Cause

	Submarines	Naval Aircraft	Army Aircraft	Mines	Miscellaneous
1942	600	100	75	—	100
1943	1,800	50	250	—	75
1944	2,990	990	250	—	100
1945	490	600	250	600	175

NOTES: Figures are approximate. Naval aircraft losses include those due to land-based naval aircraft. Mine casualties are those attributable to the B-29 mining campaign. Miscellaneous includes wrecks, sabotage, surface action, and conventional mines.

during the war, of which more than half were lost to U.S. submarines.

During the war, U.S. submarines spent 31,571 days on patrol in the Pacific. They attacked 4,112 Japanese-controlled merchant ships, expending 14,748 torpedoes in the process. This resulted in the sinking of 1,304.5 vessels, totaling 5.3 million gross tons, or an average of 359.4 tons for every torpedo expended. The "half" ship in these figures was sunk in conjunction with an air attack.

U.S. Submarine Campaign Statistics

	Japanese Warship Losses		Japanese Merchantman Losses		U.S. Submarine Patrols	U.S. Submarines Lost
	Number	Tonnage	Number	Tonnage		
1941–42	2	11.0	180.0*	725	350	7
1943	22	29.1	335.0	1,500	350	15
1944	104	405.7	603.0	2,700	520	19
1945	60	66.1	186.5	415	330	8

NOTES: Tonnage figures are in thousands, with those for warships being standard displacement tons and those for merchantmen gross registered tons. A patrol is a single submarine going out to hunt ships. Figures for 1945 go through the end of July only. Although a number of patrols were undertaken during August, no ships were sunk.
* Figure is approximate.

The submarine war was not entirely one-sided. Although the Japanese never approached the skill of Great Britain and the United States in antisubmarine warfare, casualties to submarines were significant, as can be seen from these statistics, which include losses due to all causes.

Submarine Losses in the Pacific War

British	3
Dutch	5
U.S.	49
Japanese	130

Proportionally, the highest manpower losses by any arm of the U.S. Military (surface warships, carrier pilots, infantry, artillerymen, etc.) during the war was among submarine crews, 22 percent. Japanese submarine losses do not reflect intensive submarine activity, but rather the increasing exposure of Japanese bases to U.S. carrier aircraft attacks in the later months of the war.

The devastating effect of the submarine campaign on the Japanese merchant marine can be seen not only in terms of lost vessels, but also in terms of the increasing length of voyages, due largely to the necessity of taking detours to avoid U.S. submarine and air power. This was done by increasing coastal crawl (moving as close to shore as possible), island hopping, and minimizing movements by day (when the generally smaller Japanese merchantmen would drop anchor close to shore and camouflage themselves). In addition, voyages became longer due to a growing shortage of experienced seamen, which caused ships to go to sea with a disproportionate number of green hands. When the United States began to mine Japanese waters in 1945, the effects were even more devastating. And as U.S. submarines became better, with better torpedoes and more aggressive skippers, more areas became dangerous to Japanese shipping. Because it was so expensive to build roads and railroads in mountainous Japan, much of the domestic transportation was via small coastal freighters. More often these ships were sunk, rather than damaged, by mines. Once this coastal shipping system was shut down, essential items like food and fuel could not be moved.

The Japanese never rationalized their merchant shipping. Not until early 1945 was a joint army-navy shipping commission established, far too late. As a result, for example, ships bringing military cargo to Malaya would return in ballast to the home islands, while ships bringing tin or rubber from Malaya to the home islands would return to Malaya in ballast. In effect, only half of most voyages were useful to the war effort. In addition, they never caught on to the idea that large

Length of Roundtrip Voyage from Japan* (*in days*)

Year	(*Months*)	Hong Kong	Singapore	Manila	Rabaul
1942	(April–October)	26.9	38.5	28.0	48.2
1943	(March–May)	26.9	56.4	41.5	71.2
	(June–August)	26.9	56.4	41.5	76.7
1944	(June–August)	36.4		70.5	

* Figures include time to the port in question, unloading there, and return voyage time.

convoys were better than small ones, and so most convoys consisted of two to three merchant ships with a couple of escorts.

THE KAMIKAZE

The ultimate image of Japanese determination and desperation in the war is that of the kamikaze pilot, a young man sworn to crash his airplane directly into an enemy vessel in order to destroy it. Nearly 4,000 kamikaze aircraft managed to sink or damage over 300 Allied ships and kill or injure more than 15,000 Allied sailors.

Named for the "Divine Wind," which had twice saved Japan from Mongol invasion during the thirteenth century, the Kamikaze Special Attack Corps was a logical, almost reasonable measure. Japan's prewar pilots were extraordinarily capable, perhaps the best in the world. But there were relatively few of them, and Japan had an inadequate pilot-replacement training program. So from the moment Japan entered the war it began to lose pilots faster than they could be replaced. By mid-1944 new Japanese pilots were being sent into action with less than a third of the flight training time that U.S. pilots received and were being shot down in disproportionate numbers. Meanwhile, the antiaircraft defense capability of the U.S. Navy had increased to the point that a pilot who attempted to attack a U.S. ship was more or less committing suicide anyway, and not likely to do very much damage in the process. Given the sacrificial mythos of the Japanese military the kamikaze corps was a reactively logical step. How much more practical and profitable to deliberately plunge one's aircraft into the enemy, thereby ensuring his destruction along with one's own.

And the kamikazes were actually quite effective. Indeed, they could easily have been more devastating than was the case. The first attacks were very successful. From October 24 through November 1, 1944, kamikaze attacks off Leyte in the Philippines sank one escort carrier, one destroyer, and an oceangoing tug while damaging two fleet carriers, one light carrier, seven escort carriers, one light cruiser, and three destroyers, at an expenditure of 51 kamikaze aircraft and fifteen escorting fighters. During the Philippines campaign as a whole (October 24, 1944–January 31, 1945), the Japanese sank sixteen U.S. vessels (two escort carriers, three destroyers, one small mine sweeper, plus ten smaller vessels, including a PT boat!) and damaged another eighty-seven (including seven aircraft carriers, two light aircraft carriers, thirteen escort carriers, five battleships and battle cruisers, three heavy cruisers, seven light cruisers, twenty-three destroyers, five destroyer escorts, and one small minesweeper), at a cost of 378 kamikaze aircraft and 102 escorts. Japanese air power had not done so well since Pearl Harbor. Nor was it ever to do as well again.

The success of the kamikazes off the Philippines alerted the U.S. Navy to the threat posed by this new weapon. Defensive weapons and tactics that were adequate to deal with aircraft attacking in the normal way were inadequate to cope with the kamikazes. Antiaircraft machine guns were much too light, 20mm guns only marginally better, and even 40mm guns only barely served. The problem was that these wouldn't break up an incoming airplane. Even a bullet-riddled, dying pilot could guide his plane the few extra minutes necessary to crash it into a ship. What was needed was something explosive. The most effective gun was the Navy's standard 5-inch/38 dual-purpose rapid-fire cannon. Combat air patrol was also much less effective against the kamikazes. Standard doctrine assumed that defensive fighters could handle an attacking force of roughly twice their own number, since it was your fighters against his bombers. But this didn't work with suicide attackers, for which you needed as many defenders as there were attackers and escorts.

Another asset of the kamikazes was that aircraft making such attacks had much greater reach than those making conventional attacks. After all, they weren't planning on returning to base. So kamikaze attacks were possible well beyond the range of conventional air strikes. This was particularly evident off Okinawa. During the Okinawa campaign (April–June 1945), the Japanese expended 1,465 aircraft in kamikaze attacks, sinking 21 ships and damaging 217, of which 43 were constructive total losses and 23 required at least a month's repair before returning to service. Including casualties from conventional air attacks, a total of about 4,900 U.S. Navy men were killed (more than 7 percent of total navy war dead) and 4,800 wounded during the campaign, making it the bloodiest in U.S. naval history.

Altogether about 3,900 aircraft were expended by the Japanese as kamikazes, counting army and navy attacks together and excluding escorts. Several thousand aircraft sortied on kamikaze missions but returned to base having failed to locate targets worthy of their sacrifice. Many of these were eventually used in successful attacks. These aircraft inflicted considerable damage on U.S. and Allied ships, sinking 83 and damaging some 350 others.

Casualties from Kamikazes

	Sunk	Damaged
Aircraft Carriers	0	16
Light Aircraft Carriers	0	3
Escort Carriers	3	17
Battleships and Battle Cruisers	0	15
Heavy Cruisers	0	5
Light Cruisers	0	10
Destroyers	13	87
Destroyer Escorts	1	24
Small Minesweepers	2	28
Submarines	0	1
Other	64	144
Total	83	350

Kamikazes were the most serious threat to the safety of the fleet during the war. They were also, interestingly enough, the only major development in the war that U.S. Navy brass had not anticipated during prewar planning. Actually, as bad as the experience with the kamikazes was, it could easily have been worse. The Japanese could have resorted to kamikaze tactics earlier, when antiaircraft defenses were not so good. Or they could have attempted mass attacks rather than piecemeal attacks during the Philippine campaign. Had the war lasted longer, it would most certainly have been worse. In anticipation of a U.S. invasion of the home islands, the Japanese had some nine thousand aircraft on hand, of which a third were earmarked for kamikaze attacks.

THE VERY LONG HOMECOMING PENNANTS

An astute observer on board U.S. Navy ships in 1945 could get a good sense of how soon the war was going to end by noticing how many sailors were working on "homecoming" pennants. These are long multicolored streamers that are flown from the mainmast as ships return victorious from a war. It's an old tradition, passed down by enlisted seamen, and many ships found one or more sailors beginning to sew homecoming pennants in early 1945. Most ships had theirs finished by the time Japan surrendered in August 1945, and they can be seen streaming astern of the mainmast in pictures of ships returning home after the war. By tradition, a homecoming pennant is one foot long for each day the ship was away from home. The longest belonged to "the Big E," the carrier *Enterprise,* which upon her return to the United States in late 1945, had been continuously away from the forty-eight states for well over five hundred days. Her streamer was so long, in fact, that helium balloons were needed to keep it aloft.

The U.S. submarine service preserved another very old maritime tradition. Boats returning from successful war patrols customarily wore a broom at the top of their mainmast. This custom dates back to the seventeenth century, when the Dutch seadog Michiel de Ruyter tied a broom to his mainmast to let everyone know that he had "swept" the seas of enemy ships.

There was one other hoary naval homecoming tradition, though no longer practiced in the U.S. Navy, the awarding of prize money upon the successful conclusion of a war. Originally a way to organize the division of loot, prize money had passed out of fashion in the U.S. Navy shortly after the Civil War. It was, however, still awarded in the Royal Navy, and shortly after the end of the war His Majesty's tars and jollies received rather nice little bonuses, amounting to several hundred dollars each for the common seamen and marines, and proportionately more as one went up the ranks.

7

WAR IN
THE SHADOWS

While the war was won in the factories and on the fighting fronts, there was also a lot of action going on behind the scenes—secret missions, espionage, psychological warfare, and the like.

COVERT ACTIVITY?

The pilot of the British Coastal Command PBY-Catalina, which spotted the German battleship *Bismarck* during its famous sortie into the Atlantic in May 1941, was Ensign Leonard B. Smith, USN, on loan to the RAF, as a "pilot adviser." Smith was not the only American involved in the pursuit of the German battlewagon, her movements for a time being monitored by a Coast Guard vessel which thoughtfully passed the information on to the Royal Navy. It was not until many years after the war that the United States's role in the *Bismarck* chase was revealed.

THE BOHR MISSION

One of the most distinguished physicists in the world was Niels Bohr, a Dane. Trapped in Denmark by the German invasion, Bohr lived quietly, being permitted to continue nuclear research, which was deemed useful to the German war effort. Meanwhile, of course, the

Allies were pressing ahead with their own nuclear research. In 1943 the Allies decided that they might be in need of Bohr's expertise, and with his permission arranged to rescue him. Although a supersecret operation, at the last minute the German occupation authorities got wind of it and came looking for Bohr. As a result, it was a near thing. Reportedly, as the Germans were coming in the front door, Bohr headed out the back, pausing momentarily to grab a beer bottle full of heavy water from his refrigerator. While some members of the Danish resistance provided covering fire, Bohr, who at age fifty-eight was rather old for such adventures, was taken aboard a fishing boat and ferried over to Sweden, where he was secretly landed and transported to Stockholm. Several days later, on October 7, Bohr boarded a modified Mosquito bomber at a secret airstrip for the final leg of his journey to Great Britain.

During the flight Bohr's oxygen supply failed, and he became unconscious before the pilot realized this. Thinking quickly, the pilot brought the plane down to a very low altitude, which failed to revive Bohr, but kept him alive. After two hours the Mosquito landed in Scotland, where Bohr, still clutching his bottle of heavy water, was taken to a hospital. He soon recovered and eventually made his way to the United States, where he joined the Manhattan Project. Despite Allied expectations, Bohr's actual contribution to the development of the atomic bomb proved marginal, as the American and British scientists already working on the project had surpassed Bohr's researches. The bottle of heavy water turned out to be the wrong one; it contained beer.

OPERATION BERNARD OR MAKING A DISHONEST POUND

One of the most unusual economic warfare efforts undertaken by either side during the Second World War was an attempt by the Reichssicherheitshauptamt (German Central Security Office) to counterfeit and pass £5 notes, then worth about $20 each, in an effort to ruin the British economy. The scheme, code-named Operation Bernard, was intended to counterfeit £100 million (about $1.5 billion in 1994 dollars) worth of bogus £5 notes, which would be put into circulation by secret agents in Great Britain, through neutral countries, and even by merely scattering them over the English countryside. The project was entrusted to Bernard Kruger, who was in charge of manufacturing forged documents for the numerous branches of the German secret service, such as passports, driver's licenses, ration books, identity cards, and the like.

Like all counterfeiters, Kruger (from whose given name the operation got its code name) was faced with a number of obstacles in coming up with a passable bank note. The most critical problems were to duplicate the plates and to find suitable paper. Since, unlike ordinary counterfeiters, Kruger already had an effective forgery establishment and could call upon the resources of the Reichsbank, which was already in the bank note business, his efforts proved quite successful. Kruger established several teams to work simultaneously on the various problems. Step-by-step they were resolved. While some workers used elaborate photographic techniques to examine and duplicate the design of the bank notes, others analyzed the paper and came up with a suitable substitute (allegedly paper made from dirty Turkish rags was best). The less important problems of ink color and serial numbers were resolved by other teams. The bogus bank notes were then printed by concentration camp labor (one of Kruger's sidelines was keeping Jews from being gassed by finding them jobs in his establishment).

It is unclear how many British bank notes were counterfeited by Operation Bernard before it went out of the pound business. The effort did not, of course, undermine the British economy. A £100 million was already chicken feed by World War II standards. A lot of the money did get into circulation, in a variety of ways. Proving that there's no honor among thieves, the Germans used a lot of it to pay off agents (the famous spy Cicero, an Albanian named Elias Basna who was the valet of the British ambassador to Turkey, was paid some £300,000 in bogus notes for his pains) and to bribe officials in neutral countries. In the immediate postwar period some wanted Nazis appear to have used the counterfeit notes to pay for their escape. However, most of the notes appear to have been destroyed, mostly by having been put into crates and sunk in Austrian lakes. Despite this, bogus notes kept turning up into the 1960s.

Addendum: When Operation Bernard was completed, Kruger convinced his superiors to let him work on counterfeiting Uncle Sam's greenbacks, primarily in order to save his many Jewish engravers, chemists, and printers. He was still involved in this project when the war ended.

UNCONVENTIONAL WARFARE

World War II was notable for the extent of its "unconventional warfare" operations. While previous wars had their share of raiders, commandos, and spies, this aspect of warfare was a major element in World War II, particularly on the part of the Allies. Indeed, it was the British who coined the word, and concept of *commandos*. The United States had its OSS (Office of Strategic Services, the predecessor of the CIA and Special Forces), while the British had the SOE (Special Operations Executive). During World War II guerrilla warfare was waged on a larger scale than in any previous war. The details of many of these operations are still cloaked in secrecy, fifty years after they took place. After all, some people are still alive, and in some areas passions run generations deep. However, enough details have leaked out over the years to make for some fascinating stories, and lessons, for the future.

SNEAKING IN BY AIR

Two bits of technology made the vast number of "special operations" during World War II possible. First, there were relatively lightweight, cheap, and reliable radios. Being able to keep in touch with agents deep in enemy territory eliminated a problem that had long made it difficult to keep a lot of spies, commandos, and partisans going. But equally important was the availability of air transport. Agents and supplies could be brought in at night and parachuted to their operating areas. Long-range bombers were used for much of the parachute work. B-17s and Halifax bombers could carry several tons of material and many personnel nearly anywhere in Europe. In addition, it was also possible to fly in, land deep inside enemy territory, pick up people and material, and fly out. But flying in and out was a tricky business in this period just before the introduction of the helicopter. Only aircraft that could land on unprepared fields (clover turned out to be the best vegetation to land on), and take off from them as well, were capable of this. Flying was particularly dicey in Europe, where it was nearly impossible to land inside Germany. Thus early in the war, landings were mainly in France. As the war went on and Allied ground forces advanced closer to Germany, landings could be made in more German-occupied territory. The favorite aircraft for these missions was the British Westland Lysander. This was a large (three-ton, fifty-foot wingspan) single-engine aircraft with a maximum range of 400 to 600 miles. It was a two-seater aircraft originally designed for army liaison, towing targets and gliders, and artillery spotting. Its slow speed (210 miles per hour, max) and handling characteristics allowed the Lysander to take off from a 1,200-foot-long field and land on an even smaller field. Its short range, though, prevented the Lysander from getting to key places like Poland, where an energetic and effective partisan operation was able to obtain documents and weapons parts from nearby Germany and factories inside Poland itself. The twin-engine de Havilland D.H. 98 Mosquito, nicknamed the "Wooden Wonder," was also quite suited to this sort of mission. Special versions, dubbed "moon planes," were built to maximize the effectiveness of the aircraft for such work. Faster (about 425 mph) and with a much longer range than the Lysander (about 3,500 miles), the Mosquito was valuable for long-range operations, but being big (up to ten tons, fifty-four-foot wingspan), was not always suited to many missions.

The Russians favored their slow, but agile U-2 (later Po-2) biplane. It could carry only two or three additional passengers and a quarter ton of supplies but it could land anywhere and its pilots regularly operated at night. The short range (a few hundred miles, depending on its load) was fine with the Soviets, as they had most of their partisans right behind the German front lines.

Once the Allies landed in Italy in 1943, it was possible to fly to Poland with the other two favorite special-operations aircraft, the Douglas DC-3 and the Lockheed Hudson (A-28/29). The DC-3 (or C-47 Dakota) was the workhorse transport of World War II, and over a thousand continue to fly passengers and cargo in the 1990s. But while the DC-3 had the range to get to Poland, it had about the same speed as the Lysander. For some missions, the Hudson was used, as this was originally designed as a combat aircraft and could hustle along at 250 miles an hour and take more punishment than the DC-3. Both of these heavier aircraft (the DC-3 weighed thirteen tons with a ninety-five-foot wingspan, the Hudson nine tons with a sixty-six-foot wingspan) required about three thousand feet to take off. These larger aircraft also had the capability of bringing out injured agents and larger numbers of personnel in general. This ability to get people out of enemy territory was important for morale as well as a more efficient way to support special operations.

Not a lot of aircraft were used for these landings in enemy territory, a few hundred throughout the entire war. These operations required a lot of planning and preparation. The flying was generally done at night to avoid enemy fighters and antiaircraft fire. This was hard enough, but the flying often had to be at low altitude as enemy radar got more effective. Navigating at night was difficult enough, but finding the impromptu airfield and landing on it was a breathtaking experience without all the modern navigation aids we now have. Accidents were common, and often fatal. An operation might also be compromised on the ground, with enemy troops suddenly showing up while the aircraft was still there. This sort of thing was not for the faint of heart. But in wartime, there were always pilots who would rise to the occasion, and often pay with their lives.

Some idea of the scope of this clandestine air traffic into occupied Europe may be gained by noting that in the course of the war British, American, and Free French aircraft parachuted or otherwise brought into France 198,000 Sten guns, 128,000 rifles, 20,000 Bren machine guns, 10,000 carbines, 58,000 pistols (some of them of a unique single-shot, throwaway variety), 732,000 hand grenades, 9,000 land mines, 2,700 bazookas, 285 mortars, and an enormous amount of ammunition, including a remarkable 595 tons of TNT.

FIRST THINGS FIRST

On the eve of the D-day landings the OSS and SOE stepped up their infiltration of agents into occupied Europe. Many of these men and women had interesting, often exciting experiences. But few must have been as unusual as that of a French agent parachuted into Brittany shortly before the invasion in order to help the Resistance.

The fellow came down at night, in a field. Quickly getting out of his parachute, he began to dig a hole in which to bury it. As he did so, he saw a figure approaching and gave the indicated call sign, whipping out his commando knife at the same time. Receiving the correct counter-sign, he resumed burying his parachute. Suddenly a rather attractive woman knelt by his side and began digging up the parachute.

"What are you doing? Orders are to bury parachutes!"

Without looking up, the young woman replied, "Who cares, I haven't seen silk this good since before the war."

THE BRANDENBURGERS

The British and American press played up the exploits of their commandos, leaving most people unaware that the Germans played this game too. The German army commandos were called the Branden-burgers (after the area where they trained). These were army troops, not part of the Nazi party's Waffen SS forces, and the Brandenburgers didn't get along with the SS anyway. As a result, the Nazi-controlled press kept the Brandenburgers pretty much a secret throughout the war while playing up the exploits of SS commandos and the SS in general.

Yet the Brandenburgers proved themselves a remarkably capable special warfare organization, operating on virtually all fronts (for example, Rommel's famous drive across France in 1940 was greatly facilitated by Brandenburgers, who captured bridges prior to the arrival of his spearheads). As the war went on, the number of troops assigned to the Brandenburgers increased. Many elements began operating as regular troops, and by the end of the war there was Brandenburg panzergrenadier division.

POPSKI'S PRIVATE ARMY

In any war, extraordinary individuals, by force of personality, will form and lead exotic commando-type units. One of the most exotic was officially known variously as the 1st Long Range Demolition Squadron and the 1st Special Demolition Squadron. But it was more commonly known as Popski's Private Army. Formed in North Africa at the outbreak of the war by a forty-three-year-old British officer, Vladimir "Popski" Peniakoff, it specialized in going out into the desert and raiding distant enemy bases. Peniakoff was a Belgian (with a Russian father) who had studied at Cambridge and served in the French Army during World War I. After that war, he went to Egypt and became a sugar manufacturer. While living in Egypt, Popski spent a lot of time traveling in the desert. Like T. E. Lawrence before World War I, he was much taken by desert life and became quite an expert in navigating the wastes. As World War II approached, he joined the British colonial forces in Egypt as an officer, serving in the Libyan Arab Force, which mostly performed internal security duties as the British advanced into Libya.

Popski soon tired of this dull routine work and joined the Long Range Desert Group (LRDG), a regular commando-type unit of only a few hundred men that conducted "long-range" reconnaissance operations and raids in the desert during the North African campaign. The LRDG specialized in hitting Axis air bases well behind the front and actually destroyed more enemy aircraft than did any Allied fighter squadron in the campaign. Popski, however, found this too tame, for the "long" in LRDG was not long enough. So he recruited his own specialized raiding group of about 120 men. The 1st Long Range Demolition Squadron made really deep penetration raids behind Axis lines, often striking hundreds of miles into the enemy's rear. Popski and his daredevils fought throughout the North African campaign and in Italy, making thousands of rear-area Italian and German troops decidedly uncomfortable.

A UNITED NATIONS OF RESISTANCE ORGANIZATIONS

A unique aspect of World War II was the proliferation of organized Resistance movements to the occupying enemy troops. There were many of these Resistance movements, more than most people realize.

ALBANIA. Invaded and occupied by the Italians in 1939, Albania didn't have a Resistance movement organized until after the Soviet Union was invaded in June 1941. This was because the best-organized group in the country was the Communists and they formed the core of the politically diverse Resistance. The leader was Enver Hoxha (pronounced HOD-ja). Hoxha made a deal with the new occupiers, the Germans, after the Italians surrendered in early 1943 (Hoxha's partisans grabbed most of the Italians' weapons and equipment). In 1944, with the German situation becoming more precarious elsewhere, Hoxha began attacking and by early 1945 the Germans were on their way out and Hoxha controlled most of the country. Although they had not given him much aid during the war, the Allies recognized Hoxha. Hoxha promptly purged the non-Communist elements from the Resistance, established a Communist-style police state, and died in power in 1986.

BELGIUM. Although Belgium contained a lot of Nazi sympathizers (many joined the Waffen SS to prove it), the country had an active Resistance throughout the war. The Germans, and their Belgian sympathizers, were brutal in fighting the Resistance. Over 17,000 Belgian Resistance fighters were killed, nearly all of them while engaged in sabotage and espionage operations. The Resistance was also active in saving Jews from the Nazis, and Resistance fighters were often sent to the concentration camps along with the people they were trying to protect.

BULGARIA. Although controlled by a pro-German government throughout the war, the Bulgarian people were so pro-Russian (and had always been) that the nation did not declare war on the Soviet Union and even maintained diplomatic relations with the

Soviets until 1944. The Communists did form a Resistance movement, and as the Red Army advance came closer to Bulgaria, Resistance activity picked up. When the Red Army entered Bulgaria it found a large Communist-led Resistance movement to greet it. Non-Communist elements were promptly purged and a Communist government installed which survived until 1990.

BURMA. While most of the numerous groups in Burma were indifferent to the war, and some actively collaborated with the Japanese, several ethnic minority groups, such as the Kachins, held out "for king and country" (or rather, tribe) and conducted guerrilla operations with the support of Allied advisers and equipment. Some of them are still at it.

CHINA. There were possibly more guerrillas in China than in all the other occupied countries combined. There were all sorts of guerrillas, some loyal to Chiang Kai-shek, some (the most effective) supporting Mao Tse-tung, and some working for themselves. It was all of these partisans who held down the bulk of the Japanese Army, as well as upward of twenty divisions of collaborationist troops. After the Japanese surrendered the Chinese went back to fighting each other, which was what enabled the Japanese to do so well in the first place.

CZECHOSLOVAKIA. Although Czechoslovakia was occupied by the Germans before the war began, the Czechs put together a well-organized Resistance movement. In 1942 the Resistance managed to assassinate Reinhard Heydrich, the Nazi commander in Czechoslovakia. This resulted in a massive and brutal Nazi campaign to stamp out the Resistance. Over 350,000 Czechs were sent to concentration camps, where 250,000 died. Many others died during the anti-Resistance campaign. For the rest of the war, what was left of the Czech Resistance operated primarily as an espionage organization for the Allies. At the very end of the war, the Czechs rose up against the Germans as the Red Army approached, and several thousand more Czechs were killed.

DENMARK. It took only one day for the Germans to occupy Denmark in early 1941, mainly because it is not very large, not very defensible, and had largely disarmed itself before the war anyway. The Danish government was left in place, and while the Germans controlled everything, they did so with a light touch. Except, the Germans immediately began milking the Danish economy to support the Nazi war effort and after a year this caused severe shortages for the Danish population. This in turn led to the organization of a Resistance movement. By 1943, sabotage against the Germans and espionage for the Allies became common. In that year, the Germans tried to round up the nation's Jews, but the Resistance managed to get most of them out of the country to Sweden. Plans were made for an armed uprising, but the war ended before these could be carried out.

ETHIOPIA. Occupied by the Italians in 1936, Ethiopia had a Resistance that was widespread and active from the very beginning. By the time the British got the upper hand in Ethiopia in 1941, the Italians were eager to surrender to the British rather than have to face the wrath of the tribal partisans.

EUROPE'S JEWISH POPULATION. Resistance to the German extermination policy developed rapidly among Europe's Jewish population. Jewish fugitives in forests all over Europe formed guerrilla bands that operated against German and other Axis troops, often in cooperation with local partisans but occasionally in the face of resistance from them. Jews in various ghettos armed themselves for self-defense and, in the case of the Warsaw Ghetto, conducted a heroic uprising which was crushed with great brutality. Resistance groups were even formed inside concentration camps, in which there were occasional uprisings. There was even an uprising in one of the Nazi extermination camps (Sobibor). In addition, of course, many Jews joined nationalist Resistance groups, such as the Yugoslav partisans. It's important to note that one reason why there was not more Jewish armed resistance was the gradual, and clever, way in which the Nazis introduced the "Final Solution." This extermination campaign was not even decided upon until early 1942. And even then it was kept as secret (as much as these things can be kept secret). The Germans carried on, as before, persecuting the Jews, leaving their victims to keep a low profile and wait for the war to end. Since the Jews were under constant pressure from the Nazis and local anti-Semites, there was less opportunity to sneak away and join the partisans or otherwise organize armed resistance. Nevertheless, the degree of Jewish resistance was substantial.

FRANCE. Although France was conquered in 1940, some Resistance was active from the beginning. The southern part of the country was left independent until late 1942, when the Germans occupied the entire country. There were several different Resistance organizations, including a Communist organization that became active only after the Soviet Union was invaded in June 1941 (before that the French Communists collaborated with the Nazi occupiers and the Vichy government). By 1944, the Resistance was more united, or at least better coordinated. The United States and Great Britain were supplying the arms, and de Gaulle was calling the shots, some of which were directed at Resistance groups that were reluctant to support restoration of a "bourgeois" regime. The Germans were energetic in antipartisan operations, particularly because the Resistance was the principal espionage operation in the country and responsible for getting many downed Allied pilots back to Great Britain. The Resistance began active military operations (as opposed to sabotage, espionage, and assassinations) after the Allied invasion of Normandy in June and aided the Allies in driving the Germans out of France by the end of the year.

GERMANY. Resistance in Germany to the Nazis began as soon as they took over in 1933. Many attempts on Hitler's life were made, the most famous one being the bomb blast on July 20, 1944, which Hitler miraculously survived. Before the war began in 1939, many senior German Army officers were active in trying to get rid of the Nazis. But the British and French were hesitant to cooperate and the army became less of a source of Resistance activity after the war began. While the Resistance was widespread, it was never organized on a large scale. The efficient Nazi secret police were constantly arresting actual or simply suspected Resistance members. Aside from trying to get rid of Hitler, the Resistance did provide espionage services for the Allies. When the war ended, many of the surviving Resistance participants took part in the rebuilding of the German government.

GREECE. After the German invasion of Greece in 1941, many Resistance movements sprang up. Unfortunately, the partisans spent more time fighting each other than they did going after the Germans or otherwise supporting the Allies. Allied efforts to unite the various Resistance groups was futile, and the Germans

took advantage of the situation by playing one partisan group
against the other, not too difficult when one considers that some
of the guerrillas were Communists and some were not. When
the Germans withdrew from Greece in 1944 (to avoid being cut
off by the Red Army advance to the north), the partisans
continued to fight each other and the British troops who
landed shortly thereafter. This civil war continued until the
late 1940s.

HUNGARY. A pro-Fascist government was in control in Hungary
when World War II broke out, and Hungary became an active
ally of Germany. The only resistance initially came from the
Communists, but they were ruthlessly hunted down by the secret
police. As the war went against the Axis powers (and a
Hungarian army was demolished at Stalingrad in early 1943),
the Hungarian people lost their enthusiasm for the war, and the
Germans. Strikes and demonstrations, often orchestrated by the
Communists, eventually led to the Germans occupying
the country in March 1944. At that point armed partisans
became active, while parts of the Hungarian Army went over to
the Russians. The country was in chaos until the Red
Army arrived in late 1944. Non-Communist elements were
purged from the Resistance and a Communist government
set up.

ITALY. Covert political resistance to Mussolini and the Fascist
government came to life in Italy in 1940 when many Italians
realized they had been dragged into World War II as a German
ally. Mussolini's Fascists were not quite the police state storm
troopers the German Nazis were, and a lot of open opposition
was tolerated. The Italian Fascists were also not as efficient or
bloody-minded as the Nazis. Such was the nature of the Italian
government that Mussolini was forced out of office in July 1943
in a coup engineered by the king. The Germans had by then
occupied Italy north of Naples and were far more ruthless in
dealing with opposition. At this point armed resistance began,
and there ensued nearly two years of savage fighting between
Italian anti-Fascist partisans and German troops. There were also
pro-Fascist armed groups assisting the Germans. Mussolini
himself was rescued by German commandos shortly after he
was overthrown. Later in 1945, Mussolini was caught by some
pro-Communist partisans and executed on the spot. That was not
the end of Mussolini's political influence. In the early 1990s,

one of his granddaughters was elected to the Italian parliament on a neo-Fascist ticket.

THE NETHERLANDS. The Netherlands was overrun in five days during early 1940, and many of the Dutch either sympathized with the Germans or, more often, considered the war over and the Germans the victors. As a result, there was not much resistance during the first year of occupation. But after that, increasing Allied success caused many Netherlanders to change their minds and a Resistance movement grew. Because of the presence of many German combat and secret police units in the country, armed resistance never became a major factor. But sabotage and espionage were common, coordinated by the government in exile in London. Prince Bernard, the husband of Queen Juliana, by birth a German, actually ran the Resistance from inside the Netherlands for a while. The similarity of the Dutch and German languages made it easier for the Nazis to hunt down and (usually) kill members of the Resistance. Nevertheless, 23 percent of the country's Jews were saved from Nazi death camps and the Germans were always under observation by pro-Allied Dutch spies through most of the war.

THE NETHERLANDS EAST INDIES (INDONESIA). In a masterpiece of realpolitik, when the Japanese arrived in the Netherlands East Indies, the leaders of the anti-Dutch independence movement agreed to bet on both sides. So while some of them actively collaborated with the Japanese, even raising troops for their masters, others took to the hills and, with some Allied assistance, organized a moderately successful guerrilla movement. When the Dutch returned in 1945 they discovered that both the pro-Allied guerrillas and the pro-Japanese collaborationists were lined up against them, aided by the fact that the surrendering Japanese had abandoned a lot of equipment. The result was a fairly bloody war for independence which the Dutch lost.

NORWAY. After the German invasion and occupation of Norway in early 1940, a Resistance movement was quickly organized. Unlike most Resistance movements, the Norwegian Resistance refrained from sabotage and armed activity in order to spare the civilian population reprisals (which usually included the taking and killing of hostages). The Norwegian Resistance did engage in considerable espionage activity and assisted British commando operations within the country. This caused the Germans to suspect that one of the Allied 1944 invasions would be in Norway. As a result, seventeen German divisions were stationed in Norway during most of 1944, thus tying up considerable forces in an area the Allies had no intention of invading, and making it even more difficult for the Resistance to operate.

THE PHILIPPINES. Even before the last regular U.S. and Filipino units surrendered on Bataan and Corregidor in mid-1942, many troops had fled to the mountains of the numerous Philippine islands. There they formed Resistance units and harassed the Japanese garrisons for the next two years. Since they were cut off from aid because of the long distance to the nearest Allied bases, it wasn't until 1944 that regular contact was established. U.S. submarines and aircraft then began to land weapons and agents. Most of the partisans were Philippines citizens, along with some U.S. officers and troops. Radio contact was always maintained with the Allies and the partisans were an invaluable source of information on the Japanese garrison. When the Allies invaded the Philippines in late 1944, the tens of thousands of armed partisans were a major asset in quickly defeating the Japanese ground forces. Unfortunately, some of the guerrilla bands were Communist-dominated and began a war to establish a Marxist regime which dragged on for several years.

POLAND. After Poland was invaded and carved up by Germany and the Soviets in 1939, a Resistance movement sprang up. At first, only Great Britain offered assistance, but after the German invasion of the Soviet Union in 1941, the local Communists (hitherto active collaborators with the Nazis) got into the act too. The Germans were ruthless in their efforts against the Polish Resistance, and millions of Poles were killed in the process. The Resistance was initially known as the Home Army. But because this organization was loyal to the government in exile in London, there was conflict with the Soviet-backed partisans who emerged after the Germans invaded the Soviet Union. The two partisan armies did not fight each other (at least not a lot), but the non-Communist Home Army got little support from the Soviets (who were able to fly in arms and supplies for the Communist People's Army and refused to undertake operations that might aid their opponents). When the Germans were driven out in 1945, the Home Army began fighting Soviet troops and by the late 1940s the Home Army was exterminated and a Communist government set up.

SIAM (THAILAND). In the only independent nation in Southeast Asia at the start of World War II, the Thais were leaned on by the Japanese to allow passage of Japanese troops on their way to invasions of British-held Malaya and Burma. This was not popular with a lot of the Thai people, but the government saw it as preferable to outright Japanese domination. Thus a well-organized and widely supported (even by a lot of government officials) Resistance rose from 1942 on. The partisans provided invaluable espionage services for the Allies, as well doing a little sabotage. As a result, Thailand was not treated as an enemy nation after the war, even though it was technically an ally of Japan.

THE SOVIET UNION. Partisan groups formed in the Soviet Union as soon as German units moved through conquered Soviet territory. Many of these were civilians or local Communists (in danger of immediate execution by the Germans if they were caught). Many of the Soviet soldiers cut off by the fast-moving Germans in 1941 fled into the forests and swamps to become partisans. Through 1941 and early 1942, partisan activity was largely uncoordinated and sometimes nationalist (pro-Ukrainian and anti-Communist, for example). By the end of 1942, the partisans were increasingly under the centralized control of the Soviet government. During 1943 and 1944, the Germans were hit with an increasing number of partisan attacks. The Resistance was also a valuable source of information for the Soviets, which became increasingly important as the Red Army went on the offensive. By late 1944, the partisans were a major problem for the Germans, who often undertook multidivisional operations in an attempt to clear Resistance units from the German rear areas.

VIETNAM. A French colony from the late nineteenth century, Vietnam was taken over by the Japanese more or less peacefully in late 1941. There was already a Resistance movement against the French, and this promptly shifted its operations to resist the Japanese. The partisans were Communist-led (by Ho Chi Minh), but included non-Communist groups. Armed attacks were made on the Japanese and espionage conducted for the Allies. In return, the Allies provided weapons and supplies. This was the same Resistance organization that ultimately took over all of Vietnam in 1975.

Yugoslavia. The Germans invaded Yugoslavia in early 1941, but Italians (who had attacked Albania in 1939) comprised most of the occupation troops until 1943, abetted by locally recruited Croat and Bosnian collaborators. A Resistance formed immediately, but because of the multicultural composition of Yugoslavia, and the enmity between Communists and monarchists, there was more fighting between partisans than with the occupying Italians. After Italy left the war in 1943, German troops took over the occupation. The partisans grabbed many of the Italians' weapons, and many anti-Fascist Italians even joined the partisans: One whole division more or less went over to them intact. While the Italians had usually been relatively easygoing during their occupation, the Germans were a lot tougher. Many of the non-Communist partisans collaborated with the Italians, and then with the Germans, to gain advantage over the Communist groups. Moreover, the Communist partisans were largely Serbs, while the monarchists were largely Croats. The other ethnic groups in Yugoslavia also tended to take sides against each other rather than against the occupying army. The Germans took advantage of this, to the extent that they raised two SS divisions comprised of Muslim Yugoslavs and then turned them loose on Christian civilians and partisans. Still, the partisans were a tough bunch and the Germans managed to assist the guerrillas by butchering suspected partisan sympathizers. This turned more of the population, and partisans, against the Germans. By this time, the Allies realized that, although they had been sending most of their aid to the non-Communist partisans, it was the Communist partisans led by Josip Broz (Tito) who were most energetically fighting the Germans. So by late 1943, the Allies got behind Tito and his Communist partisans. Throughout 1944, the partisans became stronger and stronger, and eventually, the Yugoslavs earned the distinction of being the only partisan army to liberate its own country without the aid of Allied troops. The Yugoslav partisans were even able to keep the Red Army out of

the country. Meanwhile, by the end of the war, the
non-Communist groups in the country were disarmed (and many
killed) and a Communist government set up.

AND WOULDN'T WE ALL LIKE TO KNOW WHY?

In her old age Erika Waag Canaris, widow of Admiral Wilhelm Canaris, wartime chief of German military intelligence (the *Abwehr*) and
a prime mover in the conspiracy to assassinate Hitler in July 1944, was
supported by an American pension apparently arranged by Allen
Dulles, who was for many years head of the CIA.

SWIMMING IN HARM'S WAY

Many technological advances in the 1920s and 1930s led to unique
new weapons systems in World War II. Perhaps the most curious was
scuba diving gear. The use of an air tank and mask allowed a swimmer
to stay underwater for an hour or more. This led to two "special
weapons": underwater commandos and manned torpedoes. The underwater commandos' primary function was gathering information of
beaches to be invaded and clearing some obstacles. This latter task was
achieved by having the swimmers attach explosives to man-made obstacles and blow them up. This was particularly useful for obstacles
lying on the bottom, but not protruding above the surface, which were
designed to rip the bottoms off landing craft. The underwater demolition teams (UDTs) first had to find these (although many were visible
during low tide) and then destroy them. The UDTs also went ashore at
night to check the condition of the beach, sometimes taking sand
samples (which, after analysis, would show what types of vehicles
could safely traverse the beach). Being able to stay underwater for long
periods gave these intruders an enormous advantage. With the primitive radars available during World War II, it was possible for small
boats or submarines to get close to heavily defended areas. Naval
minefields could be crossed by rubber boats before the divers made
their final approach underwater. So the UDTs played an important role
in the amphibious war.

Realizing, of course, that the Germans and Japanese would take the
presence of UDTs as portending an American landing, the U.S. Navy
began using them as part of deception plans. Special UDTs ("Beach

Jumpers'') were deliberately sent to explore beaches that no one had any intention of hitting so that the enemy would believe a landing was imminent. On several occasions the UDTs were particularly successful in diverting enemy attentions and resources away from a genuine objective.

The Italian Navy made extensive use of underwater commandos. Transported near an enemy port by submarine or a small craft, the divers would swim inside, place mines on ships' bottoms, and then make their getaway. This technique was particularly successful at Gibraltar, for the Italians were able to turn a merchant ship interned at a Spanish dock across the Bay of Algeciras and a nearby villa into secret underwater assault team bases. Divers would enter the water through a secret airlock cut into the ship's bottom, swim across to the British side of the bay, and plant mines on the bottoms of various ships. By timing the mines so that they went off when the ships were far out at sea, the Italians were able to confuse the British as to the causes of various sinkings. The secret base was never detected and closed down only when Italy joined the Allies.

The other development that made use of scuba gear was the so-called human torpedo. It came in two varieties, but both were essentially miniature submarines. One type might best be called an ''underwater motorcycle,'' able to carry two men astride. The Italian Navy developed this shortly before the war, as a vehicle for their UDTs. Called *Maiali* (''Pigs''), they were used with considerable success to damage British warships in heavily defended ports, the most notable being when two battleships were sunk at their moorings in the Alexandria harbor. So effective were these devices that the Royal Navy began its own experiments with human torpedoes, giving them the more dignified name ''Chariots.'' These were used with some success to sink several ships in Axis-controlled ports in the Mediterranean later in the war.

The Japanese also developed a manned torpedo, in the literal sense, a one-man suicide submarine called the ''Kaiten Weapon.'' Over three hundred of these were sent to sea to take on Allied shipping. However, they were very inefficient and not particularly useful on the high seas, so that only one Allied ship was damaged. On the other hand, some hundreds of kaitens were available to attack the invasion fleet if the United States had undertaken Operation Olympic, the invasion of Japan. Supporting them would have been thousands of suicide swimmers, men equipped with a simple breathing apparatus who were supposed to walk along the sea floor and hit the bottom of landing craft with bomb-tipped poles.

The direct descendant of these World War II scuba warriors is the U.S. Navy SEAL force, and similar commando units in many nations. The adventure continues.

TOP SECRET

The archives of the world still hold literally millions of secret documents from the Second World War. Nor is it likely that most of them will ever be declassified. There are many reasons for this. Bureaucratic inertia is one. As is the sheer physical task of sorting through all those papers. Then too, there is the danger that some documents may present to some people's lives and reputations, or those of their offspring. For example, the United States has never revealed the name of a certain loose-lipped colonel attached to Eisenhower's headquarters who was relieved and shipped home in disgrace after trying to impress a young woman with his importance by revealing that he was privy to the date of D-Day. Nor are the files relating to German, Italian, and Japanese subsidies to various fraternal, social, ethnic, and religious organizations in the United States, not to mention prominent individuals, ever likely to be revealed. The Axis powers were quite generous in subsidizing organizations and individuals in the United States that might later be influenced to repay the favor. The U.S. government thought it prudent to keep these payments secret, especially for those payees who did not engage in treasonable behavior during the war.

Consider some of the more fascinating bits of information that have come out over the years.

- **The ULTRA Secret.** Not until the mid-1970s was it revealed that, due to some impressive work by Polish military intelligence shortly before the war, the Allies were in possession of duplicate versions of the German supersecret "Enigma" code machines, which enabled them to quickly "break" new versions of the most critical German codes as they were introduced. As a result, the Allies were able regularly to read a great deal of the most secret German radio traffic, a matter that frequently proved of immense military consequence.

- **Katyn Forest.** In 1940 the Soviets slaughtered at least 15,000 Polish officers. The Germans first brought this to the world's attention, but the Soviets promptly blamed it on the Germans.

Charges flew back and forth until the Soviets admitted their culpability after the Berlin Wall fell and the Communist governments in Eastern Europe disappeared. Despite this, some die-hard apologists for the Soviets continue to deny their responsibility.

- **Magic.** As the Poles did to the Germans, so too did the U.S. Navy do to the Japanese, cracking the secret of their highest-priority codes. This resulted in numerous intelligence coups such as confirmation that the Japanese objective in their mid-1942 offensive was to be Midway, a major factor in helping the United States turn the tide of the war in the Pacific, and the information that led directly to the killing of Admiral Isoroku Yamamoto.

- **The XX Secret.** In the early 1970s the British revealed that they had successfully "turned" every intelligence agent that the Germans had managed to infiltrate into Great Britain, so that for virtually the entire war they were able to feed misleading information to the enemy.

- **Raoul Wallenberg.** The fate of this young Swedish diplomat who went to extraordinary lengths to assist Jews in escaping the Holocaust, and then disappeared in Soviet-occupied Hungary, was long a mystery. At first the Soviets denied having held him. Then they admitted that he had been arrested by mistake and had died of natural causes in prison in the late 1940s. Only recently, as the Soviet archives have become more accessible, has it been revealed that Wallenberg was executed in 1947 at the specific orders of Stalin.

- **William J. "Wild Bill" Donovan.** Only within the last few years has it been revealed that Donovan, a distinguished World War I veteran and Wall Street lawyer, had for many years conducted unofficial intelligence-gathering missions for several presidents, long before he was put in charge of what would become the OSS in mid-1941. Apparently beginning as early as World War I, Donovan regularly conducted fact-finding missions at the suggestion of the president, using his legitimate business activities to mask the purpose of his many trips abroad, including one to Ethiopia during the Italian conquest.

- **The Heisenberg Assassination.** In early 1993 documents were revealed telling of an OSS effort to assassinate the German physicist Werner Heisenberg, at the suggestion of scientists working on the Manhattan Project, for fear that he would help Hitler develop an atomic bomb. Although several attempts appear to have been made, all failed due mostly to poor timing or bad luck, which is just as well, as Heisenberg was probably more of a hindrance to the German nuclear weapons program than a help.

- **U.S. Weapons Performance.** Many reports on the shabby performance of U.S. weapons were conveniently left classified long after the war. Many of these did not come to the surface until the 1960s and 1970s. The reports concerning the experience with naval mines was one such case, the navy being somewhat embarrassed just how effective this weapon was. Not wanting this reality to interfere with postwar plans for the fleet, the reports were kept classified for several decades. The cost was paid in the Persian Gulf in the late 1980s (when warships had to steam behind a tanker because no minesweepers were available) and 1991 (when a carrier and cruiser were mined).

Masses of rather ordinary records were not unclassified until the 1960s. This made it difficult to get into the details of how the war was fought. First, these records were "unclassified" as researchers asked for them ("Need the intel summaries from the Third Army for August 1944? Okay, here they are, just let me hit them with this *unclassified* stamp first"). The clerks soon tired of this drill and tons of documents were summarily unclassified. But many similarly mundane (but vital to a historian) records remain under wraps, until some diligent researcher goes digging for them with a lawyer in tow.

Now think about what secrets may still be lying quietly in some dusty file cabinets somewhere.

8
MAKING
PEACE

When the fighting stopped, the war wasn't over. Not at all. Many loose ends remained, some immediate, some long-term. The last of these repercussions of World War II are still going on. The grandchildren of the Yugoslav partisans continue the civil war their elders began in 1941, and many lesser aftershocks continue to shake the political landscape.

"BRING THE BOYS HOME!"

Even as the army and navy struggled to find ways to get the maximum number of troops to the fighting fronts in 1942–1943, they began to plan for ways to get them back home again when the war was over. The intention was that the troops be returned to the United States and demobilized in an orderly fashion. But things didn't work out quite that way. As the demobilization plan finally evolved in 1944, it was assumed that the war in Europe would be over around mid-1945, and in the Pacific about a year later. Events overtook planning; the war in Europe ended a couple of months sooner than expected, and the Pacific fighting nearly a year earlier than expected. Moreover, while the officers planning the return of the troops tried to account for everything, they forgot the folks back home. Almost, literally, as soon as the fighting ended in Europe the folks back home began clamoring to "bring the boys home."

The army had wanted to bring the troops home in organized formations, particularly in divisions. There were several reasons for this. Some divisions were to be transferred to the Pacific, in anticipation of the invasion of Japan, scheduled for November 1945, and it seemed a good idea to keep a few additional ones together as long as possible as a strategic reserve. Also, veteran formations were thought best for occupation duties, since no one was quite certain that the Germans had not established a vast secret Resistance that would rise up if the Allies let down their guard. Then too, there was increasing concern over Soviet intentions in the postwar world. There were also logistical and managerial considerations. Bringing the troops home in their divisions would allow equipment to be collected, serviced, and stockpiled with the least pain to the army. And then there was the lure of marching up Broadway in triumph to the cheers of the crowd. This had been the way the doughboys had come home from World War I. But the 1918 victory parade meant that some men who had been in the service but a short time were demobilized before some guys who had gone "over there" with Pershing in June 1917: In fact some troops on ships bound for Europe on Armistice Day never set foot in France. America's mothers were not going to stand for that again, particularly those whose sons had been in the army since late 1940. So the army's elaborate planning pretty much went by the board, and there were few great victory parades.

Most of the troops came home as individuals, based on an elaborate system of "points." A man received a point for each month he was in the army, another for each month he was overseas, yet another for each month he was in combat, and additional ones for being married and having dependents, and so forth. The higher a man's points, the sooner he was supposed to be put on the road home. The point system eviscerated some units. For example, the 45th Infantry Division, originally scheduled to return home in August 1945 (for retraining and redeployment to the Pacific), had lost 600 officers and 11,000 enlisted men by that date, about 65 percent of its manpower. The artillery staff ended up with only one officer, the divisional artillery commander himself!

Troops began to come home almost from VE-Day and did so in almost indecent haste. At first the movement of troops was purely an army affair, as the navy, happy to be rid of the unwanted war in Europe, was rushing everything afloat to the Pacific. The initial movement involved nearly six hundred vessels of the War Shipping Board, plus some additional hired ships, most notably the two superliners *Queen Mary* and *Queen Elizabeth,* each of which could accommodate as many as 15,000 men. Then Japan collapsed, nearly a year ahead of schedule.

With Japan out of the war, the pressure to "bring the boys home" became enormous. Liberty ships, Victory ships, attack transports, and scores of warships (even battleships!) were converted to troop transports for Operation Magic Carpet. Best of all were carriers, for bunks could be stacked as many as five high in their spacious hangar decks. The *Lake Champlain,* a newly commissioned Essex class carrier was converted to carry some 3,300 troops. Some lucky guys were flown home in C-54s, C-47s, and even bombers, which could carry one or two men in addition to their crews. And so the boys came home.

Of some 5.5 million U.S. Army personnel (about two thirds of total army personnel) abroad in the respective theaters at the end of operations in Europe, only about 4 million were still overseas by VJ-Day, and only 870,000 by December 1946. Note that these figures do not account for fresh troops being sent overseas for occupation duty, so the actual number of men brought home is higher than a mere comparison of the numbers would suggest. Average movement overseas had been about 157,000 troops a month for forty-one months, movement home over the next fourteen months averaged about 430,000 men per month, with the peak month being December 1945, when 695,486 army personnel came home.

Repatriation of Army Personnel

Period	Number of Individuals
VE-Day–September 1945	1,216,750
October 1945–April 1946	3,123,394
May 1946–September 1946	127,233

In the words of George C. Marshall, "It was not a demobilization, it was a rout."

AFTERMATH

World War II was such a huge conflict that it took months to come to a complete end. The Germans surrendered in early May, although it was over a month before all German combat units were disarmed. The

Japanese fought on until mid-August. Again, it took over a month to conclude a formal surrender and even longer to disarm all Japanese troops (and even then some guys held out for years afterward, the last known one surrendering in the 1970s). But the war didn't end there, it took nearly ten years for all the guerrilla fighting to die out, and there were a lot of "supplementary wars" that followed, right into the 1990s. This lingering combat occurred because, as usually happens in a major war, there were also a lot of little wars going on at the same time. While the big nations were slugging it out, the simultaneous little wars tended to go unnoticed. But when the principal nations decided to declare the war over, many of the minor players fought on.

Typical of these little wars was the struggle between Ukrainian nationalists and the Soviet Union. This dragged on into the early 1950s, when the last multidivision operation by the Soviets eliminated the remaining organized Ukrainian partisan units. Some of these Ukrainian troops had served alongside the Germans, while some had fought against both Germans and Soviets. As this fighting overlapped the beginning of the Cold War, the CIA was air-dropping agents (and losing them) regularly through the early 1950s. These air transport operations were one of the reasons why the Soviets built such a large air defense operation over the next forty years. The Communists had their hand in many of the other "carryover" wars. The one most Americans will recognize is Vietnam.

During World War II, the Allies supported armed Vietnamese Resistance groups who fought against the Japanese. Many of these partisans in colonies kept their weapons and kept on fighting after the Japanese surrendered. The Vietnamese had to first defeat their former colonial masters, the French, and then take on the United States. The largest of these wars was in China, where the Chinese Communists received the bulk of the Japanese weapons and equipment the Soviets captured when Japanese forces in Manchuria were overrun. China had been embroiled in fighting between Japanese troops and various Chinese factions for most of the 1930s. The fighting didn't end until 1948 when the Chinese Communists triumphed.

Former anti-Axis Communist guerrillas also played a major role in the Greek Civil War, the Indonesian War for Independence, the Huk Insurrection in the Philippines, a covert war against Francoist Spain that began in 1944 and did not end until the 1950s, and the Malaya Insurgency, which ended in the early 1960s, not to mention Burma, where various groups have been cautiously in arms since before 1945, and more recently the hostilities in the former Yugoslavia. Naturally, the ultimate carryover war was the Cold War, which didn't end until 1991. Wars are, as always, easier to start than to end.

THE WAR AND THE WHITE HOUSE

A bit of military service has never been a handicap to a successful political career, particularly if one is contemplating the White House. In fact, twenty-five of the forty-one men who have been president were "veterans" of one sort or another. Seven of the last nine presidents to date served in the Second World War, a record matched only by the seven who saw service in the Civil War.

- **Dwight D. Eisenhower** (1953–1961) had, of course, commanded in the ETO and emerged from the war as a General of the Army.

- **John F. Kennedy** (1961–1963) was a junior officer in the navy, serving with distinction in the South Pacific.

- **Lyndon B. Johnson** (1963–1969) left his congressional seat to take up a commission in the navy, serving as a staff officer before returning to Congress.

- **Richard M. Nixon** (1969–1974) served as a junior officer in the navy, for a time running a rest camp for battle-weary aviators.

- **Gerald R. Ford** (1974–1977) was a naval officer.

- **James E. Carter** (1977–1981) spent most of the war as a midshipman at Annapolis, from which he graduated in 1946, and hence was the only president between 1953 and 1993 who had not seen active duty in the war.

- **Ronald Reagan** (1981–1989)) was a captain in the army, making training films in Hollywood and sleeping at home every night.

- **George Bush** (1989–1993) was the youngest combat pilot in the navy, flying Avengers in the Pacific, where he was shot down and wounded.

It is interesting to note that while most of the presidents previous to these with military service were senior officers, only Eisenhower was so distinguished among the World War II crop of veteran presidents. Moreover, while most of this Class of 1945 were navy men, all previous presidents had been army men. Of course, World War II was the first time the nation had a truly large navy relative to the army.

The Also-Rans: Two of those who lost out in the presidential sweepstakes were also veterans of the war, both, surprisingly, having been bomber pilots in the army air forces, Barry Goldwater (1964) and George McGovern (1972).

Honorable Mention: Harold Stassen, who repeatedly attempted to secure the nomination for president, had had a very distinguished career as a senior staff officer in the navy in the Pacific and was one of the first Americans to land in Japan, by parachute, so that he could arrange details of the surrender.

The last World War II veterans of prominence in American politics are Senators Robert Dole (R-Kansas) and Daniel K. Inouye (D-Hawaii). Surprisingly, both fought as infantrymen in Italy, where each lost the use of an arm.

IT IS WITH SUCH BAUBLES MEN ARE LED

The most expensive military decoration in history is probably the Soviet Order of Victory, created on November 8, 1943, for award to high officers of the Soviet and Allied forces, which consists of a platinum star two inches across enameled in blue and red and studded with 135 diamonds.

SOME NAZIS AND COLLABORATORS WHO GOT AWAY WITH IT

It's generally believed that members of the Nazi party and collaborators (people who supported the German occupation of their homelands) received appropriate, if often swift, informal, and brutal punishment when the Liberation came. Most did. Aside from the formal proceedings of the Nuremberg war crimes trials (and similar ones in the Pacific) there were numerous local proceedings, some of which continue to this day. There were even more informal acts of "judgment," often executed on the spot. Others were left to die slowly in concentration camps. This last item was most common in the Communist nations. Thus many of the guilty paid. But some didn't. In fact, some came away very well indeed.

COMMUNISTS: With the exception of the Finnish Communist party, which supported the motherland against Soviet aggression, the world's Communists loyally supported the Moscow line for most of the first two years of the war, proclaiming that it was an imperialist conflict. Communist parties in Europe actively assisted German occupation forces in France and elsewhere, organized strikes to hamper the war effort in Great Britain, Greece, and several other countries, and, in the United States, opposed ''warmonger'' Franklin D. Roosevelt's modest efforts to prepare the country for a possible war. All of this changed after June 22, 1941.

KIRSTIN FLAGSTAD, internationally famous Norwegian opera singer: The wife of a cabinet member in the Quisling government, she was outspoken in her support for the regime. Although there were some voices raised against her after the war, her prominence in opera more or less protected her from prosecution, and she resumed her career.

THE FRENCH: Save for a small band of exiles upholding the honor of France under Charles de Gaulle with the Free French and in the Resistance, most of the French (including those in colonies far beyond the reach of Vichy or the Germans) worked closely with the Nazis, collaborating in war work, the rounding up of Jews, and other activities required by the occupiers. Among the more prominent collaborators may be numbered Simone de Beauvoir, the noted feminist scholar (who became the editor of a new scholarly journal devoted to Vichyite notions of French history and culture); Maurice Chevalier, the internationally acclaimed entertainer (who found no difficulty entertaining German troops, perhaps because he had already done so in World War I); Jean-Paul Sartre, the philosopher (who lived with de Beauvoir during the war and helped get a number of other collaborators off the hook after it); and Coco Chanel, the fashion designer (who was so devoted to her high-ranking German lover that after the Liberation she moved to Switzerland so she could continue living with him).
Not until the Gaullists began parachuting agents into France and the Communists turned from being collaborators to resisters (after Hitler attacked Russia) did the underground begin to grow. And even then, there were so many collaborators that it was impolitic to attempt to prosecute them all. As a result, France, with nearly 50 million inhabitants, prosecuted only 30,000 people as collaborators, while Belgium, with about a fifth of the population of France prosecuted over 50,000. And

not until 1994 was a Frenchman convicted for assisting the Germans in genocide.

REINHARD GEHLEN, director of Foreign Armies East, the German military intelligence army responsible for information about Russia and Eastern Europe: Although deeply involved in the brutal antipartisan war on the Eastern front and in the Balkans, at the end of the war Gehlen was shielded from prosecution by U.S. and later West German authorities in exchange for his cooperation (he supposedly brought all of his agents in the Soviet Union over to the service of the West in the Cold War). Gehlen is also famous in intelligence circles for revolutionizing the way information is presented to the senior commanders. When Gehlen took over Foreign Armies East, Germany was losing the war. Hitler did not want any bad news, but Gehlen knew that unless he got the truth of the situation across to Hitler, a lot more German troops would get killed. So Gehlen went "Madison Avenue," turning his presentations into razzle-dazzle multimedia performances. It impressed Hitler, and intelligence briefings have never been the same since.

MARIJA GIMBUTAS, feminist historian: Of Lithuanian origin, Professor Gimbutas, who subsequently became famous as the advocate of the prehistoric "golden age" matriarchal society, received her doctorate from Tübingen University in Germany shortly after the war. Which means she was a politically acceptable candidate during the war, when the faculty was infested with Nazi sympathizers.

MARTIN HEIDEGGER, German philosopher: A world-renowned scholar, Heidegger became a member of the Nazi party when Hitler came to power and was rewarded by being made rector of the University of Berlin, a post that he held throughout the war, during which he faithfully maintained his party membership. He was afterward not prosecuted by the Allies because of his earlier distinguished academic record and pressure from numerous intellectuals, among whom was Jean-Paul Sartre, himself a collaborator.

HAJJ AMIN AL-HUSSEINI, the grand mufti of Jerusalem: An active collaborator with the Nazis before the war, Al-Husseini fled to Germany after the collapse of the anti-Allied (and pro-Nazi) Iraqi revolt of 1941. In Germany he became an active propagandist for the Nazis, promoted the recruitment of Bosnians and other Muslims into the Waffen SS, and advised Himmler on the "final solution to the Jewish problem," urging that it be extended as quickly as possible to Palestine. After the war Al-Husseini was left at liberty by the victorious Allies, the British being concerned that prosecuting him might cause unrest in the Islamic world. He spent the rest of his days living in various Arab capitals.

HERBERT VON KARAJAN, Austrian conductor: Becoming a member of the Nazi party shortly after the *Anschluss,* he benefited greatly from this association and suffered not in the least after the war. In the postwar era he became one of the most famous conductors in the world.

ALFRED KRUPP VON BOHLEN UND HALBECH, heir to the Krupp fortune: Actual head of the Krupp empire during the war due to the increasing debility of his aged father, the younger Krupp knowingly and actively employed slave labor, participated in the mass extermination program, and enthusiastically supported the Nazi regime. By shifting the blame to his father, whom the Allied authorities declared too senile to stand trial with the Nurenberg 21, the younger Krupp got off with a light sentence, of which he served only about a year, before returning to resume control of Krupp industries.

PHILIPP LENARD, German Nobelist in physics: An ardent Nazi and anti-Semite (he described Einstein as a "Jewish fraud"), Lenard helped purge non-Aryans from the German academic community before the war. After the war he remained undisturbed in his Nazi-conferred academic post, primarily as a result of pressure from German academic and scientific circles, which managed to explain away his crimes.

PAUL DE MAN, Belgian art critic: Actively collaborating with the Germans during the occupation, he denounced enemies of Germany and helped to identify and collect art works for shipment to the Reich. After the war he managed to brazen things out. One of the founders of "deconstructionist criticism," he subsequently became a respected figure among leftist academicians, who seem to have cared little about what he was doing from 1940 through 1945.

ERICH VON MANSTEIN, brilliant German tactician: General von Manstein actively supported Nazi occupation policies in Russia, disseminating the "Commissar Order" (directing that all Soviet political officers were to be shot out of hand, an order that most other senior commanders refused to countenance), and even dropped his Polish birth name, von Lewinski (he had been adopted into the Manstein family) to prove his Nordic racial purity. Brought to trial after the war on charges of supporting the *Einsatzgruppe* in their massacres of Jews, he lied under oath, which, in combination with a bungled prosecution and his brilliant record as a field commander, got him off.

RICHARD STRAUSS, German composer: Supporting the Nazi occupation of Austria, Strauss benefited from this in a variety of ways, becoming, for example, *Reichskapellemeister,* more or less the czar of music in Germany. He was afterward not prosecuted by the postwar Austrian government, which was notably lax in its pursuit of Nazi sympathizers and collaborators.

SWEDEN: Despite official neutrality, Sweden actively supported German military operations, allowing German troops to cross Swedish soil on numerous occasions, permitting recruiting for SS volunteer units, and selling so much raw material and military equipment to Germany as to impede planned expansion of the Swedish armed forces. As one Swedish leader put it, "If the Allies win we are a democracy, if the Germans win we are Aryans." Fortunately, many individual Swedes saw things differently.

KURT WALDHEIM, Austrian politician: Serving as a staff officer in the German Army in the Balkans, he helped supervise various atrocities, including the deportation of thousands of Jews from Salonika. Afterward concealing his war record, he eventually served as secretary general of the United Nations and president of Austria.

THE EMPEROR'S TREASURE

When Japan accepted defeat in August 1945, it went to great lengths to preserve its emperor from harm, or diminution in status. General Douglas MacArthur, the American officer in charge of postwar Japan, was willing to accommodate Japan's desires. After all, an emperor in debt to America would prove useful in keeping the peace among the emperor-worshipping Japanese. But the emperor had another reason to work closely with the U.S. conquerors; he wanted to keep his treasure under Japanese control. Allied investigators were seizing control of all Japanese government assets, and the emperor was considered part of the government. The personal fortune of the emperor was immense, and a large chunk of it had been transferred to Swiss bank accounts during the war. The Swiss, then and now, were noted for keeping the money in their banks from the prying eyes, and hands, of foreign governments. The emperor had over $100 billion (in 1994 dollars) sequestered in these Swiss accounts. He was not inclined to bring it back to Japan until, shall we say, "it was safe." The money had been steadily transferred to the Swiss accounts during the war, and the flow of this foreign currency to Switzerland increased as the tide of battle turned against the Japanese. Much of the imperial wealth had long been tied up in Japanese banks and financial institutions. The Japanese always had a knack for planning ahead, and there were many Japanese bankers, and imperial advisers, who could see beyond the catastrophe of Japan losing a war.

In the postwar years, Allied investigators were only dimly aware of this offshore wealth, and the Japanese were not about to enlighten them. As long as the emperor maintained good relations with the occupying powers (particularly MacArthur), there was little danger of the treasure being discovered, much less seized. Even if the Swiss bank accounts were uncovered, the lawyers might still be fighting the issue out in court to this day.

In the early 1950s, it was considered safe to bring this wealth back to Japan. The money certainly was needed. Although MacArthur was gone (to Korea, and then into retirement after an argument with President Truman), the Japanese economy was beginning to boom. A large part of this boom was due to the orders for goods and services to support the war raging in Korea. Because of the need for a stronger Japanese industry, and because Americans had a new enemy in Asia (the Chinese Communists), restrictions on Japanese banking were relaxed. The emperor's treasure began returning to Japan, often through the same prewar Japanese banks that had arranged its transfer to Switzerland in the first place. Today, the Japanese imperial family is still quite wealthy. While the Japanese are quite secretive about the extent of the emperor's treasure, a substantial amount of this wealth is probably still sitting in Swiss bank accounts. After all, it worked once.

UNFINISHED BUSINESS

On September 21, 1945, Georg Gaetner, a German PW, slipped out of Deming Army Air Force Base in New Mexico, apparently to avoid being shipped back to Germany. Although the FBI stopped looking for him in 1963, he remained uncaught until the late 1980s, when, having lived quietly and raised a family, he voluntarily surrendered. Gaetner received an instant pardon and afterward wrote a moderately successful book about his adventures and even visited Germany again.

Gaetner was one of millions of men who found themselves unwilling guests of their enemies during the war. Altogether, it appears that at least 8 million men were captured during the war, exclusive of the enormous hordes of German and Japanese troops who surrendered at its end. The treatment of prisoners varied greatly. The United States and Great Britain accorded their prisoners their rights under the Geneva Convention, but this was not common practice.

The record of other powers ranged from poor to criminal. While with some exceptions Germany generally respected the rights of U.S. and British prisoners of war, they treated Russian and other prisoners brutally, causing millions of men to die from starvation, exposure, and deliberate murder. The Soviets reciprocated in kind. Japanese treatment of prisoners of war was deplorable, and the death rate among American and British Commonwealth prisoners ran about 30 percent, more than three times higher that of those in German hands. This was, however, still better than the treatment generally accorded Asian troops captured by the Japanese. As word spread of the Japanese attitude toward prisoners of war, it became rather difficult for Japanese troops to surrender, in the unlikely event that they were so inclined. As a result, only a relative handful of Japanese troops became prisoners of war, although the number increased as their morale weakened toward the end of the war. German troops, particularly SS men, faced similar problems after Malmédy, where, on December 17, 1944, on the second day of the Battle of the Bulge, scores of American prisoners of war were massacred by troops of the 1st SS Panzer Division. The SS troops already had a similar problem with Canadian units because of Malmédy-like atrocities months earlier in Normandy.

About 425,000 Germans and 53,000 Italian prisoners of war were transported to the United States for incarceration during the war. Most of these men were housed in camps only a little more heavily guarded than regular army posts. In general they were treated well. Indeed in some parts of the country German PWs were distinctly more welcome than American soldiers of African ancestry.

THE LINGERING COST OF WAR

Although World War II has been over for nearly fifty years, it still has enormous potential to cause human suffering and death. Not all of the ammunition used during the war has been accounted for. Although most of it blew up as expected, some rounds were duds, while some were just misplaced, either through neglect or because enemy action buried it. So there's a lot of old ammunition lying around. And sometimes it kills.

In the early 1990s an estimated 1,500 tons of unexploded ammunition left over from World War II were discovered annually on the territory of what was until recently West Germany. Nor is the problem confined to Germany alone, as ammunition regularly turns up in most other areas where there was heavy fighting. Depending upon the environment in which the ammunition is found, and the amount found, it can be disposed of by detonation. But this is not always possible, because old ammunition keeps turning up in highly sensitive places. As a result, it must be disposed of by hand. This is a risky, often deadly business.

In early 1990 Captain Anthony Crawford and Lance Corporal Keith Porter of the Royal Engineers were awarded the Queen's Gallantry Medal after working for thirty-two hours to disarm a German 500-pound bomb, left over from Hitler's blitz, that had been found when a sewer collapsed in London. This was the second time in only a few months that the QGM had been awarded for disarming World War II ammunition, Captain Christopher Goddard and Corporal Gary Fisher having received it after working for thirty-one hours to defuse a 1-ton bomb found near Tower Bridge. These men were lucky. Since the end of World War II, 608 men of the French explosive ordnance disposal service have died in the course of removing 16 million artillery shells, 490,000 aerial bombs, and 600,000 land and maritime mines, not to mention countless grenades, poison gas canisters, and other lethal ordnance left over from World War II, as well as the two previous Franco-German wars of 1870–1871 and 1914–1918.

The problem even affects the United States. The last (or, rather, the most recent) vessel sunk as a result of German U-boat operations in World War II was the 70-ton fishing trawler *Shinnecock I*, off Southhampton, Long Island, New York, which was scuttled by U.S. Navy ordnance specialists on March 14, 1991, after she inadvertently hoisted aboard a 1,200-pound torpedo.

Surprisingly, there is no coordinated international effort to organize the identification and disposal of old ammunition. Nor is there any systematic collection of information regarding injuries resulting from it. Yet in just three incidents during 1984, the only year for which any information is available, eight people (all children) were killed and over thirty injured by explosives or poison gas left over from World War II.

THE VETERANS

In the early 1990s there remain about 8.5 million of the more than 16.3 million men and women who served in the U.S. armed forces during World War II, approximately 10 percent of whom are receiving benefits for service-connected disabilities, while another 1 million receive other forms of benefits. By 1990 the cumulative cost of veterans' benefits had exceeded the cost of the war itself, approximately $290 billion in 1940s dollars (nearly $3 trillion in rather inflated 1994 greenbacks). Based on the experience of previous wars, pensions for service in World War II will still be paid into the 2030s. The last pensions for dependents of World War II veterans will probably be paid in the 2050s. While the financial cost was huge, so too was the human cost.

Hundreds of thousands of veterans sustained injuries during their service that left them physically or emotionally crippled for the rest of their lives. Some injuries, particularly tropical diseases, did not become disabling until the veterans got older. Thus many of those who survived the war had their lives changed forever.

You pay for a war long after the joy of the victory celebrations have faded from memory.

DIRTY LITTLE WORLD WAR II TIME LINE

(In Case You Get Lost)

As you read this book you might want to get a better idea of where some item fits into the Big Picture. The following chronology of important events in World War II mentions only those that had major military significance. It is not meant to be exhaustive, simply a little enlightening.

September 18, 1931. Manchurian incident occurs (Japanese troops begin fighting with the Chinese, as an excuse for seizing more Chinese territory).

January 30, 1933. Adolf Hitler becomes chancellor of Germany.

March 4, 1933. Franklin D. Roosevelt becomes president of the United States. Roosevelt was elected to get America out of the Great Depression. But more important, he was one of those rare U.S. politicians who was not an isolationist.

May 27, 1933. Japan withdraws from the League of Nations and four days later begins the occupation of Jehol Province in China.

October 3, 1935. Italy invades Ethiopia.

March 7, 1936. Germany remilitarizes the Rhineland.

July 17, 1936. Civil war begins in Spain and continues until early 1939. This serves as a testing ground for many of the new weapons used widely during World War II.

July 7, 1937. Marco Polo Bridge incident occurs. Another Japanese provocation, this one is on a larger scale than the Manchurian incident and the beginning of large-scale and sustained Japanese military operations in China.

December 12, 1937. Panay incident occurs: A U.S. gunboat is bombed ''by accident'' by Japanese aircraft. The United States is not amused.

March 12, 1938. Germans invade Austria and annex it to Germany.

October 1, 1938. The Munich Pact: Germany invades Czechoslovakia and annexes German-populated areas.

March 28, 1939. Spanish Civil War ends.

There were nearly 500,000 dead. Most of the combatants were Spaniards, although 75,000 Italian and 19,000 German troops were involved as well as a few thousand Russians acting as advisers and about 60,000 individual foreign volunteers recruited mostly by the Communist International.

April 7, 1939. Italy invades Albania.

May-August 1939. Russians and Japanese fight a series of battles on the Manchuria-Mongolian border. The Russians win.

August 23, 1939. Germany and the Soviet Union sign a nonaggression pact.

This neutralizes the biggest bulwark against German aggression. Secret clauses in the treaty allowed Germany and Russia to help themselves to parts of Eastern Europe without interference from each other.

September 1, 1939. Germany invades Poland, overrunning it within a few weeks. Within three days, Great Britain and France declare war on Germany. Germans begin a submarine warfare campaign against Allied shipping. This causes serious problems for the British until 1943.

September 17, 1939. Russia invades Poland to grab its portion (as per the August 23 treaty).

November 30, 1939. Russia invades Finland in order to seize Finnish territory near Leningrad (St. Petersburg).

At the end of 1939, it was still unclear how dangerous Germany would be. France and Great Britain were mobilizing their considerable forces and a replay of World War I was still expected by many.

March 12, 1940. Russo-Finnish war ends. Soviets get the territory they wanted, but Finland retains its independence.

Nearly 70,000 Soviets died, compared to 25,000 Finns. The Soviets also lost 1,600 tanks and 700 aircraft, as well as whatever reputation the Red Army had for combat prowess.

April 9, 1940. Germans invade Denmark and Norway.

May 10, 1940. Germany invades France.

June 10, 1940. Italy enters war and invades France.

June 21, 1940. France surrenders. Southern France is allowed to remain an independent state (Vichy France) allied with Germany. Allies lose 90,000 dead, 1.9 million prisoners and missing. Germans lose 27,000 dead and 18,000 missing.

August 1, 1940. Baltic states (Lithuania, Latvia, and Estonia) are occupied by Soviet forces and incorporated into the Soviet Union.

August 3, 1940. Italy invades British Somaliland and takes control.

August–September 1940. Battle of Britain is fought and the Germans lose. In the Mediterranean, Axis attacks on Malta (south of Sicily) and British shipping begin and continue into 1943.

September 13, 1940. Italy invades British-controlled Egypt with a largely non-motorized army. After advancing a few miles the Italians settle into some hastily fortified positions.

October 28, 1940. Italy invades Greece from Albania, making little progress.

November 20, 1940. Hungary, Romania, and Slovakia join the Axis alliance. Bulgaria refuses.

December 9, 1940. Greek forces counterattack, forcing the Italians back into Albania.

December 9, 1940. British undertake a mechanized counterattack in North Africa. Over the next two months they force the Italians back hundreds of miles, inflicting several significant defeats.

The Allies (well, mainly Great Britain all alone) were in shock after 1940. The United States was still proclaiming neutrality, the Russians had a nonaggression pact with the Third Reich, and the German armed forces seemed unbeatable. The Battle of Britain was the one bright spot, but everyone feared further military action by the seemingly invincible German ground forces.

January 10, 1941. The United States applies trade sanctions to Japan, the first of several economic pressures seeking to halt Japanese aggression in China.

January 19, 1941. British begin a campaign to reconquer Italian territories in East Africa (Ethiopia, etc.).

February 9, 1941. Victorious British advance into Italian Libya is halted voluntarily, as many British units are withdrawn for service in Greece.

March 27, 1941. A coup by Serbian officers replaces the pro-German Yugoslav government with a neutral one. Germany decides to invade.

April 1941. German Afrika Korps goes into action against the British in Libya. The British retreat.

April 3, 1941. Pro-Nazi Arab officers seize control of the Iraqi government. British women and children are taken hostage. Germany sends combat aircraft to assist the Iraqis. The British invade and take control of Iraq by the end of May. Arab mobs riot and kill six hundred Iraqi Jews. Many Iraqi officers flee to Iran, a few notables get to sanctuary in Germany.

April 6, 1941. Germany, Italy, and Bulgaria invade Yugoslavia with 33 divisions and 1,200 aircraft, conquering the nation in a week.

April 9, 1941. Germany invades Greece and conquers the country in eleven days. The last British troops leave by April 29.

May 1941. German battleship *Bismarck* sails into the Atlantic to attack Allied shipping. She is hunted down and sunk by the British.

May 20, 1941. Germans make a parachute assault on Crete. British defenders are defeated within ten days.

June 8, 1941. British and Free French forces invade Vichy (pro-German) French–held Syria. After five weeks of hard fighting, the Vichyites surrender.

June 22, 1941. Germany invades the Soviet Union.

Thus began the largest military campaign in history, with three million German troops falling upon over four million Soviet soldiers. Within a week, Hungary and Finland also declared war on the Soviet Union.

July 2, 1941. Japan mobilizes a million men for military service. The Manchurian-based Kwantung Army is increased to 700,000 troops (from 400,000) for possible use against the Soviets.

July 21, 1941. Japan begins occupying major military bases in French Indochina. This puts Japanese troops closer to British Malaya and the U.S. Philippines.

July 22, 1941. German armies slow down after a month of combat in Russia.

After they advanced 400 to 500 miles, the next month was taken up with shuffling units around, resting troops and equipment, and preparing to advance again. Meanwhile, the decision was made to divert forces from the drive on Moscow to the south (in order to conquer the Ukraine and the Crimea).

August 24, 1941. British and Russian forces invade Iran, to replace a pro-German government.

September 12, 1941. An early snow begins to fall along most of the fighting front in Russia, heralding one of the bitterest winters in 140 years. Soviet soldiers are greatly assisted by "Marshal Winter."

However, a week later the Germans completed their conquest of the Ukraine, killing or capturing over 600,000 Soviet troops. At the same time, they also completed their encirclement of Leningrad (St. Petersburg).

October 1941. Seasonal rains turn the Russian front into a sea of mud, slowing and sometimes stopping German advances. Finland prepares to go on the defensive, a status it will maintain for the remainder of the war. Finnish offensive operations cease in December, after 25,000 Finns have been killed since June 1941. Russians introduce the T-34 tank, fresh from the factory. This marks the end of German armor superiority in Russia. At the same time, southeast of Moscow, the Germans shatter Russian forces, killing or capturing over 700,000 troops.

November 5, 1941. Unable to get the Allies to lift their oil embargo, Japan decides on war against U.S., British, and Dutch holdings in the Pacific.

November 25, 1941. Germans make one more push toward Moscow, get within nineteen miles of the city, and are stopped.

This is as far as the Germans would ever advance in the northern part of the front. During the first five months of the campaign the Germans had killed or captured over 2 million Russian troops, while losing only 750,000 of their own. It wasn't enough.

December 6, 1941. Russians mass a million fresh troops and attack the overextended Germans in front of Moscow.

In places, this two-month offensive pushed German forces back a hundred miles. By coincidence, on the same day America began work on the atomic bomb.

December 7, 1941. Japan attacks Pearl Harbor, as well as British, Dutch, and other U.S. possessions in the Pacific.

By the end of 1941, the Allies had much reason to despair. Except for the Russian winter offensive (which no one expected would destroy the Germans), everywhere else the Allies were in retreat. The Japanese were on their way to conquering Malaya and the Philippines as well as the Netherlands East Indies (Indonesia). The British were still taking a battering in North Africa and German submarines were sinking increasing numbers of Allied merchant ships in the Atlantic. For the Allied cause, this was indeed the low point of the war.

January 16, 1942. Japanese invade Burma from Thailand (which, while technically neutral, thought it prudent to cooperate with the Japanese).

The battle between British and Japanese forces in Burma continued into 1945, even though the British were forced back into India by May 1942.

February 15, 1942. Singapore (and Malaya) falls to the Japanese.

This was the major British base in southeast Asia and was thought to be impregnable.

March 10, 1942. Dutch forces in Indonesia (Netherlands East Indies) surrender to the Japanese. This gives the Japanese access to the oil that the Allied embargo has denied them.

Unfortunately, the retreating Allied troops had destroyed much of the oil facilities and the Japanese would never be able to get as much oil out of those oil fields as was the case before the war. To make matters worse, a Japanese ship bringing their technicians and engineers to the oil fields was sunk by a U.S. submarine.

April 1942. Japanese carriers rampage through the Indian Ocean, striking as far east as Ceylon (Sri Lanka).

May 4–8, 1942. Battle of the Coral Sea is fought, the first carrier battle in history. A draw.

May 1942. German forces begin to regain ground lost during the Russian winter offensive. Many of the German losses from the past eleven months' fighting are replaced and plans are made for a 1942 summer offensive.

May 6, 1942. Last U.S. forces in the Philippines (except guerrillas, who would be active throughout the war) surrender on Corregidor island.

These were the last Allied troops to surrender in the Pacific as a result of the Japanese offensive that began in early December 1941.

June 4–6, 1942. Battle of Midway is fought. Four Japanese carriers are sunk to only one U.S. loss. The Japanese also land in the Aleutian Islands off Alaska and establish two bases. (These bases will be retaken within a year.)

June 1942. The German Afrika Korps caps a series of victories by advancing into Egypt. British forces prepare to make their stand at El Alamein. The Germans are stopped and later in the year a counteroffensive pushes them back toward Tunisia. In Russia, the Germans begin their summer offensive, defeating all Russian forces they encounter. The city of Stalingrad is reached in September. Here the Russians make their stand.

August 7, 1942. U.S. Marines land on Guadalcanal, the first U.S. offensive of the Pacific War.

This attack came nine months after Pearl Harbor, a year earlier than the Japanese expected. The air, land, and naval battle for the island continued until February 1943, when the Japanese finally withdrew.

August 19, 1942. Battle for Stalingrad (Volgograd) begins.

October 23, 1942. Battle of El Alamein is fought. British forces attack the Germans and begin pushing them back all the way to Tunisia. By November 4, the German retreat is under way with the remnants of twelve Axis divisions fleeing west.

November 8, 1942. Allied (mainly American) forces began landing in Algeria and Morocco, defeating Vichy (pro-German) French forces within a week.

By the end of the month, the Germans retaliated by occupying the southern portion of France that had still been under Collaborationist (Vichy, for the city that was now France's capital) French control since 1940. Within a few months, the Axis forces held only the Tunisian city of Tunis and some surrounding countryside.

November 19, 1942. Russians launch their winter offensive against the German Sixth Army in Stalingrad. Over sixty Russian divisions attack the Axis units on the flanks.

Within a week, over half a million Russian troops had surrounded the 260,000 Germans and other Axis troops in Stalingrad. Smaller offensives were launched on the Moscow and Leningrad fronts. A German relief army got to within forty miles of Stalingrad before being forced back in the middle of December. By the end of the year, some Russian forces had advanced over a hundred miles west of Stalingrad.

The year 1942 was rather encouraging for the Allies. Axis troops were on the defensive in Russia, North Africa, and the Pacific. The Germans and the Japanese were no longer regarded as supermen and Allied victory appeared to be only a matter of time.

January 18, 1943. Russians break the German siege of Leningrad, allowing the hard-pressed garrison to be resupplied. Perhaps 900,000 citizens of Leningrad have starved to death during the blockade.

January 31, 1943. Germans surrender their forces in Stalingrad. Some resistance continues until February 2.

The Russian winter offensive continued to advance on nearly all parts of the front. Eventually, the winter offensive took Russian forces some four hundred miles west of Stalingrad.

February 9, 1943. Japanese complete their evacuation from Guadalcanal, leaving the Americans to invade the other islands between Guadalcanal and the main Japanese base to the north on Rabaul.

May 12, 1943. German and Italian forces surrender in North Africa, many withdraw to Sicily. Between North Africa and Stalingrad the Axis powers lose nearly a million men.

June 1943. German U-boat war against Allied shipping in the Atlantic is lost.

During the summer of 1943, the Allies reached the point where they were building new shipping faster than the Germans were sinking it. Allied aircraft and combat ships were destroying U-boats more quickly than the Germans could get them into action. The U-boat war would go on, but the Germans were steadily less effective as the war continued.

July 5, 1943. Germans launch their summer offensive with the battle for Kursk in central Russia. The Soviets immediately counterattack; the Germans soon are forced on the defensive and the great Nazi retreat to Berlin begins. For the rest of the war, the Russians are on the offensive.

July 9, 1943. Allied invasion of Sicily begins with an airborne assault (which did not go so well) followed the next day by an amphibious assault.

Within a week, this caused the Germans to call off their summer offensive in Russia to send units to Italy.

August 17, 1943. Allies conquer Sicily, although the Germans and Italians manage to evacuate most of their surviving troops to Italy.

August 27, 1943. Germans fight Italian troops in Slovenia as they attempt to take over that Italian-occupied area. Croatian troops assist the Germans.

September 3, 1943. Italy surrenders and (in October) switches sides. This is not announced until September 8 to give the Italians time to prepare to fight the Germans (who have been entering northern Italy for nearly a month).

The Germans managed to enter and take over Rome on September 10 anyway. Some forty-three Italian divisions (in Italy, the Balkans, and France) were disarmed or overwhelmed by the Germans, several more deserted to the Allies. Most of these divisions had to be replaced by German units taken from the Russian front, much to the Russians' relief.

September 9, 1943. Allies land in Italy at Salerno. German reaction is swift and nearly succeeds in throwing the Allied troops back into the sea. Allies recover and begin the hard fight north through the mountainous terrain of Italy.

This struggle would continue until the end of the war, when the remaining Germans surrendered in northern Italy.

November 20, 1943. In the Pacific, U.S. Marines begin their drive through the central Pacific by assaulting heavily defended Tarawa. In a bloody battle, the island is taken.

Fighting continued in the Solomons and New Guinea, where the Japanese continued to send reinforcements, and Allied troops continued to fight from one island and ridge line to another as they had since early 1942.

December 5, 1943. Allies begin using fuel drop-tanks on their P-47 and P-51 fighters to escort heavy bombers during missions deep inside Germany.

This changed the strategic bombing campaign considerably, greatly reducing bomber losses and significantly increasing German aircraft losses.

December 14, 1943. Russians launch their winter offensive (not long after their summer offensive had ground to a halt).

This advance would take them into Poland and liberate most of Russia from the Germans.

1943 was a year of constant advances and victories for the Allies. Yet the Axis forces continued to resist, and even counterattack, on occasion. While optimists saw final victory in 1944, pessimists pointed out the Axis powers still had a lot of troops, ships, and aircraft left. And the Axis leaders were unquestionably fanatic.

January 22, 1944. Allied forces land at Anzio, in an attempt to out-flank the main German defensive lines south of Rome. Timidity on the part of the Allied commanders, and quick response on the part of the Germans, dooms this effort to failure.

January 31, 1944. U.S. amphibious forces take Kwajalein (and most of the other Marshal Islands). This is the second major move of the central Pacific drive.

March 1944. Allied troops seize the Admiralty Islands, north of the major Japanese base of Rabaul (which is now isolated, and continues to be until Japan surrenders at the end of the war). This completes Operation Cartwheel, the isolation of Rabaul, and sets the stage for the advance on the Philippines.

April 1944. Japanese launch their last offensive in China. This is primarily to destroy air bases from which Allied long-range bombers are operating.

June 4, 1944. Allied troops take Rome.

June 6, 1944. Allied armies land at Normandy; the principal western Allied ground offensive of the war begins.

June 15, 1944. Saipan (in the Mariana Islands) is assaulted.
The Marianas were needed as air bases for the B-29 bombers that would attack Japan. On the same day, the first B-29s flew from Chinese bases to attack Japan. These bases would soon be overrun by Japanese ground troops. In any event, few B-29 raids could be launched from China because all fuel, bombs, and other supplies had to be flown in from India.

June 19–20, 1944. Battle of the Philippine Sea is fought. After Midway, this is the most decisive naval battle of the Pacific war. Japan commits most of its remaining fleet in an effort to chase the Allies away from the Marianas. The Japanese fail, and in the "Great Marianas Turkey Shoot" more experienced and numerous American carrier pilots destroy what is left of Japanese carrier aviation.

July 21, 1944. Army and Marine troops assault the island of Guam, a necessary way station in the drive toward the Philippines.

July 25, 1944. Allies launch a breakout from the Normandy beachhead (where Allied and German troops had been fighting furiously since early June).

Within a month, Paris was liberated and Nazi forces were beating a hasty retreat for Germany.

August 26, 1944. Bulgaria leaves the Axis alliance, disarming German troops within Bulgaria. A week later, Russia declares war and Bulgaria surrenders within twenty-four hours.

September 2, 1944. Finland agrees to an armistice with Russia, thus leaving the war.

September 1944. German troops evacuate Greece and the Aegean Islands to avoid being trapped by Russian troops advancing in the north (toward the Aegean Sea through Yugoslavia). At the same time, the first American troops enter Germany.

September 24, 1944. San Marino declares war on Germany (finally!).

The Germans had occupied San Marino in 1943 because nearly 100,000 fugitives from Nazi "justice" had taken shelter there.

October 10, 1944. Russian forces reach the Baltic, trapping Nazi troops in Latvia and parts of adjacent Russia.

October 15, 1944. The Hungarian government tries to surrender to the Allies. Germans arrest the senior officials of the government and continue to control the country.

October 20, 1944. American troops land in the Philippines, twenty-eight months after the last American troops there had surrendered.

October 23–30, 1944. Battle of Leyte Gulf is fought. The Japanese Navy makes its last attempt to stop the Americans. The Japanese fleet is essentially eliminated.

December 16, 1944. Germans launch their last offensive in the west (the Battle of the Bulge) in an attempt to stop the Allies. The attack fails.

The war didn't end in 1944, and even the optimists were not sure it would end in 1945 (particularly in the Pacific). While the Germans appeared to be on their last legs, the Japanese seemed fanatical in their determination to defend their home islands.

February 19, 1945. U.S. Marines assault Iwo Jima, to provide another airfield for the B-29 assault on Japan.

February 25, 1945. U.S. B-29s in the Pacific change their tactics to emphasize night fire bomb raids on cities rather than daytime raids on industrial centers.

This move proved devastating for Japanese war production (because many components were manufactured in small factories in residential areas of cities).

March 7, 1945. American units cross the Rhine into the German heartland.

April 1, 1945. The last major amphibious assault of the war begins with a landing on Okinawa.

April 25, 1945. Russian forces complete their encirclement of Berlin and, within a week, capture the city.

April 30, 1945. American and Russian forces link up in central Germany.

May 2, 1945. German forces in Italy surrender. In the following days, most German forces facing the Western Allies surrender. Germans fighting the Russians are less willing to give up.

May 7, 1945. All German forces surrender. The war in Europe is over. The war in the Pacific continues.

June 7, 1945. Chinese forces recapture the last of the territory taken by the Japanese during their spring offensive. The Japanese barely hold on in China, many of their best troops and units previously having been sent to the Pacific or back to Japan.

June 30, 1945. The campaign in the Philippines is declared officially over, although over 20,000 Japanese troops continue to operate in rural areas.

July 16, 1945. The first atomic bomb is detonated in New Mexico.

August 3, 1945. Blockade of Japan is complete, virtually no supplies can get in, or out, of the country.

August 4, 1945. British destroy the last Japanese units in Burma.

August 6, 1945. Atomic bomb is dropped on Hiroshima.

August 8, 1945. Russia declares war on Japan and promptly invades Manchuria and Korea.

August 9, 1945. Atomic bomb is dropped on Nagasaki.

August 15, 1945. Japan surrenders (the formalities take place the following month).

September 12, 1990. The United States, the Soviet Union, France, and Great Britain conclude a peace treaty with the German Federal Republic and the German Democratic Republic (itself about to go out of business). World War II is formally over. With the subsequent end of the Cold War, the World War II era comes to an end. Thus the events of the summer of 1914, which precipitated World War I and then led to World War II, finally come to a conclusion. This took the greater part of the twentieth century (1914–1991) and will be so recorded in future histories.

RECOMMENDED READING

Some suggestions for further inquiry into the "dirty little secrets of World War II":

This does not purport to be an exhaustive, or even extensive, bibliography of materials on the Second World War. There are literally tens of thousands of books on the subject, and even a volume equal in size to the present one would not be enough to list works in English alone. However, some works are more important, or at least more unusual, than others, and worth having a look at.

BARNETT, CORRELLI. *The Desert Generals.* 2d. ed. Bloomington: Indiana University Press, 1982. A devastating inquiry into the causes of the repeated disasters that the British Army suffered at the hands of Erwin Rommel during the North African campaign, which Barnett followed up by editing *Hitler's Generals* (London: Weidenfeld & Nicolson, 1989), a generally critical look at the careers of the principal German commanders in the war.

BROWN, ROBERT. *Warship Losses of World War Two.* New York: Sterling/Arms and Armour, 1990. A valuable compendium of all warship losses during the war, including those of the neutrals. In addition to the basic chronological presentation of ship losses, with location, circumstances, and often extensive explanatory notes, there are statistical tables and several analyses of the causes of the losses of the ships. Very handy for the serious student of World War II at sea.

DiNARDO, RICHARD L. *Mechanized Juggernaut or Military Anachronism? Horses and the German Army of World War II.* Westport, CT: Greenwood Press, 1991. The title says it all, and it's well worth it.

DUNNIGAN, JAMES F. *How to Make War.* 3d. ed. New York: William Morrow and Co., 1993. Focuses on the theory and practice of warfare in the late twentieth century, and contains much that is useful in helping to understand the conduct of the Second World War as well.

————, ed. *The War in the East.* New York: Simulations Publications, 1977. An anthology of materials on the Russo-German conflict drawn chiefly from the pages of *Strategy and Tactics,* the premier journal of military historical simulation.

————, and ALBERT A. NOFI. *Shooting Blanks.* (New York: William Morrow and Co., 1991. Looks at the problem of understanding military power, with numerous examples drawn from World War II.

DuPuy, TREVOR N. *Numbers, Predictions, and War.* Indianapolis: Bobbs-Merrill, 1979. Discusses the Quantified Judgment Model, an attempt to develop a mathematical model capable of comparing the military capabilities of various military forces, based on the experience of several dozen battles during the Second World War.

GREENBERG, ELI et al. *The Ineffective Soldier: Lessons for Management and the Nation.* 3 vols. New York: Columbia University Press, 1959. Analyzes where and how the U.S. armed forces mismanaged their manpower; one volume is subtitled *The Lost Divisions.*

HARRIS, MERION, and SUSIE HARRIS. *Soldiers of the Sun: The Rise and Fall of the Japanese Imperial Army.* New York: Random House, 1991. Although not entirely successful as a history of the imperial army, this comes into its own in a series of chapters that analyze the doctrine, character, equipment, and philosophy of the Japanese Army in the period of World War II.

KNOX, MACGREGOR. *Mussolini Unleashed, 1939–1941.* Cambridge: Cambridge University Press, 1982. Despite its limited time frame, this is the best available look at the role of Italy in the diplomatic and military events of the 1930s and early 1940s.

MILLER, EDWARD S. *War Plan Orange: The U.S. Strategy to Defeat Japan, 1897–1945.* Annapolis: United States Naval Institute,

1991. Presents a detailed analysis of U.S. planning for a war with Japan, with an examination of the personalities involved and the ways in which changing world events influenced such planning, plus a look at the ways in which the various prewar plans influenced the actual development of U.S. strategy in the Pacific war.

MILLETT, ALLAN REID, AND MURRAY WILLIAMSON, eds. *Military Effectiveness.* 3 vols. Boston: Allen & Unwin, 1988. A collection of essays by noted specialists on the military capabilities and limitations of the armed forces of each of the great powers during World War I (vol. 1), the interwar period (vol. 2), and World War II (vol. 3), with many valuable insights and much food for thought. Millett and Williamson's *Calculations: Net Assessment and the Coming of World War II* (New York: The Free Press, 1992) contains a series of essays on how each of the great powers dealt with the problem of evaluating the military capabilities and limitations of their opponents.

MORISON, SAMUEL ELIOT. *History of United States Naval Operations in World War II.* 15 vols. Boston: Little, Brown, 1947–1962. A remarkably literate, very complete treatment of the subject in sometimes extraordinary detail, which has stood the test of time rather well. For those short of the leisure to read it all, Morison's *The Two Ocean War* (Boston: Little, Brown, 1963) presents a shorter treatment of the subject.

NOFI, ALBERT A. *The War Against Hitler: Military Strategy in the West.* New York: Hippocrene, 1982. Collects a number of in-depth essays on the Second World War in Europe as it involved the Western Allies, drawn mostly from the pages of *Strategy and Tactics,* the magazine of historical conflict simulation, itself a valuable source of unusual information on the war.

OVERY, R. J. *The Air War, 1939–1945.* New York: Stein & Day, 1981. A critical analytical look at the nature of war in the air, with many valuable perspectives, such as the importance not merely of aircraft production but also of the production of spare parts.

PERRETT, GEOFFREY. *There's a War to Be Won: The United States Army in World War II.* New York: Random House, 1991. Presents a pretty good look at the U.S. Army in World War II, weaving together the diverse trends in doctrine, organization, equipment, and planning that ultimately led to the army with which the United States fought the Second World War, while looking into everything from the personalities of the army's leaders, problems and surprises in weapons development, racial policies, the medical corps, the famous maneuvers of 1940–1941, and, of course, the experience of battle.

PRANGE, GORDON R., with DONALD M. GOLDSTEIN and KATHERINE V. DILLON. *At Dawn We Slept.* New York: McGraw-Hill, 1981. Together with their *Pearl Harbor: The Verdict of History* (New York: McGraw-Hill, 1986) provides the most detailed and exhaustive inquiry into the American disaster at Pearl Harbor. Going to considerable lengths to examine the numerous conspiracy theories (some of which are remarkable indeed), the authors conclude that "there is enough blame for everyone," and not a little credit for the Japanese. Their *Miracle at Midway* (New York: McGraw-Hill, 1982) carries the story forward to the series of Japanese blunders and American successes that led to the Japanese disaster just seven months later.

READY, J. LEE. *Forgotten Allies.* 2 vols. New York: McFarland, 1985. Takes a look at the role in the war of the minor powers, and the numerous Resistance movements, with one volume about the war against Germany and the other about that against Japan. A valuable, and very neglected, book.

REYNOLDS, CLARK G. *The Fast Carriers.* New York: McGraw-Hill, 1968. Although relatively old, and rather focused on the American point of view, still the best overall treatment of the carrier war in the Pacific.

SEATON, ALBERT. *The German Army, 1933–1945.* New York: St. Martin's Press, 1982. Although superseded in some aspects, still the best single treatment of the subject.

SHIRER, WILLIAM L. *The Collapse of the Third Republic.* New York: Simon & Schuster, 1969. Also see Shirer, *The Rise and Fall of the Third Reich* (New York: Simon & Schuster, 1960). Two excellent historical treatments that integrate the political, economic, military, and social aspects of the war.

STOUFFER, SAMUEL A. et al. *The American Soldier: Studies in Social Psychology in World War II.* 2 vols. Princeton: Princeton University Press, 1949. This was written because, by an extraordinary bit of military mismanagement, upon being drafted into the army, Stouffer and several other sociologists were assigned to study the troops. The result was a series of opinion polls and surveys that are unmatched in the insight they give into the mind and attitudes of the common soldier on everything from army chow to race relations to the nature of the enemy.

The United States Army in World War II. Washington, DC: Office of the Chief, Military History, 1947–1994. A nearly 80-volume official account of the U.S. Army in the war, probably the best official history ever written. While the operational volumes are literate, well-reasoned, critical, and worth reading, the really good stuff is in the technical volumes, on matters from the procurement of aircraft to racial policies to logistical support. No other major power's official history even comes close to the objectivity, scholarship, and readability of this series.

U.S. ARMY MEDICAL SERVICE, HISTORICAL UNIT. *Wound Ballistics.* Washington, DC: Office of the Surgeon General, 1962. An analysis of the ways in which weapons kill people, based on the evidence of World War II and Korea. Not for the fainthearted.

The United States Strategic Bombing Survey. Washington, DC: United States Strategic Bombing Survey, 1945–1949. A two hundred-volume look at the war, focusing on the influence of strategic bombing, with many valuable insights.

VAN CREVELD, MARTIN. *Fighting Power: German and U.S. Army Performance, 1939–1945.* Westport, CT: Greenwood Press, 1982. Makes some comparisons that are generally not flattering to the U.S. Army.

WATT, D. CAMERON. *How War Came.* New York: Pantheon, 1989. The best available treatment of the interplay of political, diplomatic, and military maneuvers between the Munich Pact and the outbreak of the war in September 1939.

ZALOGA, STEVE, and VICTOR MADEJ. *The September Campaign.* New York: Hippocrene, 1989. The only useful treatment of the most neglected, yet in many ways most critical, campaign of the war, that in Poland in 1939.

INDEX

Note: Entries for the Great Powers and their armed forces appear so frequently in *Dirty Little Secrets of World War II* that they have been omitted from this index.